Not for consumers

"Vitsœ's furniture does not shout; it performs its function in relative anonymity alongside furniture from any designer and in homes from any era. We make the effort to produce products like this for intelligent and responsible users – not consumers – who consciously select products that they can really use. Good design must be able to coexist."

Dieter Rams, 1976

vitsoe.com

GRANTA

12 Addison Avenue, London W11 4QR | email: editorial@granta.com
To subscribe go to granta.com, or call 020 8955 7011 (free phone 0500 004 033)
in the United Kingdom, 845-267-3031 (toll-free 866-438-6150) in the United States

ISSUE 147: SPRING 2019

PUBLISHER AND EDITOR	Sigrid Rausing
DEPUTY EDITOR	Rosalind Porter
POETRY EDITOR	Rachael Allen
DIGITAL DIRECTOR	Luke Neima
ASSISTANT EDITOR	Francisco Vilhena
SENIOR DESIGNER	Daniela Silva
DEPUTY ONLINE EDITOR	Eleanor Chandler
EDITORIAL ASSISTANT	Lucy Diver
OPERATIONS AND SUBSCRIPTIONS	Mercedes Forest
MARKETING MANAGER	Simon Heafield
PUBLICITY	Pru Rowlandson
TO ADVERTISE CONTACT	Charlotte Burgess, charlotteburgess@granta.com
FINANCE	Mercedes Forest, Josephine Perez
SALES MANAGER	Katie Hayward
IT MANAGER	Mark Williams
PRODUCTION ASSOCIATE	Sarah Wasley
PROOFS	Amber Dowell, Katherine Fry, Jessica Kelly, Lesley Levene
CONTRIBUTING EDITORS	Daniel Alarcón, Anne Carson, Mohsin Hamid, Isabel Hilton, Michael Hofmann, A.M. Homes, Janet Malcolm, Adam Nicolson, Edmund White

Unplug

yourself

National Art Pass_

Ashley Cosstick
Individual

Please show your card for free admission and reduced price entry to participating museums and galleries

What will you see? Experience over 240 museums, galleries and historic places for free and enjoy 50% off entry to major exhibitions.

SEARCH NATIONAL ART PASS

Art Fund_

A DIFFERENT KIND
OF MEMBERS CLUB

The Royal Over-Seas League (ROSL) is a not-for-profit private members' organisation dedicated to championing international friendship and understanding. We help artists and musicians across the Commonwealth connect, collaborate and create. Our education work benefits communities and changes lives. Members enjoy luxury clubhouse accommodation in St James's, London, a vibrant event calendar packed with concerts, exhibitions, literary talks including collaborations with Caine Prize authors, and links to over 100 reciprocal clubs worldwide.

Join ROSL and be part of a club that's been making a difference since 1910.

HOW TO JOIN
Call **+44 (0)20 7408 0214** (ext. **214** & **216**) and quote **'Granta'**, visit **www.rosl.org.uk** or email **info@rosl.org.uk**

Royal Over-seas League, Over-Seas House, Park Place, St James's Street, London SW1A 1LR

ROSL
ROYAL OVER-SEAS LEAGUE

STRATFORD-UPON-AVON

2019 NEW WRITING

INCLUDES

CROOKED DANCES
ROBIN FRENCH

A MUSEUM IN BAGHDAD
HANNAH KHALIL

THE WHIP
JULIET GILKES ROMERO

BOOK NOW
rsc.org.uk

The work of the RSC Literary Department is generously supported by THE DRUE AND H.J. HEINZ II CHARITABLE TRUST

The work of Juliet Gilkes Romero was supported through our collaboration with the University of Birmingham

Supported using public funding by

ARTS COUNCIL ENGLAND

EMMETT
L O N D O N
112 Jermyn Street

'Masterly and brilliant ... This book could only be written by a writer with a knowledge of the geography of the Arab soul as well the Arab land.'

–Simon Sebag Montefiore, author of *Jerusalem*

ARABS
A 3,000-YEAR HISTORY OF PEOPLES, TRIBES AND EMPIRES
TIM MACKINTOSH-SMITH

OUT NOW IN HARDCOVER

YaleBooks | @yalebooks
www.yalebooks.co.uk

4th December, 1979.

Dear Mr. Burns,

Thank you for your letter. I am afraid
you are almost certain to be unable to afford me.
Anyway, I will proceed on that assumption. The
comment of Rubin Rabonvitz which you quote seems
to me dismally umpromising. It is exactly the sort
of thing that semi-literate Americans always say to
explain their feelings of puzzled inferiority when
they look at the English novel.

Yours sincerely,

Kingsley amis

Eric Burns, Esq.,
Granta,
Box 666,
King's College,
Cambridge.

CONTENTS

Introduction

This is *Granta*'s fortieth anniversary issue: a selection of fiction and essays published in the magazine between 1979 and 2013. We read our way through the back issues, and suggestions poured in – Elena Lappin's exploration of the complexities of Binjamin Wilkomirski (author of a falsified Holocaust memoir), Adrian Leftwich's account of betrayal in apartheid South Africa and Ian Jack's investigation of the shooting of two IRA suspects in Gibraltar. We discussed David Feuer's tale of his stint working as a psychiatrist in a Hasidic community in Brooklyn, and Reinaldo Arenas's harsh and even description of leaving Cuba. We also considered whether Primo Levi's 'Weightless', a meditation on gravity and falling published shortly before his death, was perhaps more interesting than 'Tadpoles', but in the end we decided on the latter. These works, and others from the longlist, are part of the online edition of the issue.

There was much to discuss. How far should we try to capture *Granta*'s original spirit by publishing a 'representative' collection – dirty realism, travel, memoir? Should we prioritise frequent contributors? Should we exclude excerpts – if Philip Roth and Don DeLillo, why not Arthur Miller on the Chelsea Hotel? What about gender? The early issues of *Granta* were startlingly male – of some fifteen writers one might be female. As late as 1994, one issue, depressingly, had not a single female contributor.

I felt James Fenton had to be in the issue, and Bruce Chatwin and Ryszard Kapuściński – they define *Granta* travel writing, narratives of place that read like short stories. We have three other African pieces in this issue: Alexandra Fuller's memoir of giving birth in Zambia, Lindsey Hilsum's reportage from the Rwandan genocide and Binyavanga Wainaina's now-famous ironic critique, 'How to Write About Africa', which began as a letter to the editor criticising *Granta*'s 1994 Africa issue.

Ved Mehta's 'Kiltykins' caused some editorial discussions. The piece reminded me of Leonard Michaels's autobiographical novel

Sylvia – a description of a dysfunctional relationship from the male point of view – but Mehta is also blind, and reflects on why he writes as though he can see. We too can never quite see or grasp who Kilty is – does she have a personality disorder, is she simply childish and manipulative, or is she the victim of Mehta's objectifying conception? We don't know, and perhaps Mehta himself isn't sure.

Edmund White, Ved Mehta and Edward W. Said all wrote about mid-twentieth century dysfunctional relationships, parental or sexual. White's and Mehta's psychoanalysts would now certainly be accused of malpractice, and Said's description of his parents' excessive interest in his physical development might be seen as a mild form of medical abuse.

It is hard to read John Gregory Dunne's description of being diagnosed with heart disease without thinking of Joan Didion's haunting memoir about the aftermath of his death, *The Year of Magical Thinking*. Dunne's voice, so vivid, so alive, reads like a kind of preface to her book – *By the way, this is what it was like for me.*

How do we think ourselves into the minds of non-human beings? Thomas Nagel might have proven the philosophical impossibility of it ('What Is It Like To Be a Bat?'), and yet I suspect there must be degrees of perception and communication. John Berger's beautiful meditation on the chimpanzees in Basel Zoo points to the profound kinship between us, while Mary Gaitskill's melancholy essay on loss and good intentions asks how far it is possible to understand those we try to help, animal and human.

I hope you will like these works as much as we do; that veteran subscribers will be reminded of other times in their lives, and that new readers will discover voices they may not be familiar with. These stories are both representative of *Granta*'s past and of our current editorial taste. Some of our choices will no doubt be controversial, but then blandness has never been part of *Granta*'s mission. We hope you will revel, instead, in the bracing pleasure of the text. ■

Sigrid Rausing

Lui 12·48

June 24

107 The Chase
London SW4 ONR

Bill Buford
Granta
King's College
Cambridge
CB2 IST

Dear Bill,

Thank you for GRANT, which looks perfectly splendid. Congratulations.

Herewith a story, COUSINS, which ought to be about 3,500 words.
It is another wolf-child child story - of course, you may not be
aware of this obseesion of mine; I have an obsession with wolf-
children, and this story is by no means the last of it. Actually,
it is really about nature and culture, but don't want to cross the
t's and dot the i's. (Well, not too much.) Obviously, it is meant to read plain and clumsy.
I can punctuate perfectly adequately when I want to. Anyway,
I hope it's okay.

Glad you liked the Updike review. Does he, and Roth, et al,
realise how sexist they are?
It beats me.

In haste, in order to catch the post - but I'm supposed to be going
to the States, next year, myself, so would like a word or two
before I go -

yours,

Angela

P.S.

COUSINS

Angela Carter

GRANTA 3: AUTUMN 1980

The people who live in its shadow have no relation to the mountain itself other than one of use, though you could say that the mountain also uses them, uses them up, exhausts not only their energies, their work, but also their imaginations. The vastness of their world oppresses them; their servitude to the elements kills them.

A girl from a small village on the lower slope of the mountain married a man who lived by himself on the far side of a certain river. She was from a fairly well-off family, he was dirt poor, he had an acre or two of stones, that was his farm, lonely beyond belief. He got her in the family way and she went off with him one early summer. They thought, when her time was near, she'd go to her widowed mother in the village for her confinement but the equinoctial storms came, thunder, lightning, and she went into labour. Since she could not go to her mother, her man went to fetch her mother to her. If the river had not swollen twice its size, due to the rain, and been washing down earth and boulders, he'd have crossed it easily but he drowned, somebody hooked his corpse out miles down, weeks later, he'd travelled further in death than he'd ever done living.

The old woman knew her daughter couldn't cross the river in her condition, in such weather. When the storm was over, the river calmed down, the old woman and her son went over to the farm themselves. The young woman lay on the straw mattress, she had bled to death.

The roof of the building had caved in during the storm. By the traces of wolf dung, they knew wolves had got in. There was no sign of the baby, except those that showed it had been born.

The old woman's son carried his sister home on his back. Absolute quiet followed the tempest; there is something mutilating about the silence of the mountain. Then the wolves began to howl. After that, it was winter. When the snow melted, it was spring. The old woman's son married the blacksmith's daughter, she moved in with them. By Christmas, there was a bouncing grandson but the old woman still crossed herself when she heard the wolves on the mountain. Time passed. Then came a granddaughter; then a stillbirth; compensated for by twins, a boy and a girl. And so on.

The summer the eldest grandson was seven, he went up with his father and their goats to the high pastures, as was the village custom, to lodge in a shelter up the mountainside while the goats gorged themselves on young grass. The boy was sitting in the sun, plaiting straws and watching the kids butt one another when he saw the shadow of what he had been told to fear most, a wolf, advancing silently along the lea of an outcrop of rock. Then another wolf, and another, while his charges frisked and nibbled on.

If they had not been the first wolves he ever saw, the boy would not have looked at them so closely; the russet-grey pelts, the lovely, plumey tails; the sharp, inquiring masks. Because he looked at them so intently, he saw, or thought he saw, a bald one, a naked one, going on all fours, as they did, but furless, though with a kind of brown mane.

He was so awestruck and fascinated by this bald wolf that he would have lost his flock, maybe himself been eaten and certainly been beaten to the bone, had not the goats themselves sniffed danger, their hooves drumming off down the slope, their terrified whinnying, so the men came, firing off guns, making hullabaloo, scaring the wolves away.

The boy was cuffed round the head and sent home in disgrace. His mother was feeding the baby and his grandmother sat at the table shelling peas into a pot.

'Grandmother, there was a little girl with the wolves,' he said. He wasn't sure why he thought it was a little girl. He just had a feeling. His grandmother went on shelling peas.

'About my age,' he said. His grandmother threw away a flat pod. 'I saw her,' he said. His grandmother tipped water into the pot and put it on the fire. There wasn't time, that night, but, next morning, she herself took the boy up to the high pastures, again, and said:

'Tell your father what you told me.'

They went to examine the wolves' tracks. On a bit of dampish ground, they found a print, not like that of a dog's paw, but even less like that of a child's footprint – yet curiously like that one of the great cats. Only, here we are high in the cool North; all the cats, here, are small, sit by the fire, and purr. But *this* print was like that of the five-toed paw of a great cat; or, more, like the beautiful and mysterious prints on the suave pelts of certain great cats, that carry markings like the glyphs of a script we cannot read.

'She was running on all fours with her arse stuck up in the air,' said the boy. 'Therefore, she'd put all her weight on the ball of her foot, wouldn't she. And splay out her toes, see . . . just like that.'

He inserted the ball of his own foot in the print, to show his father and the others how it would go, if he, too, ran habitually on all fours. His foot fitted the print perfectly.

'And, see, no use for a heel, if you run that way . . . Stands to reason. That's why there's no heel-print, see?'

They searched a long way before they found her asleep in a sandy hollow not far from the ruins of the house in which she had been born. Her head lay on the flank of a grey, grizzled, old bitch. The men banged cans and rattled sticks to keep the other wolves away; when the sleepers woke, the girl's uncle blasted the bitch to pieces with his gun. The grandmother tried to put her arms round the girl but she bit the old woman's hand. Then the other men caught hold of the girl.

She scratched, fought and bit so much they tied her wrists and ankles together with twine, then slung her from a pole and carried her, like game, back to the village. She neither screamed nor cried out, she didn't seem able to. She made only a few dull, guttural, choking sounds. Her eyes watered all the time but not as though she were crying. She was skinny, all her ribs stuck out, there was no flesh on her, not like the plump, potato-fed boy. She was burned almost black, and filthy, and she was scored and scabbed all over with dozens of the scars of sharp abrasions of rock and thorn. Her matted hair was so long it hung down to the ground as they carried her. It was stuck with burrs. She was dreadfully verminous. She stank riotously.

Solemn with wonder, her little cousin trotted behind her. Granny kept her bitten hand wrapped up in her apron. When they dumped the girl on the earth floor of her grandmother's house, the boy secretly stretched out and touched her upper arm. Her flesh felt warm but hard as wood. She had given up struggling, now; she lay on the floor, trussed up, and pretended to be dead.

Granny's house had the one big room, half byre, half home, the beasts who lived with them in winter segregated by a wood partition from where the family lived. There was a ladder up to the hayloft. There was soup on the fire and the table laid, it was now about supper time but still light; night comes late on the summer mountain.

'Untie her,' said Grandmother.

Her son wasn't willing but she would not be denied. He got the bread knife and cut the rope round the girl's ankles. All she did was kick out a bit. But when he cut the rope round her wrists, it was as if he had let a fiend loose. The onlookers ran out of the door, the family ran for the ladder to the hayloft and roosted there, out of her way, all of them but Gran and the eldest boy, who both made for the door to pull it to and shoot the bolt, to keep her in.

The trapped one knocked round the room, bang, over went the table, crash, dishes shattering, bang, crash, the dresser fell on its face. Over went the meal barrel; she coughed, she sneezed just like a human being sneezes, she bounded around, bewildered, in a white cloud until the flour settled. She made little rushes here and there, all her movements were jagged, violent, illogical. She was mad with terror.

She never rose up on two legs; she crouched, all the time, on her hands and the tips of her feet, yet it was not quite like crouching, you could see how all fours, now, came naturally to her, as though she had made a different pact with gravity than we have. You could see how strong the muscles in her thighs had grown, how taut and twanging the arches of her feet were, how she used her heels only when she sat back on her haunches. She growled; now and then, she hiccuped out those thick grunts of distress. All you could see of her rolling eyes were the whites. Several times, her bowels opened, apparently involuntarily.

She careered into the hearth, yelped with burned pain, and knocked over the pan hanging on the hook. The spilled contents of the pan put out the fire; hot soup spilled over her forelegs. When the soup scalded her, she was shocked rigid. Then, squatting on her hindquarters, holding up her hurt paw before her, dangling piteously from its wrist, she howled, she howled, she howled. It sounded like the birth of tragedy.

Even the old woman, who had contracted with herself to love the child of her dead, beloved daughter, was afraid when she heard that.

But the grandson was not afraid; he hardly heard it, he could not take his eyes off the crevice of her child's sex, that was perfectly visible to him as she sat square on the base of her spine. Her purple inner lips opened up as she howled; she offered him a view of a set of Chinese boxes of whorled flesh that opened one upon the other into herself, perpetually receding, his first, devastating intimation of infinity.

You could see a white thread of moon in the blond sky through the chimney hole. It was neither dark nor light in the room but the boy could see her genitals clearly.

She howled. From the bald mountain, first singly, then in complex polyphony, answered at last voices in the same language. She howled for a long time. Soon it was impossible for the occupants of the house to deny to themselves that the answering howling was coming closer and closer to them.

When all the air outside was full of the sound of wolves, she seemed consoled, sank down, laid her head on her paws so that her hair trailed in the cooling soup, and waited. The household gun hung on a nail over the fireplace, where the man of the house had put it when he came in. When he put his foot on the top of the ladder in order to come down and retrieve it, the girl jumped up, yapping, snarling and showing long, yellow canines; he stayed where he was. Now the howling outside was mixed with the shrieks of terrified domestic beasts. All the other villagers had locked themselves up fast in these houses that could convert to fortresses. It was a siege, but their enemy was bolted inside with this family.

The girl began to howl, again, but in a different way. She squatted in the middle of the floor, pointed her nose to the roof and howled with a kind of wild triumph. An answering howling now came from directly outside the door. The stout door shuddered; a sharp snout poked underneath. Her son leant out of the hayloft and said to his mother: 'Come up.'

She took hold of her grandson's hand with the one of hers that had not been bitten, that was not throbbing. The howling girl allowed them to pass by. The boy pushed his grandmother up the ladder in front of him and drew it up behind them.

The door shook with the impact of many furry shoulders throwing themselves against it. It was secured on the inside by an iron bar that rocked in its socket. The ambiguous light, not night nor day, filled the room like transparent milk, but the boy could not see his cousin's cunt any more, he was at the wrong angle. He looked, instead, at her nakedness, that was, unlike human nakedness, beyond innocence or display. He was filled with a terrified excitement.

Now she stopped howling, leapt at this side of the door, and began to worry and rattle the iron bar with her muzzle and forepaws. The carnivorous wind-band of the mountain encouraged her. It was only a matter of a few moments before she worried the bar out of its socket and the door flew open.

The family in the hayloft, staring as if tranced down through the trap, felt themselves to be on a precarious cloud floating above a sudden whirlpool. The whirlpool had eyes and teeth and red mouths and ululated like all the winds of winter caught in a bag. The fur and wild swirled round the house. A gaunt, brindled dog, four feet through his shoulders, reared on his haunches; in the loft, the baby started whimpering and its mother stuffed her nipple in its mouth to hush it. Below, the girl threw her leg over the dog's back and hugged his thick neck.

The last glimpse the grandson had of her was of her clotted hair shifting with speed as the tide of wolves swept outdoors.

Leaving behind wrecked furniture, smashed crocks, a stench of urine, irremediable silence.

The grandson thought the old woman would cry, now, but she seemed unmoved. When all was safe, they came down the ladder one by one. Although it was well past midnight, the old woman and her daughter-in-law went to the river for water to scrub the house out, they did not want to sleep in a place that smelled of wolves. They threw away the broken things; the man nailed the table and the dresser back together. While they worked, the neighbours came out into the frail moonlight and chattered about the strangeness of the night. The wolves had not taken so much as a single chicken from any village coop. No goat, nor ox, nor cow, nor donkey was a mite harmed.

People brought out beer, and the schnapps they made from potatoes, and snacks, because the excitement made everybody hungry. Soon there was a grand, impromptu party going on but Granny said nothing, although you could see her injured hand was hurting her.

Next day, she went to the graveyard and sat for a while by the wooden cross over the place where her daughter was buried, but she did not pray. Then she went home and started chopping cabbage for the evening meal but had to leave off because her right hand was festering.

That winter, when there was more leisure, her grandson went to the priest to learn to read and write because his parents decided it was high time somebody in the family could do so. It was as though the incident with the wolves had somehow precipitated them all forwards; as though they realised the key to its inexplicability lay elsewhere than on the mountain. The boy learned his letters so quickly and with such enthusiasm that he continued to visit the priest for lessons in mathematics, Latin, and then Greek as his duties with the herd permitted. The summer he was fourteen, the priest told his father and mother their eldest son had exhausted his own store of knowledge and now should go to the seminary in the town and, perhaps, one day become a priest himself. Gran was dead, by then.

The boy's parents were now prosperous and had five strong young sons, altogether, besides three daughters. They could easily spare the eldest, indeed, perhaps had hopes of him. Although he did not want to be a priest, he knew the seminary was the only way off the mountain. It was decided the priest should take the boy the twenty-mile walk to the seminary and make the arrangements for his schooling there after the goats came down from the high pasture for the winter.

The journey would take a day and a half; the priest was old. The nights were already chilly. The priest and the boy lit a fire, ate bread and cheese they brought with them, and talked for a while about some problems in Greek grammar the boy was encountering. The fire would keep wild beasts away. They slept, but the boy was agitated by nervous dreams. He wanted to leave the mountain but was afraid of doing so. In the first light that no more than clarifies the dark, they woke and went to the river for water.

On the other side, a wolf crouched, lapping water that contained mauve cloud; her mouth seemed to liquify the sky. Two cubs played on the bank near her, rolling and cuffing one another. All silent as a dream. At first, in the weird dawn, you did not see how her pelt was the wrong colour for a wolf; that she was tailless; and had no ears. Then she lifted her round head towards them.

Indeed, she had become abundantly hairy. Her forearms were thick with hair, so were her loins and legs, and the hair on her head hung over her face in such a way you could hardly make out her features and these had suffered a feral change, a girl who lived without mirrors, who did not acknowledge the reflection in the river as that of herself, a face the mirror of a different consciousness than ours. Her eyes, the fruit of night on the mountain, were extraordinarily luminous. The priest involuntarily mumbled something in Latin. She cocked her head at the vague, river-washed sound. The scared cubs left off playing and ran to her, to burrow their heads in her sides.

The boy started to tremble violently. She soon decided there was no danger and lowered her muzzle, again, to the surface of the water that took hold of her hair and spread it round her head in a wide circle. When she had finished her drink, she retreated a few paces, shaking her wet head; the boy saw how the little cubs now fastened their mouths on her dangling breasts.

He could not help it, he broke out crying. Tears rolled down his face and splashed on the grass. He took a few steps forward, into the river, with his arms held open, intending to cross over to her, perhaps to embrace her, perhaps to exorcise the vertiginous memory of the depths within depths he had once glimpsed within her.

But his cousin took fright at the sudden movement, wrenched the teats away from the cubs, and ran off. The cubs scampered, squeaking after. She ran on hands and feet as if it were the only way to run, towards the higher ground, into the pale maze of the unfinished dawn.

The boy scrubbed his face with his sleeve, sat down, took off his boots, and dried his feet and legs on the tail of his shirt. Then he and his companion ate something and continued on towards the seminary in silence. There was no language in which they could speak of what they had seen. The boy walked barefoot, carrying his soaked boots slung on his back by the laces. It was the last time he would ever walk barefoot.

The birds woke up and began singing. The sun came up and the mountain, which now lay behind them, began to acquire a two-dimensional look, to recede to manageable proportions, to seem more and more like a piece of *mise en scène*, a backdrop for the emblematic display of fabulous events.

The boy shot one glance over his shoulder, saw how the mountain shrank and thought: 'If I look back again, I shall turn into a pillar of salt.'

As if his life depended on it, he began to babble away about Greek irregular verbs. ■

© GOLBANOU MOGHADDAS

Poster from the Greater Japan National Defense Women's Association, early 1940s. A woman welcomes home the Imperial Japanese Navy. The sash she is wearing and the flag behind her both bear the association's name.

THE SUMMER AFTER
THE WAR

Kazuo Ishiguro

GRANTA 7: SPRING 1983

Something like a torn blanket – I could not see clearly through the evening gloom – had caught high in the limbs of a tree and was billowing gently in the wind. Another tree had fallen and tumbled over the shrubs. Leaves and broken branches lay scattered everywhere. I thought of the war, of the destruction and waste I had seen throughout my earliest years, and I stared at the garden, saying nothing, while my grandmother explained how a typhoon had passed through Kagoshima that morning.

Within a few days, the garden had been tidied, the broken tree piled against a wall together with all the branches and dead foliage. Only then did I notice for the first time the stepping stones which wound a passage through the shrubs towards the trees at the back of the garden. Those shrubs bore a few signs of the assault so recently endured; they were in full bloom, their foliage rich and strangely coloured – in shades of red, orange and purple unlike anything I had encountered in Tokyo. In all, the garden ceased to hold much resemblance to that defeated place I had glimpsed on the night of my arrival.

Between the veranda of the house and the start of the stepping stones was a flat area of turf. There, each morning before the sun had fully risen, my grandfather would lay out his straw mat and exercise.

I would awake to the sounds coming from the garden, dress quickly, and go out onto the veranda. I would then see my grandfather's figure, clad in a loose kimono, moving in the early light. He would bend and stretch with some vigour, and his step was light when he ran on the spot. I would sit waiting quietly through these routine movements. Eventually, the sun would have risen high enough to fall over the wall and into the garden; and all around me, the polished planks of the veranda would become covered in patches of sunlight. Then at last, my grandfather's face would turn stern, and he would begin the judo sequences: swift turns, frozen postures, and – best of all – the throwing motions, each throw accompanied by a short shout. As I watched, I could see vividly the invisible assailants who came at him from all sides, only to fall helplessly in the face of such prowess.

At the end of each session, my grandfather would follow the stepping stones to the back of the garden to confront the largest of the trees that grew by the wall. He would stand before the tree for several seconds, absolutely still. Then, with an abrupt shout, he would pounce on it and attempt to throw it over his hip. He would repeat the attack four or five times, beginning each time with those few seconds of contemplative silence, as if that way he would catch the tree by surprise.

As soon as my grandfather had gone inside to change, I would go into the garden and attempt to reproduce the movements I had just seen. This would end with my constructing elaborate scenarios around the movements – scenarios which were always variations on the same plot. They always began with my grandfather and I walking home at night, along the alley behind the Kagoshima railway station. From out of the darkness would emerge figures, and we would be obliged to stop. Their leader would step forward – a man with drunken, slovenly speech – demanding we hand over money. My grandfather would quietly warn them they should let us pass or they would come to harm. At this, voices would laugh in the darkness all around us – dirty, leering laughs. My grandfather and I would exchange an unworried glance, then take up positions back to back.

Then they would come, an unlimited number from all sides. And there in the garden I would enact their destruction; my grandfather and I, a smoothly co-ordinated team, rendering them harmless one by one. Finally, we would survey with gravity the bodies all around us. He would then nod, and we would go on our way. Of course, we would show no untoward excitement about the matter and continue home without discussing it.

There were times midway through such a battle when Noriko, my grandparents' housemaid, called me in to breakfast. But otherwise, I would conclude my programme as my grandfather did; I would go to the tree, stand before it silently for those vital few seconds, then embrace it with appropriate suddenness. I did at times act out a scenario in which, before my grandfather's startled gaze, I would actually uproot the tree and send it tumbling over the shrubs. But the tree was infinitely more solid than the one broken by the typhoon, and even as a boy of seven, I accepted this particular scenario as unlikely, not of the same realm of possibility as the other.

I do not think my grandfather was an especially wealthy man, but life at his house seemed very comfortable after the conditions I had known in Tokyo. There were shopping expeditions with Noriko to buy toys, books and new clothes; and there were many kinds of food – though commonplace enough today – which I tasted for the first time in my life. The house too seemed spacious, despite a whole side of it being so damaged as to be uninhabitable. One afternoon soon after my arrival, my grandmother took me around it to show me the paintings and ornaments which adorned the rooms. Whenever I saw a painting I liked, I would point and ask: 'Did my grandfather do that?' But in the end, though we must have inspected each of the many paintings displayed around the house, not one turned out to be an example of my grandfather's work.

'But I thought Oji was a famous painter,' I said. 'Where are his paintings?'

'Perhaps you would care for something to eat, Ichiro-san?'

'Oji's paintings! Bring them at once!'

My grandmother looked at me with a curious expression. 'I wonder now,' she said. 'I suppose it was Ichiro's aunt who told him about his grandfather.'

Something in her manner caused me to become silent.

'I wonder what else Ichiro's aunt told him,' she continued. 'Yes, I do wonder.'

'She just said Oji was a famous painter. Why aren't his paintings here?'

'What else did she say, Ichiro-san?'

'Why aren't his paintings here? I want an answer!'

My grandmother smiled. 'I expect they've been tidied away. We can look for them another time. But your aunt was saying how keen you were yourself on drawing and painting. Most talented, she told me. If you were to ask your grandfather, Ichiro-san, I'm sure he'd be honoured to teach you.'

'I don't need a teacher.'

'Forgive me, it was merely a suggestion. Now, perhaps, you would care for something to eat.'

As it was, my grandfather began helping me to paint without my having to ask him. I was sitting on the veranda one hot day, trying to compose a picture with my water paints. The picture was going badly, and I was about to screw it up in anger when my grandfather came out onto the veranda, placed a cushion near me, and sat down.

'Don't let me stop you working, Ichiro.' He leaned over to see the picture, but I hid it with my arm. 'All right,' he said, with a laugh. 'I'll see it once it's finished.'

Noriko brought out some tea, poured it, and left. My grandfather continued to sit there with a contented air, sipping tea and looking out onto his garden. His presence made me self-conscious, and I made a show of working at my picture. After some minutes, however, the frustration overtook me again, and I hurled my paintbrush across the veranda. My grandfather turned to me.

'Ichiro,' he said, quite calmly, 'you're throwing paint everywhere. If Noriki-san sees that, she'll be very angry with you.'

'I don't care.'

He gave a laugh and once more leaned over to look at my painting. I tried to hide it again, but he held my arm aside.

'Not so bad. Why are you so angry with it?'

'Give it back. I want to tear it up.'

He held the picture beyond my reach and continued looking at it. 'Not so bad at all,' he said, thoughtfully. 'You shouldn't give up so easily. Look, Oji will help you a little. Then you try and finish it.'

The brush had bounced across the floorboards to a point some distance from us, and my grandfather rose to retrieve it. When he picked it up, he touched the end with his fingertips as if to heal it, then came back and sat down. He studied the picture carefully for a moment, dipped the brush into the water, then touched it against two or three of the colours. And then, in one smooth movement, he passed the dripping brush across the surface of my picture, and a trail of tiny leaves had appeared in its wake: lights and shades, folds and clusters, all in one smooth movement.

'There. Now you try and finish it.'

I did my best to look unimpressed, but my enthusiasm could not help being rekindled by such a feat. Once my grandfather had returned to sipping his tea and looking out at the garden, I dipped the brush in paint and water, then tried to emulate what I had just witnessed.

I succeeded in painting a number of thick wet lines across the paper. My grandfather saw this and shook his head, believing I had been erasing my picture.

Initially, I had assumed that the damage to the house had been caused by the typhoon, but I soon discovered that most of it originated from the war. My grandfather had been in the process of rebuilding that side of the house, when the typhoon had demolished the scaffolding and ruined much of what he had achieved over the past year. He showed little frustration over what had occurred, and during the weeks after my arrival, continued to work on the house at a steady pace – perhaps two or three hours each day. At times, workmen would come to assist him, but usually he worked alone, hammering and sawing. There was no sense of urgency about the matter. There was plenty of room in the rest of the house, and, in any case, progress was necessarily impeded by the scarcity of materials. Sometimes, he would wait days for a box of nails or a certain piece of wood.

The only room in use on the damaged side of the house was the bathroom. It was very bare; the floor was concrete, with channels cut into it to allow water to flow out under the outer wall; and the windows looked out onto the rubble and scaffolding outside, so that one felt one was standing in an annex of the house rather than within it. But in one corner, my grandfather had built a deep wooden box into which could be poured three or four feet of steaming water. Each night before going to bed, I would call to my grandfather through the screen and, sliding it back, would discover the room filled with steam. There would be a smell, like that of dried fish, which I thought appropriate to the body of a grown man, and my grandfather would be in his bath, up to his neck in hot water. And each night, I would stand in that steam-filled room and talk to him – often of matters I would never mention elsewhere. My grandfather would listen, then answer me with sparse, reassuring words from behind the clouds of steam.

'This is your home now, Ichiro,' he would say. 'No need to leave until you've grown up. Even then, you may want to stay here. No need to worry. No need at all.'

On one such evening in that bathroom, I remarked to my grandfather: 'Japanese soldiers were the best fighters in the war.'

'Our soldiers certainly were the most determined,' he said. 'The most courageous, perhaps. Very brave soldiers. But even the finest of soldiers are sometimes defeated.'

'Because there's too many of the enemy.'

'Because there's too many of the enemy. And because the enemy have more weapons.'

'Japanese soldiers could fight on even when they were badly wounded, couldn't they? Because they were determined.'

'Yes. Our soldiers fought even when they were badly hurt.'

'Oji, watch!'

There in the bathroom, I began to act out a scenario of a soldier surrounded by enemies, engaged in unarmed combat. Whenever a bullet struck me, I would halt briefly, then continue fighting. 'Yah! Yah!'

My grandfather laughed, raised his hands from the water and applauded. Encouraged, I fought on – eight, nine, ten bullets. When I stopped for a moment to catch my breath, my grandfather was still clapping and laughing to himself.

'Oji, do you know who I am?'

He closed his eyes again, and sank deeper into the water. 'A soldier. A very brave Japanese soldier.'

'Yes, but who? Which soldier? Watch, Oji. You guess.'

I pressed a hand painfully against my wounds and recommenced the battle. The large number of bullets I had received in my chest and stomach obliged me to forego my more flamboyant techniques. 'Yah! Yah! Who am I, Oji? Guess! Guess!'

Then I noticed that my grandfather had opened his eyes and was staring at me through the steam. He was staring at me as if I were a ghost, and a chill went through me. I stopped and stared back at him. Then his face smiled again, but the strange look remained in his eyes.

'Enough now,' he said, reclining again in the water. 'Too many enemies. Too many.'

I remained standing still.

'What's the matter, Ichiro?' he asked, and gave a laugh. 'Suddenly so quiet.'

I did not reply. My grandfather closed his eyes again and sighed.

'What an awful thing war is, Ichiro,' he said, tiredly. 'An awful thing. But never mind. You're here now. This is your home. No need to worry.'

O ne evening at the height of the summer, I came in to find an extra place set for supper. My grandmother said in a low voice: 'Your grandfather has a visitor. They'll be through in a moment.'

For some time, my grandmother, Noriko and I sat waiting around the supper table. When I began to show impatience, Noriko told me to keep my voice down. 'The gentleman's only just arrived. You can't expect him to be ready so soon.'

My grandmother nodded. 'I expect they have much to say to each other after all this time.'

At last, my grandfather appeared with the guest. He was perhaps around forty – I had little sense of adults' ages then – a stocky man, with eyebrows so black they looked as if they were inked in. During the meal, he and my grandfather talked much of the past. A name would be mentioned, and my grandfather would repeat it and nod gravely. Soon, a solemn atmosphere hung over the table. Once, my grandmother began to congratulate the visitor on his new job, but he stopped her.

'No, no, madam. You're most kind, but too hasty. The appointment is by no means certain.'

'But as you say,' my grandfather put in, 'you have no real rivals. You're by far the best qualified for the post.'

'You're much too kind, Sensei,' the visitor said. 'But it's by no means certain. I can only hope and wait.'

'If this were a few years ago,' said my grandfather, 'I could have put in a good word for you. But I don't expect my opinion carries much weight these days.'

'Really, Sensei,' said the visitor, 'you do yourself a grave injustice. A man of your achievements must always be respected.'

At this, my grandfather laughed rather oddly.

A fter supper, I asked my grandmother: 'Why does he call Oji "Sensei"?'

'The gentleman was once your grandfather's pupil. A most brilliant one.'

'When Oji was a famous painter?'

'Yes. The gentleman is a very splendid artist. One of your grandfather's most brilliant pupils.'

The visitor's presence meant I was deprived of my grandfather's attention, and this put me in a bad mood. During the days which followed, I avoided the visitor as much as I could and spoke barely a word to him. Then one afternoon, I overheard the conversation which took place on the veranda.

At the top of my grandfather's house was a Western-style room with high chairs and tables. The balcony of the room overlooked the garden, and the veranda was two floors below. I had been amusing myself in the room, and had been conscious for some time of the voices below me. Then something caught my attention – something in the tone of the exchange – and I went out onto the balcony to listen. Sure enough, my grandfather and his guest were in disagreement; as I understood it, the matter involved some letter the visitor wished my grandfather to write.

'Surely, Sensei,' the man was saying, 'it's hardly unreasonable of me. For a long time, I believed my career to be at an end. Surely, Sensei wouldn't wish to see me burdened down by what happened in the past.'

There was silence for a while, then the visitor spoke again: 'Please don't misunderstand, Sensei. I'm as proud as ever to have my name associated with yours. It's merely for the purpose of satisfying the committee, nothing more.'

'So this is why you've come to see me.' My grandfather's voice sounded more weary than angry. 'So this is why you've come after all this time. But why do you wish to lie about yourself? You did what you did with pride and brilliance. A mistake or not, a man should not lie about himself.'

'But, Sensei, perhaps you've forgotten. Do you remember that evening in Kobe? After the banquet for Kinoshita-san? You became angry with me that night because I dared to disagree with you. Don't you remember, Sensei?'

'The banquet for Kinoshita? I'm afraid I don't. What did we quarrel about?'

'We quarrelled because I dared to suggest the school had taken a wrong direction. Don't you remember, Sensei? I said that it was no business of ours to employ our talents like that. And you were furious at me. Don't you remember that, Sensei?'

There was silence again.

'Ah yes,' my grandfather said, eventually. 'I remember now. It was at the time of the China campaign. A crucial time for the nation. It would have been irresponsible to carry on working as we once had.'

'But I always disagreed with you, Sensei. And I felt so strongly about it, I actually told you to your face. All I'm asking now is simply that you acknowledge that fact to the committee. Simply state what my view was from the beginning, and that I went so far as to disagree with you openly. Surely, that's not unreasonable, Sensei.'

There was another pause, then my grandfather said: 'You benefited much from my name while it was revered. Now the world has a different opinion of me, you must face up to it.'

There was silence for some time, then I could hear movement and the sliding shut of screens.

At supper, I searched for signs of conflict between my grandfather and the visitor, but they behaved towards each other with perfect politeness. That night, in the steam-filled bathroom, I asked my grandfather: 'Oji, why don't you paint any more?'

At first, he was silent. Then he said: 'Sometimes, when you paint your pictures and things don't go well, you get angry, don't you? You want to tear the pictures up and Oji has to stop you. Isn't that so?'

'Yes,' I said, and waited. His eyes remained closed, his voice slow and tired. 'It was rather like that for your grandfather. He didn't do things so well, so he decided to put it aside.'

'But you always tell me not to tear up pictures. You always make me finish them.'

'That's true. But then you're very young, Ichiro. You'll get so much better.'

The next morning, the sun was already high when I went out to the veranda to watch my grandfather. Shortly after I had sat down, there was a sound behind me, and the visitor appeared, dressed in a dark kimono. He greeted me, and when I said nothing, laughed and strode past me to the edge of the veranda. My grandfather saw him and stopped exercising.

'Ah! Up so early. I didn't disturb you, I hope.' My grandfather reached down to roll up his straw mat.

'Not at all, Sensei. I slept splendidly. But please don't let me stop you. Noriko-san was telling me you do this every morning, summer or winter. Highly admirable. No, please, really. I was so impressed, I promised myself I'd get up this morning and see for myself. I'd never forgive myself if I were the reason for Sensei breaking his routine. Sensei, please.'

In the end, my grandfather continued his exercises – he had been running on the spot – with an air of reluctance. He stopped again almost immediately and said: 'Thank you for being so patient. Really, that will do for this morning.'

'But Sensei, the little gentleman here will be disappointed. I heard how much he enjoys your judo training. Now isn't that so, Ichiro-san?'

I pretended not to have heard.

'It will do no harm to miss them this morning,' said my grandfather. 'Let's go inside and wait for breakfast.'

'But I too would be disappointed, Sensei. I was hoping to be reminded of your prowess. Do you remember you tried to teach me judo once?'

'Really? Yes, I seem to remember something like that.'

'Murasaki was with us then. And Ishida. At that sports hall in Yokohama. You remember that, Sensei? However I tried to throw you, I'd end up flat on my back. I was so dejected afterwards. Come, Sensei – Ichiro and I would like to see you practising.'

My grandfather laughed and held up his hands. He was standing rather awkwardly at the centre of his mat. 'But really, I gave up serious training a long time ago.'

'You know, Sensei, during the war I became quite an expert myself. We trained a lot in unarmed combat.' As he said this, the visitor glanced towards me.

'I'm sure you were very well trained in the army,' my grandfather said.

'As I say, I became quite an expert. Still, if I were to take on Sensei again, I'm sure my fate would be no different from before. I'd be flat on my back in no time.'

They both laughed.

'I'm sure you had excellent training,' my grandfather said.

The visitor turned towards me again, and I saw his eyes were smiling in an odd way. 'But against a man of Sensei's experience, all that training would be of little use. I'm sure my fate would be just as it was in that sports hall.'

My grandfather remained standing on his mat. Then the visitor said: 'Please, Sensei, don't let me disturb you. Exercise as if I weren't here.'

'No, really. That will do for this morning.' My grandfather dropped down onto one knee and began rolling up his mat.

The visitor leaned his shoulder against the veranda post and looked up at the sky.

'Murasaki, Ishida . . . That seems a long time ago now.' He appeared to be talking to himself, but he spoke loudly enough for my grandfather to hear. My grandfather's back was turned to us as he continued gathering up the mat.

'All of them gone now,' the visitor said. 'You and I, Sensei. We seem to be the only ones left from those days.'

My grandfather paused. 'Yes,' he said, without turning. 'Yes, it's tragic.'

'That war was such a waste. Such a mistake.' The visitor was staring at my grandfather's back.

'Yes, it's tragic,' my grandfather repeated, quietly. I could see him gazing at a spot on the ground, the straw mat half-rolled before him.

The visitor left that day after breakfast, and I was never to see him again. My grandfather was reluctant to talk about him and would tell me only what I knew already. I did, however, learn something from Noriko.

I often accompanied her when she went shopping for groceries, and during one such outing, I asked: 'Noriko, what was the China campaign?'

She obviously assumed I had asked an 'education' question, for she replied in the pleased, patient manner she adopted when I asked her such questions as where frogs went in winter. Before the outbreak of the Pacific War, she explained, the Japanese army had undertaken a campaign of some success through China. I asked her if there had been something wrong about it and for the first time she looked at me curiously. No, there had been nothing wrong about it, but there had been a lot of argument at the time. And now, some people were saying there would not have been a war if the army had not pressed on into China. I asked again if the army had been wrong to invade China. Noriko said there was nothing wrong as such, but there had been a lot of argument about it. War was not a good thing, everyone knew that now.

As the summer went on, my grandfather spent more and more time with me – so much so that he had almost ceased to work on the repairs to the damaged side of the house. With his encouragement, my interest in painting and sketching grew into a genuine enthusiasm. He would take me on day outings, and on reaching our destination, we would sit in the sunshine while I sketched with my coloured crayons. Usually, we would go somewhere far away from people – perhaps to some hill slope with tall grass and a splendid view. Or we would go to the shipyards, or the site of some new factory. Then on the tram going home, we would look through the sketches I had done that day.

Our days would still begin with my going out to the veranda to watch my grandfather exercise. But we had by then added a new feature to the morning's routine. When my grandfather had completed his round of exercises on the mat, he would call up to me: 'Come on then. Let's see if you're any tougher today.' And I would step down from the veranda, go to his mat, and hold his kimono as he had shown me – one hand gripping the collar, the other the sleeve close to the elbow. I would then try to execute the throw he had taught me, and after several attempts would succeed in getting my grandfather onto his back. Although I realised he was allowing me to throw him, I would nonetheless be overcome with pride when he finally went over. My grandfather would see to it though that I would have to try a little harder each time before succeeding. Then one morning, however much I tried, my grandfather would not oblige by going over.

'Come on, Ichiro, don't give up. You're not holding the kimono correctly, are you?'

I readjusted the grip.

'Good. Now try again.'

I turned and tried once more.

'Nearly. You have to put your whole hip into it. Oji is a big man. You won't do it with just your hands.'

I tried yet again; my grandfather still would not go over. Disheartened, I let go.

'Now, come on, Ichiro. Don't give up so easily. Just once more. Do everything right. That's right. There, now I'm helpless. Now throw.'

This time my grandfather gave no resistance and tumbled over my heel and onto his back. He lay on the mat with his eyes closed.

'You let me do it,' I said, sulkily.

My grandfather did not open his eyes. I laughed, deciding he was pretending to be dead. My grandfather still gave no response.

'Oji?'

He opened his eyes, then noticing me, smiled. He sat up slowly, a puzzled expression on his face, and rubbed a hand over the back of his neck. 'Well, well,' he said. 'Now that was a proper throw.' He touched my arm, but immediately his hand returned to the back of his neck. Then he gave a laugh and got to his feet. 'Breakfast now.'

'Aren't you going to the tree?'

'Not today. You've given Oji enough for one morning.'

A great sense of triumph was rising in me; for the first time, I thought, I had thrown my grandfather without his letting me.

'I'm going to practise with the tree,' I said.

'No, no.' My grandfather ushered me towards him, one hand still rubbing his neck. 'Come and eat now. Men have to eat or they'll lose their strength.'

It was not until the early months of autumn that I finally saw an example of my grandfather's work. I had been helping Noriko store away some old books in the Western room at the top of the house, when I noticed, protruding from a box in a cupboard, several large rolled sheets of paper. I pulled one out and unrolled it on the floor. What I had found resembled a cinema poster. I tried to examine it more closely, but it had spent so much time rolled up, I could not hold it flat without it curling. I asked Noriko to hold one end, and I moved round to hold down the other.

We both looked at the poster. It showed a samurai holding up a sword; behind him was the Japanese military flag. The picture was set against a deep red background which gave me an uneasy feeling, reminding me of the colour of wounds when I fell and injured my leg. Down one edge were bold kanji characters, of which I only recognised those reading 'Japan'. I asked Noriko what the poster said. She was examining another section of it with interest, and read off the heading rather distractedly: ' "No time for cowardly talking. Japan must go forward." '

'What is it?'

'Something your grandfather did. A long time ago.'

'Oji?' I was disappointed, for I disliked the poster and I had always imagined his work to have been of a quite different nature.

'Yes, a long time ago. See, here's his signature in the corner.'

There was more writing towards the bottom of the sheet. Noriko turned her head and began to read.

'What does it say?' I asked.

She continued to read with a serious expression.

'What does it say, Noriko?'

She released her end of the sheet, and it immediately rolled over my hand. I tried to spread it open again, but Noriko was no longer interested.

'What does it say, Noriko?'

'I don't know,' she said, returning to the books. 'It's very old. Before the war.'

I did not persist with the matter, but resolved to find out more from my grandfather.

That evening, as usual, I went to the bathroom and called to him through the partition. There was no reply, and I called more loudly. Then I put my ear to the screen and listened. Everything inside seemed very still. The thought occurred to me that my grandfather had discovered about my seeing the poster and was angry with me. But then a fear passed through me, and I slid back the partition and looked inside.

The bathroom was filled with steam, and for a moment I could not make things out clearly. Then I saw, over by the wall, my grandfather trying to get out of his bath. I could see through the steam his elbow and shoulder, locked in an effort to heave the body out of the water. His face was bowed over, almost touching the rim of the bath. He was absolutely still, as if he could go no further and his body had locked itself. I ran to him.

'Oji!'

My grandfather remained still. I reached out and touched him, but did so cautiously, afraid the shoulder would collapse and he would fall back into the water.

'Oji! Oji!'

Noriko came hurrying into the room, then my grandmother. One of them pulled me aside, and they both struggled with my grandfather. Whenever I tried to help, I was told to stand away. They lifted my grandfather out of the bath with considerable difficulty, then I was ordered out of the room.

I went to my own room and listened to the commotion around the house. There were voices I did not recognise, and whenever I slid open my door and tried to step out, someone would tell me angrily to return to bed. I lay awake for a long time.

During the days that followed, I was not allowed to see my grandfather and he did not emerge from his room. A nurse came to the house each morning and would stay all day. My questions always received the same reply: my grandfather was ill, but would be all right again. It was only natural that he, like anyone else, should fall ill from time to time.

I continued each morning to get up early and go to the veranda, hoping to find my grandfather recovered and exercising again. When he did not appear, I would remain in the garden, not giving up hope, until Noriko called me in to breakfast.

Then one evening, I was told I could visit my grandfather's room. I was warned I could see him only briefly, and when I went in, Noriko sat beside me as if she would take me away should I do anything out of place. The nurse was sat in the far corner, and there was a smell of chemicals in the room.

My grandfather was lying on his side. He smiled at me, made a small motion with his head, but said nothing. I sensed a formality about the occasion and became inhibited. In the end, I said: 'Oji, you're to get better soon.'

Again, he smiled, but said nothing.

'I drew the maple tree yesterday,' I said. 'I brought it for you. I'll leave it here.'

'Let me see it,' he said, quietly.

I held out the sketch. My grandfather took it and turned onto his back. As he did so, Noriko stirred uneasily beside me.

'Good,' he said. 'Well done.'

Noriko reached forward quickly and took the sketch from him.

'Leave it here with me,' my grandfather said. 'It'll help me get better.'

Noriko placed the sketch on the tatami close to him, then led me out of the room.

Weeks passed without my being allowed to see him. I still awoke each morning in the hope of finding him in the garden, but he would not be there, and my days became long and empty.

Then one morning, I was in the garden as usual, when my grandfather appeared on the veranda. He was seating himself as I ran up to him and hugged him.

'So what have you been up to, Ichiro?'

Somewhat ashamed of my show of emotion, I composed myself and sat beside him in what I considered a manly posture.

'Just walking around the garden,' I said. 'Taking the air a little before breakfast.'

'I see.' My grandfather's eyes were roving around the garden, as if to study each shrub and tree. I followed his gaze. It was well into autumn by then; the sky above the wall was grey, the garden full of fallen leaves.

'Tell me, Ichiro,' he said, still looking at the garden. 'What will you be when you grow up?'

I thought for a moment. 'A policeman,' I said.

'A policeman?' My grandfather turned to me and smiled. 'Now that's a real man's job.'

'I'll need to practise hard if I want to be successful.'

'Practise? What will you practise to become a policeman?'

'Judo. I've been practising some mornings. Before breakfast.'

My grandfather's eyes returned to the garden. 'Indeed,' he said, quietly. 'A real man's job.'

I watched my grandfather for a while. 'Oji,' I asked, 'what did you want to be when you were my age?'

'When I was your age?' For some moments, he continued to gaze at the garden. Then he said: 'Why, I suppose I wanted to be a painter. I don't remember a time when I wished to be anything else.'

'I want to be a painter too.'

'Really? You're very good already, Ichiro. I wasn't as good at your age.'

'Oji, watch!'

'Where are you off to?' he called after me.

THE SUMMER AFTER THE WAR

'Oji, watch. Watch!'

I ran to the back of the garden and stood before my grandfather's tree.

'Yah!' I gripped it round the trunk and heaved my hip against it. 'Yah! Yah!'

I looked up and my grandfather was laughing. He raised both hands and applauded. I laughed also, overcome with happiness that my grandfather had been returned to me. Then I turned back to the tree and challenged it once more.

'Yah! Yah!'

From the veranda came the sounds of my grandfather's laughter and the clapping of his hands. ■

EVENSONG

Todd McEwen

GRANTA 8: AUTUMN 1983

Leave my wife alone I said. No he said I will not leave your wife alone, I love her. And so saying he went from the doorstep and taking a small green tent he set it up in the garden and every morning thereafter I was irritated awake by the smell of his infernal little cookstove and a bit later tortured by that of his squalid fried breakfast. He hired a small boy to bring love letters to the front door sixteen times a day, hourly. My wife gave the boy 5p every time; this angered me but as she said it is not the boy's fault. Besides he is from a poor family. But at 5p x 16 hrs = 80p per diem might I not end up in the poorhouse myself? But it was not the money. It was the situation. And the smell every morning. My wife's one pronouncement was It is just a phase. But a phase for who? I said And how long? She, lovely, went to the other side of the garden and planted leeks in silence. While she planted the leeks I was left to answer the door and pay the boy the 5p every hour. Can't you see she's just over there by the hedge? I said after he had handed me the third letter. He smiled at me mutely. So he was retarded as well as poor! Darling, I love you, I can't live without you, be mine. Your worshipper. I stopped reading the letters, they were all the same. And the envelopes were all the same, addressed merely to She. In the morning the letters were often stained with cooking fat or some kind of jam. The letters that came at midday were relatively clean (I think he ate only salads for lunch, made from herbs and flowers growing on the cat's grave by the tent). The evening letters often smelled of whisky or canned beer and potato crisps. I left the letters in a neat pile on my wife's table. She would come in from planting leeks and glance at the letters, occasionally sifting through them to see if the message varied which as I have said it did not. Characteristically my wife refused to be drawn into the situation while I became obsessed with it. Even the coalmen stepped around the tent without disturbing him while they made their delivery. It's probably just a phase! one of them whispered to me. One evening as I sat and watched the smoke from his wretched stove drift past the window I said to my wife Don't you realise we are tenants of a noble? A man with a title? He'll take care of this. My wife sewed placidly. She refused to be drawn into the situation but I had become obsessed with it. I dialled the castle. What! groaned a voice. I I I want to talk to His Lordship I said This is me at the west farm. What's the matter with you? said the voice Do you know what time it is? I do I said What's the matter with you? His Lordship is asleep said the voice and is always asleep at this hour. Dog's life, being a life peer I snarled. What is the nature of your business? said the voice. There is a man in a tent in my garden I said. Squatter eh? said the voice. Most indubitably I said feeling I was getting somewhere. Why don't you tell him to clear off? said the voice. I have I said. Why don't you call the police? said the voice. There's no point I said As you well know only His Lordship can evict someone from *feudal* land. With the *f* I filled the mouthpiece with foam. Is he causing trouble? said the voice. He writes love letters to my wife I said. Oh? said the voice lighting a cigarette. He was interested now. Hourly I said They are delivered by a little backward boy who lives down the road. Yes I know the place said the voice His father was gamekeeper to His Lordship for many years. Isn't that marvellous? I said. The estate cannot mix in affairs of the heart said the voice It's not good business. It's not an affair of the heart I said. My wife wants nothing to do with him or the letters. Well perhaps she's pursuing the best course then eh? said the voice I must

ring off now but it has been most interesting. He hung up. I hung up
and looked at my wife who was trying to tune in her radio. I put on
my hat and stamped out of the house and out the gate slamming it for
effect of which there was none and glaring at the tent I stalked down
the road toward Muckhart's house. Muckhart was cleaning his nose,
absorbed in its reflection in the window over his kitchen sink. Because
of complicated lighting conditions the window acted as a mirror in
the interior of the house but approaching from the road I could see
Muckhart cleaning his nose. I banged on the door and Muckhart
opened it. His dog barked at me immediately and without cessation.
Muckhart! I shouted over the dog din Muckhart! Realising the dog
would not stop barking Muckhart came out onto the step and closed
the door behind him. Immediately the barking stopped. He gave me
a merry look and turned toward the door again but as soon as his
touch had disturbed the mechanism of the doorknob the furious
barking began again. We'd best stay out here! I shouted and he nodded
and turned back to me. Muckhart I said There is a man in my garden
in a tent. Aye I've seen that he said Friend o yours? Not at all I said He
is a squatter. Och! A squatter? said Muckhart. Yes I said feeling I was
getting somewhere. Weel hae ye askit him tae leave? said Muckhart.
It's more complicated than that I said He's writing love letters to my
wife, once an hour, delivered by a retarded boy. Muckhart scratched
his head. Aye that would be the wee boy fae the cottage by the water.
I suppose so I said impatiently. Weel dinnae fash yerseel said
Muckhart I'll awa and hae a blether wi his mam in the mornin. No! I
said No No No! Not the boy. Oh so ye dinna mind aboot the letters?
said Muckhart queerly. I do mind! I said turning red But it's the man
in the tent! I want you to get rid of the man in the tent. But I cannae
do onythin aboot that spluttered Muckhart suddenly resentful Ye
kens it's ony the laird as can evict a squatter. He made to enter the
kitchen but I stayed him. Listen I said Can't you arrange to (here I
moved my clawlike hands in a foolish imitation of quotation marks)
'accidentally' run over the tent with your tractor? Muckhart eyed my
gesture without comprehension but took his hand away from the

doorknob. He looked out at the evening and taking a pipe out of his pocket he sat down on the step. I sat down beside him and watched him fill the pipe. He tamped the tobacco firmly with his alarming brown thumb which had been in India during the war. He lit the pipe and smoked, silent, staring at the byre. No he said eventually I cannae do that. Why not? I whined. Ye ask me if I couldnae arrange tae accidentally run ooer the tent wi ma tractor and the onser tae that is no. Ye see said Muckhart If I *arranged* tae dae it it wouldnae be an accident noo would it? And I micht truly accidentally run ooer the tent but I couldnae predict it and indeed the possibility is verrry verrry slim considering (here he got up) yer gairden is separatit fae the road by a ditch and yer wife's flooers and the grave of yer puir auld puss. He knocked his pipe against the step. Evenin to ye he said and went inside. I was left alone with my thoughts and the road home. It was twilight. Approaching my house and the tent with its accursed tin chimney I suddenly hied into the ditch which rendered me invisible from the garden. I prised up a large stone from the moocky bottom and hurled it at the tent. To my delight it struck the tin chimney, knocking off its little Chinese hat. Hey! came a cry from the tent. Woo! I said Woo! Who's there? he said still inside. I rustled the weeds on the garden side of the ditch in a supernatural manner. Woo! I said I am the Spirit of this Place. There is great danger here. Woo! He put his head out of the tent, frightened. Woo! I said Leave this place leave this place leave this place. Woo! For God's sake! he cried Who's there? Woo! I said It's me, an awful raw-head bloody-bones! Fly for your life! Woo! The head disappeared into the tent and I heard nothing. Rummaging in the ditch I felt another stone which to my disgust turned out to be a dead toad. Yet I flung it and managed to knock down the tent pole. With a tremendous clatter the whole of him emerged from the collapsed tent. He was wearing an overcoat and had a rope tied around him from which hung his damned pots and pans. He stood and looked with uncertainty at the lifeless toad on the tent, the whole of which was catching fire owing to the stove being upset. *Woo!* I howled like the wind. *Wah!* With a shriek he leaped over the fence and began to hurry down the road. Every few yards he tripped over the pans, some of which were very large. I continued to wail until he had disappeared down the road to the south. Bloody Sassenach. I had difficulty in extracting my legs from the mud in the ditch but eventually got up to the garden hauling myself by thistles and brambles. I stood and watched his tent burn and made up incantations which I recited. When I entered the house my wife was still trying to tune her radio. She had refused to be drawn into the situation while I on the other hand had become obsessed with it. The next morning the retarded boy knocked at the door but he had no letter. I was almost happy to see him. I gave him 50p and told him to go home but he came back in an hour, again with no letter and the next hour and the next and the next and the next and the next. ■

Bruce Chatwin in Paris, France, 1984

A COUP

Bruce Chatwin

GRANTA 10: SPRING 1984

The coup began at seven on Sunday morning. It was a grey and windless dawn and the grey Atlantic rollers broke in long even lines along the beach. The palms above the tidemark shivered in a current of cooler air that blew in off the breakers. Out at sea – beyond the surf – there were several black fishing canoes. Buzzards were spiralling above the market, swooping now and then to snatch up scraps of offal. The butchers were slaughtering, even on a Sunday.

We were in a taxi when the coup began, on our way to another country. We had passed the Hôtel de la Plage, passed the Sûreté Nationale, and then we drove under a limply flapping banner which said, in red letters, that Marxism–Leninism was the one and only guide. In front of the Presidential Palace was a roadblock. A soldier waved us to a halt, and then waved us on.

'*Pourriture!*' said my friend, Domingo, and grinned.

Domingo was a young, honey-coloured mulatto with a flat and friendly face, a curly moustache and a set of dazzling teeth. He was the direct descendant of Francisco Félix de Souza, the Chacha of Ouidah, a Brazilian slaver who lived and died in Dahomey, and about whom I was writing a book.

Domingo had two wives. The first wife was old and the skin hung in loose folds off her back. The second wife was hardly more than a child. We were on our way to Togo, to watch a football game, and visit his great-uncle who knew a lot of old stories about the Chacha.

The taxi was jammed with football fans. On my right sat a very black old man wrapped in green and orange cotton. His teeth were also orange from chewing cola nuts, and from time to time he spat.

Outside the Presidential Palace hung an overblown poster of the Head of State, and two much smaller posters of Lenin and Kim Il-sung. Beyond the roadblock, we took a right fork, on through the old European section where there were bungalows and baulks of bougainvillaea by the gates. Along the sides of the tarmac, market women walked in single file with basins and baskets balanced on their head.

'What's that?' I asked. I could see some kind of commotion, up ahead, towards the airport.

'Accident!' Domingo shrugged, and grinned again.

Then all the women were screaming, and scattering their yams and pineapples, and rushing for the shelter of the gardens. A white Peugeot shot down the middle of the road, swerving right and left to miss the women. The driver waved for us to turn back, and just then, we heard the crack of gunfire.

'*C'est la guerre!*' our driver shouted, and spun the taxi round.

'I knew it.' Domingo grabbed my arm. 'I knew it.'

The sun was up by the time we got to downtown Cotonou. In the taxi park the crowd had panicked and overturned a brazier, and a stack of crates had caught fire. A policeman blew his whistle and bawled for water. Above the rooftops, there was a column of black smoke, rising.

'They're burning the palace,' said Domingo. 'Quick! Run!'

We ran, bumped into other running figures, and ran on. A man shouted 'Mercenary!' and lunged for my shoulder. I ducked and we dodged down a sidestreet. A boy in a red shirt beckoned me into a bar. It was dark inside. People were clustered round a radio. Then the bartender screamed, wildly, in African, at me, and at the boy. And then I was out again on the dusty red street, shielding my head with my arms, pushed and pummelled against the corrugated building by four hard, acridly sweating men until the gendarmes came to fetch me in a jeep.

'For your own proper protection,' their officer said, as the handcuffs snapped around my wrists.

The last I ever saw of Domingo he was standing in the street, crying, as the jeep drove off, and he vanished in a clash of coloured cottons.

In the barracks guardroom a skinny boy, stripped to a pair of purple underpants, sat hunched against the wall. His hands and feet were bound with rope, and he had the greyish look Africans get when they are truly frightened. A gecko hung motionless on the dirty whitewash. Outside the door there was a papaya with a tall scaly trunk and yellowish fruit. A mud wall ran along the far side of the compound. Beyond the wall the noise of gunfire continued, and the high-pitched wailing of women.

A corporal came in and searched me. He was small, wiry, angular, and his cheekbones shone. He took my watch, wallet, passport and notebook.

'Mercenary!' he said, pointing to the patch-pocket on the leg of my khaki trousers. His gums were spongy and his breath was foul.

'No,' I said, submissively. 'I'm a tourist.'

'Mercenary!' he shrieked, and slapped my face – not hard, but hard enough to hurt.

He held up my fountain pen. 'What?'

'A pen,' I said. It was a black Montblanc.

'What for?'

'To write with.'

'A gun?'

'Not a gun.'

'Yes, a gun!'

I sat on a bench, staring at the skinny boy who continued to stare at his toes. The corporal sat cross-legged in the doorway with his sub-machine gun trained on me. Outside in the yard, two sergeants were distributing rifles, and a truck was loading with troops. The troops sat down with the barrels sticking up from their crotches. The colonel came out of his office and took the salute. The truck lurched off, and he came over, lumpily, towards the guardroom.

The corporal snapped to attention and said, 'Mercenary, Comrade Colonel!'

'From today,' said the colonel, 'there are no more comrades in our country.'

'Yes, Comrade Colonel,' the man nodded; but checked himself and added, 'Yes, my Colonel.'

The colonel waved him aside and surveyed me gloomily. He wore an exquisitely pressed pair of paratrooper fatigues, a red star on his cap, and another red star in his lapel. A roll of fat stood out around the back of his neck; his thick lips drooped at the corners; his eyes were hooded. He looked, I thought, so like a sad hippopotamus. I told myself I mustn't think he looks like a sad hippopotamus. Whatever happens, he mustn't think I think he looks like a sad hippopotamus.

'*Ah, monsieur!*' he said, in a quiet dispirited voice. 'What are you doing in this poor country of ours?'

'I came here as a tourist.'

'You are English?'

'Yes.'

'But you speak an excellent French.'

'Passable,' I said.

'With a Parisian accent I should have said.'

'I have lived in Paris.'

'I, also, have visited Paris. A wonderful city!'

'The most wonderful city.'

'But you have mistimed your visit to Benin.'

'Yes,' I faltered. 'I seem to have run into trouble.'

'You have been here before?'

'Once,' I said. 'Five years ago.'

'When Benin was Dahomey.'

'Yes,' I said. 'I used to think Benin was in Nigeria.'

'Benin is in Nigeria and now we have it here.'

'I think I understand.'

'Calm yourself, monsieur.' His fingers reached to unlock my handcuffs. 'We are having another little change of politics. Nothing more! In these situations one must keep calm. You understand? Calm!'

Some boys had come through the barracks' gate and were creeping forward to peer at the prisoner. The colonel appeared in the doorway, and they scampered off.

'Come,' he said. 'You will be safer if you stay with me. Come, let us listen to the Head of State.'

We walked across the parade ground to his office where he sat me in a chair and reached for a portable radio. Above his desk hung a photo of the Head of State, in a Fidel Castro cap. His cheeks were a basketwork of scarifications.

'The Head of State,' said the colonel, 'is always speaking over the radio. We call it the *journal parlé*. It is a crime in this country *not* to listen to the *journal parlé*.'

He turned the knob. The military music came in cracking bursts.

> Citizens of Benin . . . the hour is grave. At seven hours this morning, an unidentified DC-8 jet aircraft landed at our International Airport of Cotonou, carrying a crapulous crowd of mercenaries . . . black and white . . . financed by the lackeys of international imperialism . . . A vile plot to destroy our democratic and operational regime.

The colonel laid his jowls on his hands and sighed, 'The Sombas! The Sombas!'

The Sombas came from the far north-west of the country. They filed their teeth to points and once, not so long ago, were cannibals.

'. . . launched a vicious attack on our Presidential Palace . . .'

I glanced up again at the wall. The Head of State was a Somba – and the colonel was a Fon.

'. . . the population is requested to arm itself with stones and knives to kill this crapulous . . .'

'A recorded message,' said the colonel, and turned the volume down. 'It was recorded yesterday.'

'You mean . . .'

'Calm yourself, monsieur. You do not understand. In this country one understands nothing.'

Certainly, as this morning wore on, the colonel understood less and less. He did not, for example, understand why, on the nine o'clock communiqué, the mercenaries had landed in a DC-8 jet, while at ten the plane had changed to a DC-7 turbo-prop. Around eleven the music cut off again and the Head of State announced a victory for the government forces. The enemy, he said, were retreating en catastrophe for the marshes of Ouidah.

'There has been a mistake,' said the colonel, looking very shaken. 'Excuse me, monsieur. I must leave you.'

He hesitated on the threshold and then stepped out into the sunlight. The hawks made swift spiralling shadows on the ground. I helped myself to a drink from his water flask. The shooting sounded further off now, and the town was quieter. Ten minutes later, the corporal marched into the office. I put my hands above my head, and he escorted me back to the guardroom.

It was very hot. The skinny boy had been taken away and, on the bench at the back, sat a Frenchman.

Outside, tied to the papaya, a springer spaniel was panting and straining at its leash. A pair of soldiers squatted on their hams and were trying to dismantle the Frenchman's shotgun. A third soldier, rummaging in his game bag, was laying out a few brace of partridge and a guinea fowl.

'Will you please give that dog some water?' the Frenchman asked.

'Eh?' The corporal bared his gums.

'The dog,' he pointed. 'Water!'

'No.'

'What's going on?' I asked.

'The monkeys are wrecking my gun and killing my dog.'

'Out there, I mean.'

'*Coup monté.*'

'Which means?'

'You hire a plane-load of mercenaries to shoot up the town. See who your friends are and who are your enemies. Shoot the enemies. Simple!'

'Clever.'

'Very.'

'And us?'

'They might need a corpse or two. As proof!'

'Thank you,' I said.

'I was joking.'

'Thanks all the same.'

The Frenchman was a water engineer. He worked upcountry, on artesian wells, and was down in the capital on leave. He was a short, muscular man, tending to paunch, with cropped grey hair and a web of white laugh lines over his leathery cheeks. He had dressed himself en mercenaire, in fake python-skin camouflage, to shoot a few game birds in the forest on the outskirts of town.

'What do you think of my costume?' he asked.

'Suitable,' I said.

'Thank you.'

The sun was vertical. The colour of the parade ground had bleached to a pinkish orange, and the soldiers strutted back and forth in their own pools of shade. Along the wall the vultures flexed their wings.

'Waiting,' joked the Frenchman.

'Thank you.'

'Don't mention it.'

Our view of the morning's entertainment was restricted by the width of the door frame. We were, however, able to witness a group of soldiers treating their ex-colonel in a most shabby fashion. We wondered how he could still be alive as they dragged him out and bundled him into the back of a jeep. The corporal had taken the colonel's radio, and was cradling it on his knee. The Head of State was baying for blood – '*Mort aux mercenaires soit qu'ils sont noirs ou blancs* ...' The urchins, too, were back in force, jumping up and down, drawing their fingers across their throats, and chanting in unison, '*Mort-aux-mercenaires! ... Mort-aux-mercenaires! ...*'

Around noon, the jeep came back. A lithe young woman jumped out and started screeching orders at an infantry platoon. She was wearing a mud-stained battledress. A nest of plaits curled, like snakes, from under her beret.

'So,' said my companion. 'The new colonel.'

'An Amazon colonel,' I said.

'I always said it,' he said. 'Never trust a teenage Amazon colonel.'

He passed me a cigarette. There were two in the packet and I took one of them.

'Thanks,' I said. 'I don't smoke.'

He lit mine, and then his, and blew a smoke ring at the rafters. The gecko on the wall hadn't budged.

'My name's Jacques,' he said.

I told him my own name and he said, 'I don't like the look of this.'

'Nor I,' I said.

'No,' he said. 'There are no rules in this country.'

Nor were there any rules, none that one could think of, when the corporal came back from conferring with the Amazon and ordered us, also, to strip to our underpants. I hesitated. I was unsure whether I was wearing underpants. But a barrel in the small of my back convinced me, underpants or no, that my trousers would have to come down – only to find that I did, after all, have on a pair of pink-and-white boxer shorts from Brooks Brothers.

Jacques was wearing green string pants. We must have looked a pretty couple – my back welted all over with mosquito bites, he with his paunch flopping over the elastic, as the corporal marched us out, barefoot over the burning ground, and stood us, hands up, against the wall which the vultures had fouled with their ash-white, ammonia-smelling droppings.

'*Merde!*' said Jacques. 'Now what?'

What indeed? I was not frightened. I was tired and hot. My arms ached, my knees sagged, my tongue felt like leather, and my temples throbbed. But this was not frightening. It was too like a B-grade movie to be frightening. I began to count the flecks of millet chaff embedded in the mud-plaster wall . . .

I remembered the morning, five years earlier, my first morning in Dahomey, under the tall trees in Parakou. I'd had a rough night, coming down from the desert in the back of a crowded truck, and at breakfast time, at the *café-routier*, I'd asked the waiter what there was to see in town.

'Patrice.'

'Patrice?'

'That's me,' he grinned. 'And, monsieur, there are hundreds of other beautiful young girls and boys who walk, all the time, up and down the streets of Parakou.'

I remembered, too, the girl who sold pineapples at Dassa-Zoumbé station. It had been a stifling day, the train slow and the country burnt. I had been reading Gide's *Les Nourritures terrestres* and, as we drew into Dassa, had come to the line, '*Ô cafés! – où notre démence s'est continuée très avant dans la nuit . . .*' No, I thought, this will never do, and looked out of the carriage window. A basket of pineapples had halted outside. The girl underneath the basket smiled and, when I gave her the Gide, gasped, lobbed all six pineapples into the carriage, and ran off to show her friends – who in turn came skipping down the tracks, clamouring, 'A book, please? A book? A book!' So *out* went a dog-eared thriller and Saint-Exupéry's *Vol de nuit*, and *in* came *Fruits of the Earth* – the real ones – pawpaws, guavas, more pineapples, a raunch of grilled swamp rat, and a palm-leaf hat.

'Those girls,' I remember scribbling in my notebook, 'are the ultimate products of the lycée system.'

A nd now what?

The Amazon was squawking at the platoon and we strained our ears for the click of safety catches.

'I think they're playing games,' Jacques said, squinting sideways.

'I should hope so,' I muttered. I liked Jacques. It was good, if one had to be here, to be here with him. He was an old Africa hand and had been through coups before.

'That is,' he added glumly, 'if they don't get drunk.'

'Thank you,' I said, and looked over my shoulder at the drill squad.

'No look!' the corporal barked. He was standing beside us, his shirt front open to the navel. Obviously, he was anxious to cut a fine figure.

'Stick your belly button in,' I muttered in English.

'No speak!' he threatened.

'I won't speak.' I held the words within my teeth. 'But stay there. Don't leave me. I need you.'

Maddened by the heat and excitement, the crowds who had come to gawp were clamouring, '*Mort-aux-mercenaires! ... Mort-aux-mercenaires!*' and my mind went racing back over the horrors of Old Dahomey, before the French came. I thought, the slave wars, the human sacrifices, the piles of broken skulls. I thought of Domingo's other uncle, 'The Brazilian', who received us on his rocking chair dressed in white ducks and a topee. 'Yes,' he sighed, 'the Dahomeans are a charming and intelligent people. Their only weakness is a certain nostalgia for taking heads.'

No. This was not my Africa. Not this rainy, rotten-fruit Africa. Not this Africa of blood and laughter. The Africa I loved was the long undulating savannah country to the north, the 'leopard-spotted land', where flat-topped acacias stretched as far as the eye could see, and there were black-and-white hornbills and tall red termitaries. For whenever I went back to that Africa, and saw a camel caravan, a view of white tents, or a single blue turban far off in the heat haze, I knew that, no matter what the Persians said, Paradise never was a garden but a waste of white thorns.

'I am dreaming,' said Jacques, suddenly, 'of *perdrix aux choux*.'

'I'd take a dozen Belons and a bottle of Krug.'

'No speak!' The corporal waved his gun, and I braced myself, half expecting the butt to crash down on my skull.

And so what? What would it matter when already I felt as if my skull were split clean open? Was this, I wondered, sunstroke? How strange, too, as I tried to focus on the wall, that each bit of chaff should bring back some clear specific memory of food or drink?

There was a lake in central Sweden and, in the lake, there was an island where the ospreys nested. On the first day of the crayfish season we rowed to the fisherman's hut and rowed back towing twelve dozen crayfish in a live net. That evening, they came in from the kitchen, a scarlet mountain smothered in dill. The northern sunlight bounced off the lake into the bright white room. We drank akvavit from thimble-sized glasses and we ended the meal with a tart made of cloudberries. I could taste again the grilled sardines we ate on the quay at Douarnenez and see my father demonstrating how his father ate sardines *à la mordecai*: you took a live sardine by the tail and swallowed it. Or the elvers we had in Madrid, fried in oil with garlic and half a red pepper. It had been a cold spring morning, and we'd spent two hours in the Prado, gazing at the Velázquezes, hugging one another it was so good to be alive: we had cancelled our bookings on a plane that had crashed. Or the lobsters we bought at Cape Split Harbor, Maine. There was a noticeboard in the shack on the jetty and, pinned to it, a card on which a widow thanked her husband's friends for their contributions, and prayed, prayed to the Lord, that they lashed themselves to the boat when hauling in the pots.

How long, O Lord, how long? How long, when all the world was wheeling, could I stay on my feet . . .?

How long I shall never know, because the next thing I remember I was staggering groggily across the parade ground, with one arm over the corporal's shoulder and the other over Jacques's.

Jacques then gave me a glass of water and, after that, he helped me into my clothes.

'You passed out,' he said.

'Thank you,' I said.

'Don't worry,' he said. 'They *are* only playing games.'

It was late afternoon now. The corporal was in a better mood and allowed us to sit outside the guardroom. The sun was still hot. My head was still aching, but the crowd had simmered down and fortunately, for us, this particular section of the Benin Proletarian Army had found a new source of amusement – in the form of three Belgian ornithologists, whom they had taken prisoner in a swamp, along with a Leica lens the shape and size of a mortar.

The leader of the expedition was a beefy, red-bearded fellow. He believed, apparently, that the only way to deal with Africans was to shout. Jacques advised him to shut his mouth; but when one of the subalterns started tinkering with the Leica, the Belgian went off his head. How dare they? How dare they touch his camera? How dare they think they were mercenaries? Did they look like mercenaries?

'And I suppose they're mercenaries, too?' He waved his arms at us.

'I told you to shut your mouth,' Jacques repeated.

The Belgian took no notice and went on bellowing to be set free. *At once! Now! Or else! Did he hear that?*

Yes. The subaltern had heard, and smashed his fist into the Belgian's face. I never saw anyone crumple so quickly. The blood gushed down his beard, and he fell. The subaltern kicked him when he was down. He lay on the dirt floor, whimpering.

'Idiot!' Jacques growled.

'Poor Belgium,' I said.

The next few hours I would prefer to forget. I do, however, remember that when the corporal brought back my things I cursed, 'Christ, they've nicked my traveller's cheques,' – and Jacques, squeezing my arm very tightly, whispered, 'Now *you* keep your mouth shut!' I remember 'John Brown's Body' playing loudly over the radio, and the Head of State inviting the population, this time, to gather up the corpses. *Ramasser les cadavres* is what he said, in a voice so hoarse and sinister you knew a great many people had died, or would do. And I remember, at sunset, being driven by minibus to the Gezo Barracks where hundreds of soldiers, all elated by victory, were embracing one another, and kissing.

Our new guards made us undress again, and we were shut up, with other suspected mercenaries, in a disused ammunition shed. 'Well,' I thought, at the sight of so many naked bodies, 'there must be some safety in numbers.'

It was stifling in the shed. The other whites seemed cheerful, but the blacks hung their heads between their knees, and shook. After dark, a missionary doctor, who was an old man, collapsed and died of a heart attack. The guards took him out on a stretcher, and we were taken to the Sûreté for questioning.

Our interrogator was a gaunt man with hollow temples, a cap of woolly white hair and bloodshot slits for eyes. He sat sprawled behind his desk, caressing with his fingertips the blade of his bowie knife. Jacques made me stand a pace behind him. When his turn came, he said loudly that he was employed by such-and-such a French engineering company and that I, he added, was an old friend.

'Pass!' snapped the officer. 'Next!'

The officer snatched my passport, thumbed through the pages and began blaming me, personally, for certain events in southern Africa.

'What are you doing in our country?'

'I'm a tourist.'

'Your case is more complicated. Stand over there.'

I stood like a schoolboy, in the corner, until a female sergeant took me away for fingerprinting. She was a very large sergeant. My head was throbbing; and when I tried to manoeuvre my little finger onto the inkpad, she bent it back double; I yelled 'Ayee!', and her boot slammed down on my sandalled foot.

That night there were nine of us, all white, cooped up in a ramshackle office. The president's picture hung aslant on a bright blue wall and, beside it, were a broken guitar and a stuffed civet cat, nailed in mockery of the Crucifixion, with its tail and hind legs together, and its forelegs splayed apart.

In addition to the mosquito bites, my back had come up in watery blisters. My toe was very sore. The guard kicked me awake whenever I nodded off. His cheeks were cicatrised, and I remember thinking how remote his voice sounded when he said, '*On va vous fusiler.*' At two or three in the morning, there was a burst of machine-gun fire close by, and we all thought, This is it. It was only a soldier, drunk or trigger-happy, discharging his magazine at the stars.

None of us was sad to see the first light of day.

It was another greasy dawn and the wind was blowing hard onshore, buffeting the buzzards and bending the coco palms. Across the compound a big crowd was jamming the gate. Jacques then caught sight of his houseboy and when he waved, the boy waved back. At nine, the French Vice Consul put in an appearance, under guard. He was a fat, suet-faced man, who kept wiping the sweat from his forehead and glancing over his shoulder at the bayonet points behind.

'*Messieurs,*' he stammered, 'this situation is perhaps a little less disagreeable for me than for you. Unfortunately, although we do have stratagems for your release, I am not permitted to discuss your liberty, only the question of food.'

'*Eh bien!*' Jacques grinned. 'You see my boy over there? Send him to the Boulangerie Gerbe d'Or and bring us sandwiches of jambon, paté and saucisson sec, enough croissants for everyone, and three petits pains au chocolat for me.'

'*Oui,*' said the Vice Consul weakly.

I then scribbled my name and passport number on a scrap of paper, and asked him to telex the British embassy in Lagos.

'I cannot,' he said. 'I cannot be mixed up in this affair.'

He turned his back, and waddled off the way he'd come, with the pair of bayonets following.

'Charming,' I said to Jacques.

'Remember Waterloo,' Jacques said. 'And, besides, you may be a mercenary!'

Half an hour later, Jacques's bright-eyed boy came back with a basket of provisions. Jacques gave the guard a sandwich, spread the rest on the office table, sank his teeth into a petit pain au chocolat, and murmured, '*Byzance*!'

The sight of food had a wonderfully revivifying effect on the Belgian ornithologists. All through the night the three had been weepy and hysterical, and now they were wolfing the sandwiches. They were not my idea of company. I was left alone with them, when, around noon, the citizens of France were set at liberty.

'Don't worry,' Jacques squeezed my hand. 'I'll do what I can.'

He had hardly been gone ten minutes before a big German, with a red face and sweeps of fair hair, came striding across the compound, shouting at the soldiers and brushing the bayonets aside.

He introduced himself as the Counsellor of the German embassy.

'I'm so sorry you've landed in this mess,' he said in faultless English. 'Our ambassador has made a formal protest. From what I understand, you'll have to pass before some kind of military tribunal. Nothing to worry about! The commander is a nice chap. He's embarrassed about the whole business. But we'll watch you going into the building, and watch you coming out.'

'Thanks,' I said.

'Anyway,' he added, 'the embassy car is outside, and we're not leaving until everyone's out.'

'Can you tell me what *is* going on?'

The German lowered his voice: 'Better leave it alone.'

The tribunal began its work at one. I was among the first prisoners to be called. A young zealot started mouthing anti-capitalist formulae until he was silenced by the colonel in charge. The colonel then asked a few perfunctory questions, wearily apologised for the inconvenience, signed my pass, and hoped I would continue to enjoy my holiday in the People's Republic.

'I hope so,' I said.

Outside the gate, I thanked the German who sat in the back of his air-conditioned Mercedes. He smiled, and went on reading the *Frankfurter Zeitung.*

It was grey and muggy and there were not many people on the street. I bought the government newspaper and read its account of the glorious victory. There were pictures of three dead mercenaries – a white man who appeared to be sleeping, and two very mangled blacks. Then I went to the hotel where my bag was in storage.

The manager's wife looked worn and jittery. I checked my bag and found the two traveller's cheques I'd hidden in a sock. I cashed a hundred dollars, took a room, and lay down.

I kept off the streets to avoid the vigilante groups that roamed the town making citizen's arrests. My toenail was turning black and my head still ached. I ate in the room, and read, and tried to sleep. All the other guests were either Guinean or Algerian.

Around eleven next morning, I was reading the sad story of Mrs Marmeladov in *Crime and Punishment,* and heard the thud of gunfire coming from the Gezo Barracks. I looked from the window at the palms, the hawks, a woman selling mangoes, and a nun coming out of the convent.

Seconds later, the fruit stall had overturned, the nun bolted, and two armoured cars went roaring up the street.

There was a knock on the door. It was the manager.

'Please, monsieur. You must not look.'

'What's happening?'

'Please,' he pleaded, 'you must shut the window.'

I closed the shutter. The electricity had cut off. A few bars of sunlight squeezed through the slats, but it was too dark to read, so I lay back and listened to the salvoes. There must have been a lot of people dying.

There was another knock.

'Come in.'

A soldier came into the room. He was very young and smartly turned out. His fatigues were criss-crossed with ammunition belts and his teeth shone. He seemed extremely nervous. His finger quivered round the trigger-guard. I raised my hands and got up off the bed.

'In there!' He pointed the barrel at the bathroom door.

The walls of the bathroom were covered with blue tiles and, on the blue plastic shower curtain, was a design of tropical fish.

'Money,' said the soldier.

'Sure!' I said. 'How much?'

He said nothing. I glanced at the mirror and saw the gaping whites of his eyes. He was breathing heavily.

I eased my fingers down my trouser pocket: my impulse was to give him all I had. Then I separated one banknote from the rest, and put it in his outstretched palm.

'*Merci, monsieur!*' His lips expanded in an astonished smile.

'*Merci,*' he repeated, and unlocked the bathroom door. '*Merci,*' he kept repeating, as he bowed and pointed his own way out into the passage.

That young man, it struck me, really had very nice manners.

The Algerians and Guineans were men in brown suits who sat all day in the bar, sucking soft drinks through straws and giving me dirty looks whenever I went in. I decided to move to the Hôtel de la Plage where there were other Europeans, and a swimming pool. I took a towel to go swimming and went into the garden. The pool had been drained: on the morning of the coup, a sniper had taken a pot-shot at a Canadian boy who happened to be swimming his lengths.

The frontiers of the country were closed, and the airport.

That evening I ate with a Norwegian oil man, who insisted that the coup had been a fake. He had seen the mercenaries shelling the palace. He had watched them drinking opposite in the bar of the Hôtel de Cocotiers.

'All of it I saw,' he said, his neck reddening with indignation. 'The palace had been deserted. The army had been in the barracks. The mercenaries had shot innocent people. Then they all went back to the airport and flew away.

'All of it,' he said, 'was fake.'

'Well,' I said, 'if it was a fake, it certainly took me in.'

It took another day for the airport to open, and another two before I got a seat on the Abidjan plane. I had a mild attack of bronchitis and was aching to leave the country.

O n my last morning I looked in at the Paris-Snack, which, in the old days when Dahomey was Dahomey, was owned by a Corsican called Guerini. He had gone back to Corsica while the going was good. The bar stools were covered in red leather, and the barman wore a solid gold bracelet round his wrist.

Two Nigerian businessmen were seated at lunch with a pair of whores. At a table in the corner I saw Jacques.

'*Tiens?*' he said, grinning. 'Still alive?'

'Thanks to you,' I said, 'and the Germans.'

'*Braves Bosches!*' He beckoned me to the banquette. 'Very intelligent people.'

'*Braves Bosches!*' I agreed.

'Let's have a bottle of champagne.'

'I haven't got much money.'

'Lunch is on me,' he insisted. 'Pierrot!'

The barman tilted his head, coquettishly, and tittered.

'Yes, Monsieur Jacques.'

'This is an English gentleman and we must find him a very special bottle of champagne. You have Krug?'

'No, Monsieur Jacques. We have Roederer. We have Bollinger, and we have Mumm.'

'Bollinger,' I said.

Jacques pulled a face: 'And in Guerini's time you could have had your oysters. Flown in twice a week from *Paris ... Belons ... Claires ... Portugaises ...*'

'I remember him.'

'He was a character.'

'Tell me,' I leaned over. 'What *was* going on?'

'Sssh!' His lips tightened. 'There are two theories and, if I think anyone's listening, I shall change the subject.'

I nodded and looked at the menu.

'In the official version,' Jacques said, 'the mercenaries were recruited by Dahomean émigrés in Paris. The plane took off from a military airfield in Morocco, refuelled in Abidjan . . .'

One of the whores got up from her table and lurched down the restaurant towards the Ladies.

''66 was a wonderful year,' said Jacques, decisively.

'I like it even older,' I said, as the whore brushed past, 'dark and almost flat . . .'

'The plane flew to Gabon to pick up the commander . . . who is supposed to be an adviser to President Bongo . . .' He then explained how, at Libreville, the pilot of the chartered DC-8 refused to go on, and the mercenaries had to switch to a DC-7.

'So their arrival was expected at the airport?'

'Precisely,' Jacques agreed. 'Now the second scenario . . .'

The door of the Ladies swung open. The whore winked at us. Jacques pushed his face up to the menu.

'What'll you have?' he asked.

'Stuffed crab,' I said.

'The second scenario,' he continued quietly, 'calls for Czech and East German mercenaries. The plane, a DC-7, takes off from a military airfield in Algeria, refuels at Conakry . . . you understand?'

'Yes,' I said, when he'd finished. 'I think I get it. And which one do you believe?'

'Both,' he said.

'That,' I said, 'is a very sophisticated analysis.'

'This,' he said, 'is a very sophisticated country.'

'I know it.'

'You heard the shooting at Camp Gezo?'

'What was that?'

'Settling old scores,' he shrugged. 'And now the Guineans have taken over the Secret Police.'

'Clever.'

'This is Africa.'

'I know and I'm leaving.'

'For England?'

'No,' I said. 'For Brazil. I've a book to write.'

'Beautiful country, Brazil.'

'I hope so.'

'Beautiful women.'

'So I'm told.'

'So what is this book?'

'It's about the slave trade.'

'In Benin?'

'Also in Brazil.'

'*Eh bien!*' The champagne had come and he filled my glass. 'You have material!'

'Yes,' I agreed. 'I do have material.' ∎

24 Gondar Gardens
London N.W 6

21st January 1985

Dear Bill,

Right, I've found the copy of <u>Granta</u>.

The title: Yes, it is quite awful.

The bottom of page 54: you left, after:
her father was prepared to forgive her, "She never
forgave him." ~~Thx~~ It should go back in.   This
excision was just part of the way you felt impelled
to remove all the small bits and phrases that gave
my mother a bit more. Why?

Yes, I should have fought much harder:
a lot came out which should not.

The problem here is that I do have a
strong reluctance to writing it at all, which disarms
me; but you, I think, dislike a style which is
natural to me - between the two of us, we have
produced a curious lifelessness. Which I look
at various phrases which you wanted to take out,
and which I insisted should stay in - if <u>they</u> had
come out, the piece really would have been dead.

Anyway: I'm off, as you know, and I think
I won't be able to tackle the second piece for quite
a bit.   I'll try and do it in the gap between
Norway and Australia.

I hope all goes well.

I think the issue as a whole is very
creditable.

See you -

D ais

James Fenton, 1985

THE FALL OF SAIGON

James Fenton

GRANTA 15: SPRING 1985

In the summer of 1973 I had a dream in which, to my great distress, I died. I was alone in a friend's house at the time and, not knowing what to do, I hid the body in her deep freeze. When everyone returned, I explained to them what had taken place: 'Something terrible happened when you were out. I – I died.'

My friends were very sympathetic. 'But what did you do with the body?' they asked.

I was ashamed to tell them. 'I don't know where it is,' I said, and we all set out to search the house for my corpse. Upstairs and downstairs we looked, until finally, unable to bear the deception any longer, I took my hostess aside and confessed. 'There wasn't anything else in the compartment,' I said, 'and I just didn't know what to do.' We went to the deep freeze and opened it. As the curled and frozen shape was revealed, I woke up.

I was glad to be going off on a journey. I had been awarded a bursary for the purpose of travelling and writing poetry; I intended to stay out of England a long time. Looking at what the world had to offer, I thought either Africa or Indochina would be the place to go. I chose Indochina partly on a whim, and partly because, after the Paris Peace Accords in January of that same year, it looked as if it was in for some very big changes. The essence of the agreement was that it removed American military personnel from Indochina and stopped the B-52 bombing raids. The question was how long could the American-backed regime last without that accustomed support. I wanted to see Vietnam for myself. I wanted to see a war, and I wanted to see a communist victory, which I presumed to be inevitable. I wanted to see the fall of a city.

I wanted to see a communist victory because, in common with many people, I believed that the Americans had not the slightest justification for their interference in Indochina. I admired the Vietcong and, by extension, the Khmer Rouge, but I subscribed to a philosophy that prided itself on taking a cool, critical look at the liberation movements of the Third World. I, and many others like me, supported these movements against the ambitions of American foreign policy. We supported them as nationalist movements. We did not support their political character, which we perceived as Stalinist in the case of the Vietnamese, and in the case of the Cambodians . . . I don't know. The theory was, and is, that when a genuine movement of national liberation was fighting against imperialism it received our unconditional support. When such a movement had won, then it might well take its place among the governments we execrated – those who ruled by sophisticated tyranny in the name of socialism.

There was also an argument that Stalinism was not a simple equivalent of Fascism, that it contained what was called a partial negation of capitalism. Further, under certain conditions it might even lay down the foundations of a socialist organisation of society. In the Third World, Stalinism might do the job which the bourgeois revolutions had done in Europe. Even Stalinism had its progressive features.

Our attitudes may have looked cynical in the extreme. In fact they were the formulation of a dilemma. After all, we had not invented the Indochina War, and it was not for us to conjure out of thin air a movement that would match up to our own aspirations for Britain. To remain neutral over Vietnam was to support the Americans. To argue for an end to all US involvement, and leave the matter at that, was to ignore the consequences of one's own argument. If there was a conflict on which one had to choose sides, then it was only right to choose sides honestly, and say: 'Stalinists they may be, but we support them.' The slogans of the Vietnam movement were crude stuff indeed – 'One side right, one side wrong, victory to . . . Vi-et-cong!' – but the justice of the cause was deeply felt.

This feeling was shared by many people who were not socialists or communists by any stretch of the imagination, and who did not have any other political axe to grind. Such people had merely to look at what was being done to Vietnam in the name of the Free World to know that the Free World was in the wrong. The broadest support for the anti-war movement was engendered by a disgust at what the Americans were doing. In Britain, the Communist Party made precious few gains in this period. The tradition to which the students looked was broadly or narrowly Trotskyist, a fact that no doubt intrigued the Vietnamese communists, who had taken care to bump off their own Trotskyists a long time before. But the Trotskyist emphasis, like the general emphasis, was again in opposition to American imperialism. Very few people idolised the Vietcong, or the North Vietnamese, or Uncle Ho, in quite the same way that, for instance, the French Left did. Indeed, it might be fairly said that the Left in Britain was not terribly curious about or enamoured of the Vietnamese movement it was supporting.

By the time I was about to go to Indochina, the issue had fallen from prominence. When the Indochina Solidarity Conference was held in London that year, my own group, the International Socialists, did not bother to send a delegation. There were other, more important campaigns: against the Tories, against the Industrial Relations Act, against racism. Our movement had grown up: it was to be working class in character; it had graduated from what it thought of as student issues. It had not abandoned Vietnam, but it had other fish to fry. At the conference itself, I remember two speeches of interest. One was by I.F. Stone, who was hissed by the audience (which included an unusually large number of Maoists) when he attacked Chairman Mao for shaking hands with a murderer like Nixon. The other was by Noam Chomsky, who warned against the assumption that the war was over, and that direct US intervention in Vietnam would cease. Chomsky argued that the Left were wrong to dismiss the 'Domino Theory' out of hand. As stated by the Cold Warriors it might not measure up to the facts, but there was another formulation which did indeed make sense; it was US foreign policy, rather than Russian expansionism, which knocked over the dominoes: countries might be forced into positions where the only alternative to accepting American domination was to go over to the opposite camp and would thus be drawn into the power struggle whether they liked it or not.

I mention such arguments because I do not wish to give the impression that I was completely wide-eyed about the Vietnamese communists when I set out. I considered myself a revolutionary socialist, of the kind who believes in no Fatherland of the Revolution, and has no cult hero. My political beliefs were fairly broadly based and instinctively grasped, but they were not, I hope, religiously held.

But I wanted very much to see a communist victory. Although I had a few journalist commissions, I was not going primarily as a journalist. I wanted to see a war and the fall of a city because – because I wanted to see what such things were like. I had once seen a man dying, from natural causes, and my first reaction, as I realised what was taking place, was that I was glad to be *there*. This is what happens, I thought, so watch it carefully, don't miss a detail. The first time I saw a surgical operation (it was in Cambodia) I experienced the same sensation, and no doubt when I see a child born it will be even more powerful. The point is simply in being there and seeing it. The experience has no essential value beyond itself.

I spent a long time on my preparations and, as my dream of dying might indicate, I had developed some fairly morbid apprehensions. The journey itself was to be utterly selfish. I was going to do exactly as I pleased. As far as political beliefs were concerned, they were going to remain 'on the table'. Everything was negotiable. But the fear of death, which had begun for the first time to enter my calculations, followed me on my journey. As I went through the passport check at Heathrow, I glanced at the Sunday papers and saw that the poet I most admired, W.H. Auden, had just died in Vienna. People were talking about him in the passenger lounge, or rather they weren't talking about him, they were talking about his face.

I kept seeing the face, on the plane, in the transit lounges, on the empty seat next to mine, and I kept remembering Auden. From the start he had willed himself into old age, and it was not surprising that he had not lived longer. He had courted death, cultivated first eccentricity and then what looked to the world very much like senility. It was not senility, but it was a useful cover for his despair of living, the deep unhappiness which he kept concealed. He had held the world very much at arm's length, and had paid a heavy price for doing so.

Between sleeping and reading, I found myself passing through a depression compounded of one part loneliness, one part uneager anticipation, one part fright and two parts obscure self-pity. In Bombay the depression began to lift: I slept all morning at the Sea Palace Hotel, then, surrendering to the good offices of a driver and guide, set off to see the sights. The evening light was first a muddy yellow; next it turned green. On the Malabar Hill, I paid my respects to the spectacular view, the vultures picking the bones on the Parsee tower, the lights along the waterfront ('Queen Victoria's Necklace') and the couples sitting on the lawns of the Hanging Gardens, in attitudes reminiscent of a Mogul miniature. The most impressive sight was a vast open-air laundry, a yard full of boiling vats between which, through the dark and steam, one could scarcely make out the moving figures of the workers. There was a steamy warmth everywhere, which I liked immediately. Waking the next morning, I looked down on a wide meandering river, either the Salween or the Irrawaddy, whose muddy waters spread out for miles into the sea. Seen from the plane, the landscape of the Far East was dazzling, silver and blue. You could tell you had arrived in Indochina when you saw the rows and rows of yellow circles, where muddy water had filled the bomb craters.

Fear of Madness: November 1973

'I know not whether others share my feelings on this point,' wrote De Quincey, 'but I have often thought that if I were compelled to forego England, and to live in China, and among Chinese manners and modes of life and scenery, I should go mad.' I read this sentence the other day, for the first time, and as I came to the last clause I was struck once again with the full nausea of my first trip to Vietnam. 'The causes of my horror lie deep,' De Quincey went on. But he set them forth beautifully:

> No man can pretend that the wild, barbarous, and capricious superstitions of Africa, or of savage tribes elsewhere, affect him in the way that he is affected by the ancient, monumental, cruel, and elaborate religions of Indostan, etc. The mere antiquity of Asiatic things, of their institutions, histories, modes of faith, &c. is so impressive, that to me the vast age of the race and name overpowers the sense of youth in the individual. A young Chinese seems to me an antediluvian renewed . . . Man is a weed in those regions.

I was impressed, overawed, by the scale and age of the subject: a war that had been going on for longer than I had been alive, a people about whose history and traditions I knew so little. I had read some books in preparation, but the effect of doing so was only to make the country recede further. So much had been written about Vietnam. I hadn't even had the application to finish Frances FitzGerald's *Fire in the Lake*. The purpose of the book seemed to be to warn you off the subject.

I could well have believed that somebody was trying to tell me something when I came out of my room on the first morning in Saigon and stepped over the decapitated corpse of a rat. I was staying, as most British journalists did, in the Hotel Royale, but even there I felt something of an intruder. I had to find work, I had to sell some stories, but I was afraid of trespassing on somebody else's patch. There was an epidemic of infectious neurosis at the time: as soon as one journalist had shaken it off, another would succumb. It would attack without warning – in the middle of an otherwise amiable meal, in the bars, in your room. And it could be recurrent, like malaria.

The reason for the neurosis was not far to seek; indeed it sought you out, and pursued you throughout the day: Saigon was an addicted city, and we were the drug; the corruption of children, the mutilation of young men, the prostitution of women, the humiliation of the old, the division of the family, the division of the country – it had all been done in our name. People looked back to the French Saigon with a sentimental warmth, as if the problem had begun with the Americans. But the French city, the 'Saigon of the piastre' as Lucien Bodard called it, had represented the opium stage of the addiction. With the Americans had begun the heroin phase, and what I was seeing now was the first symptoms of withdrawal. There was a desperate edge to life. It was impossible to relax for a moment. The last of the American troops had left at the end of March, six months before I arrived, and what I saw now was what they left behind: a vast service industry clamouring for the attention of a dwindling number of customers: Hey, you! American! Change money, buy *Time* magazine, give me back *Time* magazine I sell you yesterday, buy *Stars and Stripes*, give me back *Stars and Stripes*, you number one, you number ten, you number ten thousand Yankee, you want number one fuck, you want *Quiet American*, you want *Ugly American*, you give me money I shine shoes, number one, no sweat . . . on and on, the passionate pursuit of money.

The bar at the Royale was half-open to the street. The coffee at breakfast tasted of diarrhoea. You washed it down with Bireley's orangeade ('Refreshing . . . and no carbonation!'). Through the windows peered the shoeshine boys – Hey! You! It was starting up again. One morning I was ignoring a particularly revolting specimen when he picked up a handful of sand which he pretended to eat: 'You! You no give me money, you want I eat shit!' His expression, as he brought the dirt to his mouth, was most horrible. It was impossible to imagine how a boy of that age had acquired such features: he was about ten, but his face contained at least thirty years of degeneration and misery. A few days later I did give him my boots to clean. He sat down in the corner of the bar and set to work, first with a matchstick and a little water, meticulously removing all the mud and dust from the welt, then with the polish. The whole process took about half an hour, and the barman and I watched him throughout, in fascination. He was determined to show his superiority to all other contestants in the trade. I was amused, and gave him a large sum. He was furious; it wasn't nearly enough. We haggled for a while, but I finally gave in. I gave him about a pound. The next day, at the same time, he came into the bar; his eyes were rolling back in their sockets and he staggered helplessly around the tables and chairs. I do not know what he had taken, but I knew how he had bought it.

O f all the ingenious and desperate forms of raising money, the practice of drugging your baby and laying the thing on the pavement in front of the visitor seemed to me the most repulsive. It did not take long to see that none of these children was ever awake during the day, or that, if asleep, something was amiss. Among the foreigners, stories circulated about the same baby being seen in the arms of five different mothers in one week, but the beggar who regularly sat outside the Royale always had the same child, a girl of eighteen months or so. I never gave any money either to the girl and her 'mother', or to any of the other teams.

One day, however, I was returning from a good lunch when I saw that a crowd had formed around the old woman, who was wailing and gesticulating. The child was more than usually grey, and there were traces of vomit around her face. People were turning her over, slapping her, trying to force her eyes open. At one point she and the old woman were bundled into a taxi. Then they were taken out again and the slapping was repeated. I went into the hotel and told the girl at reception to call a doctor.

'No,' she replied.

'But the child is sick.'

'If baby go to hospital or doctor' – and here she imitated an injection – 'then baby die.'

'No,' I replied, 'if baby don't go to hospital maybe baby die.'

'No.'

I took the girl out into the street, where the scene had become grotesque. All the beggars I had ever seen in Saigon seemed to have gathered, and from their filthy garments they were producing pins and sticking them under the child's toenails. 'You see,' I said to the girl, 'no good, number ten. Baby need number one hospital.'

'No, my grandmother had same-same thing. She need this – number one.' And the receptionist produced a small phial of eucalyptus oil.

'That's not number one,' I said, 'that's number ten. Number ten thousand,' I added for emphasis. But it was no good insisting or appealing to other members of the crowd. Everybody was adamant that if the child was taken to hospital, the doctor would kill it with an injection. While I correspondingly became convinced that a moment's delay would cost the child's life.

Finally, after a long eucalyptus massage and repeated pricking of the fingers and toes had produced no visible results, I seemed to win. If I would pay for taxi and hospital, the woman would come. I pushed my way through the crowd and dragged her towards the taxi – a battered old Renault tied together with string. The baby was wrapped in tarpaulin and her face covered with a red handkerchief. Every time I tried to remove the handkerchief, from which came the most ominous dry gaspings, the woman replaced it. I directed the taxi-man to take us to number one hospital and we set off.

From the start everything went wrong. Within a hundred yards we had to stop for petrol. Then a van stalled in front of us, trapping the taxi. Next, to my amazement, we came to what must have been, I thought, the only level crossing in Saigon, where as it happened a train was expected in the near future. And around here we were hit by the side effects of Typhoon Sarah, which at the time was causing havoc in the northern provinces. We also split a tyre, though this was not noticed till later. Driving on through the cloudburst, the taxi-man seemed strangely unwilling to hurry. So I sat in the back seat keeping one hand on the horn and with the other attempting to ease the baby's breathing by loosening the tarpaulin around her neck. I also recall from time to time producing a third arm with which to comfort the old woman, and I remember that her shoulder, when my hand rested on it, was very small and very hard. Everything, I said, was going to be number one, OK: number one hospital, number one doctor, baby-san OK. We were travelling through Cholon, the Chinese quarter, on an errand of Western mercy.

All things considered, it took a long time for it to dawn on me that we were not going to a hospital at all. We even passed a first-aid post without the taxi-man giving it a glance. In my mind there was an image of the sort of thing required: a large cool building dating from French times, recently refurbished by American aid and charity, with some of the best equipment in the East. I could even imagine the sententious plaques on the walls. Perhaps there would be a ward named after the former US Ambassador. It would be called the Bunker Ward.

It was when the old woman began giving directions that I saw I had been duped. We were threading our way through some modern slums, which looked like the Chinese equivalent of the Isle of Dogs. 'Where is the hospital? This is no hospital,' I said.

'Yes, yes,' the taxi-man replied, 'we are going to hospital, number one doctor.'

We stopped by a row of shops and the taxi-man got out. I jumped from the car and seized him by the arm, shouting: 'I said number one hospital. You lie. You cheap charlie. You number ten thousand Saigon.' We were surrounded by children, in the pouring rain, the taxi-man tugging himself free, and me gripping him by the arm. It was left to the woman, carrying the little bundle of tarpaulin, to find out exactly where the doctor lived. Finally I gave in, and followed her up some steps, then along an open corridor lined with tailors and merchants. At least, I thought, when the baby dies I can't be blamed. And once I had had that thought, it turned into a wish: a little cough would have done it, a pathetic gurgle, then silence, and my point about Western medicine would have been proved to my own satisfaction. I should have behaved very well, and would have paid for the funeral.

In retrospect it was easy to see how the establishment would command confidence: the dark main room with its traditional furnishings, the walls lined with photographs of ancestors in traditional Vietnamese robes, a framed jigsaw of the Italian lakes. And in the back room (it would, of course, have to be a back room) a plump, middle-aged lady was massaging the back of another plump, middle-aged lady. They paid hardly any attention when we came in. There was not the slightest element of drama. Indeed, I began to see that I was now the only person who was panicking. When she had finished the massage, the doctor turned her attention to the baby. First she took some ointment from a dirty bowl at her elbow, and rubbed it all over the little grey body. Then from another bowl she produced some pink substance resembling Euthymol toothpaste, with which she proceeded to line the mouth. In a matter of minutes, the child was slightly sick, began to cry, and recovered. I had never been more furious in my life. To complete my humiliation, the doctor refused any payment. She provided the old woman with a prescription wrapped in newspaper, and we left.

We drove to the miserable shelter in which the old woman lived.

'Sit down,' she said, indicating the wooden bed which was the only feature of her home apart from the roof (there were no walls).

In any other mood I might have been moved by the fact that the only English she knew beyond the terrible pidgin currency of the beggars was a phrase of hospitality. But I so deeply hated her at that moment that I could only give her a couple of pounds, plus some useless advice about keeping the baby warm and off the pavements, and go.

I left the taxi-man at a garage not far from the Royale, where I also gave him some money towards repairing the split tyre.

'You number one, Saigon,' he said, with a slight note of terror in his voice.

The weather had cleared up, and I left him, strolling along past the market stalls. Here, you could buy US Army foot powder in bulk, K-rations, lurp-rations (for Long Range Reconnaissance Patrols), souvenir Zippo lighters (engraved YEA THOUGH I WALK THROUGH THE VALLEY OF THE SHADOW OF DEATH I SHALL FEAR NO EVIL, FOR I AM THE EVILEST SONOFABITCH IN THE VALLEY), khaki toothbrushes and flannels, and model helicopters constructed out of used hypodermics. You could also buy jackets brightly embroidered with the words WHEN I DIE I SHALL GO TO HEAVEN, FOR I HAVE SPENT MY TIME IN HELL – SAIGON, and a collection of GI cartoons and jokes called *Sorry 'bout that,Vietnam*. Five years ago, there had been over 500,000 American GIs. Now there were none.

As I approached the hotel people began asking how the baby was, and smiling when I replied, 'OK.' I began to think: Supposing they were all in it together? Suppose the old woman, the taxi driver, the man whose van stalled, the engine driver – suppose they were all now dividing the proceeds and having a good laugh at my expense, congratulating the child on the way it had played its role? That evening I would be telling the story to some old Saigon hand when a strange pitying smile would come over his face. 'You went to Cholon, did you? Describe the doctor . . . uh-huh . . . Was there a jigsaw puzzle of the Italian Lakes? Well, well, well. So they even used the toothpaste trick. Funny how the oldest gags are still the best . . .'

Indeed I did have rather that conversation a few days later, with an American girl, a weaver. It began: 'You realise, of course, first of all that the taxi driver was the husband of the old woman . . .' But I do not think there was a conspiracy. Worse, I should rather conclude that the principals involved were quite right not to trust the hospital doctors with a beggar's child. It was for this reason that the hotel receptionist had countermanded my orders to the taxi-man, I learned afterwards, and many people agreed with her.

When the old woman came back on the streets, I hardly recognised either her or the child, who for the first time looked conscious and well. 'Baby-san OK now, no sick,' she said, gazing at me with an awful adoring expression, though the hand was not stretched out for money. And when I didn't reply she turned to the child and told it something in the same unctuous tones. This performance went on for the rest of my stay: whenever I was around the child would be made to look at the kind foreigner who had saved its life. I had indeed wanted to save the child's life, but not in that way, not on the old woman's terms.

I was disgusted, not just at what I saw around me, but at what I saw in myself. I saw how perilously thin was the line between the charitable and the murderous impulse, how strong the force of righteous indignation. I could well imagine that most of those who came to Vietnam to fight were not the evilest sons-of-bitches in the valley. It was just that, beyond the bright circle illuminated by their intelligence, in which everything was under their control and every person a compliant object, they came across a second person – a being or a nation with a will of its own, with its own medicine, whether Fishing Pills or pink toothpaste, and its own ideas for the future. And in the ensuing encounter everything had turned to justifiable ashes. It was impossible in Saigon to be the passive observer. Saigon cast you, inevitably, into the role of the American. ■

Primo Levi, *c.*1950

TADPOLES

Primo Levi

TRANSLATED FROM THE ITALIAN BY SIMON REES

GRANTA 18: SPRING 1986

O ur summer holiday lasted the whole length of the school
vacation: about three months. Preparations began early, usually
on St Joseph's Day (19 March): since we weren't rich enough to
afford a hotel, my parents would tour the still snow-clad valleys of
Piedmont looking for lodgings to rent – preferably somewhere served
by the railway and not too far from Turin. We didn't have a car (this
was the early thirties, and almost no one did) and for my father, who
hated the sultriness of summer anyway, time off was restricted to
three days around the August bank holiday. So, just to sleep with the
family and in the cool, he would subject himself to the drudgery of a
twice-daily train journey out to Torre Pellice or Meana, or any of the
other modest villages within a hundred or so kilometres of the city.
For our part we went every evening to the station to wait for him.
At daybreak he set out again, even on Saturdays, to be in the office
by eight.

My mother began the packing around the middle of June.
Apart from bags and suitcases, the main load consisted of three
wicker trunks, which when full must each have weighed at least
two hundredweight; the removal men came and hoisted them
miraculously onto their backs and carried them downstairs sweating
and cursing. The trunks contained everything: bedclothes, pots and

pans, toys, books, provisions, winter and summer clothing, shoes, medicines, utensils – as if we were departing for the Antipodes. Usually we arranged our destination together with other families – relations or friends; it was less lonely like that. In this way we took a part of our city along with us.

The three months went by slowly, and quietly, and dully, and punctuated by the abominable sadism of holiday homework: a contradiction in terms! My father spent only Sundays with us, and those in his own fashion. He was a thorough-going urbanite: the countryside did not agree with him. He disliked the emptiness of the fields, the steepness of the paths, the silence, the flies, the discomforts. The mornings he would spend reading, taciturn and cross; in the afternoon he dragged us off for an ice cream at the only cafe in the village, and then he would retire to play the tarot with the miller and his wife. But for my sister and me the months in the country meant a regularly renewed union with nature: humble plants and flowers whose names it was fun to learn in Italian and dialect; the birds, each with their own song; insects; spiders. On one occasion in the washbasin, a leech, no less, graceful in its swimming, undulating as if in a dance. Another time, a bat that zigzagged dementedly about the bedroom, or a stone marten glimpsed in the twilight, or a mole cricket, a monstrous, obese little insect, neither mole nor cricket, repugnant and menacing. In the courtyard garden well-disciplined tribes of ants rushed about their business, and it was enthralling to observe their cunning and their stubborn stupidity. They were held up as an example in our schoolbooks: 'Go to the ant, thou sluggard; consider her ways, and be wise' (Proverbs 6:6). They never took summer holidays. Yes, they may have been virtuous little creatures, but it was the obligatory virtue of prisoners.

The stream was the most interesting place of all. My mother took us down every morning to sunbathe and to paddle in the clear, clean water, while she got on with her knitting in the shade of a willow. You could wade the stream safely from bank to bank, and it was a haven to creatures the like of which we had never seen. On the riverbed black insects staggered along resembling huge ants, each one dragging behind it a cylindrical case made of tiny pebbles or little pieces of vegetation, into which it had threaded its abdomen; only its head and claws poked out. When disturbed, the creatures recoiled like a shot into their little mobile homes.

In mid-air hovered wondrous dragonflies, frozen in flight, iridescent in metallic turquoise; even their buzzing was metallic, mechanical, bellicose. They were miniature war machines, dropping in one stroke, dart-like, on some invisible prey. On the dry, sandy banks green beetles ran nimbly to and fro; the conical traps of the ant lion sprang open. Such ambushes we witnessed with a secret sense of complicity, and hence of guilt, to the extent that my sister, overwhelmed every so often with pity, would use a twig to divert some poor ant on the point of a sudden and cruel death.

Alongside the left bank the water teemed with tadpoles in their thousands. Why only on the left? After much fruitless discussion about sun and shade we noticed that along that side ran a footpath much used by anglers; the trout were wise to this, and kept to the safety of the right bank. Accordingly, to avoid the trout, the tadpoles had established themselves on the left. They aroused conflicting feelings: laughter and tenderness – like puppies, newborn babies and all creatures whose heads seem too big for their bodies – and indignation, because every so often they ate each other. They were chimaeras, impossible creations, yet they sailed along swiftly and surely, propelling themselves with elegant flicks of the tail. Between head and tail they had no body, and this was what seemed incomprehensible and monstrous; all the same, the head had eyes and a mouth – a voracious mouth curiously downturned as if sulking – ever in search of food. We brought a dozen back home and put them, to my mother's disapproval, in the portable 'camping' bidet, slung on its trestle – we had covered the bottom with sand from the bed of the stream. The tadpoles seemed at home there, and sure enough after a few days they began their metamorphosis. This was a novel spectacle, as full of mystery as a birth or a death – enough to make us forget our holiday homework, and for the days to seem fleeting and the nights interminable.

Every morning, indeed, had a surprise in store. The tail of one tadpole began to thicken, close to its root, into a small knot. The knot enlarged, and in two or three days out pushed a pair of webbed feet – but the little creature made no use of them: it let them hang limp, and carried on waggling its tail. A few more days, and a pustule formed on one side of its head; this swelled up, then burst like an abscess, and out came a forelimb already perfectly formed, minute, transparent – a tiny glass hand, already treading water. A little later, and the same happened to the other side, while the tail was already starting to shrink.

This was a dramatic time: one could see that at a glance. It was a harsh and brutal puberty: the tiny creatures began to fret, as if an inner sense had forewarned them of the torment in store for those who change their shape, and they were confounded in mind and body: perhaps they no longer knew who they were. Their swimming was frantic and bewildered, their tails growing ever shorter and their four legs still too weak to use. They circled around in search of something – air for their new lungs, perhaps, or maybe a landing place from which to set forth into the world. I realised that the sides of the bidet were too steep for the tadpoles to climb out, as was clearly their wish, and so I positioned in the water two or three small wooden ramps.

It was the right idea, and some of the tadpoles took advantage of it – but could you still call them tadpoles? Not any more: the larvae had gone; now there were brown frogs as big as beans – but frogs with two arms and two legs, folk like us, who swam breaststroke with difficulty but in the correct style. And they no longer ate each other, so we felt differently towards them, like a mother and father: in some way they were our children, even if our part in their metamorphosis had been more of a hindrance than a help. I sat one in the palm of my hand: it had an ugly mug, but a face nevertheless; it looked at me, winked, and its mouth gaped open. Was it gasping for air, or was it trying to tell me something? Another time it set off determinedly along my finger, as if along a springboard. The next instant it was gone, with one senseless hop into the void.

B ringing up tadpoles, then, was not so easy. Only a few of them cottoned on to our little safety ramps and got out onto dry land. The rest, already deprived of the gills provided for their aquatic infancy, we would find in the morning, drowned, worn out by too much swimming, just like a human swimmer trapped inside a lock. And even those who had understood the purpose of the landing stage, the more intelligent ones, did not always live long. The tadpoles responded to a perfectly natural instinct – the same instinct that has driven us to the moon, that is epitomised in the commandment, 'Multiply and replenish the earth' – which spurred them to forsake the stretch of water where they had completed their metamorphosis. It did not matter whither – anywhere else but there. In the wild, for every likely pool, for every bend in the stream, there will be another not far away, or perhaps a damp meadow or a marsh. Thus some do survive, by migrating and colonising new surroundings. Still, even in the most favourable conditions a large proportion of these neo-frogs are bound to die. And it is for this reason that the mother frog exhausts herself laying interminable strings of eggs: she 'knows' that the infant mortality rate will be breathtakingly high, and she allows for this as our country forebears did.

Our surviving tadpoles dispersed around the courtyard garden in search of water that wasn't there. We tried to keep track of them through the grass and the gravel. The boldest, labouring to cross the granite pavement in clumsy hops, was spotted by a robin, who made a quick meal of him. And that very instant the white kitten, our gentle little playmate, who had watched all this transfixed, took a prodigious leap and pounced on the bird, whose mind was still on its lucky catch. She half-killed it, as cats do, and took it off into a corner to toy with its agony. ■

New Gourna, Egypt, 1987

THE IMAM AND THE INDIAN

Amitav Ghosh

GRANTA 20: WINTER 1986

I met the Imam of the village and Khamees the Rat at about the same time. I don't exactly remember now – it happened more than six years ago – but I think I met the Imam first.

But this is not quite accurate. I didn't really 'meet' the Imam: I inflicted myself upon him. Perhaps that explains what happened.

Still, there was nothing else I could have done. As the man who led the daily prayers in the mosque, he was a leading figure in the village, and since I, a foreigner, had come to live there, he may well for all I knew have been offended had I neglected to pay him a call. Besides, I wanted to meet him; I was intrigued by what I'd heard about him.

People didn't often talk about the Imam in the village, but when they did, they usually spoke of him somewhat dismissively, but also a little wistfully, as they might of some old, half-forgotten thing, like the annual flooding of the Nile. Listening to my friends speak of him, I had an inkling, long before I actually met him, that he already belonged, in a way, to the village's past. I thought I knew this for certain when I heard that apart from being an imam he was also, by profession, a barber and a healer. People said he knew a great deal about herbs and poultices and the old kind of medicine. This interested me. This was Tradition: I knew that in rural Egypt imams and other religious figures are often by custom associated with those two professions.

The trouble was that these accomplishments bought the Imam very little credit in the village. The villagers didn't any longer want an Imam who was also a barber and a healer. The older people wanted someone who had studied at al-Azhar and could quote from Jamal ad-Din Afghani and Mohammad Abduh as fluently as he could from the Hadith, and the younger men wanted a fierce, black-bearded orator, someone whose voice would thunder from the mimbar and reveal to them their destiny. No one had time for old-fashioned imams who made themselves ridiculous by boiling herbs and cutting hair.

Yet Ustad Ahmed, who taught in the village's secondary school and was as well-read a man as I have ever met, often said – and this was not something he said of many people – that the old Imam read a lot. A lot of what? Politics, theology, even popular science . . . that kind of thing.

This made me all the more determined to meet him, and one evening, a few months after I first came to the village, I found my way to his house. He lived in the centre of the village, on the edge of the dusty open square which had the mosque in its middle. This was the oldest part of the village: a maze of low mud huts huddled together like confectionery on a tray, each hut crowned with a billowing, tousled head of straw.

When I knocked on the door the Imam opened it himself. He was a big man, with very bright brown eyes, set deep in a wrinkled, weather-beaten face. Like the room behind him, he was distinctly untidy: his blue jallabeyya was mud-stained and unwashed and his turban had been knotted anyhow around his head. But his beard, short and white and neatly trimmed, was everything a barber's beard should be. Age had been harsh on his face, but there was a certain energy in the way he arched his shoulders, in the clarity of his eyes and in the way he fidgeted constantly, was never still: it was plain that he was a vigorous, restive kind of person.

'Welcome,' he said, courteous but unsmiling, and stood aside and waved me in. It was a long dark room, with sloping walls and a very low ceiling. There was a bed in it and a couple of mats but little else, apart from a few, scattered books: everything bore that dull patina of grime which speaks of years of neglect. Later, I learned that the Imam had divorced his first wife and his second had left him, so that now he lived quite alone and had his meals with his son's family who lived across the square.

'Welcome,' he said again, formally.

'Welcome to you,' I said, giving him the formal response, and then we began on the long, reassuring litany of Arabic phrases of greeting.

'How are you?'

'How are you?'

'You have brought blessings?'

'May God bless you.'

'Welcome.'

'Welcome to you.'

'You have brought light.'

'The light is yours.'

'How are you?'

'How are you?'

He was very polite, very proper. In a moment he produced a kerosene stove and began to brew tea. But even in the performance of that little ritual there was something about him that was guarded, watchful.

'You're the *doktor al-Hindi*,' he said to me at last, 'aren't you? The Indian doctor?'

I nodded, for that was the name the village had given me. Then I told him that I wanted to talk to him about the methods of his system of medicine.

He looked very surprised and for a while he was silent. Then he put his right hand to his heart and began again on the ritual of greetings and responses, but in a markedly different way this time; one that I had learned to recognise as a means of changing the subject.

'Welcome.'

'Welcome to you.'

'You have brought light.'

'The light is yours.'

And so on.

At the end of it I repeated what I had said.

'Why do you want to hear about *my* herbs?' he retorted. 'Why don't you go back to your country and find out about your own?'

'I will,' I said. 'Soon. But right now . . .'

'No, no,' he said restlessly. 'Forget about all that; I'm trying to forget about it myself.'

And then I knew that he would never talk to me about his craft, not just because he had taken a dislike to me for some reason of his own, but because his medicines were as discredited in his own eyes as they were in his clients'; because he knew as well as anybody else that the people who came to him now did so only because of old habits; because he bitterly regretted his inherited association with these relics of the past.

'Instead,' he said, 'let me tell you about what I have been learning over the last few years. Then you can go back to your country and tell them all about it.'

He jumped up, his eyes shining, reached under his bed and brought out a glistening new biscuit tin.

'Here!' he said, opening it. 'Look!'

Inside the box was a hypodermic syringe and a couple of glass phials. This is what he had been learning, he told me: the art of mixing and giving injections. And there was a huge market for it too, in the village: everybody wanted injections, for coughs, colds, fevers, whatever. There was a good living in it. He wanted to demonstrate his skill to me right there, on my arm, and when I protested that I wasn't ill, that I didn't need an injection just then, he was offended. 'All right,' he said curtly, standing up. 'I have to go to the mosque right now. Perhaps we can talk about this some other day.'

That was the end of my interview. I walked with him to the mosque and there, with an air of calculated finality, he took my hand in his, gave it a perfunctory shake and vanished up the stairs.

K hamees the Rat I met one morning when I was walking through the rice fields that lay behind the village, watching people transplant their seedlings. Everybody I met was cheerful and busy and the flooded rice fields were sparkling in the clear sunlight. If I shut my ears to the language, I thought, and stretch the date palms a bit and give them a few coconuts, I could easily be back somewhere in Bengal.

I was a long way from the village and not quite sure of my bearings, when I spotted a group of people who had finished their work and were sitting on the path, passing around a hookah.

'*Ahlan!*' a man in a brown jallabeyya called out to me. 'Hullo! Aren't you the Indian *doktor*?'

'Yes,' I called back. 'And who're you?'

'He's a rat,' someone answered, raising a gale of laughter. 'Don't go anywhere near him.'

'Tell me, *ya doktor*,' the Rat said, 'if I get onto my donkey and ride steadily for thirty days will I make it to India?'

'No,' I said. 'You wouldn't make it in thirty months.'

'Thirty months!' he said. 'You must have come a long way.'

'Yes.'

'As for me,' he declared, 'I've never even been as far as Alexandria and if I can help it I never will.'

I laughed: it did not occur to me to believe him.

When I first came to that quiet corner of the Nile Delta I had expected to find on that most ancient and most settled of soils a settled and restful people. I couldn't have been more wrong.

The men of the village had all the busy restlessness of airline passengers in a transit lounge. Many of them had worked and travelled in the sheikhdoms of the Persian Gulf, others had been in Libya and Jordan and Syria, some had been to the Yemen as soldiers, others to Saudi Arabia as pilgrims, a few had visited Europe: some of them had passports so thick they opened out like ink-blackened concertinas. And none of this was new: their grandparents and ancestors and relatives had travelled and migrated too, in much the same way as mine had, in the Indian subcontinent – because of wars, or for money and jobs, or perhaps simply because they got tired of living always in one place. You could read the history of this restlessness in the villagers' surnames: they had names which derived from cities in the Levant, from Turkey, from faraway towns in Nubia; it was as though people had drifted here from every corner of the Middle East. The wanderlust of its founders had been ploughed into the soil of the village: it seemed to me sometimes that every man in it was a traveller. Everyone, that is, except Khamees the Rat, and even his surname, as I discovered later, meant 'of Sudan'.

'Well, never mind, *ya doktor*,' Khamees said to me now, 'since you're not going to make it back to your country by sundown anyway, why don't you come and sit with us for a while?'

He smiled and moved up to make room for me.

I liked him at once. He was about my age, in the early twenties, scrawny, with a thin, mobile face deeply scorched by the sun. He had that brightness of eye and the quick, slightly sardonic turn to his mouth that I associated with faces in the coffee houses of universities in Delhi and Calcutta; he seemed to belong to a world of late-night rehearsals and black coffee and lecture rooms, even though, in fact, unlike most people in the village, he was completely illiterate. Later I learned that he was called the Rat – Khamees the Rat – because he was said to gnaw away at things with his tongue, like a rat did with its teeth. He laughed at everything, people said – at his father, the village's patron saint, the village elders, the Imam, everything.

That day he decided to laugh at me.

'All right, *ya doktor*,' he said to me as soon as I had seated myself. 'Tell me, is it true what they say, that in your country you burn your dead?'

No sooner had he said it than the women of the group clasped their hands to their hearts and muttered in breathless horror: '*Haram! Haram!*'

My heart sank. This was a conversation I usually went through at least once a day and I was desperately tired of it. 'Yes,' I said, 'it's true; some people in my country burn their dead.'

'You mean,' said Khamees in mock horror, 'that you put them on heaps of wood and just light them up?'

'Yes,' I said, hoping that he would tire of this sport if I humoured him.

'Why?' he said. 'Is there a shortage of kindling in your country?'

'No,' I said helplessly, 'you don't understand.' Somewhere in the limitless riches of the Arabic language a word such as 'cremate' must exist, but if it does, I never succeeded in finding it. Instead, for lack of any other, I had to use the word 'burn'. That was unfortunate, for 'burn' was the word for what happened to wood and straw and the eternally damned.

Khamees the Rat turned to his spellbound listeners. 'I'll tell you why they do it,' he said. 'They do it so that their bodies can't be punished after the Day of Judgement.'

Everybody burst into wonderstruck laughter. 'Why, how clever,' cried one of the younger girls. 'What a good idea! We ought to start doing it ourselves. That way we can do exactly what we like and when we die and the Day of Judgement comes, there'll be nothing there to judge.'

Khamees had got his laugh. Now he gestured to them to be quiet again.

'All right then, *ya doktor*,' he said. 'Tell me something else: is it true that you are a Magian? That in your country everybody worships cows? Is it true that the other day when you were walking through the fields you saw a man beating a cow and you were so upset that you burst into tears and ran back to your room?'

'No, it's not true,' I said, but without much hope: I had heard this story before and knew that there was nothing I could say which would effectively give it the lie. 'You're wrong. In my country people beat their cows all the time; I promise you.'

I could see that no one believed me.

'Everything's upside down in their country,' said a dark, aquiline young woman who, I was told later, was Khamees's wife. 'Tell us, *ya doktor*: in your country, do you have crops and fields and canals like we do?'

'Yes,' I said, 'we have crops and fields, but we don't always have canals. In some parts of my country they aren't needed because it rains all the year round.'

'*Ya salám*,' she cried, striking her forehead with the heel of her palm. 'Do you hear that, oh you people? Oh, the Protector, oh, the Lord! It rains all the year round in his country.'

She had gone pale with amazement. 'So tell us then,' she demanded, 'do you have night and day like we do?'

'Shut up, woman,' said Khamees. 'Of course they don't. It's day all the time over there, didn't you know? They arranged it like that so that they wouldn't have to spend any money on lamps.'

We all laughed, and then someone pointed to a baby lying in the shade of a tree swaddled in a sheet of cloth. 'That's Khamees's baby,' I was told. 'He was born last month.'

'That's wonderful,' I said. 'Khamees must be very happy.'

Khamees gave a cry of delight. 'The Indian knows I'm happy because I've had a son,' he said to the others. 'He understands that people are happy when they have children: he's not as upside down as we thought.'

He slapped me on the knee and lit up the hookah and from that moment we were friends.

One evening, perhaps a month or so after I first met Khamees, he and his brothers and I were walking back to the village from the fields when he spotted the old Imam sitting on the steps that led to the mosque.

'Listen,' he said to me, 'you know the old Imam, don't you? I saw you talking to him once.'

'Yes,' I said. 'I talked to him once.'

'My wife's ill,' Khamees said. 'I want the Imam to come to my house to give her an injection. He won't come if I ask him, he doesn't like me. You go and ask.'

'He doesn't like me either,' I said.

'Never mind,' Khamees insisted. 'He'll come if you ask him – he knows you're a foreigner. He'll listen to you.'

While Khamees waited on the edge of the square with his brothers I went across to the Imam. I could tell that he had seen me – and Khamees – from a long way off, that he knew I was crossing the square to talk to him. But he would not look in my direction. Instead, he pretended to be deep in conversation with a man who was sitting beside him, an elderly and pious shopkeeper whom I knew slightly.

When I reached them I said 'Good evening' very pointedly to the Imam. He could not ignore me any longer then, but his response was short and curt, and he turned back at once to resume his conversation.

The old shopkeeper was embarrassed now, for he was a courteous, gracious man in the way that seemed to come so naturally to the elders of the village. 'Please sit down,' he said to me. 'Do sit. Shall we get you a chair?'

Then he turned to the Imam and said, slightly puzzled: 'You know the Indian *doktor*, don't you? He's come all the way from India to be a student at the University of Alexandria.'

'I know him,' said the Imam. 'He came around to ask me questions. But as for this student business, I don't know. What's he going to study? He doesn't even write in Arabic.'

'Well,' said the shopkeeper judiciously, 'that's true; but after all he writes his own languages and he knows English.'

'Oh, those,' said the Imam. 'What's the use of *those* languages? They're the easiest languages in the world. Anyone can write those.'

He turned to face me for the first time. His eyes were very bright and his mouth was twitching with anger. 'Tell me,' he said, 'why do you worship cows?'

I was so taken aback that I began to stammer. The Imam ignored me. He turned to the old shopkeeper and said: 'That's what they do in his country – did you know? – they worship cows.'

He shot me a glance from the corner of his eyes. 'And shall I tell you what else they do?' he said to the shopkeeper.

He let the question hang for a moment. And then, very loudly, he hissed: 'They burn their dead.'

The shopkeeper recoiled as though he had been slapped. His hands flew to his mouth. 'Oh God!' he muttered. '*Ya Allah.*'

'That's what they do,' said the Imam. 'They burn their dead.'

Then suddenly he turned to me and said, very rapidly: 'Why do you allow it? Can't you see that it's a primitive and backward custom? Are you savages that you permit something like that? Look at you: you've had some kind of education; you should know better. How will your country ever progress if you carry on doing these things? You've even been to the West; you've seen how advanced they are. Now tell me: have you ever seen them burning their dead?'

The Imam was shouting now and a circle of young men and boys had gathered around us. Under the pressure of their interested eyes my tongue began to trip, even on syllables I thought I had mastered. I found myself growing angry – as much with my own incompetence as the Imam.

'Yes, they do burn their dead in the West,' I managed to say somehow. I raised my voice too now. 'They have special electric furnaces meant just for that.'

The Imam could see that he had stung me. He turned away and laughed. 'He's lying,' he said to the crowd. 'They don't burn their dead in the West. They're not an ignorant people. They're advanced, they're educated, they have science, they have guns and tanks and bombs.'

'We have them too!' I shouted back at him. I was as confused now as I was angry. 'In my country we have all those things too,' I said to the crowd. 'We have guns and tanks and bombs. And they're better than anything you have – we're way ahead of you.'

The Imam could no longer disguise his anger. 'I tell you, he's lying,' he said. 'Our guns and bombs are much better than theirs. Ours are second only to the West's.'

'It's you who's lying,' I said. 'You know nothing about this. Ours are much better. Why, in my country we've even had a nuclear explosion. You won't be able to match that in a hundred years.'

So there we were, the Imam and I, delegates from two superseded civilisations vying with each other to lay claim to the violence of the West.

At that moment, despite the vast gap that lay between us, we understood each other perfectly. We were both travelling, he and I: we were travelling in the West. The only difference was that I had actually been there, in person: I could have told him about the ancient English university I had won a scholarship to, about punk dons with safety pins in their mortarboards, about superhighways and sex shops and Picasso. But none of it would have mattered. We would have known, both of us, that all that was mere fluff: at the bottom, for him as for me and millions and millions of people on the land masses around us, the West meant only this – science and tanks and guns and bombs.

And we recognised too the inescapability of these things, their strength, their power – evident in nothing so much as this: that even for him, a man of God, and for me, a student of the 'humane' sciences, they had usurped the place of all other languages of argument. He knew, just as I did, that he could no longer say to me, as Ibn Battuta might have when he travelled to India in the fourteenth century: 'You should do this or that because it is right or good or because God wills it so.' He could not have said it because that language is dead: those things are no longer sayable; they sound absurd. Instead he had had, of necessity, to use that other language, so universal that it extended equally to him, an old-fashioned village imam, and great leaders at SALT conferences: he had had to say to me: 'You ought not to do this because otherwise you will not have guns and tanks and bombs.'

Since he was a man of God his was the greater defeat.

For a moment then I was desperately envious. The Imam would not have said any of those things to me had I been a Westerner. He would not have dared. Whether I wanted it or not, I would have had around me the protective aura of an inherited expertise in the technology of violence. That aura would have surrounded me, I thought, with a sheet of clear glass, like a bulletproof screen; or perhaps it would have worked as a talisman, like a press card, armed with which I could have gone off to what were said to be the most terrible places in the world that month, to gaze and wonder. And then perhaps I too would one day have had enough material for a book which would have had for its epigraph the line, *The horror! The horror!* – for the virtue of a sheet of glass is that it does not require one to look within.

But that still leaves Khamees the Rat waiting on the edge of the square.

In the end it was he and his brothers who led me away from the Imam. They took me home with them, and there, while Khamees's wife cooked dinner for us – she was not so ill after all – Khamees said to me: 'Do not be upset, *ya doktor*. Forget about all those guns and things. I'll tell you what: *I'll* come to visit you in your country, even though I've never been anywhere. I'll come all the way.'

He slipped a finger under his skullcap and scratched his head, thinking hard.

Then he added: 'But if I die, you must bury me.' ∎

Edinburgh International Book Festival

10–26 August 2019

The World, in Words.
900 events featuring 1000
authors, poets, musicians and
artists, plus cafés, bookshops
and bars all in one central leafy
tented village in Edinburgh's
beautiful New Town.

Programme launch: 6 June
Tickets on sale from 25 June

edbookfest.co.uk
@edbookfest

MENUDO

Raymond Carver

GRANTA 21: SPRING 1987

I can't sleep, but when I'm sure my wife Vicky is asleep, I get up and look through our bedroom window, across the street, at Oliver and Amanda's house. Oliver has been gone for three days, but his wife Amanda is awake. She can't sleep either. It's four in the morning, and there's not a sound outside – no wind, no cars, no moon even – just Oliver and Amanda's place with the lights on, leaves heaped up under the front windows.

A couple of days ago, when I couldn't sit still, I raked our yard – Vicky's and mine. I gathered all the leaves into bags, tied off the tops, and put the bags alongside the curb. I had an urge then to cross the street and rake over there, but I didn't follow through. It's my fault things are the way they are across the street.

I've only slept a few hours since Oliver left. Vicky saw me moping around the house, looking anxious, and decided to put two and two together. She's on her side of the bed now, scrunched onto about ten inches of mattress. She got into bed and tried to position herself so she wouldn't accidentally roll into me while she slept. She hasn't moved since she lay down, sobbed, and then dropped into sleep. She's exhausted. I'm exhausted too.

I've taken nearly all of Vicky's pills, but I still can't sleep. I'm keyed up. But maybe if I keep looking I'll catch a glimpse of Amanda moving around inside her house, or else find her peering from behind a curtain, trying to see what she can see over here.

What if I do see her? So what? What then?

Vicky says I'm crazy. She said worse things too last night. But who could blame her? I told her – I had to – but I didn't tell her it was Amanda. When Amanda's name came up, I insisted it wasn't her. Vicky suspects, but I wouldn't name names. I wouldn't say who, even though she kept pressing and then hit me a few times in the head.

'What's it matter *who*?' I said. 'You've never met the woman,' I lied. 'You don't know her.' That's when she started hitting me.

I feel *wired*. That's what my painter friend Alfredo used to call it when he talked about friends of his coming down off something. *Wired*. I'm wired.

This thing is nuts. I know it is, but I can't stop thinking about Amanda. Things are so bad just now I even find myself thinking about my first wife, Molly. I loved Molly, I thought, more than my own life.

I keep picturing Amanda in her pink nightgown, the one I like on her so much, along with her pink slippers. And I feel certain she's in the big leather chair right now, under the brass reading lamp. She's smoking cigarettes, one after the other. There are two ashtrays close at hand, and they're both full. To the left of her chair, next to the lamp, there's an end table stacked with magazines – the usual magazines that nice people read. We're nice people, all of us, to a point. Right this minute, Amanda is, I imagine, paging through a magazine, stopping every so often to look at an illustration or a cartoon.

Two days ago, in the afternoon, Amanda said to me, 'I can't read books anymore. Who has the time?' It was the day after Oliver had left, and we were in this little cafe in the industrial part of the city. 'Who can concentrate anymore?' she said, stirring her coffee. 'Who reads? Do you read?' (I shook my head.) 'Somebody must read, I guess. You see all these books around in store windows, and there are those clubs. Somebody's reading,' she said. 'Who? I don't know anybody who reads.'

That's what she said, apropos of nothing – that is, we weren't talking about books, we were talking about our *lives*. Books had nothing to do with it.

'What did Oliver say when you told him?'

Then it struck me that what we were saying – the tense, watchful expressions we wore – belonged to the people on afternoon TV programs that I'd never done more than switch on and then off.

Amanda looked down and shook her head, as if she couldn't bear to remember.

'You didn't admit who it was you were involved with, did you?'

She shook her head again.

'You're sure of that?' I waited until she looked up from her coffee.

'I didn't mention any names, if that's what you mean.'

'Did he say where he was going, or how long he'd be away?' I said, wishing I didn't have to hear myself. This was my neighbor I was talking about. Oliver Porter. A man I'd helped drive out of his home.

'He didn't say where. A hotel. He said I should make my arrangements and be gone – *be gone*, he said. It was like biblical the way he said it – out of his house, out of his *life*, in a week's time. I guess he's coming back then. So we have to decide something real important, real soon, honey. You and I have to make up our minds pretty damn quick.'

It was her turn to look at me now, and I know she was looking for a sign of lifelong commitment. 'A week,' I said. I looked at my coffee, which had gotten cold. A lot had happened in a little while, and we were trying to take it in. I don't know what long-term things, if any, we'd thought about those months as we moved from flirtation to love, and then afternoon assignations. In any case, we were in a serious fix now. Very serious. We'd never expected – not in a hundred years – to be hiding out in a cafe, in the middle of the afternoon, trying to decide matters like this.

I raised my eyes, and Amanda began stirring her coffee. She kept stirring it. I touched her hand, and the spoon dropped out of her fingers. She picked it up and began stirring again. We could have been anybody drinking coffee at a table under fluorescent lights in a run-down cafe. Anybody, just about. I took Amanda's hand and held it, and it seemed to make a difference.

Vicky's still sleeping on her side when I go downstairs. I plan to heat some milk and drink that. I used to drink whiskey when I couldn't sleep, but I gave it up. Now it's strictly hot milk. In the whiskey days I'd wake up with this tremendous thirst in the middle of the night. But, back then, I was always looking ahead: I kept a bottle of water in the fridge, for instance. I'd be dehydrated, sweating from head to toe when I woke, but I'd wander out to the kitchen and could count on finding that bottle of cold water in the fridge. I'd drink it, all of it, down the hatch, an entire quart of water. Once in a while I'd use a glass, but not often. Suddenly I'd be drunk all over again and weaving around the kitchen. I can't begin to account for it – sober one minute, drunk the next.

The drinking was part of my destiny – according to Molly, anyway. She put a lot of stock in destiny.

I feel wild from lack of sleep. I'd give anything, just about, to be able to go to sleep, and sleep the sleep of an honest man.

Why do we have to sleep anyway? And why do we tend to sleep less during some crises and more during others? For instance, that time my dad had his stroke. He woke up after a coma – seven days and nights in a hospital bed – and calmly said 'Hello' to the people in his room. Then his eyes picked me out. 'Hello, son,' he said. Five minutes later, he died. Just like that – he died. But, during that whole crisis, I never took my clothes off and didn't go to bed. I may have catnapped in a waiting-room chair from time to time, but I never went to bed and *slept*.

And then a year or so ago I found out Vicky was seeing somebody else. Instead of confronting *her*, I went to bed when I heard about it, and stayed there. I didn't get up for days, a week maybe – I don't know. I mean, I got up to go to the bathroom, or else to the kitchen to make a sandwich. I even went out to the living room in my pajamas, in the afternoon, and tried to read the papers. But I'd fall asleep sitting up. Then I'd stir, open my eyes and go back to bed and sleep some more. I couldn't get enough sleep.

It passed. We weathered it. Vicky quit her boyfriend, or he quit her, I never found out. I just know she went away from me for a while, and then she came back. But I have the feeling we're not going to weather this business. This thing is different. Oliver has given Amanda that ultimatum.

Still, isn't it possible that Oliver himself is awake at this moment and writing a letter to Amanda, urging reconciliation? Even now he might be scribbling away, trying to persuade her that what she's doing to him and their daughter Beth is foolish, disastrous, and finally a tragic thing for the three of them.

No, that's insane. I know Oliver. He's relentless, unforgiving. He could slam a croquet ball into the next block – and has. He isn't going to write any such letter. He gave her an ultimatum, right? – a diktat – and that's that. A week. Four days now. Or is it three? Oliver may be awake, but if he is, he's sitting in a chair in his hotel room with a glass of iced vodka in his hand, his feet on the bed, TV turned on low. He's dressed, except for his shoes. He's not wearing shoes – that's the only concession he makes. That and the fact he's loosened his tie.

Oliver is relentless.

I heat the milk, spoon the membrane from the surface and pour it up. Then I turn off the kitchen light and take the cup into the living room and sit on the sofa, where I can look across the street at the lighted windows. But I can hardly sit still. I keep fidgeting, crossing one leg and then the other. I feel like I could throw off sparks, or break a window – maybe rearrange all the furniture.

The things that go through your mind when you can't sleep! Earlier, thinking about Molly, for a moment I couldn't even remember what she *looked* like, for Christ's sake, yet we were together for years, more or less continuously, since we were kids. Molly, who said she'd love me forever. The only thing left was the memory of her sitting and weeping at the kitchen table, her shoulders bent forward, and her hands covering her face. *Forever*, she said. But it hadn't worked out that way. Finally, she said, it didn't matter, it was of no real concern to her, if she and I lived together the rest of our lives or not. Our love existed on a 'higher plane'. That's what she said to Vicky over the phone that time, after Vicky and I had set up housekeeping together. Molly called, got hold of Vicky, and said, 'You have your relationship with him, but I'll always have mine. His destiny and mine are linked.'

My first wife, Molly, she talked like that. 'Our destinies are linked.' She didn't talk like that in the beginning. It was only later, after so much had happened, that she started using words like 'cosmic' and 'empowerment' and so forth. But our destinies are *not* linked – not now, anyway, if they ever were. I don't even know where she is now, not for certain.

I think I could put my finger on the exact time, the real turning point, when it came undone for Molly. It was after I started seeing Vicky, and Molly found out. They called me up one day from the high school where Molly taught and said, 'Please. Your wife is doing handsprings in front of the school. You'd better get down here.' It was after I took her home that I began hearing about 'higher power' and 'going with the flow' – stuff of that sort. Our destiny had been 'revised'. And if I'd been hesitating before, well, I left her then as fast as I could – this woman I'd known all my life, the one who'd been my best friend for years, my intimate, my confidante. I bailed out on her. For one thing, I was scared. *Scared.*

This girl I'd started out with in life, this sweet thing, this gentle soul, she wound up going to fortune-tellers, palm readers, *crystal-ball gazers*, looking for answers, trying to figure out what she should do with her life. She quit her job, drew out her teacher's retirement money, and thereafter never made a decision without consulting the I Ching. She began wearing strange clothes – clothes with permanent wrinkles and a lot of burgundy and orange. She even got involved with a group that sat around, I'm not kidding, trying to levitate.

When Molly and I were growing up together, she was a part of me and, sure, I was a part of her, too. We loved each other. It *was* our destiny. I believed in it then myself. But now I don't know what to believe in. I'm not complaining, simply stating a fact. I'm down to nothing. And I have to go on like this. No destiny. Just the next thing meaning whatever you think it does. Compulsion and error, just like everybody else.

Amanda? I'd like to believe in her, bless her heart. But she was looking for somebody when she met me. That's the way with people when they get restless: they start up something, knowing that's going to change things for good.

I'd like to go out in the front yard and shout something. 'None of this is worth it!' That's what I'd like people to hear.

'Destiny,' Molly said. For all I know she's still talking about it.

All the lights are off over there now, except for that light in the kitchen. I could try calling Amanda on the phone. I could do that and see how far it gets me! What if Vicky heard me dialing or talking on the phone and came downstairs? What if she lifted the receiver upstairs and listened? Besides, there's always the chance Beth might pick up the phone. I don't want to talk to any kids this morning. I don't want to talk to anybody. Actually, I'd talk to Molly, if I could, but I can't any longer – she's somebody else now. She isn't *Molly* anymore. But – what can I say? – I'm somebody else, too.

I wish I could be like everybody else in this neighborhood – your basic, normal, unaccomplished person – and go up to my bedroom, and lie down, and sleep. It's going to be a big day today, and I'd like to be ready for it. I wish I could sleep and wake up and find everything in my life different. Not necessarily just the big things, like this thing with Amanda or the past with Molly. But things clearly within my power.

Take the situation with my mother: I used to send money every month. But then I started sending her the same amount in twice-yearly sums. I gave her money on her birthday, and I gave her money at Christmas. I thought: I won't have to worry about forgetting her birthday, and I won't have to worry about sending her a Christmas present. I won't have to worry, period. It went like clockwork for a long time.

Then last year she asked me – it was in between money times, it was in March, or maybe April – for a radio. A radio, she said, would make a difference to her.

What she wanted was a little clock radio. She could put it in her kitchen and have it out there to listen to while she was fixing something to eat in the evening. And she'd have the clock to look at too, so she'd know when something was supposed to come out of the oven, or how long it was until one of her programs started.

A little clock radio.

She hinted around at first. She said, 'I'd sure like to have a radio. But I can't afford one. I guess I'll have to wait for my birthday. That little radio I had, it fell and broke. I miss a radio.' *I miss a radio.* That's what she said when we talked on the phone, or else she'd bring it up when she'd write.

Finally – what'd I say? I said to her over the phone that I couldn't afford any radios. I said it in a letter too, so she'd be sure and understand. *I can't afford any radios,* is what I wrote. I can't do any more, I said, than I'm doing. Those were my very words.

But it wasn't true! I could have done more. I just said I couldn't. I could have afforded to buy a radio for her. What would it have cost me? Thirty-five dollars? Forty dollars or less, including tax. I could have sent her a radio through the mail. I could have had somebody in the store do it, if I didn't want to go to the trouble myself. Or else I could have sent her a forty-dollar check along with a note saying, *This money is for your radio, Mother.*

I could have handled it in any case. Forty dollars – are you kidding? But I didn't. I wouldn't part with it. It seemed there was a *principle* involved. That's what I told myself anyway – there's a principle involved here.

Ha.

Then what happened? She died. She *died.* She was walking home from the grocery store, back to her apartment, carrying her sack of groceries, and she fell into somebody's bushes and died.

I took a flight out there to make the arrangements. She was still at the coroner's, and they had her purse and her groceries behind the desk in the office. I didn't bother to look in the purse they handed me. But what she had from the grocery store was a jar of Metamucil, two grapefruits, a carton of cottage cheese, a quart of buttermilk, some potatoes and onions and a package of ground meat that was beginning to change color.

Boy! I cried when I saw those things. I couldn't stop. I didn't think I'd ever quit crying. The woman who worked at the desk was embarrassed and brought me a glass of water. They gave me a bag for my mother's groceries and another bag for her personal effects – her purse and her dentures. Later, I put the dentures in my coat pocket and drove them down in a rental car and gave them to somebody at the funeral home.

The light in Amanda's kitchen is still on. It's a bright light that spills out onto all those leaves. Maybe she's like I am, and she's scared. Maybe she left that light burning as a night light. Or maybe she's still awake and is at the kitchen table, under the light, writing me a letter. Amanda is writing me a letter, and somehow she'll get it into my hands later on when the real day starts.

Come to think of it, I've never had a letter from her since we've known each other. All the time we've been involved – six months, eight months – and I've never once seen a scrap of her handwriting. I don't even know if she's *literate* that way.

I think she is. Sure, she is. She talks about books, doesn't she? It doesn't matter of course. Well, a little, I suppose. I love her in any case, right?

But I've never written anything to her, either. We always talked on the phone or else face-to-face.

Molly, she was the letter writer. She used to write me even after we weren't living together. Vicky would bring her letters in from the box and leave them on the kitchen table without a word. Finally the letters dwindled away, became more and more infrequent and bizarre. When she did write, the letters gave me a chill. They were full of talk about 'auras' and 'signs'. Occasionally she reported a voice that was telling her something she ought to do or some place she should go. And once she told me that no matter what happened, we were still 'on the same frequency'. She always knew exactly what I felt, she said. She 'beamed in on me', she said, from time to time. Reading those letters of hers, the hair on the back of my neck would tingle. She also had a new word for destiny: *karma*. 'I'm following out my karma,' she wrote. 'Your karma has taken a bad turn.'

I'd like to go to sleep, but what's the point? People will be getting up soon. Vicky's alarm will go off before much longer. I wish I could go upstairs and get back in bed with my wife, tell her I'm sorry, there's been a mistake, let's forget all this – then go to sleep and wake up with her in my arms. But I've forfeited that right. I'm outside all that now, and I can't get back inside! But say I did that. Say I went upstairs and slid into bed with Vicky as I'd like to do. She might wake up and say, *You bastard. Don't you dare touch me, son of a bitch.*

What's she talking about, anyway? I wouldn't touch her. Not in that way, I wouldn't.

After I left Molly, after I'd pulled out on her, about two months after, then Molly really did it. She had her real collapse then, the one that'd been coming on. Her sister saw to it that she got the care she needed. What am I saying? *They put her away.* They had to, they said. They put my wife away. By then I was living with Vicky, and trying not to drink whiskey. I couldn't do anything for Molly. I mean, she was there, I was here, and I couldn't have gotten her out of that place if I'd wanted to. But the fact is, I didn't want to. She was in there, they said, because she *needed* to be in there. Nobody said anything about destiny. Things had gone beyond that.

And I didn't even go visit her – not once! At the time, I didn't think I could stand seeing her in there. But, Christ, what was I? A fair-weather friend? We'd been through plenty. But what on earth would I have said to her? *I'm sorry about all this, honey.* I could have said that, I guess. I intended to write, but I didn't. Not a word. Anyway, when you get right down to it, what could I have said in a letter? *How are they treating you, baby? I'm sorry you're where you are, but don't give up. Remember all the good times? Remember when we were happy together? Hey, I'm sorry they've done this to you. I'm sorry it turned out this way. I'm sorry everything is just garbage now. I'm sorry, Molly.*

I didn't write. I think I was trying to forget about her, to pretend she didn't exist. Molly who?

I left my wife and took somebody else's: Vicky. Now I think maybe I've lost Vicky, too. But Vicky won't be going away to any summer camp for the mentally disabled. She's a hard case. She left her former husband, Joe Kraft, and didn't bat an eye; I don't think she ever lost a night's sleep over it.

Vicky Kraft-Hughes. Amanda Porter. This is where my destiny has brought me? To this street in this neighborhood, messing up the lives of these women?

Amanda's kitchen light went off when I wasn't looking. The room that was there is gone now, like the others. Only the porch light is still burning. Amanda must have forgotten it, I guess. Hey, Amanda.

Once, when Molly was away in that place and I wasn't in my right mind – let's face it, I was crazy too – one night I was at my friend Alfredo's house, a bunch of us drinking and listening to records. I didn't care any longer what happened to me. Everything, I thought, that could happen had happened. I felt unbalanced. I felt lost. Anyway there I was at Alfredo's. His paintings of tropical birds and animals hung on every wall in his house, and there were paintings standing around in the rooms, leaning against things – table legs, say, or his brick-and-board bookcase, as well as being stacked on his back porch. The kitchen served as his studio, and I was sitting at the kitchen table with a drink in front of me. An easel stood off to one side in front of the window that overlooked the alley, and there were crumpled tubes of paint, a palette and some brushes lying at one end of the table. Alfredo was making himself a drink at the counter a few feet away. I loved the shabby economy of that little room. The stereo music that came from the living room was turned up, filling the house with so much sound the kitchen windows rattled in their frames. Suddenly I began to shake. First my hands began to shake, and then my arms and shoulders, too. My teeth started to chatter. I couldn't hold the glass.

'What's going on, man?' Alfredo said, when he turned and saw the state I was in. 'Hey, man, what is it? What's going on with you?'

I couldn't tell him. What could I say? I thought I was having some kind of an attack. I managed to raise my shoulders and let them drop.

Then Alfredo came over, took a chair and sat down beside me at the kitchen table. He put his big painter's hand on my shoulder. I went on shaking. He could feel me shaking.

'What's wrong with you, man? I'm real sorry about everything, man. I know it's real hard right now.' Then he said he was going to fix *menudo* for me. He said it would be good for what ailed me. 'Help your nerves, man,' he said. 'Calm you right down.' He had all the ingredients for *menudo*, he said, and he'd been wanting to make some anyway.

'You listen to me. Listen to what I say, man. I'm your family now, man,' Alfredo said.

It was two in the morning, we were drunk, there were these other drunk people in the house and the stereo was going full blast. But Alfredo went to his fridge and opened it and took some stuff out. He closed the fridge door and looked in his freezer compartment. He found something in a package. Then he looked around in his cupboards. He took a big pan from the cabinet under the sink, and he was ready.

Tripe. He started with tripe and about a gallon of water. Then he chopped onions and added them to the water, which had started to boil. He put chorizo sausage in the pot. After that, he dropped peppercorns into the boiling water and sprinkled in some chili powder. Then came the olive oil. He opened a big can of tomato sauce and poured that in. He added cloves of garlic, some slices of white bread, salt and lemon juice. He opened another can – it was hominy – and poured that in the pot, too. He put it all in, and then he turned the heat down and put a lid on the pot.

I watched him. I sat there shaking while Alfredo stood at the stove making *menudo*, talking – I didn't have any idea what he was saying – and, from time to time, he'd shake his head, or else start whistling to himself. Now and then people drifted into the kitchen for beer. But all the while Alfredo went on very seriously looking after his *menudo*. He could have been home, in Morelia, making *menudo* for his family on New Year's Day.

People hung around in the kitchen for a while, joking, but Alfredo didn't joke back when they kidded him about cooking *menudo* in the middle of the night. Pretty soon they left us alone. Finally, while the *menudo* was cooking and Alfredo stood at the stove with a spoon in his hand, watching me, I got up slowly from the table. I walked out of the kitchen into the bathroom, and then opened another door off the bathroom to the spare room – where I lay down on the bed and fell asleep. When I woke it was mid-afternoon. The *menudo* was gone. The pot was in the sink, soaking. Those other people must have eaten it! They must have eaten it and grown calm. Everyone was gone, and the house was quiet. The house where the *menudo* had been cooking.

I never saw Alfredo more than once or twice afterwards. After that night, our lives took us in separate directions. And those other people who were there – who knows where they went? I'll probably die without ever tasting *menudo*. But who can say?

Is this what it all comes down to then? A middle-aged man involved with his neighbor's wife, linked to an angry ultimatum? What kind of destiny is that? A week, Oliver said. Three or four days now.

A car passes outside with its lights on. The sky is turning gray, and I hear some birds starting up. I decide I can't wait any longer. I can't just sit here, doing nothing – that's all there is to it. I can't keep waiting. I've waited and waited and where's it gotten me? Vicky's alarm will go off soon, Beth will get up and dress for school, Amanda will wake up, too. The entire neighborhood.

On the back porch I find some old jeans and a sweatshirt, and I change out of my pajamas. Then I put on my white canvas shoes – 'wino' shoes Alfredo would have called them. Alfredo, where are you?

I go outside to the garage, and find the rake and some lawn bags. By the time I get around to the front of the house with the rake, ready to begin, I feel I don't have a choice in the matter any longer. It's light out – light enough at any rate for what I have to do. And then, without thinking about it anymore, I start to rake. I rake our yard, every inch of it. It's important it be done right, too. I set the rake right down into the turf and pull hard. It must feel to the grass like it does to us whenever someone gives our hair a hard jerk. Now and then a car passes in the street and slows, but I don't look up from my work. I know what the people in the cars must be thinking, but they're dead wrong – they don't know the half of it. How could they? I'm happy, raking.

I finish our yard and put the bag out next to the curb. Then I begin next door on the Baxters' yard. In a few minutes Mrs Baxter comes out on her porch, wearing her bathrobe. I don't acknowledge her. I'm not embarrassed, and I don't want to appear unfriendly. I just want to keep on with what I'm doing.

She doesn't say anything for a while, and then she says, 'Good morning, Mr Hughes. How are you this morning?'

I stop what I'm doing and run my arm across my forehead. 'I'll be through in a little while,' I say. 'I hope you don't mind.'

'We don't mind,' Mrs Baxter says. 'Go right ahead, I guess.' I see Mr Baxter standing in the doorway behind her. He's already dressed for work in his slacks and sports coat and tie. But he doesn't venture onto the porch. Then Mrs Baxter turns and looks at Mr Baxter, who shrugs.

It's OK, I've finished here anyway. There are other yards, more important yards for that matter. I kneel, and, taking a grip low down on the rake handle, I pull the last of the leaves into my bag and tie off the top. Then, I can't help it, I just stay there, kneeling on the grass with the rake in my hand. When I look up, I see the Baxters come down the porch steps together and move slowly toward me through the wet, sweet-smelling grass. They stop a few feet away and look at me closely.

'There now,' I hear Mrs Baxter say. She's still in her robe and slippers. It's nippy out; she holds her robe at the throat. 'You did a real fine job for us, yes, you did.'

I don't say anything. I don't even say, 'You're welcome.'

They stand in front of me a while longer, and none of us says anything more. It's as if we've come to an agreement on something. In a minute, they turn around and go back to their house. High over my head, in the branches of the old maple – the place where these leaves come from – birds call out to each other. At least I think they're calling to each other.

Suddenly a car door slams. Mr Baxter is in his car in the drive with the window rolled down. Mrs Baxter says something to him from the front porch which causes Mr Baxter to nod slowly and turn his head in my direction. He sees me kneeling there with the rake, and a look crosses his face. He frowns. In his better moments, Mr Baxter is a decent, ordinary guy – a guy you wouldn't mistake for anyone special. But he is special. In my book, he is. For one thing he has a full night's sleep behind him, and he's just embraced his wife before leaving for work. But even before he goes, he's already expected home a set number of hours later. True, in the grander scheme of things, his return will be an event of small moment – but an event nonetheless.

Baxter starts his car and races the engine for a minute. Then he backs effortlessly out of the drive, brakes and changes gears. As he passes on the street, he slows and looks briefly in my direction. He lifts his hand off the steering wheel. It could be a salute or a sign of dismissal. It's a sign, in any case. And then he looks away toward the city. I get up and raise my hand, too – not a wave, exactly, but close to it. Some other cars drive past. One of the drivers must think he knows me because he gives his horn a friendly little tap. I look both ways and then cross the street. ∎

Philip Roth revisiting Newark, New Jersey, 1968

HIS ROTH

Philip Roth

GRANTA 24: SUMMER 1988

One day in late October 1944, I was astonished to find my father, whose workday ordinarily began at seven and many nights didn't end until ten, sitting alone at the kitchen table in the middle of the afternoon. He was going into the hospital unexpectedly to have his appendix removed. Though he had already packed a bag to take with him, he had waited for my brother, Sandy, and me to get home from school to tell us not to be alarmed. 'Nothing to it,' he assured us, though we all knew that two of his brothers had died back in the 1920s from complications following difficult appendectomies. My mother, the president that year of our school's parent–teacher association, happened, quite unusually, to be away overnight in Atlantic City at a statewide PTA convention. My father had phoned her hotel, however, to tell her the news, and she had immediately begun preparations to return home. That would do it, I was sure: my mother's domestic ingenuity was on a par with Robinson Crusoe's, and as for nursing us all through our illnesses, we couldn't have received much better care from Florence Nightingale. As was usual in our household, everything was now under control.

By the time her train pulled into Newark that evening, the surgeon had opened him up, seen the mess, and despaired for my father's chances. At the age of forty-three, he was put on the critical list and given less than a fifty-fifty chance to survive.

Only the adults knew how bad things were. Sandy and I were allowed to go on believing that a father was indestructible – and ours turned out to be just that. Despite a raw emotional nature that makes him prey to intractable worry, his life has been distinguished by the power of resurgence. I've never intimately known anyone else – aside from my brother and me – to swing as swiftly through so wide a range of moods, anyone else to take things so hard, to be so openly racked by a serious setback, and yet, after the blow has reverberated down to the quick, to clamber back so aggressively, to recover lost ground and get going again.

He was saved by the new sulfa powder, developed during the early years of the war to treat battlefront wounds. Surviving was an awful ordeal nonetheless, his weakness from the near-fatal peritonitis exacerbated by a ten-day siege of hiccups during which he was unable to sleep or to keep down food. After he'd lost nearly thirty pounds, his shrunken face disclosed itself to us as a replica of my elderly grandmother's, the face of the mother whom he and all his brothers adored (toward the father – laconic, authoritarian, remote, an immigrant who'd trained in Galicia to be a rabbi but worked in America in a hat factory – their feelings were more confused). Bertha Zahnstecker Roth was a simple old-country woman, good-hearted, given to neither melancholy nor complaint, yet her everyday facial expression made it plain that she nursed no illusions about life's being easy. My father's resemblance to his mother would not appear so eerily again until he himself reached his eighties, and then only when he was in the grip of a struggle that stripped an otherwise physically youthful old man of his seeming impregnability, leaving him bewildered not so much because of the eye problem or the difficulty with his gait that had made serious inroads on his self-sufficiency but because he felt all at once abandoned by the masterful accomplice and overturner of obstacles, his determination.

When he was driven home from Newark's Beth Israel Hospital after six weeks in bed there, he barely had the strength, even with our

HIS ROTH

assistance, to make it up the short back staircase to our second-story apartment. It was December 1944 by then, a cold winter day, but through the windows the sunlight illuminated my parents' bedroom. Sandy and I came in to talk to him, both of us shy and grateful and, of course, stunned by how helpless he appeared seated weakly in a lone chair in the corner of the room. Seeing his sons together like that, my father could no longer control himself and began to sob. He was alive, the sun was shining, his wife was not widowed nor his boys fatherless – family life would now resume. It was not so complicated that an eleven-year-old couldn't understand his father's tears. I just didn't see, as he so clearly could, why or how it should have turned out differently.

I knew only two boys in our neighborhood whose families were fatherless, and thought of them as no less blighted than the blind girl who attended our school for a while and had to be read to and shepherded everywhere. The fatherless boys seemed almost equally marked and set apart; in the aftermath of their fathers' deaths, they too struck me as scary and a little taboo. Though one was a model of obedience and the other a troublemaker, everything either of them did or said seemed determined by his being a boy with a dead father and, however innocently I arrived at this notion, I was probably right.

I knew no child whose family was divided by divorce. Outside of the movie magazines and the tabloid headlines, it didn't exist, certainly not among Jews like us. Jews didn't get divorced – not because divorce was forbidden by Jewish law but because that was the way they were. If Jewish fathers didn't come home drunk and beat their wives – and in our neighborhood, which was Jewry to me, I'd never heard of any who did – that too was because of the way they were. In our lore, the Jewish family was an inviolate haven against every form of menace, from personal isolation to gentile hostility. Regardless of internal friction and strife, it was assumed to be an indissoluble consolidation. *Hear, O Israel, the family is God, the family is One.*

Family indivisibility, the first commandment.

In the late 1940s, when my father's younger brother, Bernie, proclaimed his intention of divorcing the wife of nearly twenty years who was the mother of his two daughters, my mother and father were as stunned as if they'd heard that he'd killed somebody. Had Bernie committed murder and gone to jail for life, they would probably have rallied behind him despite the abominable, inexplicable deed. But when he made up his mind not merely to divorce but to do so to marry a younger woman, their support went instantly to the 'victims', the sister-in-law and the nieces. For his transgression, a breach of faith with his wife, his children, his entire clan – a dereliction of his duty as a Jew *and* as a Roth – Bernie encountered virtually universal condemnation.

That family rupture only began to mend when time revealed that no one had been destroyed by the divorce; in fact, anguished as they were by the breakup of their household, Bernie's ex-wife and his two girls were never remotely as indignant as the rest of the relatives. The healing owed a lot to Bernie himself, a more diplomatic man than most of his judges, but also to the fact that for my father the demands of family solidarity and the bond of family history exceeded even *his* admonishing instincts. It was to be another forty-odd years, however, before the two brothers threw their arms around each other and hungrily embraced in an unmistakable act of unqualified reconciliation. This occurred a few weeks before Bernie's death, in his late seventies, when his heart was failing rapidly and nobody, beginning with himself, expected him to last much longer.

I had driven my father over to see Bernie and his wife, Ruth, in their condominium in a retirement village in northwestern Connecticut, twenty miles from my own home. It was Bernie's turn now to wear the little face of his unillusioned, stoical old mother; when he came to the door to let us in, there in his features was that stark resemblance that seemed to emerge in all the Roth brothers when they were up against it.

O rdinarily the two men would have met with a handshake, but when my father stepped into the hallway, so much was clear both about the time that was left to Bernie and about all those decades, seemingly stretching back to the beginning of time, during which they had been alive as their parents' offspring, that the handshake was swallowed up in a forceful hug that lasted minutes and left them in tears. They seemed to be saying goodbye to everyone already gone as well as to each other, the last two surviving children of the dour hat-blocker Sender and the imperturbable *balabusta* Bertha. Safely in his brother's arms, Bernie seemed also to be saying goodbye to himself. There was nothing to guard against or defend against or resent anymore, nothing even to remember. In these brothers, men so deeply swayed, despite their dissimilarity, by identical strains of family emotion, everything remembered had been distilled into pure, barely bearable feeling.

In the car afterwards my father said, 'We haven't held each other like that since we were small boys. My brother's dying, Philip. I used to push him around in his carriage. There were nine of us, with my mother and father. I'll be the last one left.'

While we drove back to my house (where he was staying in the upstairs back bedroom, a room in which he says he never fails to sleep like a baby) he recounted the struggles of each of his five brothers – with bankruptcies, illnesses, and in-laws, with marital dissension and bad loans, and with children, with their Gonerils, their Regans, and their Cordelias. He recalled for me the martyrdom of his only sister, what she and all the family had gone through when her husband the bookkeeper who liked the horses had served a little time for embezzlement.

It wasn't exactly the first time I was hearing these stories. Narrative is the form that his knowledge takes, and his repertoire has never been large: family, family, family, Newark, Newark, Newark, Jew, Jew, Jew. Somewhat like mine.

I naively believed as a child that I would always have a father present, and the truth seems to be that I always will. However awkward the union may sometimes have been, vulnerable to differences of opinion, to false expectations, to radically divergent experiences of America, strained by the colliding of two impatient, equally willful temperaments and marred by masculine clumsiness, the link to him has been omnipresent. What's more, now, when he no longer commands my attention by his bulging biceps and his moral strictures, now, when he is no longer the biggest man I have to contend with – and when I am not all that far from being an old man myself – I am able to laugh at his jokes and hold his hand and concern myself with his well-being, I'm able to love him the way I wanted to when I was sixteen, seventeen and eighteen but when, what with dealing with him and feeling at odds with him, it was simply an impossibility. *The* impossibility, for all that I always respected him for his particular burden and his struggle within a system that he didn't choose. The mythological role of a Jewish boy growing up in a family like mine – to become the hero one's father failed to be – I may even have achieved by now, but not at all in the way that was preordained. After nearly forty years of living far from home, I'm equipped at last to be the most loving of sons – just, however, when he has another agenda. He is trying to die. He doesn't say that, nor, probably, does he think of it in those words, but that's his job now and, fight as he will to survive, he understands, as he always has, what the real work is.

Trying to die isn't like trying to commit suicide – it may actually be harder, because what you are trying to do is what you least want to have happen; you dread it but there it is and it must be done, and by no one but you. Twice in the last few years he has taken a shot at it, on two different occasions suddenly became so ill that I, who was then living abroad half the year, flew back to America to find him with barely enough strength to walk from the sofa to the TV set without clutching at every chair in between. And though each time the doctor, after a painstaking examination, was unable to find anything wrong with him, he nonetheless went to bed every night expecting not to awaken in the morning and, when he did awaken in the morning, he was fifteen minutes just getting himself into a sitting position on the edge of the bed and another hour shaving and dressing. Then, for God knows how long, he slouched unmoving over a bowl of cereal for which he had absolutely no appetite.

I was as certain as he was that this was it, yet neither time could he pull it off and, over a period of weeks, he recovered his strength and became himself again, loathing Reagan, defending Israel, phoning relatives, attending funerals, writing to newspapers, castigating William Buckley, watching MacNeil–Lehrer, exhorting his grown grandchildren, remembering in detail our own dead, and relentlessly, exactingly – and without having been asked – monitoring the caloric intake of the nice woman he lives with. It would seem that to prevail here, to try dying and to *do* it, he will have to work even harder than he did in the insurance business, where he achieved a remarkable success for a man with his social and educational handicaps. Of course, here too he'll eventually succeed – though clearly, despite his record of assiduous application to every job he has ever been assigned, things won't be easy. But then they never have been.

Needless to say, the link to my father was never so voluptuously tangible as the colossal bond to my mother's flesh, whose metamorphosed incarnation was a sleek black sealskin coat into which I, the younger, the privileged, the pampered papoose, blissfully wormed myself whenever my father chauffeured us home to New Jersey on a winter Sunday from our semi-annual excursion to Radio City Music Hall and Manhattan's Chinatown: the unnameable animal-me bearing her dead father's name, the protoplasm-me, boy-baby, and body-burrower-in-training, joined by every nerve ending to her smile and her sealskin coat, while his resolute dutifulness, his relentless industriousness, his unreasoning obstinacy and harsh resentments, his illusions, his innocence, his allegiances, his fears were to constitute the original mold for the American, Jew, citizen, man, even for the writer, I would become. To be at all is to be her Philip, but in the embroilment with the buffeting world, my history still takes its spin from beginning as his Roth. ∎

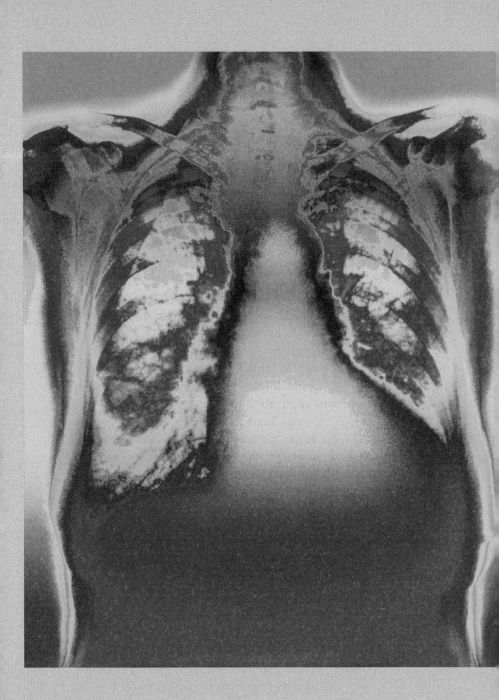

Coloured X-ray of the human chest showing left ventricular failure of the heart.

GLITCHES

John Gregory Dunne

GRANTA 27: SUMMER 1989

1

Anton Siodmak played tennis for a living. He was not on the circuit and he was not exactly a hustler, but his ability on the court made him welcome at the better weekend tennis parties and gave him permanent access to the more elaborate north/south courts in Beverly Hills and Bel Air and Holmby Hills and Trousdale and Malibu. He charmed the men and occasionally slept, especially when he was younger, with the wives of inattentive husbands. There were even husbands, it was said, who implicitly encouraged this attention, because their tastes had become more catholic as the attractions of home and family had begun to pale.

Besides his lob – a stroke perfected as he edged past sixty and one that maddened younger, stronger but less talented players – Anton's most negotiable asset was his smile. He supplemented his income from the court, and the occasional bonbon from those bored and grateful wives, as a greeter in one or two of the more fashionable restaurants frequented by Hollywood royalty. He could be found just inside the door, where he would plant a kiss on both cheeks, in the European style, and laugh and exchange gossip and rearrange his date book for the following weekend – singles here, doubles there and the private screening on Sunday night, Marty's rough cut with a wild music track because Bernie Herrmann's score isn't ready, drinks at seven, dinner seven-thirty, we'll run the picture at eight, Costa's coming by if his plane gets in on time, and Sydney and Claire, and next Sunday, you cocksucker, it won't be love, love, I'll take two games . . .

I did not know Anton all that well – I once made a stab at tennis but was glad to give it up when I broke my elbow – but I would see him at the odd screening and when I ate at the restaurant he would kiss me on both cheeks and call me 'Zhannee' and say that the dailies on so-and-so's picture were so lousy that the crew had stopped wearing the T-shirts with the film's title printed on them.

When I learned that Anton had been killed in a waterskiing accident in Portugal, where he went every summer to play tennis, I felt genuinely sad. He was an essential figure in the local community, because he had the gift of making people feel it was all right occasionally to be frivolous. His memorial service was held, fittingly, on a private tennis court in Beverly Hills, a vast complex complete with its own bleachers, at the foot of a mogul's estate, a court to which Anton had a key and where he could give lessons or bring the pigeons who thought they could take a set from him. The court was covered that day with AstroTurf to protect the playing surface, and instead of seats in rows for the mourners there were restaurant tables with bright cloths and a bar and gay waiters from the various restaurants where Anton had kissed the favored on both cheeks and passed on the latest scandal. It would be a party, we were told, not a wake. Anton would have wanted it that way.

I came directly from a doctor's appointment in Santa Monica and met my wife Joan at the service, and as I sat there under the hot August sun, death was very much on my mind. I thought Anton had actually died under the best possible circumstances for him, a moment of terror as he realized the inevitable outcome of the accident, then an instant later the eternal dark. I did not like to think of him sick or paralyzed, his smile and his serve no longer negotiable. The eulogists, all tennis partners or opponents, thought differently. They praised Anton's independence, which they claimed to envy, his ability to march to his own beat, free of all the responsibilities that came under the heading of 'making a living'. What most of the mourners, or celebrants, because this after all was a party, considered the highest praise came from a producer who said that in twenty-five years of friendship, a quarter of a century of foot-faults and let balls, Anton 'never once offered me a script'. This was a code they all understood, implying that most damning breach of the local etiquette, the favor demanded by a retainer: the subtext was that Anton knew his place.

The service ended and the parking attendant brought my car. As we drove away, my wife said, 'What did the doctor say?'

There had not been an appropriate moment to mention my visit to the doctor in Santa Monica. 'He scared the shit out of me.'

'What did he say?'

'He said I was a candidate for a catastrophic cardiovascular event.'

Internal Affairs Investigation

Q: True?

A: More or less.

Q: More? Or less.

A: A name changed. A certain dramatic restructuring.

Q: Time collapsed?

A: By about two hours. But all the same day. And I am not sure whether it was that doctor or another doctor who said I was a candidate for a catastrophic cardiovascular event. I was on my way to Europe. A doctor, maybe this one, maybe another one the next day, asked how long I planned to be gone. I said seven weeks, including a month in New York. He asked where I was going in Europe. I said Germany and Ireland. He said do you speak German. I said no. He said how many good hospitals do you think you can find in the wilds of western Ireland. I said I have a feeling you don't think I should go. He said I think you'd be mad. He said I'm not going to say you're going to have a heart attack. You could live to be eighty without having a heart attack. I wouldn't bet on it, but it's possible. You have a history. Your father died at fifty-two of heart disease, your uncle at fifty. At this point, I think I mentioned George Santayana, you know, those who forget history are condemned to repeat it, but I am not sure. In any event I am sure he would not have known who Santayana was. He was about eight feet tall and blond and very pleased with himself, really thrilled. He had that look like he thought he could fuck every nurse in his office and then go out and do the Santa Monica ten-kilometre run. So whether it was this guy, this cardiologist, or my own internist the next day who said I was a candidate et cetera, I am not sure. It just seemed to fit better here.

Q: That's what you mean by dramatic restructuring?

A: If I did it, yes.

Q: Anything else?

A: When I told my wife he scared the shit out of me, I started to cry.

Q: Anything else?

A: I thought I was going to run into John Sweeney at the service.

Q: Who is John Sweeney?

A: He is the son of a bitch who murdered my niece Dominique.

Q: Could you elaborate?

A: In late October 1982, John Sweeney wrapped his fingers around the neck of my niece, Dominique Dunne, and strangled her for three and one-half minutes, choking the life from her body. He was tried for murder and convicted of voluntary manslaughter; he was sentenced to six and a half years in prison. With time off for time served and with good time – one day reduced from his sentence for every day served with no serious breach of penitentiary rules – he was released from the California state prison at Susanville in two and a half years. I did not attend the trial. A murder trial is an ugly spectacle, and if my own daughter had been the victim I would like to think I still would not have

attended the proceedings. I have watched too many murder
trials, known too many lawyers and too many judges and too
many prosecutors to have many illusions about the criminal
justice system. Any trial is a ritual complete with its own totems.
Calumny is the language spoken, the lie accepted, the half-truth
chiseled on stone. In the real world, most prosecutors crave
to be in private practice, where they would defend the same
people whose crimes they claim, as prosecutors, debase society,
offering the same extenuating circumstances that are the object
of their prosecutorial scorn. Before the first preliminary hearing,
I could predict that the counsel for the accused would present
the standard defense strategy in cases of this sort: the victim,
unable to speak for herself, would be put on trial, and presented
in effect as a co-conspirator in her own murder. The prosecuting
attorney was equally aware that this would be the defense tactic;
if he had been defending he would have made the same decision.
The greatest offense of which John Sweeney might have been
convicted was murder in the second degree, and in California a
conviction for murder in the second degree does not carry the
death penalty. If John Sweeney was not therefore a candidate for
capital punishment, then the state would have me believe that
other lives were more valuable than Dominique's. This is an idea I
cannot accept. I would have been quite willing myself to do bodily
harm to John Sweeney (or perhaps, to be more honest and less
bombastic, I think in a moment of rage I might have been willing),
and with a certain ambivalence to have the state of California put
him to death in the gas chamber at San Quentin. When the state,
however, and its servitors decide that one life is more valuable
than another, that one murder is more heinous than another,
that there are degrees of murder – some murders not even called
murders but manslaughter – then capital punishment becomes
a matter of bureaucratic whim, an intolerable idea. I would like
to believe, nonetheless, in a justice regnant. I have worked what
Edith Wharton called the underside of the social tapestry for most

of my professional life. I know that the laws of nature, however aberrant, rule in any penitentiary system. I would like to believe that John Sweeney was buggered in prison – he was young and soft, perfect material for the cell-block punk – and if so, that at least one of the cons who sodomized him – no: fucked him up the ass – had Aids, and infected him with it. It is an ignoble thought. So be it. I wish him every ill. I hope he dies a death as miserable as the one he inflicted on my niece.

Q: And why did you think that John Sweeney would be at the service?

A: Because he was out of prison and working as a chef in some restaurant in LA. He knew Anton Siodmak. All those restaurant people know each other. He had worked for a lot of the people who were doing the catering that day. I just thought he might show up. As a matter of fact, one of his former employers called and asked if I were going to the service. I had the sense he was sounding me out so he could let Sweeney know whether I was going or not.

Q: What would you have done?

A: Left. I wouldn't have caused a scene. I was still shaking from what that doctor said. Also it was Anton's day for tribute, and a scene would have laid a heavy trip on his wife. She said the most poignant thing at the service. You had him during the day and in the evening, she said. I had him at night. At night, alone, then I think Anton would really have been interesting. At night he wouldn't have had to smile.

2

It all started the day I received, unsolicited, a letter from my insurance agent. I have had a life insurance policy for over twenty years. I really do not know why. I have always distrusted life insurance as bad luck, a red flag waved in the face of fate. I pay my premiums quarterly and try to ignore the fact that there is only one way anyone is ever going to collect. I am not exactly afraid of dying, although there are moments when I dream of becoming the first to beat the rap. Which was why I opened this letter from my insurance agent – a gentleman I had never met – with a certain reluctance.

To my surprise, the letter said that my insurer, 'in light of the many changes in interest rates and product design' (I especially liked 'product design' as a life insurance concept), proposed to increase the value of my policy by 50 per cent, with no raise in the cost of my annual premium. I have never thought of the insurance industry as a consortium of altruists and knew there had to be some benefit to them in this new product design, but a 50 per cent increase was not to be dismissed lightly. There was nothing I had to do. A paramedic would come to my house, take my blood pressure, ask a few questions, fill out a form, nothing to it.

And so it seemed. The paramedic, a young woman, did make an appointment, did take my blood pressure, did ask the requisite questions: was I taking any medication, had I the usual string of childhood illnesses (measles, chickenpox), were my bowel movements regular and stool color consistent (I would rather be asked about venereal symptoms, about whether I ever had the clap or worse, than about my bowels; my childhood stammer returns and I avoid looking at the questioner as I try to guess what's a great stool color in the earth tones), had I ever had diabetes? As a matter of fact, I had tested as a borderline diabetic several months earlier, but I had gone on a diet and stopped drinking and my glucose levels returned to an acceptable plateau. No problem, said the paramedic. She would pass the results of my examination – it hardly seemed that, just twenty minutes in my library – to the insurer, who would check with my internist.

A month or so later, a second paramedic, also a woman, came to the house to repeat the tests, the first signal that perhaps I did not quite fit within the parameters of the new product design after all. The problem was that earlier glucose test; the possibility, if it existed, of an onset of diabetes could disqualify me from the program. Would I see my doctor for a complete physical? Of course. A month later I took the physical. You don't have diabetes, my internist said, but it's time for your annual physical anyway, so let's put you on the treadmill and do an exercise ECG, which had not been on the agenda. Twelve minutes on the treadmill, a heavy sweat. Breathing heavily, still hitched to the monitors, I sat on a gurney as my internist read the printout.

'You have a glitch,' he said after a moment.

What kind of glitch? 'An abnormality,' he said. It was the first of the terrible words with which I would become so familiar. As he tried to explain the significance of the squiggly lines on the ECG printout, I kept nodding sagely, feigning understanding, even though they were no more intelligible to me than the seismological charts you see on television after an earthquake.

Is it important? I asked, still trying to appear casual. He was already dialing a number on the examining-room telephone.

'I want you to see a cardiologist today.'

I did not get the insurance. But if it had not been for the change in the product design of my old policy, I would not have taken that ECG. I prefer not to speculate about what might have happened if I had not taken the ECG.

Right off I was exposed to the Armageddon rhetoric of cardiology. What I had, according to the examining cardiologist, was a 'critical lesion' in my left anterior descending artery, 'a hemodynamically significant lesion', according to my internist. 'Lesion' is one of those words, like 'biopsy', that one can learn to hate very quickly. Another doctor, with what I can only construe as high cardiological good humor, told me that in the trade the left anterior descending artery was called 'the widow-maker'. I had a number of amiable conversations with my various doctors about the possibility of my dying. It is a subject that tends to concentrate the mind wonderfully. Quickly I fell into the trade lingo, casually referring to that left anterior descending artery as the LAD; it was a way of distancing one's self from the diagnosis, as if I were not the patient under discussion but, because of my familiarity with the arterial chat, a member of the medical team which was going to do its goddamnedest to lengthen those odds, we can't afford to lose this one, he's too important to the nation. No, to the world. I was voluble in singing the praises of my doctors – 'They're the best, everyone says so, there's a medical conference in Shanghai, these guys are over there telling those Chinamen how to do it' – even though I had no empirical evidence that they were any more worthy medically than the pecker checkers who milked me down when I had my army pre-induction physical. Their putative ability simply became an article of faith; it made me feel safe to believe it, and feeling safe was the priority of the moment. I even praised the prints in their office, as if the quality of the artwork purchased by some medical decorator sanctified their professional skills. There was a Jim Dine in one examining room – 'I know Jim and Nancy,' I assured a nurse in that room one day, as if to tell her that the Dines were on my case too, and watching out for me, making the painter's equivalent of a novena; she seemed never to have heard of Jim Dine – and in another examining room a print of Dunster House at Harvard; better Harvard than Chico State, I told myself.

B eing a writer, I knew this was good material, and after Anton Siodmak's memorial service I began taking voluminous notes on every medical appointment and on all the wild thoughts that ran through my head, storing them in a file I called 'Cardiac' on my computer. When my doctors used a term I did not understand, I would ask them to explain in detail, a tactic that sometimes made them annoyed, especially when I carefully wrote the answer down on a yellow legal pad, as it seemed to suggest that I was already preparing a malpractice suit. After I got home, I would check out what they said against the *Merck Manual* and the various medical dictionaries we kept in the house. I likened the situation to the time when my house was robbed twice within a period of six months: I got two pieces out of those robberies, and earned far more from them than the burglars did.

What I felt, oddly enough, was a sense of guilt, mixed with shame and embarrassment. It was as if I had been caught cheating or in a public lie. One or more of my coronary arteries seemed to be occluded: it was my fault; I had put them at risk, in harm's way, because of my own bad habits, my failure to pay attention to my genetic history. Life halted. My wife had to go to New York to deliver a lecture, and to Miami to appear on a television show. The doctors had advised against my flying. 'Go with her,' I was advised by a friend with a cardiac history of his own. 'If you stay here alone, you'll start writing your will in your head.'

In effect, I already had. I was not exactly afraid. There was just a sense of constant apprehension, a feeling that I was living on borrowed time, that death was a constant companion. Every muscle spasm, every shortness of breath after the slightest exertion induced an anxiety symptom. I found myself thinking I wanted to live until I was sixty, which was more than a hop, skip and a jump away. There is something about having a '6' as the first digit of your age in your obituary. It is as if you have lived a full life and did not miss the allotted three score and ten by all that much. I began to make small bargains with myself: I just want to see how that Senate Contra aid vote comes out; I just want to wear my new suit from Sill's, it's all paid for, and I haven't worn it; I just want to give that reading at the 92nd Street Y in October; I just want, I just want. I saw omens everywhere. By accident I erased Susan Sontag's name and address from my computer telephone directory; she had written *Illness and Metaphor*, I was going to die. The next day, by some electronic miracle I did not understand, I was able to retrieve her file: I was going to live. I did not answer my mail; I did not want a letter to arrive after, the specifically unspecified after. I was ever aware of mundane last times: this was the last time I would have dinner at Morton's, the last time I would have a lube job on the Volvo, the last time I would have kung pao shrimp, the last time I would go to Dodger Stadium, the last time I would see a perfect pair of tits. Ah, sex, the last time this, the last time that, the last fucking hard-on.

'Milk it,' I wrote in the 'Cardiac' directory, 'but no excessive melodramatics.'

3

O n the second Sunday in February, seventeen months after an angioplasty, four months after a MUGA bicycle test – nineteen minutes of heavy-duty exercise stress, 'excellent ex capacity', according to the diagnostic report ('A man ten years younger than you without your history doesn't do half that well, Chief,' my cardiologist Tim said) – I went for my morning walk in the park. It was a time of contemplation.

Since it was Sunday, there were no cars in the park and I took a different route, up the steep grade of Cedar Hill on the roadway behind the Metropolitan Museum, knees pumping, sweat pouring. And then the knees would not work, the breath would not come. I rested, hands on my knees, joggers to the left and to the right and in front and behind, just rest here until I catch my breath. Then: why was I lying on the asphalt? I did not recall going down. Oh, shit, I must have blacked out. Two seconds, four, five – enough time anyway to slide from hands on my knees to stretched out on the road, like a deadbeat drunk or a homeless person lying on a grate in front of Ralph Lauren's on Madison Avenue across the street from my apartment, a source of embarrassment to the joggers who looked away, pretended not to see, this deadbeat with black sweatpants, the word PRINCETON in white and orange stitched on the left leg, going back, going back, going back to Nassau Hall, no longer in control, the ultimate degradation.

'Are you all right?' A Samaritan, not a jogger, with a canvas backpack book bag.

'I think so.' The breath was coming back. I was sitting now, brushing gravel from my sweats, hoping the joggers would think I had only taken a nasty fall, the perils of keeping fit. On my feet. The

Samaritan said he would call a cab on one of the emergency phones. No: I'll just wait here for a moment, thanks anyway. Off the road there was what appeared to be a reviewing stand, and I sat there for a few moments, taking in the museum and the cold blue Sunday sky, taking stock, what to do, what next, I'd really hate to cancel dinner tonight, dinner out with an anchorman and a big-time agent and a sports tsar and a political commentator, I'm breathing normally now, it's OK, A-OK, I won't even tell my wife, nor Tim, especially not Tim, I feel fit as a fiddle now. And fit as a fiddle I walked home. In the distance I saw my wife walking the big, shaggy, pain-in-the-ass Bouvier down another path, his post-prandial mark and dump. And I knew I would tell her: we had not stayed married for twenty-five years by keeping secrets, however unpleasant, from one another.

I called Tim, I told Joan. We went to dinner with the anchorman, the big-time agent, the sports tsar and the political commentator. My mind was elsewhere.

Tim's test the next day replicated the exercise conditions in the park. Another blackout. You've got a problem, Chief, Tim said. Aggressive diagnostics, and I suspect some surgery, Tim said. Replace that valve – the valve that had not even been much of a factor in the earlier disagreeable episode – and as long as they are in there, a bypass, and then you're fit as a fiddle and ready for love.

OK.

'I think I know how to end this thing now,' I said to my wife on the walk home from Tim's. I knew I did not have to spell it out to her.

'Terrific,' she said, the novelist in her taking precedence over the wife who knew her husband too well ever to express the concern she felt, the husband who was so volatile except in times of crisis.

'It's a hell of an ending,' I said. ■

International Summer Programmes

7 July - 17 August 2019
Our open-access programmes
for adults are made up from over
200 courses taught by leading
academics. To complete the
experience you can stay in
a historic College.

+44 (0)1223 760850
intenq@ice.cam.ac.uk
www.ice.cam.ac.uk/intsummer

UNIVERSITY OF CAMBRIDGE

Ryszard Kapuściński in his office, Warsaw, Poland, 1982

THE SNOW IN GHANA

Ryszard Kapuściński

TRANSLATED FROM THE POLISH BY WILLIAM BRAND

GRANTA 28: AUTUMN 1989

The fire stood between us and linked us together. A boy added wood and the flames rose higher, illuminating our faces.

'What is the name of your country?'

'Poland.'

Poland was distant, beyond the Sahara, beyond the sea, to the north and to the east. The *Nana* repeated the name aloud. 'Is that how it is pronounced?' he asked.

'That's the way,' I answered. 'That's correct.'

'They have snow there,' Kwesi said. Kwesi worked in town, in Kumasi, and he had come here on vacation. Once, on the movie screen, snow had fallen. The kids applauded and cried merrily, '*Anko! Anko!*' asking to see the snow again. That was great – the white puffs fell and fell. Those are lucky countries. They do not need to grow cotton: the cotton falls from the sky. They call it snow and they walk on it and even throw it into the river.

We were stuck there by chance. The driver, my friend Kofi from Accra, and I. It was already dark when the tire blew – the third tire, rotten luck. It happened on a side road, in the bush, near the village of Mpango in Ghana. Too dark to fix it. You have no idea how dark the night can be. You stick out your hand and you cannot see that hand. Here they have nights like that. We walked into the village.

The *Nana* received us. There is a *Nana* in every village, because *Nana* means boss, head man. The head man is a sort of village mayor but he has more authority. If you and Maryna want to get married back home the village mayor cannot stop you, but the *Nana* can. He has a Council of Elders. These old guys meet, govern, ponder disputes. Once upon a time the *Nana* was a god. But now there is the independent government in Accra. The government passes laws and the *Nana* has to execute them. A *Nana* who does not carry them out is acting like a feudal lord and they get rid of him. The government is trying to make all *Nanas* join the party, and many *Nanas* are the secretaries of their village party organizations. In such cases the party dues always get paid because the *Nana* takes them out of people's taxes.

The *Nana* from Mpango was skinny and bald, with thin Sudanese lips. Kofi presented us: my driver and me. He explained where I was from, and that they were to treat me as a friend.

'I know him,' Kofi said. 'He's an African.'

That is the highest compliment that a European can receive. It opens every door for him.

The *Nana* smiled and we shook hands. You always greet a *Nana* by pressing his right hand between both of your own palms. This shows respect for him. He sat us down by the fire, where the elders were just holding a meeting. He said boastfully that they met often, which did not sound strange to me. This bonfire was burning in the middle of the village and to the left and right, along the road, other fires were burning. As many fires as huts, because there are no kitchens in the huts and people need to cook. Perhaps twenty. So the fires, the moving figures of women and men, and the outlines of the clay huts were visible, all immersed in the depths of a night so dark that it felt like a weight, oppressive.

The bush had disappeared, yet the bush was everywhere; it began a hundred meters away, an immobile massiveness, a tightly-packed, coarse thicket surrounding the village, and us, and the fire. The bush screamed and cried, it stamped and crackled, it was alive, it existed, it bred and gnawed, it smelled of wilted greenery, it terrified and tempted, you could touch it and be wounded and die, but you couldn't look at it; on this night you couldn't see it.

Poland. They did not know of any such country.

The elders looked at me uncertainly or suspiciously; some of them were interested. I wanted to break their mistrust somehow. I did not know how and I was tired.

'Where are your colonies located?' the *Nana* asked.

My eyes were closing, but now I regained consciousness. People often asked that question. Kofi had asked it first, long ago. I explained it to him. It was a revelation to him and from then on he always lay in wait for the question about the Polish colonies so that he could make a concise speech demonstrating its absurdity.

Kofi answered: 'They don't have colonies, *Nana*. Not all white countries have colonies. Not all whites are colonialists. You have to understand that whites often colonized whites.'

That sounded shocking. The elders shuddered and smacked their lips: tsk, tsk, tsk. They were surprised. In the past I would have been surprised that they were surprised. But not anymore. I can't bear that language, that white, black, yellow. The myth of race is disgusting. What does it mean? Because somebody is white, is he more important? So far, the majority of scoundrels have had white skin. I cannot see how anybody is either happy or upset about being this or that. Nobody gets to choose. The one important thing is the heart. Nothing else counts.

Kofi explained later: 'For a hundred years they taught us that the white is somebody higher, super, extra. They had their clubs, their swimming pools, their neighborhoods. Their whores, cars and their burbling language. We knew that England was the only country in the world, that God is English, that only the English travel around the globe. We knew exactly as much as they wanted us to know. Now it's hard to change.'

Kofi and I stuck up for each other, we no longer spoke about the subject of skin, but here, among new faces, the matter had to come up.

One of the elders asked, 'Are all the women in your country white?'

'All of them.'

'Are they beautiful?'

'They're very beautiful,' I answered.

'Do you know what he told me, *Nana*?' Kofi interjected. 'That when they have their summer, their women take off their clothes and lie in the sun to get black skin. The ones that become dark are proud of it, and others admire them for being as tanned as Negroes.'

Very good! So, Kofi, you hit the bull's eye! You got to them. The elders' eyes lit up at the thought of those bodies darkening in the sun, because – you know how it is – men are the same all over the world: they like that sort of thing. The elders rubbed their hands together, smiled; women's bodies in the sun; the fire here was driving away their rheumatism; they snuggled up inside their loose *kente* robes modeled on Roman togas.

'My country has no colonies,' I said, 'and there was a time when my country was a colony. I respect what you've suffered, but we had it horrible: there were trams, restaurants, districts *nur für Deutsch*. There were camps, war, executions. You don't know camps, war and executions. That was what we called fascism. It's the worst colonialism.'

They listened, frowning and closing their eyes. Strange things had been said, which they had to digest. Two whites and they could not ride in the same tram.

'Tell me, what does a tram look like?'

The concrete is important. Perhaps there was not enough room. No, it had nothing to do with room; it was contempt. One person stepping on another. Not only Africa is a cursed land. Every land can be like that – Europe, America, many places in the world. The world depends on people. Of course, people fall into types. For instance, a person in the skin of a snake. A snake is neither black nor white. It is slippery. A person in a slippery skin. That is the worst.

'But *Nana*, we were free afterwards. We built cities and ran lights into the villages. Whoever couldn't, learned how to read.'

The *Nana* stood up and grasped my hand. The rest of the elders did the same. Now we were friends, *przyjaciele, amigos*. I wanted to eat. I could smell meat in the air. There was no scent of jungle, of palm or of coconuts, but only of our sausage that costs 11.60 złoty at an inn in the Mazury. And a large beer.

Instead of that, we ate goat.

Poland – snow falling, women in the sun, no colonies, there had been a war, building homes, somebody teaching somebody to read.

At least I had told them something, I rationalized inwardly. It's too late to go into details, I want to go to sleep, we are leaving at dawn, staying to deliver a lecture is impossible.

Suddenly I felt shame, some sort of shortcoming, a sense of having missed the mark. What I had described was not my country. Now, snow and the lack of colonies – that's accurate at least. But it is nothing, nothing of what we know, of what we carry around within ourselves without even wondering about: nothing of our pride and despair, of our life, nothing of what we breathe, of our death.

So, snow – that's the truth, *Nana,* snow is marvelous and terrible, it sets you free with your skis in the mountains and it kills the drunkard lying by the fence. Snow, because January, the January 1945 offensive, ashes, everything in ashes: Warsaw, Wrocław and Szczecin, a brick, a brick, freezing hands, warmth-giving vodka, people laying bricks, this is where the bed will stand, and the wardrobe right here, people filtering back into the center of the city, ice on the windowpanes, ice on the Vistula, no water, holidays at the waterside, at the seashore, the sand, the woods, the heat wave, sand, tents and Mielno, I'm sleeping with you, with you, with you, somebody's weeping, not here, it's deserted and it's night so I'm crying, those nights, our meetings till dawn, tough discussions, everybody having his say, Comrades! the sky lit up and the stars, because Silesia, blast furnaces, August, seventy degrees Celsius in front of the blast furnaces, the tropic, our Africa, black and hot, hot sausage, why did you give me a cold one, hang on friend, is this your solo, not jazz, but a speech, Sienkiewicz and Kurylewicz, cellars, damp, the potatoes are rotting, get a move on, woman, and turn those spuds over, the market women at Nowolipki, keep moving along, there are no miracles, what do you mean there aren't, what a lovely little war, shut up about the war already, we want to enjoy things, to be happy, I'll tell you something, you are my happiness, an apartment, a television, no, a motorcycle first, the noise when it revs, the children in the park wake up instead of sleeping, what air, not a cloud in the sky, no turning back, if Herr Adenauer thinks, too many graves, we can fight and we can drink so why can't we work, unless we learn how, our ships are sailing on every sea, successes in exports, successes in boxing, youngsters in gloves, wet gloves pulling tractors out of the mud, Nowa Huta, we have to build, Tychy and Wizow, cheery bright apartment houses, up with the country, upward mobility, a cowherd yesterday and an engineer today, sliding through the polytechnic, do you call that an engineer, and the whole tram bursts out laughing (tell me what a tram looks like), it's very simple: four wheels, an electrical pick-up, enough already, enough, it's all a code, nothing but signs in the bush, in Mpango, and the key to the code is in my pocket.

We always carry it to foreign countries, all over the world, to other people, and it is the key of our pride and our powerlessness. We know its configuration, but there is no way to make it accessible to others. We'll never get it right, even when we really want to. Something, the most important, the most significant thing, will remain unsaid.

Relate one year of my country, it does not matter which one, let us say 1957, just one month of that year, take July, just one day, let us say the sixth.

No way.

Yet nevertheless that day, month and year exist in us, they have to exist, because after all we were there, we were walking along the street, we were digging coal, we were cutting the forest, we were walking along the street, and how can you describe one street in one city (it could be Kraków) so that they can feel its movement, its atmosphere, its persistence and changeability, its smell and its hum, so that they can see it?

They cannot see it, nothing can be seen, the night, Mpango, the dense bush, Ghana, they're putting out the fires, the elders are going off to sleep and so are we (departure at dawn), the *Nana* is dozing off, snow is falling somewhere, women like Negroes, he thinks, they are learning to read, he said something, the *Nana* thinks, they had a war, whew, a war, he said, yes, no colonies, no colonies, that country, Poland, white and they have no colonies, he thinks, the bush screams, what a strange world. ∎

Cardiff - 2.9.94.

SS Monthermer Rd,
Cardiff.

9 Grange Close,
Guildford,
Surrey.
tel. Guildford 71315
6th Dec. 1979.

Dear Mr Buford, I learnt recently from Malcolm Bradbury that you are currently re-vamping 'Granta', and so am sending you GETTING POISONED in hopes that it may be of interest. Would you please consider it for your magazine? I would be grateful for any comments you may have. Thank you kindly for your time and attention.

Yours Sincerely,

(Mr) Kazuo Ishiguro.

PS I enclose s.a.e.

© ALBERTO ORTEGA
Baseball game, 2017
Courtesy of Blue Spiral 1 Gallery

THE LITTLE WINTER

Joy Williams

GRANTA 28: AUTUMN 1989

She was in the airport, waiting for her flight to be called, when a woman came to a phone near her chair. The woman stood there, dialing, and after a while began talking in a flat, aggrieved voice. Gloria couldn't hear everything by any means, but she did hear her say, 'If anything happens to this plane, I hope you'll be satisfied.' The woman spoke monotonously and without mercy. She was tall and disheveled and looked the very picture of someone who recently had ceased to be cherished. Nevertheless, she was still being mollified on the other end of the phone. Gloria heard with astounding clarity the part about the plane being repeated several times. The woman then slammed down the receiver and boarded Gloria's flight, flinging herself down in a first-class seat. Gloria proceeded to the rear of the plane and sat quietly, thinking that every person is on the brink of eternity every moment, that the ways and means of leaving this world are innumerable and often inconceivable. She thought in this manner for a while, then ordered a drink.

The plane pushed through the sky and the drink made her think of the way, as a child, she had enjoyed chewing on the collars of her dresses. The first drink of the day did not always bring this to mind but frequently it did. Then she began thinking of the desert which she was leaving behind and how much she liked it. Once she had liked the sea and felt she could not live without it but now missed it almost not at all.

The plane continued. Gloria ordered another drink, no longer resigned to believing that the woman was going to blow it up. Now she began thinking of where she was going and what she was going to do. She was going to visit Jean, a friend of hers, who was having a hard time – a third divorce, after all, Jean had a lot of energy – but that was only for a day or two. Jean had a child named Gwendal. Gloria hadn't seen them for over a year, she probably wouldn't even recognize Gwendal, who would be almost ten by now. Then she would just keep moving around until it happened. She was thinking of looking for a dog to get. She'd had a number of dogs but hadn't had very good luck with them. This was the thing about pets, of course, you knew that something dreadful was going to befall them, that it was not going to end well. Two of her dogs had been hit by cars, one had been epileptic and another was diagnosed early on as having hip dysplasia. That one she had bought from the same litter that Kafka's great-niece had bought hers from. Kafka's great-niece! Vets had never done very well by Gloria's dogs, much as doctors weren't doing very well by Gloria now. She thought frequently about doctors, though she wasn't going to see them anymore. Under the circumstances, she probably shouldn't acquire a dog, but she felt she wanted one. Let the dog get stuck for a change, she thought.

At the airport, Gloria rented a car. She decided to drive until just outside Jean's town and check into a motel. Jean was a talker. A day with Jean would be enough. A day and a night would be too much. Just outside Jean's town was a monastery where the monks raised dogs. Maybe she would find her dog there tomorrow. She would go over to the monastery early in the morning and spend the rest of the day with Jean. But that was it, other than that, there wasn't much of a plan.

The day was cloudy and there was a great deal of traffic. The land falling back from the highway was green and still. It seemed to her a slightly morbid landscape, obelisks and cemeteries, thick drooping forests, the evergreens dying from the top down. Of course there was hardly any place to live these days. A winding old road ran parallel to the highway and Gloria turned off and drove along it until she came to a group of cabins. The cabins were white with little porches but the office was in a structure built to resemble a tepee. There was a dilapidated miniature golf course and a wooden tower from the top of which you could see into three states. But the tower leaned and the handrail curving optimistically upward was splintered and warped, and only five steps from the ground a rusted chain prevented further ascension. Gloria liked places like this.

In the tepee, a woman in a housedress stood behind a pink formica counter. A glass hummingbird coated with greasy dust hung in one window. Gloria could smell meatloaf cooking. The woman had red cheeks and white hair, and she greeted Gloria extravagantly, but as soon as Gloria paid for her cabin she became morose. She gazed at Gloria glumly as though perceiving her as one who had already walked off with the blankets, the lamp and the painting of the waterfall.

The key Gloria had been given did not work. It fitted into the lock and turned, but did not do the job of opening the door. She walked back to the office and a small dog with short legs and a fluffy tail fell in step beside her. Back in the tepee, Gloria said, 'I can't seem to make this key work.' The smell of the meatloaf was now clangorous. The woman was old, but she came around the counter fast.

The dog was standing in the middle of the turnabout in front of the cabins.

'Is that your dog?' Gloria asked.

'I've never seen it before,' the woman said. 'It sure is not,' she added. 'Go home!' she shrieked at the dog. She turned the key in the lock of Gloria's cabin and then gave the door a sharp kick with her sneaker. The door flew open. She stomped back to the office. 'Go home!' she screamed again at the dog.

Gloria made herself an iceless drink in a paper cup and called Jean.

'I can't wait to see you,' Jean said. 'How are you?'

'I'm all right,' Gloria said.

'Tell me.'

'Really,' Gloria said.

'I can't wait to see you,' Jean said. 'I've had the most god-awful time. I know it's silly.'

'How is Gwendal doing?'

'She never liked Chuckie anyway. She's Luke's, you know. But she's not a bit like Luke. You know Gwendal.'

Gloria barely remembered the child. She sipped from the paper cup and looked through the screen at the dog which was gazing over the ruined golf course to the valley beyond.

'I don't know how I manage to pick them,' Jean was saying. She was talking about the last one.

'I'll be there by lunch tomorrow,' Gloria said.

'Not until then! Well, we'll bring some lunch over to Bill's and eat with him. You haven't met him, have you? I want you to meet him.'

Bill was Jean's first ex-husband. She had just bought a house in town where two of her old ex-husbands and her new ex-husband lived. Gloria knew she had quite a day cut out for herself tomorrow. Jean gave her directions and Gloria hung up and made herself a fresh drink in the paper cup. She stood out on the porch. Dark clouds had massed over the mountains. Traffic thundered invisibly past in the distance, beyond the trees. In the town in the valley below, there were tiny hard lights in the enlarging darkness. The light, which had changed, was disappearing, but there was still a lot of light. That's the way it was with light. If you were out in it while it was going you could still see enough for longer. When it was completely dark, Gloria said, 'Well, goodnight.'

She woke mid-morning with a terrible headache. She was not supposed to drink but what difference did it make, really. It didn't make any difference. She took her pills. Sometimes she thought it had been useless for her to grow older. She was thirty-five. She lay in the musty cabin. Everything seemed perfectly clear. Then it seemed equivocal again. She dressed and went to the office where she paid for another night. The woman took the money and looked at Gloria worriedly as though she were already saying goodbye to those towels and that old willow chair with the cushion.

It began to rain. The road to the monastery was gravel and wound up the side of a mountain. There were orchards, fields of young corn . . . the rain fell upon it all in a fury. Gloria drove slowly, barely able to make out the road. She imagined it snowing out there, not rain but snow, filling everything up. She imagined thinking – *it was dark now but still snowing* – a line like that, as in a story. A line like that was lovely, she thought. When she was small they had lived in a place where the little winter came first. That's what everyone called it. There was the little winter, then there were pleasant days, sometimes weeks. Then the big winter came. She felt dreamy and cold, a little disconnected from everything. She was on the monastery's grounds now and there were wooden buildings with turreted roofs and minarets. Someone had planted birches. She parked in front of a sign that said INFORMATION / GIFT SHOP and dashed from the car to the door. She was laughing and shaking the water from her hair as she entered.

The situation was that there were no dogs available, or rather that the brother whose duty was the dogs, who knew about the dogs, was away and would not return until tomorrow. She could come back tomorrow. The monk who told her this had a beard and wore a soiled apron. His interest in her questions did not seem intense. He had appeared from a back room, a room that seemed part smokehouse, part kitchen. This was the monk who smoked chickens, hams and cheese. There was always cheese in this life. The monastery had a substantial mail-order business; the monks smoked things, the nuns made cheesecakes. The monk seemed slightly impatient with Gloria and she was aware that her questions about the dogs seemed desultory. He had given up a great deal, no doubt, in order to be here. The gift shop was crowded with half-priced icons and dog beds. In a corner there was a glass case filled with the nuns' cheesecakes. Gloria looked in there, at the white boxes, stacked.

'The Deluxe is a standard favorite,' the monk said. 'The Kahlúa is encased in a chocolate cookie-crumb crust, the rich liqueur from sunny Mexico blending naturally with the nuns' original recipe.' The monk droned on as though at matins. 'The Chocolate is a must for chocolate-fanciers. The Chocolate Amaretto is considered by the nuns to be their *pièce de résistance.*'

Gloria bought the Chocolate Amaretto and left. How gloomy, she thought. The experience had seemed vaguely familiar as though she had surrendered passively to it in the past. She supposed it was a belief in appearances. She put the cheesecake in the car and walked around the grounds. It was raining less heavily now but even so her hair was plastered to her skull. She passed the chapel and then turned back and went inside. She picked up a candlestick and jammed it into her coat pocket. This place made her mad. Then she took the candlestick out and set it on the floor. Outside, she wandered around, hearing nothing but the highway which was humming like something in her head. She finally found the kennels and opened the door and went in. This is the way she thought it would be, nothing closed to her at all. There were four dogs, all young ones, maybe three months old, German shepherds. She watched them for a while. It would be easy to take one, she thought. She could just do it.

She drove back down the mountain into town, where she pulled into a shopping center that had a liquor store. She bought gin and some wine for Jean, then drove down to Jean's house in the valley. She felt tired. There was something pounding behind her eyes. Jean's house was a dirty peach color with a bush in front. Everything was pounding, the house, even the grass. Then the pounding stopped.

'Oh my God,' Jean exclaimed. 'You've brought the *pièce de résistance!*' Apparently everyone was familiar with the nuns' cheesecakes. They didn't know about the dogs except that there were dogs up there, they knew that. Jean and Gloria hugged each other. 'You look good,' Jean said. 'They got it all, thank God, right? The things that happen . . . there aren't even names for half of what happens, I swear. You know my second husband, Andy, the one who died? He went in and he never came out again and he just submitted to it, but no one could ever figure out what it was. It was something complicated and obscure and the only thing they knew was that he was dying from it. It might have been some insect that bit him. But the worst thing – well, not the worst thing, but the thing I remember because it had to do with me, which is bad of me, I suppose, but that's just human nature. The worst thing was what happened just before he died. He was very fussy. Everything had to be just so.'

'This is Andy,' Gloria said.

'Andy,' Jean agreed. 'He had an excellent vocabulary and was very precise. How I got involved with him I'll never know. But he was my husband and I was devastated. I *lived* at the hospital, week after week. He liked me to read to him. I was there that afternoon and I had adjusted the shade and plumped the pillows and I was reading to him. And there he was, quietly slipping away right then, I guess, looking back on it. I was reading and I got to this part about someone being the master of a highly circumscribed universe and he opened his eyes and said, "Circumscribed." "What, darling?" I said. And he said, "Circumscribed, not circumcised . . . you said circumcised." And I said, "I'm sure I didn't, darling," and he gave me this long look and then he gave a big sigh and died. Isn't that awful?'

Gloria giggled, then shook her head.

Jean's eyes darted around the room, which was in high disorder. Peeling wallpaper, cracked linoleum. Cardboard boxes everywhere. Shards of glass had been swept into one corner and a broken croquet mallet propped one window open. 'So what do you think of this place?' Jean said.

'It's some place,' Gloria said.

'Everyone says I shouldn't have. It needs some work, I know, but I found this wonderful man, or he found me. He came up to the door and looked at all this and I said, "Can you help me? Do you do work like this?"

'And he nodded and said, "I puttah." Isn't that wonderful! "I puttah . . . "'

Gloria looked at the sagging floor and the windows loose in their frames. The mantel was blackened by smoke and grooved with cigarette burns. It was clear that the previous occupants had led lives of grinding boredom here and that they had not led them with composure. He'd better start puttahing soon, Gloria thought. 'Don't marry him,' she said, and laughed.

'Oh, I know you think I marry everybody,' Jean said, 'but I don't. There have only been four. The last one, and I mean the last, was the worst. What a rodent Chuckie was. No, he's more like a big predator, a crow or a weasel or something. Cruel, lazy, deceitful.' Jean shuddered. 'The best thing about him was his hair.' Jean was frequently undone by hair. 'He has great hair. He wears it in a sort of fifties full flat-top.'

Gloria felt hollow and happy. Nothing mattered much.

'Love is a chimera,' Jean said earnestly.

Gloria laughed.

'I'm pronouncing that right, aren't I?' Jean said, laughing.

'You actually bought this place?' Gloria said.

'Oh, it's crazy,' Jean said, 'but Gwendal and I needed a home. I've heard that *faux* is the new trend. I'm going to do it all *faux* when I get organized. Do you want to see the upstairs? Gwendal's room is upstairs. Hers is the neatest.'

They went up the stairs to a room where a fat girl sat on a bed writing in a book.

'I'm doing my autobiography,' Gwendal said, 'but I think I'm going to change my approach.' She turned to Gloria. 'Would you like to be my biographer?'

Jean said, 'Say hello to Gloria. You remember Gloria.'

Gloria gave the girl a hug. Gwendal smelled good and had small gray eyes. The room wasn't clean at all, but there was very little in it. Gloria supposed it was the neatest. Conversation lagged.

'Let's go out and sit on the lawn,' Jean suggested.

'I don't want to,' Gwendal said.

The two women went downstairs. Gloria needed to use the bathroom but Jean said she had to go outside as the plumbing wasn't all it should be. There was a steep brushy bank behind the house and Gloria crouched there. The day was clear and warm now. At the bottom of the bank, a flat stream moved laboriously around vine-covered trees. The mud glistened in the sun. Blackberries grew in the brush. This place had a lot of candor, Gloria thought.

J ean had laid a blanket on the grass and was sitting there, eating a wedge of cheesecake from a plastic plate. Gloria decided on a drink over cake.

'We'll go to Bill's house for lunch,' Jean said. 'Then we'll go to Fred's house for a swim.' Fred was an old husband too. Gwendal's father was the only one who wasn't around. He lived in Las Vegas. Andy wasn't around either, of course.

Gwendal came out of the house into the sloppy yard. She stopped in the middle of a rhubarb patch, exclaiming silently and waving her arms.

Jean sighed. 'It's hard being a single mother.'

'You haven't been single for long,' Gloria said.

Jean laughed loudly at this. 'Poor Gwendal,' she said, 'I love her dearly.'

'A lovely child,' Gloria murmured.

'I just wish she wouldn't make up so much stuff sometimes.'

'She's young,' Gloria said, swallowing her drink. Really, she hardly knew what she was saying. 'What *is* she doing?' she asked Jean.

Gwendal leaped quietly around in the rhubarb.

'Whatever it is, it needs to be translated,' Jean said. 'Gwendal needs a good translator.'

'She's pretending something or other,' Gloria offered, thinking she would very much like another drink.

'I'm going to put on a fresh dress for visiting Bill,' Jean said. 'Do you want to put on a fresh dress?'

Gloria shook her head. She was watching Gwendal. When Jean went into the house, the girl trotted over to the blanket. 'Why don't you kidnap me?' she said.

'Why don't you kidnap *me*?' Gloria said, laughing. What an odd kid, she thought. 'I don't want to kidnap you,' she said.

'I'd like to see your house,' Gwendal said.

'I don't have a house. I live in an apartment.'

'Apartments aren't interesting,' Gwendal said. 'Dump it. We could get a van. The kind with the ladder that goes up the back. We could get a wheel-cover that says MESS WITH THE BEST, LOSE LIKE THE REST.'

There was something truly terrifying about girls on the verge of puberty, Gloria thought. She laughed.

'You drink too much,' Gwendal said. 'You're always drinking something.'

This hurt Gloria's feelings. 'I'm dying,' she said. 'I have a brain tumor. I can do what I want.'

'If you're dying you can do anything you want?' Gwendal said. 'I didn't know that. That's a new one. So there are compensations.'

Gloria couldn't believe she'd told Gwendal she was dying. 'You're fat,' she said glumly.

Gwendal ignored this. She wasn't all that fat. Somewhat fat, perhaps, but not grotesquely so.

'Oh, to hell with it,' Gloria said. 'You want me to stop drinking, I'll stop drinking.'

'It doesn't matter to me,' Gwendal said.

Gloria's mouth trembled. I'm drunk, she thought.

'Some simple pleasures are just a bit too simple, you know,' Gwendal said.

Gloria felt that she had been handling her upcoming death pretty well. Now she wasn't sure, in fact, she felt awful. What was she doing spending what might be one of her last days sitting on a scratchy blanket in a weedy yard while a fat child insulted her? Her problem was that she had never figured out where it was exactly she wanted to go to die. Some people knew and planned accordingly. The desert, say, or Nantucket. Or a good hotel somewhere. But she hadn't figured it out. En route was the closest she'd come.

Gwendal said, 'Listen, I have an idea. We could do it the other way around. Instead of you being my biographer, I'll be yours. *Gloria by Gwendal.*' She wrote in the air with her finger. She did not have a particularly flourishing hand, Gloria noted. 'Your life as told to Gwendal Crawley. I'll write it all down. At least that's something. We can always spice it up.'

'I haven't had a very interesting life,' Gloria said modestly. But it was true, she thought. When her parents had named her, they must have been happy. They must have thought something was going to happen now.

'I'm sure you must be having some interesting reflections though,' Gwendal said. 'And if you're really dying, I bet you'll feel like doing everything once.' She was wringing her hands in delight.

Jean walked towards them from the house.

'C'mon,' Gwendal hissed. 'Let me go with you. You didn't come all this way just to stay here, did you?'

'Gloria and I are going to visit Bill,' Jean said. 'Let's all go,' she said to Gwendal.

'I don't want to,' Gwendal said.

'If I don't see you again, goodbye,' Gloria said to Gwendal. The kid stared at her.

Jean was driving, turning this way and that, passing the houses of those she had once loved.

'That's Chuckie's house,' Jean said. 'The one with the hair.' They drove slowly by, looking at Chuckie's house. 'Charming on the outside but sleazy inside, just like Chuckie. He broke my heart, literally broke my heart. Well, his foot is going to slide in due time as they say and I want to be around for that. That's why I've decided to stay.' She said a moment later, 'It's not really.'

They passed Fred's house. Everybody had a house.

'Fred has a pond,' Jean said. 'We can go for a swim there later. I always use Fred's pond. He used to own a whole quarry, can you imagine? This was before our time with him, Gwendal's and mine, but the kids were always getting in there and drowning. He put up big signs and barbed wire and everything but they still got in. It got to be too much trouble, so he sold it.'

'Too much trouble!' Gloria said.

Death seemed preposterous. Totally unacceptable. Those silly kids, Gloria thought. She was elated and knew that she would feel tired soon and uneasy, but maybe it wouldn't happen this time. The day was bright, clean after the rain. Leaves lay on the streets, green and fresh.

'Those were Fred's words, the too much trouble. Can't I pick them? I can really pick them.' Jean shook her head.

They drove to Bill's house. Next to it was a pasture with horses in it. 'Those aren't Bill's horses, but they're pretty, aren't they?' Jean said. 'You're going to love Bill. He's gotten a little strange but he always was a little strange. We are who we are, aren't we? He carves ducks.'

Bill was obviously not expecting them. He was a big man with long hair wearing boxer shorts and smoking a cigar. He looked at Jean warily.

'This used to be the love of my life,' Jean said. To Bill, she said, 'This is Gloria, my dearest friend.'

Gloria felt she should demur, but smiled instead. Her situation didn't make her any more honest, she had found.

'Beautiful messengers, bad news,' Bill said.

'We just thought we'd stop by,' Jean said.

'Let me put on my pants,' he said.

The two women sat in the living room, surrounded by wooden ducks. The ducks, exquisite and oppressive, nested on every surface. Buffleheads, canvas-back, scaup, blue-winged teal. Gloria picked one up. It looked heavy but was light. Shoveler, mallard, merganser. The names kept coming to her.

'I forgot the lunch so we'll just stay a minute,' Jean whispered. 'I was *mad* about this man. Don't you ever wonder where it all goes?'

Bill returned, wearing trousers and a checked shirt. He had put his cigar somewhere.

'I *love* these ducks,' Jean said. 'You're getting so good.'

'You want a duck,' Bill said.

'Oh yes!' Jean said.

'I wasn't offering you one. I just figured that you did.' He winked at Gloria.

'Oh you,' Jean said.

'Take one, take one,' Bill sighed.

Jean picked up the nearest duck and put it in her lap.

'That's a harlequin,' Bill said.

'It's bizarre, I love it.' Jean gripped the duck tightly.

'You want a duck?' Bill said to Gloria.

'No,' Gloria said.

'Oh, take one!' Jean said excitedly.

'Decoys have always been particularly abhorrent to me,' Gloria said, 'since they are objects designed to lure a living thing to its destruction with the false promise of safety, companionship and rest.'

They both looked at her, startled.

'Oh wow, Gloria,' Jean said.

'These aren't decoys,' Bill said mildly. 'People don't use them for decoys anymore, they use them for decoration. There are hardly any more ducks to hunt. Ducks are on their way out. They're in a free fall.'

'Diminishing habitat,' Jean said.

'There you go,' Bill said.

Black duck, pintail, widgeon. The names kept moving toward Gloria, then past.

'I'm more interested in creating dramas now,' Bill said. 'I'm getting away from the static stuff. I want to make dramatic moments. They have to be a little less than life-sized, but otherwise it's all there . . . the whole situation.' He stood up. 'Just a second,' he said.

Once he was out of the room, Jean turned to her. 'Gloria?' she said.

Bill returned carrying a large object covered by a sheet. He set it down on the floor and took off the sheet.

'I like it so far,' Jean said after a moment.

'Interpret away,' Bill said.

'Well,' Jean said, 'I don't think you should make it too busy.'

'I said interpret, not criticize,' Bill said.

'I just think the temptation would be to make something like that too busy. The temptation would be to put stuff in all those little spaces.'

Bill appeared unmoved by this possible judgment, but he replaced the sheet.

In the car, Jean said, 'Wasn't that *awful*? He should stick to ducks.' According to Bill, the situation the object represented seemed to be the acceptance of inexorable fate, this acceptance containing within it, however, a heroic gesture of defiance. This was the situation, ideally always the situation, and it had been transformed, more or less abstractly, by Bill, into wood.

'He liked you.'

'Jean, why would he like me?'

'He was flirting with you, I think. Wouldn't it be something if you two got together and we were all here in this one place?'

'Oh my God,' Gloria said, putting her hands over her face. Jean glanced at her absent-mindedly. 'I should be getting back,' Gloria said. 'I'm a little tired.'

'But you just got here, and we have to take a swim at Fred's. The pond is wonderful, you'll love the pond. Actually, listen, do you want to go over to my parents' for lunch? Or it should be dinner, I guess. They have this big television. My mother can make us something nice for dinner.'

'Your parents live around here too?' Gloria asked.

Jean looked frightened for a moment. 'It's crazy, isn't it? They're so sweet. You'd love my parents. Oh, I wish you'd talk,' she exclaimed. 'You're my friend. I wish you'd open up some.'

They drove past Chuckie's house again. 'Whose car is that now?' Jean wondered.

'I remember trying to feed my mother a spoonful of dust once,' Gloria said.

'Why!' Jean said. 'Tell!'

'I was little, maybe four. She told me that I had grown in her stomach because she'd eaten some dust.'

'No!' Jean said. 'The things they tell you when they know you don't know.'

'I wanted there to be another baby, someone else, a brother or a sister. So I had my little teaspoon. "Eat this," I said. "It's not a bit dirty. Don't be afraid." '

'How out of control!' Jean cried.

'She looked at it and said she'd been talking about a different kind of dust, the sort of dust there was on flowers.'

'She was just getting in deeper and deeper, wasn't she?' Jean said. She waited for Gloria to say more but the story seemed to be over. 'That's a nice little story,' Jean said.

It was dark when she got back to the cabins. There were no lights on anywhere. She remembered being happy off and on that day, and then looking at things and finding it all unkind. It had gotten harder for her to talk, and harder to listen to, but she was alone now and she felt a little better. Still, she didn't feel right. She knew she would never be steady. It would never seem all of a piece for her. It would come and go until it stopped.

She pushed open the door and turned on the lamp beside the bed. There were three sockets in the lamp but only one bulb. There had been more bulbs in the lamp last night. She also thought there had been more furniture in the room, another chair. Reading would have been difficult, if she had wanted to read, but she was tired of reading, tired of books. After they had told her the first time and even after they had told her the other times in different ways, she had wanted to read, she didn't want to just stand around gaping at everything, but she couldn't pick the habit up again, it wasn't the same.

The screen behind the lamp was a mottled bluish green, a coppery, oceanic color. She thought of herself as a child with the spoonful of dust, but it was just a memory of her telling it now. She stood close to the screen, to its raw, metallic smell.

In the middle of the night she woke, soaked with sweat. Someone was just outside, she thought. Then this feeling vanished. She gathered up her things and put everything in the car. She did this all hurriedly, and then drove quickly to Jean's house. She parked out front and turned the lights off. After a few moments, Gwendal appeared. She was wearing an ugly dress and carrying a suitcase. There were creases down one side of her face as though she'd been sleeping hard before she woke. 'Where to first?' Gwendal said.

What they did first was to drive to the monastery and steal a dog. Gloria suspected that fatality made her more or less invisible and this seemed to be the case. She drove directly to the kennel, went in and walked out with a dog. She put him in the back seat and they drove off.

'We'll avoid the highway,' Gloria said. 'We'll stick to the back roads.'

'Fine with me,' Gwendal said.

Neither of them said anything for miles, then Gwendal asked, 'Would you say he had drop-dead good looks?'

'He's a dog,' Gloria said. Gwendal was really mixed up. She was worse than her mother, Gloria thought.

They pulled into a diner and had breakfast. Then they went to a store and bought notebooks, pencils, dog food and gin. They bought sunglasses. It was full day now. They kept driving until dusk. They were quite a distance from Jean's house. Gloria felt sorry for Jean. She liked to have everyone around her, even funny little Gwendal, and now she didn't.

Gwendal had been sleeping. Suddenly she woke up. 'Do you want to hear my dream?' she asked.

'Absolutely,' Gloria said.

'Someone, it wasn't you, told me not to touch this funny-looking animal, it wasn't him,' Gwendal said, gesturing toward the dog. 'Every time I'd pat it, it would bite off a piece of my arm or a piece of my chest. I just had to keep going, "It's cute," and keep petting it.'

'Oh.' Gloria said. She had no idea what to say.

'Tell me one of your dreams,' Gwendal said, yawning.

'I haven't been dreaming lately,' Gloria said.

'That's not good,' Gwendal said. 'That shows a lack of imagination.

Readiness, it shows a lack of readiness maybe. Well, I can put the dreams in later. Don't worry about it.' She chose a pencil and opened her notebook. 'OK,' she said. 'Married?'

'No.'

'Any children?'

'No.'

'Allergies?'

Gloria looked at her.

'Do you want to start at the beginning or do you want to work backward from the Big Surprise?' Gwendal asked.

They were on the outskirts of a town, stopped at a traffic light. Gloria looked straight ahead. Beginnings. She couldn't remember any beginnings.

'Hey,' someone said. 'Hey!'

She looked to her left at a dented yellow car full of young men. One of them threw a can of beer at her. It bounced off the door and they sped off, howling.

'Everyone knows if someone yells "hey" you don't look at them,' Gwendal said.

'Let's stop for the night,' Gloria said.

'How are you feeling?' Gwendal asked . . . not all that solicitously, Gloria thought.

They pulled into the first motel they saw. Gloria fed the dog and had a drink while Gwendal bounced on the bed. He seemed a most equable dog. He drank from the toilet bowl and gnawed peaceably on the bed-rail. Gloria and Gwendal ate pancakes in a brightly lit restaurant and strolled around a swimming-pool which had a filthy rubber cover rolled across it. Back in the room, Gloria lay down on one bed while Gwendal sat on the other.

'Do you want me to paint your nails or do your hair?' Gwendal asked.

'No,' Gloria said. She was recalling a bad thought she'd had once, a very bad thought. It had caused no damage, however, as far as she knew.

'I wouldn't know how to do your hair actually,' Gwendal said. With a little training this kid could be a mortician, Gloria thought.

That night Gloria dreamed. She dreamed she was going to the funeral of some woman who had been indifferent to her. There was no need for her to be there. She was standing with a group of people. She felt like a criminal, undetected, but she felt chosen too, to be here when she shouldn't be. Then she was lying across the opening of a cement pipe. When she woke, she was filled with relief, knowing she would forget the dream immediately. It was morning again. Gwendal was outside by the unpleasant pool, writing in her notebook.

'*This was happiness then,*' she said to Gloria, scribbling away. 'Where's the dog?' Gloria asked. 'Isn't he with you?'

'I don't know,' Gwendal said. 'I let him out and he took off for parts unknown.'

'What do you mean!' Gloria said. She ran back to the room, went to the car, ran across the cement parking lot and around the motel. Gloria didn't have any name to call the dog with. It had just disappeared without having ever been hers. She got Gwendal in the car and they drove down the roads around the motel. She squinted, frightened, at black heaps along the shoulder and in the littered grass, but it was tires, rags, tires. Cars sped by them. Along the median strip, dead trees were planted at fifty-foot intervals. The dog wasn't anywhere that she could find. Gloria glared at Gwendal.

'It was an accident,' Gwendal said.

'You have your own ideas about how this should be, don't you?'

'He was a distraction in many ways,' Gwendal said. Gloria's head hurt. Back in the desert, just before she had made this trip, she had had her little winter. Her heart had pounded like a fist on a door. But it was false, all false, for she had survived it.

Gwendal had the hateful notebook on her lap. It had a splatter black cover with the word COMPOSITION on it. 'Now we can get started,' she said. 'Today's the day. Favorite color?' she asked. 'Favorite show tune?' A childish blue barette was stuck haphazardly in her hair, exposing part of a large, pale ear.

Gloria wasn't going to talk to her.

After a while, Gwendal said, *'They were unaware that the fugitive was in their midst.'* She wrote it down. Gwendal scribbled in the book all day long and asked Gloria to buy her another one. She sometimes referred to Gloria's imminent condition as the Great Adventure.

Gloria was distracted. Hours went by and she was driving, though she could barely recall what they passed. 'I'm going to pull in early tonight,' she said.

The motel they stopped at late that afternoon was much like the one before. It was called the Motel Lark. Gloria lay on one bed and Gwendal sat on the other. Gloria missed having a dog. A dog wouldn't let the stranger in, she thought, knowing she was being sentimental. Whereas Gwendal would in a minute.

'We should be able to talk,' Gwendal said.

'Why should we be able to talk?' Gloria said. 'There's no reason we should be able to talk.'

'You're not open is your problem. You don't want to share. It's hard to imagine what's real all by yourself, you know.'

'It is not!' Gloria said hotly. They were bickering like an old married couple.

'This isn't working out,' Gloria said. 'This is crazy. We should call your mother.'

'I'll give you a few more days, but it's true,' Gwendal said. 'I thought this would be a more mystical experience. I thought you'd tell me something. You don't even know about makeup. I bet you don't even know how to check the oil in that car. I've never seen you check the oil.'

'I know how to check the oil,' Gloria said.

'How about an electrical problem? Would you know how to fix an electrical problem?'

'No!' Gloria yelled.

Gwendal was quiet. She stared at her fat knees.

'I'm going to take a bath,' Gloria said.

She went into the bathroom and shut the door. The tile was turquoise and the stopper to the tub hung on a chain. This was the Motel Lark, she thought. She dropped the rubber stopper in the drain and ran the water. A few tiles were missing and the wall showed a gray, failed adhesive. She wanted to say something but even that wasn't it. She didn't want to say anything. She wanted to realize something she couldn't say. She heard a voice, it must have been Gwendal's, in the bedroom. Gloria lay down in the tub. The water wasn't as warm as she expected. *Your silence is no deterrent to me, Gloria,* the voice said. She reached for the hot-water faucet but it ran in cold. If she let it run, it might get warm, she thought. That's what they say. Or again, that might be it. ■

AT YANKEE STADIUM

Don DeLillo

ISSUE 34: AUTUMN 1990

Here they come, marching into American sunlight. They are grouped in twos, eternal boy-girl, stepping out of the runway beyond the fence in left-center field. The music draws them across the grass, dozens, hundreds, already too many to count. They assemble themselves so tightly, crossing the vast arc of the outfield, that the effect is one of transformation. From a series of linked couples they become one continuous wave, larger all the time, covering the open spaces in navy and white.

Karen's daddy, watching from the grandstand, can't help thinking this is the point. They're one body now, an undifferentiated mass, and this makes him uneasy. He focuses his binoculars on a young woman, another, still another. So many columns set so closely. He has never seen anything like this or ever imagined it could happen. He hasn't come here for the spectacle but it is starting to astonish him. They're in the thousands now, approaching division strength, and the old seemly tear-jerk music begins to sound sardonic. Wife Maureen is sitting next to him. She is bold and bright today, wearing candy colours to offset the damp she feels in her heart. Rodge understands completely. They had almost no warning. Grabbed a flight, got a hotel, took the subway, passed through the metal-detector and here they are, trying to comprehend. Rodge is not unequipped for the

177

rude turns of normal fraught experience. He's got a degree and a business and a tax attorney and a cardiologist and a mutual fund and whole-life and major medical. But do the assurances always apply? There is a strangeness down there that he never thought he'd see in a ballpark. They take a time-honored event and repeat it, repeat it, repeat it until something new enters the world.

Look at the girl in the front row, about twenty couples in from the left. He adjusts the eyepiece lever and zooms to max power, hoping to see her features through the bridal veil.

There are still more couples coming out of the runway and folding into the crowd, although crowd is not the right word. He doesn't know what to call them. He imagines they are uniformly smiling, showing the face they squeeze out with the toothpaste every morning. The bridegrooms in identical blue suits, the brides in lace and satin gowns. Maureen looks around at the people in the stands. Parents are easy enough to spot and there are curiosity-seekers scattered about, ordinary slouchers and loiterers, others deeper in the mystery, dark-eyed and separate, secretly alert, people who seem to be wearing everything they own, layered and mounded in garments with missing parts, city nomads more strange to her than herdsmen in the Sahel, who at least turn up on the documentary channel. There is no admission fee and gangs of boys roam the far reaches, setting off firecrackers that carry a robust acoustical wallop, barrel bombs and ash cans booming along the concrete ramps and sending people into self-protective spasms. Maureen concentrates on the parents and other relatives, some of the women done up touchingly in best dress and white corsage, staring dead-eyed out of tinted faces. She reports to Rodge that there's a lot of looking back and forth. Nobody knows how to feel and they're checking around for hints. Rodge stays fixed to his binoculars. Six thousand five hundred couples and their daughter is down there somewhere about to marry a man she met two days ago. He's either Japanese or Korean. Rodge didn't get it straight. And he knows about eight words of English. He and Karen spoke through an interpreter, who taught them how to say Hello, it is Tuesday, here is my passport. Fifteen minutes in a bare room and they're chain-linked for life.

He works his glasses across the mass, the crowd, the movement, the membership, the flock, the following. It would make him feel a little better if he could find her.

'You know what it's as though?' Maureen says.

'Let me concentrate.'

'It's as though they designed this to the maximum degree of let the relatives squirm.'

'We can do our moaning at the hotel.'

'I'm simply stating.'

'I did suggest, did I not, that you stay at home.'

'How could I not come? What's my excuse?'

'I see a lot of faces that don't look American. They send them out in missionary teams. Maybe they think we've sunk to the status of less-developed country. They're here to show us the way and the light.'

'And make sharp investments. After, can we take in a play?'

'Let me look, OK. I want to find her.'

'We're here. We may as well avail ourselves.'

'It's hard for the mind to conceive. Thirteen-thousand people.'

'What are you going to do when you find her?'

'Who the hell thought it up? What does it mean?'

'What are you going to do when you find her? Wave goodbye?'

'I just need to know she's here,' Rodge says. 'I want to document it, OK.'

'Because that's what it is. If it hasn't been goodbye up to this point, it certainly is now.'

'Hey, Maureen? Shut up.'

From the bandstand at home plate the Mendelssohn march carries a stadium echo, with lost notes drifting back from the recesses between tiers. Flags and bunting everywhere. The blessed couples face the infield, where their true father, Master Moon, stands in three dimensions. He looks down at them from a railed pulpit that rides above a platform of silver and crimson. He wears a white silk robe and a high crown figured with stylized irises. They know him at molecular level. He lives in them like chains of matter that determine who they are. This is a man of chunky build who saw Jesus on a mountainside. He spent nine years praying and wept so long and hard his tears formed puddles and soaked through the floor and dripped into the room below and filtered through the foundation of the house into the earth. The couples know there are things he must leave unsaid, words whose planetary impact no one could bear. He is the messianic secret, ordinary-looking, his skin a weathered bronze. When the Communists sent him to a labor camp the other inmates knew who he was because they'd dreamed about him before he got there. He gave away half his food but never grew weak. He worked seventeen hours a day in the mines but always found time to pray, to keep his body clean and tuck in his shirt. The blessed couples eat kiddie food and use baby names because they feel so small in his presence. This is a man who lived in a hut made of US Army ration tins and now he is here, in American light, come to lead them to the end of human history.

The brides and grooms exchange rings and vows and many people in the grandstand are taking pictures, standing in the aisles and crowding the rails, whole families snapping anxiously, trying to shape a response or organize a memory, trying to neutralize the event, drain it of eeriness and power. Master chants the ritual in Korean. The couples file past the platform and he sprinkles water on their heads. Rodge sees the brides lift their veils and he zooms in urgently, feeling at the same moment a growing distance from events, a sorriness of spirit. But he watches and muses. When the Old God leaves the world, what happens to all the unexpended faith? He looks at each sweet face, round face, long, wrong, darkish, plain. They are a nation, he supposes, founded on the principle of easy belief. A unit fuelled by credulousness. They speak a half-language, a set of ready-made terms and empty repetitions. All things, the sum of the knowable, everything true, it all comes down to a few simple formulas copied and memorized and passed on. And here is the drama of mechanical routine played out with living figures. It knocks him back in awe, the loss of scale and intimacy, the way love and sex are multiplied out, the numbers and shaped crowd. This really scares him, a mass of people turned into a sculptured object. It is like a toy with 13,000 parts, just tootling along, an innocent and menacing thing. He keeps the glasses trained, feeling a slight desperation now, a need to find her and remind himself who she is. Healthy, intelligent, twenty-one, serious-sided, possessed of a selfness, a teeming soul, nuance and shadow, grids of pinpoint singularities they will never drill out of her. Or so he hopes and prays, wondering about the power of their own massed prayer. When the Old God goes, they pray to flies and bottle tops. The terrible thing is they follow the man because he gives them what they need. He answers their yearning, unburdens them of free will and independent thought. See how happy they look.

Around the great stadium the tenement barrens stretch, miles of delirium, men sitting in tipped-back chairs against the walls of hollow buildings, sofas burning in the lots, and there is a sense these chanting thousands have, wincing in the sun, that the future is pressing in, collapsing toward them, that they are everywhere surrounded by signs of the fated landscape and human struggle of the Last Days, and here in the middle of their columned body, lank-haired and up close, stands Karen Janney, holding a cluster of starry jasmine and thinking of the blood-storm to come. She is waiting to file past Master and sees him with the single floating eye of the crowd, inseparable from her own apparatus of vision but sharper-sighted, able to perceive more deeply. She feels intact, rayed with well-being. They all feel the same, young people from fifty countries, immunized against the language of self. They're forgetting who they are under their clothes, leaving behind all the small banes and body woes, the day-long list of sore gums and sweaty nape and need to pee, ancient rumbles in the gut, momentary chills and tics, the fungoid dampness between the toes, the deep spasm near the shoulder blade that's charged with mortal reckoning. All gone now. They stand and chant, fortified by the blood of numbers.

Karen glances over at Kim Jo Pak, soft-eyed and plump in his nice new suit and boxy shoes, husband-for-eternity.

She knows her flesh parents are in the stands somewhere. Knows what they're saying, sees the gestures and expressions. Dad trying to use old college logic to make sense of it all. Mom wearing the haunted stare that means she was put on earth strictly to suffer. They're all around us, parents in the thousands, afraid of our intensity. This is what frightens them. We really believe. They bring us up to believe but when we show them true belief they call out psychiatrists and police. We know who God is. This makes us crazy in the world.

Karen's mind-stream sometimes slows down, veering into sets of whole words. They take a funny snub-nosed form, the rudimentary English spoken by some of the Master's chief assistants.

They have God once-week. Do not understand. Must sacrifice together. Build with hands God's home on earth.

Karen says to Kim, 'This is where the Yankees play.'

He nods and smiles, blankly. Nothing about him strikes her so forcefully as his hair, which is shiny and fine and ink-black, with a Sunday comics look. It is the thing that makes him real to her.

'Baseball,' she says, using the word to sum up a hundred happy abstractions, themes that flare to life in the crowd shout and diamond symmetry, in the details of a dusty slide. The word has resonance if you're American, a sense of shared heart and untranslatable lore. But she only means to suggest the democratic clamor, a history of sweat and play on sun-dazed afternoons, an openness of form that makes the game a kind of welcome-to-my-country.

The other word is cult. How they love to use it against us. Gives them the false term they need to define us as eerie-eyed children. And how they hate our willingness to work and struggle. They want to snatch us back to the land of lawns. That we are willing to live on the road, sleep on the floor, crowd into vans and drive all night, fundraising, serving Master. That our true father is a foreigner and non-white. How they silently despise. They keep our rooms ready. They have our names on their lips. But we're a lifetime away, weeping through hours of fist-pounding prayer.

World in pieces. It is shock of shocks. But there is plan. Pali-pali. Bring hurry-up time to all man.

She does not dream anymore except about Master. They all dream about him. They see him in visions. He stands in the room with them when his three-dimensional body is thousands of miles away. They talk about him and weep. The tears roll down their faces and form puddles on the floor and drip into the room below. He is part of the structure of their protein. He lifts them out of ordinary strips of space and time and then shows them the blessedness of lives devoted to the ordinary, to work, prayer and obedience.

Rodge offers the binoculars to Maureen. She shakes her head firmly. It is like looking for the body of a loved one after a typhoon.

Balloons in clusters rise by the thousands, sailing past the rim of the upper deck. Karen lifts her veil and passes below the pulpit, which is rimmed on three sides by bullet-proof panels. She feels the blast of Master's being, the solar force of a charismatic soul. Never so close before. He sprinkles mist from a holy bottle in her face. She sees Kim move his lips, following Master's chant word for word. She's close enough to the grandstand to see people crowding the rails, standing everywhere to take pictures. Did she ever think she'd find herself in a stadium in New York, photographed by thousands of people? There may be as many people taking pictures as there are brides and grooms. One of them for every one of us. Clickety-click. The thought makes the couples a little giddy. They feel that space is contagious. They're here but also there, already in the albums and slide projectors, filling picture frames with their microcosmic bodies, the minikin selves they are trying to become.

They veer back to the outfield grass to resume formation. There are folk troupes near both dugouts dancing to gongs and drums. Karen fades into the thousands, the columned mass. She feels the metre of their breathing. They're a world family now, each marriage a channel to salvation. Master chooses every mate, seeing in a vision how backgrounds and characters match. It is a mandate from heaven, preordained, each person put here to meet the perfect other. Forty days of separation before they're alone in a room, allowed to touch and love. Or longer. Or years if Master sees the need. Take cold showers. It is this rigor that draws the strong. Their self-control cuts deep against the age, against the private ciphers, the systems of isolated craving. Husband and wife agree to live in different countries, doing missionary work, extending the breadth of the body common. Satan hates cold showers.

The crowd-eye hangs brightly above them like the triangle eye on a dollar bill.

A firecracker goes off, another M-80 banging out of an exit ramp with a hard flat impact that drives people's heads into their torsos. Maureen looks battle-stunned. There are lines of boys wending through empty rows high in the upper deck, some of them only ten or twelve years old, moving with the princely swagger of famous street felons. She decides she doesn't see them.

'I'll tell you this,' Rodge says. 'I fully intend to examine this organization. Hit the libraries, get on the phone, contact parents, truly delve. You hear about support groups that people call for all kinds of things.'

'We need support. I grant you that. But you're light years too late.'

'I think we ought to change our flight as soon as we get back to the hotel and then check out and get going.'

'They'll charge us for the room for tonight anyway. We may as well get tickets to something.'

'The sooner we get started on this.'

'Raring to go. Oh boy. What fun.'

'I want to read everything I can get my hands on. Only did some skimming but that's because I didn't know she was involved in something so grandiose. We ought to get some hotline numbers and see who's out there that we can talk to.'

'You sound like one of those people, you know, when they get struck down by some rare disease they learn every inch of material they can find in the medical books and phone up doctors on three continents and hunt day and night for people with the same awful thing.'

'Makes good sense, Maureen.'

'They fly to Houston to see the top man. The top man is always in Houston.'

'What's wrong with learning everything you can?'

'You don't have to *enjoy* it.'

'It's not a question of enjoy it. It's our responsibility to Karen.'

'Where is she by the way?'

'I fully intend.'

'You were scanning so duteously. What, bored already?'

A wind springs up, causing veils to rustle and lift. Couples cry out, surprised, caught in a sudden lightsome glide, a buoyancy. They remember they are kids, mostly, and not altogether done with infections of glee. They have a shared past after all. Karen thinks of all those nights she slept in a van or crowded room, rising at five for prayer condition, then into the streets with her flower team. There was a girl named June who felt she was shrinking, falling back to child size. They called her Junette. Her hands could not grip the midget bars of soap in the motel toilets of America. This did not seem unreasonable to the rest of the team. She was only seeing what was really there, the slinking shape of eternity beneath the paint layers and glutamates of physical earth.

All those lost landscapes. Nights downtown, live nude shows in cinder-block bunkers, slums with their dumpster garbage. All those depopulated streets in subdivisions at the edge of Metroplex, waist-high trees and fresh tar smoking in the driveways and nice-size rattlers that cozy out of the rocks behind the last split-level. Karen worked to make the $400-a-day standard, peddling mainly bud roses and sweet williams. Just dream-walking into places and dashing out. Rows of neat homes in crashing rain. People drooped over tables at 5 a.m. at casinos in the desert. PROGRESSIVE SLOT JACKPOTS. WELCOME TEAMSTERS. She fasted on liquids for a week, then fell upon a stack of Big Macs. Through revolving doors into hotel lobbies and department stores until security came scurrying with their walkie-talkies and beepers and combat magnums.

They prayed kneeling with hands crossed at forehead, bowed deep, folded like unborn young.

In the van everything mattered, every word counted, sometimes fifteen, sixteen sisters packed in tight, singing you are my sunshine, row row row, chanting their monetary goal. Satan owns the fallen world.

She stacked bundles of baby yellows in groups of seven, the number-symbol of perfection. There were times when she not only thought in broken English but spoke aloud in the voices of the workshops and training sessions, lecturing the sisters in the van, pressing them to sell, make the goal, grab the cash, and they didn't know whether to be inspired by the uncanny mimicry or report her for disrespect.

Junette was a whirlwind of awe. Everything was too much for her, too large and living. The sisters prayed with her and wept. Water rocked in the flower buckets. They had twenty-one-day selling contests, three hours' sleep. When a sister ran off, they holy-salted the clothes she'd left behind. They chanted: We're the greatest, there's no doubt; heavenly father, we'll sell out.

After midnight in some bar in that winter stillness called the inner city. God's own lonely call. Buy a carnation, sir. Karen welcomed the chance to walk among the lower-downs, the sort of legions of the night. She slipped into semi-trance, detached and martyrish, passing through those bare-looking storefronts, the air jangly with other-mindedness. A number of dug-in drinkers bought a flower or two, men with long flat fingers and pearly nails, awake to the novelty, or hat-wearing men with looks of high scruple, staring hard at the rainslickered girl. What new harassment they pushing in off the street? An old hoocher told her funny things, a line of sweat sitting on his upper lip. She got the bum's rush fairly often. Don't be so subjective, sir. Then scanned the street for another weary saloon.

Team leader said: Gotta get goin', kids. Pali-pali.

In the van every truth was magnified, everything they said and did separated them from the misery jig going on out there. They looked through the windows and saw the faces of fallen-world people. It totalized their attachment to true father. Pray all night at times, all of them, chanting, shouting out, leaping up from prayer stance, lovely moaning prayers to Master, oh *please*, oh *yes*, huddled in motel room in nowhere part of Denver.

Karen said to them, Which you like to sleep, five hour or four?

FOUR.

She said, Which you like to sleep, four hour or three?

THREE.

She said, Which you like to sleep, three hour or none?

NONE.

In the van every rule counted double, every sister was subject to routine scrutiny in the way she dressed, prayed, brushed her hair, brushed her teeth. They knew there was only one way to leave the van without risking the horror of lifetime drift and guilt. Follow the wrist-slashing fad. Or walk out a high-rise window. It's better to enter gray space than disappoint Master.

Team leader said: Pre-think your total day. Then jump it, jump it, jump it.

Oatmeal and water. Bread and jelly. Row row row your boat. Karen said to them: Lose sleep, it is for sins. Lose weight, it is for sins. Lose hair, lose nail off finger, lose whole hand, whole arm, it go on scale to stand against sins.

The man in Indiana who ate the rose she sold him.

Racing through malls at sundown to reach the daily goal. Blitzing the coin laundries and bus terminals. Door-to-door in police-dog projects, saying the money's for drug centers ma'am. Junette kidnapped by her parents in Skokie, Illinois. Scotch-taping limp flowers to make them half-way saleable. Crazy weather on the plains. Falling asleep at meals, heavy-eyed, dozing on the toilet, sneaking some Zs, catching forty winks, nodding off, hitting the hay, crashing where you can, flaked-out, dead to the world, sleep like a top, like a log, desperate for some shut-eye, some sack time, anything for beddy-bye, a cat nap, a snooze, a minute with the sandman. Prayer condition helped them jump it to the limit, got the sorry blood pounding. Aware of all the nego media, which multiplied a ton of doubt for less-committed sisters. Doing the hokey-pokey. Coldest winter in these parts since they started keeping records. Chanting the monetary goal.

Team leader said: Gotta hurry hurry hurry. Pali-pali, kids.

R odge sits there in his rumpled sport coat, pockets crammed with traveler's cheques, credit cards and subway maps, and he looks through the precision glasses, and looks and looks, and all he sees is repetition and despair. They are chanting again, one word this time, over and over, and he can't tell if it is English or some other known language or some football holler from heaven. No sign of Karen. He puts down the binoculars. People are still taking pictures. He half expects the chanting mass of bodies to rise in the air, all 13,000 ascending slowly to the height of the stadium roof, lifted by the picture-taking, the forming of aura, radiant brides clutching their bouquets, grooms showing sunny teeth. A smoke bomb sails out of the bleachers, releasing a trail of Day-Glo fog.

Master leads the chant, *Mansei*, ten thousand years of victory. The blessed couples move their lips in unison, matching the echo of his amplified voice. There is stark awareness in their faces, a near pain of rapt adoration. He is Lord of the Second Advent, the unriddling of many ills. His voice leads them out past love and joy, past the beauty of their mission, out past miracles and surrendered self. There is something in the chant, the fact of chanting, the being-one, that transports them with its power. Their voices grow in intensity. They are carried on the sound, the soar and fall. The chant becomes the boundaries of the world. They see their Master frozen in his whiteness against the patches and shadows, the towering sweep of the stadium. He raises his arms and the chant grows louder and the young arms rise. He leads them out past religion and history, thousands weeping now, all arms high. They are gripped by the force of a longing. They know at once, they feel it, all of them together, a longing deep in time, running in the earthly blood. This is what people have wanted since consciousness became corrupt. The chant brings the End Time closer. The chant is the End Time. They feel the power of the human voice, the power of a single word repeated as it moves them deeper into oneness. They chant for world-shattering rapture, for the truth of prophecies and astonishments. They chant for new life, peace eternal, the end of soul-lonely pain. Someone on the bandstand beats a massive drum. They chant for one language, one word, for the time when names are lost.

Karen, strangely, is daydreaming. It will take some getting used to, a husband named Kim. She has known girls named Kim since she was a squirt in a sunsuit. Quite a few really. Kimberleys and plain Kims. Look at his hair gleaming in the sun. My husband, weird as it sounds. They will pray together, whole-skinned, and memorize every word of Master's teaching.

The thousands stand and chant. Around them in the world, people ride escalators going up and sneak secret glances at the faces coming down. People dangle tea bags over hot water in white cups. Cars run silently on the autobahns, streaks of painted light. People sit at desks and stare at office walls. They smell their shirts and drop them in the hamper. People bind themselves into numbered seats and fly across time zones and high cirrus and deep night, knowing there is something they've forgotten to do.

The future belongs to crowds. ■

Congo the chimpanzee painting a picture, London Zoo, 1958

Painting by Còngo, late 1950s

THE ZOO IN BASEL

John Berger

GRANTA 35: SPRING 1991

In memory of Peter Fuller and our many conversations about the chain of being and neo-Darwinism.

In Basel the zoo is almost next to the railway station. Most of the larger birds in the zoo are free-flying, and so it can happen that you see a stork or a cormorant flying home over the marshalling yards. Equally unexpected is the ape house. It is constructed like a circular theatre with three stages: one for the gorillas, another for the orang-utans and a third for the chimpanzees.

You take your place on one of the tiers – as in a Greek theatre – or you can go to the very front of the pit and press your forehead against the soundproof plate glass. The lack of sound makes the spectacle on the other side, in a certain way, sharper, like mime. It also allows the apes to be less bothered by the public. We are mute to them too.

All my life I have visited zoos, perhaps because going to the zoo is one of my few happy childhood memories. My father used to take me. We didn't talk much, but we shared each other's pleasure and I was aware that his was largely based on mine. Together we used to watch the apes, losing all sense of time, each of us, in his fashion, pondering the mystery of progeniture. My mother, on the rare occasions she came with us, refused the higher primates. She preferred the newly discovered pandas.

I tried to pull her towards the chimpanzees, but she would reply – following her own logic: 'I'm a vegetarian and I only gave it up, the practice not the principle, for the sake of you boys and for Daddy.' Bears were another animal she liked. Apes, I can see now, reminded her of the passions which lead to the spilling of blood.

The audience in Basel is of all ages. From toddlers to pensioners. No other spectacle in the world can attract such a spectrum of the public. Some sit, like my father and I once did, lost to the passing of time. Others drop in for a few moments. There are habitués who come every day and whom the actors recognise. But on nobody – not even the youngest toddler – is the dramatic evolutionary riddle lost: how is it that they are so like us and yet not us?

This is the question which dominates the dramas on each of the three stages. Today the gorillas' play is a social one about coming to terms with imprisonment: life sentences. On the second stage, the chimpanzees' show is cabaret: each performer has her or his own number. The orang-utans are performing *Werther* without words – soulful and dreamy. I am exaggerating? Of course, because I do not yet know how to define the real drama of the theatre in Basel.

Is any theatre possible without a conscious ritual of re-enactment? All theatre repeats, again and again, what once happened. Often those who are dead are brought back to life on the stage. Mere reflex actions do not make theatre; but wait –

Each stage has at least one private recess where an animal can go, if she or he wishes to leave the public, and from time to time they do so. Sometimes for quite long periods. When they come out to face the audience again, they are perhaps not so far from a practice of re-enactment. In the London zoo chimps pretend to eat and drink off invisible plates with non-existent glasses. A pantomime.

We can see that chimpanzees are as familiar as we are with fear. The Dutch zoologist Dr Kortlandt believes that in fact they have intimations of mortality. We are at least on the threshold of theatre.

In the first half of the century there were attempts to teach chimpanzees to talk – until it was discovered that the form of their vocal tract was unsuitable for the production of the necessary range of sounds. Later they were taught a deaf and dumb language, and a chimp called Washoe in Ellensburg near Seattle called a duck a water bird. Did this mean that Washoe had broken through a language barrier or had she just learned by rote? A heated debate followed (the distinction of man was at stake!) about what constitutes or doesn't a language for animals.

It was already known – thanks to the extraordinary work of Jane Goodall with her chimpanzees in Tanzania – that these animals used tools, and that, language or no language, their ability to communicate with one another was both wide-ranging and subtle.

Another chimpanzee in the United States, named Sarah, underwent a series of tests conducted by Douglas Gillan, which were designed to show whether or not she could reason. Contrary to what Descartes believed, a verbal language may not be indispensable for the process of reasoning. Sarah was shown a video of her trainer playing the part of being locked in a cage and desperately trying to get out! After the film she was offered a series of pictures of varying objects to choose from. One, for instance, showed a lighted match. The picture she chose was of a key – the only object which would have been useful for the situation she had seen enacted on the video screen.

In Basel we are watching a strange theatre in which, on both sides of the glass, the performers may believe they are an audience. On both sides the drama begins with resemblance and the uneasy relationship that exists between resemblance and closeness.

The idea of evolution is very old. Hunters believed that animals – and especially the ones they hunted – were, in some mysterious way, their brothers. Aristotle argued that all the forms of nature constituted a series, a chain of being, which began with the simple and became more and more complex, striving towards the perfect. In the Latin *evolution* means unfolding.

A group of handicapped patients from a local institution come into the theatre. Some have to be helped up the tiers; others manage by themselves; one or two are in wheelchairs. They form a different kind of audience – or rather, an audience with different reactions. They are less puzzled, less astounded but more amused. Like children? Not at all. They are less puzzled, because they are more familiar with what is out of the ordinary. Or, to put it another way, their sense of the normal is far wider.

What was new and outrageous in *The Origin of Species*, when it was first published in 1859, was Darwin's argument that all animal species had evolved from the same prototype and that this immensely slow evolution had taken place through certain accidental mutations being favoured by natural selection, which had worked according to the principle of the survival of the fittest. A series of accidents. Without design or purpose and without experience counting. (Darwin rejected Jean Baptiste Lamarck's thesis that acquired characteristics could be inherited.) The precondition for Darwin's theory being plausible was something even more shocking: the wastes of empty time required – about 500 million years!

Until the nineteenth century it was generally, if not universally, believed that the world was a few thousand years old – something that could be measured by the timescale of human generations – as in the fifth chapter of Genesis. But in 1830 Charles Lyell published *Principles of Geology* and proposed that the earth, with 'no vestige of a beginning – no prospect of an end', was millions, perhaps hundreds of millions of years old.

Darwin's thinking was a creative response to the terrifying immensity of what had just been revealed. And the sadness of Darwinism – for no other scientific revolution when it was made, broadcast so little hope – derived, I think, from the desolation of the distances involved. The sadness, the desolation, is there in the last sentence of *The Descent of Man*, published in 1871: 'We must, however, acknowledge, as it seems to me, that man with all his noble qualities, still bears in his bodily frame the indelible stamp of his lowly origin.' 'The indelible stamp' speaks volumes. *Indelible* in the sense that (unfortunately) it cannot be washed out. *Stamp* meaning brand, mark, stain. And in the word *lowly* during the nineteenth century, as in Britain today, there is shame.

The liberty of the newly revealed universe with its expanses of space and time brought with it a feeling of insignificance and *pudeur*, from which the best that could be redeemed was the virtue of intellectual courage, the virtue of being unflinching. And courageous the thinkers of that time were!

Whenever an actor, who is not a baby, wants to piss or shit, he or she gets up and goes to the edge of a balcony or deck and there defecates or urinates below, so as to remain clean. An habitual act which we seldom see enacted on the stage. And the effect is surprising. The public watch with a kind of pride. An altogether legitimate one.

Mostly the thinkers of the nineteenth century thought mechanically, for theirs was the century of machines. They thought in terms of chains, branches, lines, comparative anatomies, clockworks, grids. They knew about power, resistance, speed, competition. Consequently they discovered a great deal about the material world, about tools and production. What they knew less about is what we still don't know much about: the way brains work. I can't get this out of my mind: it's somewhere at the centre of the theatre we're watching.

Apes don't live entirely within the needs and impulses of their own bodies – like the cats do. (It may be different in the wild, but this is true on the stage.) They have a gratuitous curiosity. All animals play, but the others play at being themselves, whereas the apes experiment. They suffer from a surplus of curiosity. They can momentarily forget their needs and are not restricted to a single, unchanging role. A young female will pretend to be a mother cuddling a baby lent by its real mother. 'Babysitting' the zoologists call it.

Their surplus of curiosity, their research (every animal searches, only apes research), make them suffer in two evident ways – and probably also in others, invisibly. Their bodies, forgotten, suddenly nag, twinge and irritate. They become impatient with their own skin – like Marat suffering from eczema.

And then, too, starved of events, they suffer boredom. Baudelaire's *l'ennui*. Not at the same level of self-doubt, but nevertheless with pain, apathy. The signs of boredom may resemble those of simple drowsiness. But *l'ennui* has its unmistakable lassitude. The body, instead of relaxing, huddles; the eyes stare painfully without focus; the hands, finding nothing new to touch or do, become like gloves worn by a creature drowning.

'If it could be demonstrated,' Darwin wrote, 'that any complex organ existed which could not possibly have been formed by numerous, successive slight modifications, my theory would absolutely break down.'

If the apes are partly victims of their own bodies – the price they pay, like man, for not being confined to their immediate needs – they have found a consolation, which Europe has forgotten. My mother used to say the chimps were looking for fleas and that, when they found one, they put it between their teeth and bit it. But it goes further than Mother thought – as I guessed even then. The chimpanzees touch and caress and scratch each other for hours on end (and according to the etiquette rules of a strict group hierarchy) not only for purposes of hygiene, but to give pleasure. 'Grooming', as it is called, is one of their principal ways of appeasing the troublesome body.

This one is scratching inside her own ear with her little finger. Now she has stopped scratching to examine minutely her small nail. Her gestures are intimately familiar and strikingly remote. (The same is true for most actions on any theatre stage.) An orang-utan is preparing a bed for herself. Suddenly she hesitates before placing her armful of straw on the floor, as if she has heard a siren. Not only are the apes' functional gestures familiar, but also their expressive ones.

Gestures which denote surprise, amusement, tenderness, irritation, pleasure, indifference, desire, fear.

Their movements are different from ours. Everything which derives from the apes' skill in swinging from branches – *brachiation* as the zoologists call it – sets them apart. In evolutionary history, however, this difference is in fact a link. Monkeys walk on all fours along the tops of branches and use their tails for hanging. The common ancestors of man and apes began, instead, to use their arms – began to become *brachiators*. This gave them the advantage of being able to reach the fruit at the ends of the branches!

I must have been two years old when I had my first cuddly toy. It was a monkey. A chimpanzee, in fact. I think I called him Jackie. To be certain, I'd have to ask my mother. She would remember. But my mother is dead. There is just a chance – one in a hundred million (about the same as a chance mutation being favoured by natural selection) – that a reader may be able to tell me, for we had visitors to our home in Highams Park, in east London, sixty years ago, and I presented my chimp to everyone who came through the front door. I think his name was Jackie.

Slowly, the hanging position, favoured by natural selection, changed the anatomy of the *brachiators'* torsos so that finally they became half-upright animals – although not yet as upright as us. It is thanks to hanging from trees that we have long collarbones which keep our arms away from our chests, wrists which allow our hands to bend backwards and sideways and shoulder sockets that let our arms rotate. It is thanks to hanging from trees that one of the actors can throw himself into the arms of a mother and now cry. *Brachiation* gave us breasts to beat and to be held against. No other animal can do these things.

When Darwin thought about the eyes of mammals, he admitted that he broke out in a cold sweat. The complexity of the eye was hard to explain within the logic of his theory, for it implied the coordination of so many evolutionary 'accidents'. If the eye is to work at all, all the elements have to be there, tear glands, eyelid, cornea, pupil, retina, millions of light-sensitive rods and cones which transmit to the brain millions of electrical impulses per second. Before they constituted an eye, these intricate parts would have been useless, so why should they have been favoured by natural selection? The existence of the eye perfidiously suggests an evolutionary aim, an intention.

Darwin finally got over the problem by going back to the existence of light-sensitive spots on one-celled organisms. These, he claimed, could have been 'the first eye' from which the evolution of our complex eyes began.

I have the impression that the oldest gorilla may be blind. Like Beckett's Pozzo. I ask his keeper, a young woman with fair hair.

Yes, she says, he's almost blind.

How old is he? I ask.

She looks at me hard. About your age, she replies, in his early sixties.

Recently, molecular biologists have shown that we share with apes 99 per cent of their DNA. Only 1 per cent of his genetic code separates man from the chimpanzee or the gorilla. The orang-utan, which means in the language of the people of Borneo 'man of the forest', is fractionally further removed. If we take another animal family, in order to emphasise how small the 1 per cent is, a dog differs from a raccoon by 12 per cent. The genetic closeness between man and ape – apart from making our theatre possible – strongly suggests that their common ancestor existed, not 20 million years ago as the neo-Darwinist palaeontologists believed, but maybe only 4 million years ago. This molecular evidence has been contested because there are no fossil proofs to support it. But in evolutionary theory, fossils, it seems to me, have usually been notable by their absence!

In the Anglo-Saxon world today, the creationists, who take the Genesis story of the Creation as the literal truth, are increasingly vocal and insist that their version be taught in schools alongside the neo-Darwinist one. The orang-utan is like he is, say the creationists, because that's the way God made him, once and for all, 5,000 years ago! He is like he is, reply the neo-Darwinists, because he has been efficient in the ceaseless struggle for survival!

Her orang-utan eyes operate exactly like mine – each retina with its 130 million rods and cones. But her expression is the oldest I've ever seen. Approach it at your peril, for you can fall into a kind of maelstrom of ageing.

Not far up the Rhine from Basel, Angelus Silesius, the seventeenth-century German doctor of medicine, studied in Strasbourg, and he once wrote:

> *Anybody who passes more than a day in eternity is as old as*
> *God could ever be.*

I look at her with her eyelids which are so pale that when she closes them they're like eye cups, and I wonder.

The conceptual framework in which the neo-Darwinists and the creationists debate is of such limited imagination that the contrast with the immensity of the process whose origin they are searching is flagrant. They are like two bands of seven-year-olds who, having discovered a packet of love letters in an attic, try to piece together the story behind the correspondence. Both bands are ingenious and argue ferociously with one another, but the passion of the letters is beyond their competence.

Perhaps it is objectively true that only poetry can talk of birth and origin. Because true poetry invokes the whole of language (it breathes with everything it has not said), just as the origin invokes the whole of life, the whole of Being.

The mother orang-utan has come back, this time with her baby. She is sitting right up against the glass. The children in the audience have come close to watch her. Suddenly I think of a Madonna and Child by Cosimo Tura. I'm not indulging in a sentimental confusion. I haven't forgotten I'm talking about apes, any more than I've forgotten I'm watching a theatre. The more one emphasises the millions of years, the more extraordinary the expressive gestures become. Arms, fingers, eyes, always eyes . . . A certain way of being protective, a certain gentleness – if one could feel the fingers on one's neck, one would say a certain *tenderness* – which has endured for 5 million years.

A species that did not protect its young would not survive comes the answer. Indisputably. But the answer does not explain the theatre.

I ask myself about the theatre – about its mystery and its essence. It's to do with time. The theatre, more tangibly than any other art, presents us with the past. Paintings may show what the past looked like, but they are like traces or footprints; they no longer move. With each theatre performance, what once happened is re-enacted. Each time we keep the same rendezvous: with Macbeth who can't wake up from his downfall; with Antigone who must do her duty. And each night in the theatre, Antigone, who died three millennia ago, says: 'We have only a short time to please the living, all eternity to please the dead.'

Theatre depends upon two times physically coexisting. The hour of the performance and the moment of the drama. If you read a novel, you leave the present; in the theatre you never leave the present. The past becomes the present in the only way that it is possible for this to happen. And this unique possibility is theatre.

The creationists, like all bigots, derive their fervour from rejection – the more they can reject, the more righteous they themselves feel. The neo-Darwinists are trapped within the machine of their theory, in which there can be no place for creation as an act of love. (Their theory was born of the nineteenth century, the most orphaned of centuries.)

The ape theatre in Basel, with its two times, suggests an alternative view. The evolutionary process unfolded, more or less as the evolutionists suppose, within time. The fabric of its duration has been stretched to breaking point by billions of years. Outside time, God is still (present tense) creating the universe.

Silesius, after he left Strasbourg, to return to Cracow, wrote: 'God is still creating the world. Does that seem strange to you? You must suppose that in him there is no before nor after, as there is here.'

How can the timeless enter the temporal? the gorilla now asks me.

Can we think of time as a field magnetised by eternity? I'm no scientist. (As I say that, I can see the real ones smiling!)

Which are they?

The ones up there on a ladder, looking for something. Now they're coming down to take a bow . . .

As I say, I'm no scientist, but I have the impression that scientists today, when dealing with phenomena whose time or spatial scale is either immense or very small (a full set of human genes contains about 6 billion bases: bases being the units – the signs – of the genetic language), are on the point of breaking through space and time to discover another axis on which events may be strung, and that, in face of the hidden scales of nature, they resort increasingly to the model of a brain or mind to explain the universe.

'Can't God find what he is looking for?' To this question, Silesius replied: 'From eternity he is searching for what is lost, far from him, in time.'

The orang-utan mother presses the baby's head against her chest.

Birth begins the process of learning to be separate. The separation is hard to believe or accept. Yet, as we accept it, our imagination grows – imagination which is the capacity to reconnect, to bring together, that which is separate. Metaphor finds the traces which indicate that all is one. Acts of solidarity, compassion, self-sacrifice, generosity are attempts to re-establish – or at least a refusal to forget – a once-known unity. Death is the hardest test of accepting the separation which life has incurred.

You're playing with words!

Who said that?

Jackie!

The act of creation implies a separation. Something that remains attached to the creator is only half created. To create is to let take over something which did not exist before and is therefore new. And the new is inseparable from pain, for it is alone.

One of the male chimps is suddenly angry. Histrionically. Everything he can pick up, he throws. He tries to pull down the stage trees. He is like Samson at the temple. But unlike Samson, he is not high up in the group hierarchy of the cage. The other actors are nonetheless impressed by his fury.

Alone, we are forced to recognise that we have been created, like everything else. Only our souls, when encouraged, remember the origin, wordlessly.

Silesius's master was Johannes Eckhart, who, further down the Rhine beyond Strasbourg, in Cologne, wrote during the thirteenth century: 'God becomes God when the animals say: God.'

Are these the words which the play, behind the soundproof plate glass, is about?

In any case, I can't find better. ∎

Havana, Cuba

DREAMS FOR HIRE

Gabriel García Márquez

TRANSLATED FROM THE SPANISH BY NICK CAISTOR

GRANTA 41: AUTUMN 1992

At nine o'clock in the morning, while we were having breakfast on the terrace of the Hotel Riviera in Havana, a terrifying wave appeared out of nowhere – the day was sunny and calm – and came crashing upon us. It lifted the cars that had been passing along the seafront, as well as several others that had been parked nearby, and tossed them into the air, smashing one into the side of our hotel. It was like an explosion of dynamite, spreading panic up and down the twenty floors of our building and transforming the lobby into a pile of broken glass, where many of the hotel guests were hurled through the air like the furniture. Several were wounded in the hail of glass shards. It must have been a tidal wave of monumental size: the hotel is protected from the sea by a wall and the wide two-way avenue that passes before it, but the wave had erupted with such force that it obliterated the glass lobby.

Cuban volunteers, with the help of the local fire brigade, set to sweeping up the damage, and in less than six hours, after closing off the hotel's seafront entrance and opening up an alternative, everything was back to normal. Throughout the morning no one paid any attention to the car that had been smashed against the wall of the hotel, believing it had been among the vehicles parked along the avenue. But by the time it was eventually removed by a crane, the body of a woman was discovered inside, moored to the driving seat by her seat belt. The blow had been so great that there wasn't a bone in her body which was left unbroken. Her face was messy and unrecognisable, her ankle boots had burst at the seams, her clothes were in tatters. But there was a ring, still worn on her finger, which remained intact: it was made in the shape of a serpent and had emeralds for eyes. The police established that she was the housekeeper for the new Portuguese ambassador and his wife. In fact she had arrived with them only fifteen days before and had that morning left for the market in their new car. Her name meant nothing to me when I read about the incident in the papers, but I was intrigued by that ring, made in the shape of a serpent with emeralds for its eyes. I was, unfortunately, unable to find out on which finger the ring had been worn.

It was an essential detail: I feared that this woman might be someone I knew and whom I would never forget, even though I never learned her real name. She, too, had a ring made in the shape of a serpent, with emeralds for its eyes, but she always wore it on the first finger of her right hand, which was unusual, especially then. I had met her forty-six years ago in Vienna, eating sausages and boiled potatoes and drinking beer straight from the barrel, in a tavern frequented by Latin American students. I had arrived from Rome that morning, and I still recall that first impression made by her ample opera-singer's bosom, the drooping fox tails gathered round the collar of her coat and that Egyptian ring made in the shape of a serpent. She spoke a rudimentary Spanish, in a breathless shopkeeper's accent, and I assumed that she must be Austrian, the only one at that long wooden table. I was wrong: she had been born in Colombia and between the wars had travelled to Austria to study music and singing. When I met her she must have been around thirty, and she had begun ageing before her time. Even so, she was magical: and, also, among the most fearsome people I've ever met.

At that time – the late forties – Vienna was nothing more than an ancient imperial city that history had reduced to a remote provincial capital, located between the two irreconcilable worlds left by the Second World War, a paradise for the black market and international espionage. I couldn't imagine surroundings better suited to my fugitive compatriot, who went on eating in the students' tavern on the corner only out of nostalgia for her roots, because she had more than enough money to buy the whole place, its diners included. She never told us her real name; we always referred to her by the German tongue-twister that the Latin American students in Vienna had invented for her: Frau Frida. No sooner had we been introduced than I committed the fortuitous imprudence of asking her how she came to find herself in a part of the world so distant and different from the windy heights of the Quindío region in Colombia. She replied matter-of-factly: 'I hire myself out to dream.'

That was her profession. She was the third of eleven children of a prosperous shopkeeper from the old region of Caldas, and by the time she learned to speak, she had established the habit of telling all her dreams before breakfast, when, she said, her powers of premonition were at their most pure. At the age of seven, she dreamt that one of her brothers had been swept away by a raging torrent. The mother, simply out of a nervous superstitiousness, refused to allow her son to do what he most enjoyed, swimming in the local gorge. But Frau Frida had already developed her own system of interpreting her prophecies.

'What the dream means,' she explained, 'is not that he is going to drown, but that he mustn't eat sweets.'

The interpretation amounted to a terrible punishment, especially for a five-year-old boy who could not imagine life without his Sunday treats. But the mother, convinced of her daughter's divinatory powers, ensured that her injunction was adhered to. Unfortunately, following a moment's inattention, the son choked on a gobstopper that he had been eating in secret, and it proved impossible to save him.

Frau Frida had never thought that it would be possible to earn a living from her talent until life took her by the scruff of the neck and, during a harsh Viennese winter, she rang the bell of the first house where she wanted to live, and, when asked what she could do, offered the simple reply: 'I dream.' After only a brief explanation, the lady of the house took her on, at a wage that was little more than pocket money, but with a decent room and three meals a day. Above all, there was a breakfast, the time when the members of the family sat down to learn their immediate destinies: the father, a sophisticated *rentier*; the mother, a jolly woman with a passion for Romantic chamber music; and the two children, aged eleven and nine. All of them were religious and therefore susceptible to archaic superstitions, and they were delighted to welcome Frau Frida into their home, on the sole condition that every day she revealed the family's destiny through her dreams.

She did well, especially during the war years that followed, when reality was more sinister than any nightmare. At the breakfast table every morning, she alone decided what each member of the family was to do that day, and how it was to be done, until eventually her prognostications became the house's sole voice of authority. Her domination of the family was absolute: even the slightest sigh was made on her orders. The father had died just prior to my stay in Vienna, and he had had the good grace to leave Frau Frida a part of his fortune, again on the condition that she continued dreaming for the family until she was unable to dream any more.

I spent a month in Vienna, living the frugal life of a student while waiting for money which never arrived. The unexpected and generous visits that Frau Frida paid to our tavern were like fiestas in our otherwise penurious regime. One night, the powerful smell of beer about us, she whispered something in my ear with such conviction that I found it impossible to ignore.

'I came here specially to tell you that last night I saw you in my dreams,' she said. 'You must leave Vienna at once and not come back here for at least five years.'

Such was her conviction that I was put, that same night, on the last train for Rome. I was so shaken that I have since come to believe that I survived a disaster I never encountered. To this day I have not set foot in Vienna again.

B efore the incident in Havana I met up with Frau Frida once more, in Barcelona, in an encounter so unexpected that it seemed to me especially mysterious. It was the day that Pablo Neruda set foot on Spanish soil for the first time since the Civil War, during a stopover on a long sea journey to Valparaíso in Chile. He spent the morning with us, big-game hunting in the antiquarian bookshops, buying eventually a faded book with torn covers for which he paid what must have been the equivalent of two months' salary for the Chilean consulate in Rangoon. He lumbered along like a rheumatic elephant, showing a childlike interest in the internal workings of every object he came across. The world always appeared to him as a giant clockwork toy.

I have never known anyone who approximated so closely the received idea of a Renaissance pope – that mixture of gluttony and refinement – who, even against his will, would dominate and preside over any table. Matilde, his wife, wrapped him in a bib which looked more like an apron from a barbershop than a napkin from a restaurant, but it was the only way to prevent him from being bathed in sauces. That day Neruda ate three lobsters in their entirety, dismembering them with the precision of a surgeon, while concurrently devouring everyone else's dishes with his eyes, until he was unable to resist picking from each plate, with a relish and an appetite that everyone found contagious: clams from Galicia, barnacle geese from Cantabria, prawns from Alicante, swordfish from the Costa Brava. All the while he was talking, just like the French, about other culinary delights, especially the prehistoric shellfish of Chile that were his heart's favourite. And then suddenly he stopped eating, pricked up his ears like the antennae of a lobster, and whispered to me: 'There's someone behind me who keeps staring at me.'

I looked over his shoulder. It was true. Behind him, three tables back, a woman, unabashed in an old-fashioned felt hat and a purple scarf, was slowly chewing her food with her eyes fixed on Neruda. I recognised her at once. She was older and bigger, but it was her, with the ring made in the form of a serpent on her first finger.

She had travelled from Naples on the same boat as the Nerudas, but they had not met on board. We asked her to join us for coffee, and I invited her to talk about her dreams, if only to entertain the poet. But the poet would have none of it, declaring outright that he did not believe in the divination of dreams.

'Only poetry is clairvoyant,' he said.

After lunch, and the inevitable walk along the Ramblas, I deliberately fell in with Frau Frida so that we could renew our acquaintance without the others hearing. She told me that she had sold her properties in Austria and, having retired to Porto, in Portugal, was now living in a house that she described as a fake castle perched on a cliff from where she could see the whole Atlantic as far as America. It was clear, although she didn't say as much explicitly, that, from one dream to another, she had ended up in possession of the entire fortune of her once unlikely Viennese employers. Even so, I remained unimpressed, only because I had always thought that her dreams were no more than a contrivance to make ends meet. I told her as much.

She laughed her mocking laugh. 'You're as shameless as ever,' she said. The rest of our group had now stopped to wait for Neruda who was speaking in Chilean slang to the parrots in the bird market. When we renewed our conversation, Frau Frida had changed the subject.

'By the way,' she said, 'you can go back to Vienna if you like.'

I then realised that thirteen years had passed since we first met.

'Even if your dreams aren't true, I will never return,' I told her, 'just in case.'

At three o'clock we parted in order to accompany Neruda to his sacred siesta, which he took at our house, following a number of solemn preparatory rituals that, for some reason, reminded me of the Japanese tea ceremony. Windows had to be opened, others closed – an exact temperature was essential – and only a certain kind of light from only a certain direction could be tolerated. And then: an absolute silence. Neruda fell asleep at once, waking ten minutes later, like children do, when we expected it least. He appeared in the living room, refreshed, the monogram of the pillowcase impressed on his cheek.

'I dreamt of that woman who dreams,' he said.

Matilde asked him to tell us about the dream.

'I dreamt she was dreaming of me,' he said.

'That sounds like Borges,' I said.

He looked at me, crestfallen. 'Has he already written it?'

'If he hasn't, he's bound to write it one day,' I said. 'It'll be one of his labyrinths.'

As soon as Neruda was back on board ship at six that afternoon, he said his farewells to us, went to sit at an out-of-the-way table and began writing verses with the same pen of green ink that he had been using to draw flowers, fish and birds in the dedications he signed in his own books. With the first announcement to disembark, we sought out Frau Frida and found her finally on the tourist deck just as we were about to give up. She, too, had just woken from a siesta.

'I dreamt of your poet,' she told us.

Astonished, I asked her to tell me about the dream.

'I dreamt he was dreaming about me,' she said, and my look of disbelief confused her. 'What do you expect? Sometimes among all the dreams there has to be one that bears no relation to real life.'

I never saw or thought about her again until I heard about the ring made in the form of a serpent on the finger of the woman who died in the sea disaster at the Hotel Riviera. I could not resist asking the Portuguese ambassador about it when we met up a few months later at a diplomatic reception.

The ambassador spoke of her with enthusiasm and tremendous admiration. 'You can't imagine how extraordinary she was,' he said. 'You would have been unable to resist wanting to write a story about her.' And he continued in the same spirit, on and on, with some occasional, surprising details, but without an end in sight.

'Tell me then,' I said finally, interrupting him, 'what exactly did she do?'

'Nothing,' he replied, with a shrug of resignation. 'She was a dreamer.' ∎

© DON McCULLIN
Bill Buford, 1983

EDITORIAL

Bill Buford

GRANTA 50: SUMMER 1995

Three months ago, I did a thing that, for a long time, I had regarded as inconceivable: I resigned from *Granta*. Even now, the logic implicit in that ordinary, adult statement – I, an employee of a publishing company, resigned from my position in it – seems to me inadmissible, if only because I find it impossible to think of *Granta* as a place of work. No one edits a literary magazine because it's a good job. And, as a rule, no one leaves. The editor stays with the ship until – well, until it goes down (which, finally, it always seems to do).

Why edit a literary magazine in the first place? The question was one of the first ones put to me by our first accountant, who – our dark balance sheet spread across the table of the pub – patiently explained why businesses exist: 'So that,' he said, 'the people who own them can make money from them. This clearly is not the reason you started *Granta*. Why, then, do you believe *Granta* is a business? Do you have any idea?'

I had none. But does any editor? The wall of my sitting room at home is taken up almost exclusively with literary magazines. And while I have only skimmed through most, they are, all of them, a reassuring sight. My wall represents ten years in the life of John Lehmann (when he made Penguin's *New Writing*), Cyril Connolly (*Horizon*), Ted Solotaroff (*New American Review*), Charles Newman (*TriQuarterly*) and Ben Sonnenberg's noble *Grand Street* (a neat

213

decade being the conventional life, it would seem, of the successful literary magazine); as well as three years when Saul Bellow wasn't writing a novel (*The Noble Savage*), the fifteen years when T.S. Eliot wasn't writing a poem (the *Criterion*), the twenty-five years when Daniel Halpern wasn't writing enough (*Antaeus*) and the eighteen months when Craig Raine was not writing anything at all (*Quarto*); and, as profound, the months of anguish suffered silently by the other editors whose labours were not allowed to endure past the first, crushing consequences of the first printer's invoice. For me, the comfort in this sight is in knowing that we all know what we've been through. Only the editors of literary magazines understand that it's a prepostcrous thing to cdit a litcrary magazinc. Thcy know thc labour that goes into making one – I still don't know why it should be so much work; what can be so difficult? My wall represents late nights and spilt ashtrays and bottles of drink that shouldn't have been drunk, not then and not in such quantity; and other editors know how much time is spent on everything except editing: on worrying about money, usually, and invariably on the subject of its insistent absence. And they also appreciate the exquisite, even philosophical arbitrariness with which a magazine comes into existence: the transition from nothing, that terrifying condition of no pages, to something, a physical object that exists in the world, in a bookshop, in a parcel delivered by the Royal Mail, in someone's hands on the Underground on the way to work, on a shelf in my sitting room.

But, in anticipation of the business at hand, filling up the empty pages of this fiftieth issue of *Granta*, my last, I've also been reading through the final issues of my collection – the goodbye editorials – and find that most don't match my experience now. In a crucial respect, of course, this is simply because *Granta* is different: it has been publishing not for ten years, or three years, or eighteen months, or two weeks, but for nearly sixteen years; and, more importantly, this issue is not the last one; *Granta* will continue; and anything I write is not therefore a requiem – the gardens of the West are not closing – but a leave-taking. But I also feel that the inevitable defensiveness that characterizes most of these final editorials – chronicles of what has been achieved, or apologies, or expressions of exhaustion, or twitchy, nervous laments arising out of being unable to pay the salaries – misses something essential.

I can't think of *Granta* as employment, as a job that I'm leaving, because *Granta* has been my life, my 'me', a thing inseparable from what I am: the normal boundaries between labour (what you do during weekdays so that something regularly enters your bank account) and self (what you are during the rest of the time) don't exist. And for some time I thought this confusion arose out of my particular circumstances. I became involved in *Granta* when I was twenty-four, a student, an American who had been in Britain all of fourteen months. I became an adult in the magazine I created, and formed the most important relationships in my life – and with my newly adopted country – through the work that I then did. It was inevitable – was it not? – that I should become confused with the magazine I made, if only because the magazine had done so much in making me. But this week I came to realize that I am not exceptional.

This week, I returned to *Granta*'s original offices. *Granta* now occupies an elegant building in north London, with space and windows and plenty of light. It has heating. But for ten years, *Granta* was published out of an attic above a Cambridge hairdresser's – the powerful smells of shampoos and peroxides and all kinds of pastel-coloured goos still permeate the original space, still empty and unrented since *Granta* moved from it five years ago. The space has no heating – it was where I learned how to type wearing gloves – and one small window that opens only by removing the frame, which became essential during English summers, however brief. There was no insulation in the roof – during windy periods dust cascaded from it, covering everything, manuscripts, your telephone, your hair, with a fine layer of dark grit – and, thus, when it was hot, it became very hot: oven hot, insufferably hot, impossible-to-work-in hot. And yet we worked there. Me alone for a time. Then me and an assistant, part-time. And then three people, five, six, eventually as many as twelve, putting in impossible hours under impossible conditions, regularly staying up until dawn to finish an issue. Why?

Because it was fun. And it was fun because it was a privilege.

There was a time when I felt there could be nothing more alienating or dispiriting than editing a literary magazine. I was a student in the United States, bewildered by the more than five hundred American literary magazines produced mainly by universities and English faculties, printed in small, heavily subsidized print runs and read by very few people. Why put such effort into something with so few consequences? But the converse is also true: what could be more satisfying than a literary magazine that was read?

Cyril Connolly, in his last editorial, described the vocation of *Horizon* as feeling 'its way to what is, in the best sense of the word, contemporary', and endeavouring to 'print what many years hence will be recognized as alive and original'. A modest vocation, and yet it is everything. To be in the position of making a magazine that, having felt its way to representing the contemporary, prints the most alive and original writing of the culture and finds readers for it, not just in this country but all over the world – the world's smartest and most literate strangers; to know that you are publishing what is probably the most widely read literary magazine in the world: to be in such a position is unique; it is a monumental privilege. It is not a job; it is never simply work; and it has never simply been me.

Granta exists because it has had the fortune of enjoying fifteen years of people who, like me, have been so confused that, at one time or another, they have been unable to separate themselves from the work they do: people for whom making a magazine of the best writing in the English language was an endeavour as serious as any endeavour could possibly be.

This issue is dedicated to all the people who have worked at *Granta* with me. For most, working at *Granta* was a first job, and it is gratifying to know that many have gone on to be writers or journalists or publishers: that the experience, I would like to think, has somehow never left them. Many were at *Granta* for years. I can't think of one who wasn't essential to what the magazine has become. ■

MARTHA GELLHORN
CATSCRADLE
NEWCHURCH WEST
CHEPSTOW
GWENT NP6 6DA
WALES

Dearest William; Thank you very much for editing job. I used a
lot of it. Am truly gaga now and truly nicotine posioned as
well. Have sent off the Afterword to Ms LuAnn (can it be?)
Walther of NAL on the assumption that you have got a contract
and it's okay. Dear God, if only I could finish this Welsh
horror.

Your contract does not sound like you or Granta. It soundes
like dreaded Penguin. There are things I don,t understand but
what I do understand is that, since most sales will come via
the mag, I will get 5% royalties on everything, and little else.
I mistrust the contract (not you, but them) and have sent it
to the Society of Authors to be vetted and also explained.
I hate to see you so much in the pocket of these Penguin people
which you are. You're a feather in their lousy cap, you
know; and your books will not get any more care than anything of
theirs does, unless it's a bestseller. William, please think
hard about all this: about what they can do to the mag (have done
on the Cavendish thing) and to your publishing house, and also
about whether you are not becoming like Agatha Runcible (read
"Vile Bodies" again.)

The mag only has to look neglected or dubious for a few
issues for it to lose its shine. Be very careful now.

Love,

Martha

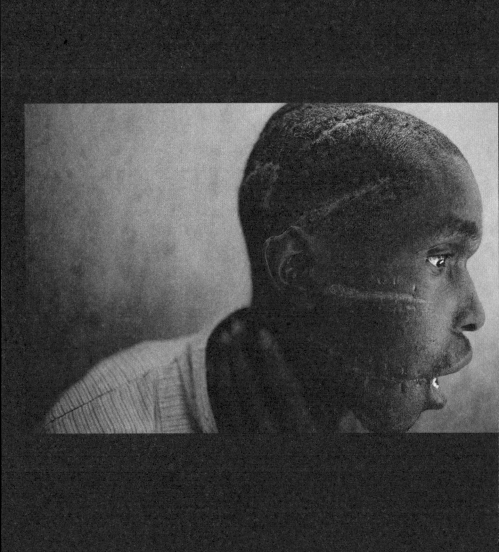

Hutu man who was attacked with machetes after refusing to support the genocide.
Rwanda, 1994

WHERE IS KIGALI?

Lindsey Hilsum

GRANTA 51: AUTUMN 1995

1

Evariste was the nightwatchman. He and I were alone in the house in Kigali, the capital of Rwanda, when the killing started. It was on the night of 6 April 1994. A plane carrying the presidents of Rwanda and its neighbouring state Burundi had been shot down, and everybody on board had died. In Kigali, there was confusion. Bands of men armed with machetes, rocks and clubs were roaming the town. Beyond the foliage that enclosed our garden, Kigali shook with rocket fire and grenade explosions.

I listened to the strokes of Evariste's broom as he swept the terrace at the back of the house. He filled his hours cleaning, making tea and listening to the radio. I was usually on the phone, talking to people elsewhere in Kigali to find out what was going on, and calling London to report.

Every hour or so, I would go out on the terrace, and we would listen to the gunfire and exchange anxious platitudes.

'It's terrible, isn't it?'

'Yes, it's terrible.'

'It sounds as if it's getting worse.'

I tried to open the front gate and look outside. Two soldiers patrolling the dirt road waved their rifles to tell me to get back into the house.

During the day, I was too busy to feel scared. At night, I lay in bed and wondered if I would ever get out of Kigali. Evariste slept outside. Each day started with the crack and sputter of shooting. He showed no fear.

At first – isolated in the house with the taciturn Evariste – I didn't understand that terror lay in the quiet times, when the killers moved undisturbed around the suburbs.

How many men, women and children were killed in Rwanda that year? Half a million? A million? Various organisations give various estimates, but nobody can be certain; for certainty you would require teams of reliable body-counters and grave-excavators, neutral statisticians free of the political need to exaggerate or diminish the number. And the total dead would take no account of the mutilated: men minus arms, children without legs. All I know is that the killing began in earnest during the time I spent trapped in the house with Evariste. My notebook doesn't reveal much about those days; a few phrases, a few 'facts' which I relayed to the BBC and which later turned out (as is sometimes the way with facts reported from places of terror and confusion) to be not quite true. I still dream about that time – the dreams usually involve pits and writhing bodies. When I first got back to London, my friends were concerned. Had I had counselling? Surely I should talk to someone? I didn't see how this would help – a therapeutic conversation with a well-meaning person in a consulting room in London – because the only proper reaction of the therapist would be horror; there would be no way of learning to 'deal' with it. What I witnessed in Rwanda was genocide – a word that needs to be used carefully, but which I use as Primo Levi defined it: as the 'monstrous modern goal of erasing entire peoples and cultures from the world'.

In Rwanda, I couldn't stop the smallest part of it. I am only slowly beginning to understand it. At the time, I could only watch and survive.

Why was I there? Because freelance journalism can be an unreliable and therefore varied trade. For the past ten years, I'd worked mainly out of Africa as a reporter. Occasionally, I work for aid agencies in what they call 'emergency countries', where war has brought destitution, hunger and disease. I'd never visited Rwanda. During the 1980s, when I was based in Nairobi, the journalists I met said it was boring – a place where farmers farmed and the government governed. It was the most densely populated country in Africa, more than seven million people trying to live off the land in a country no bigger than Wales. Coffee was its main export. Rwandans were obedient – only the Jehovah's Witnesses refused to perform *umuganda*, the obligatory unpaid communal labour that enabled the government to build a national network of roads, plant forests and construct terraces to contain soil erosion on the hillsides. Aid agencies were well disposed to Rwanda in those days. President Juvénal Habyarimana's regime was seen as authoritarian, but efficient. Society was so constrained that there was little corruption – if money was provided for clinics, then clinics were built. The Swiss, seeing a society in Africa as disciplined as their own, gave more money to Rwanda than to any other country on the continent.

Last year, I was offered a two-month contract in Rwanda with Unicef, the United Nations Children's Fund. I was to produce a newsletter which was supposed to help the dozens of aid agencies in Rwanda and Burundi work together more effectively, and to help them understand the politics of both countries.

There had, of course, been four years of war. But that had ended in a peace accord, and when I arrived in Kigali in February 1994, two months before the president's plane came down, the country was peaceful except for sporadic grenade attacks and the occasional political assassination. Outside Rwanda, those hardly counted as news. Inside Rwanda, everyone was waiting for something to happen: for political accords to be implemented, for the war to restart, for something to give.

K igali is scattered across a series of hills and, when I arrived, the country around it was covered in crops and flowers, and everything was a lush green. The city, however, was ugly. Paint peeled off the walls of the concrete blocks, and in the afternoons, the torrential rains that came each day would wash mud down the steep roads. When I walked in town, children followed me, calling '*Mzungu, mzungu*' – 'white person', signalling a lack of sophistication that you wouldn't find in Nairobi or Kampala or even in Bujumbura, the capital of Burundi. Food purloined from aid consignments was on sale in the market – square cans of cooking oil marked with the Canadian maple leaf or the stars of the European Union. If you knew whom to ask, you could get a hand grenade for three US dollars.

'Political power,' an African diplomat told me one evening, 'is the only way to wealth in Rwanda. Most of the politicians here don't even have farms to go back to. If they lose power, they'll have nothing.'

The diplomat took me to dinner at a restaurant owned by a Maronite Lebanese called Afif, whose chief business was construction. We were the only diners. A handful of musicians, in robes intended to represent traditional Rwandan dress, played mood music. The mood was glum. The Ministry of Public Works owed Afif money, and he couldn't get his hands on it. 'Since democracy, you can't even drink the water,' he said. He and the diplomat spent much of the evening on the phone, calling politicians to discover what deals had been brokered to shore up the government. I asked Afif about his contacts. He said he had bribed most government ministers, and they were afraid of him.

My daytime conversations were different. Western aid workers preferred to take another view of Rwanda, a humanitarian attitude expressed in terms of how many bags of food had been delivered the previous week and how many children had been immunised. Politics, how Rwandans thought and felt about their present and future, hardly existed in this world. The map on the office wall showed clusters of camps, inhabited by two sorts of refugee: in the north, those displaced by Rwanda's war; in the south, those who had

fled a coup attempt in Burundi a few months before. There was a
drought in some places, incipient famine, and malaria was on the
rise. Nearly half the pregnant women in towns were HIV-positive.
The population was growing; land was scarce. Talk of food sacks and
immunisation programmes was a way of avoiding the what-is-to-be-
done conversation, the indulgence of despair.

Most of the Rwandans who worked at Unicef simply refused to talk
about politics at all. The secretaries showed me how the computers
worked and promised to introduce me to their dressmakers. They
shrugged off my questions. 'Rwandans are terrible,' said one. 'They
will just lie to you.'

And then one day, I made a mistake. Compiling my first Unicef
newsletter, I quoted an internal report by the Catholic Relief Services
in south-western Rwanda on the problems faced by the country's tiny
population of forest or pygmy people, the Twa. 'The Twa cannot find
work as farm labourers because of the drought, so they have taken to
stealing. When they are caught, they are killed.'

My draft came back from Unicef with a line through the
offending quotation. I was told to expunge the reference and never to
mention the Twa. Or Hutus. Or Tutsis. Referring to people's ethnic
group – their *ethnie* – was too sensitive, too dangerous. If one or other
group was attacked, or suffered disproportionately, I shouldn't draw
attention to it. All the people of Rwanda were Rwandans.

This denied a truth that was obvious to the most ignorant outsider,
though it was a well-meaning denial. When a foreigner comes to
Africa and sees something cruel and ugly, perpetrated between
citizens of the same country, then the easiest explanation is contained
by the phrase 'ancient tribal hatred' and the idea that the neat colonial
boundaries of Africa, drawn up by Europeans, are no more than a
result of cartography; that they have disguised, but never resolved,
long-standing struggles for territory or power between different
peoples – tribes if you like – who happened to find themselves under
the same flag of a new nation state. Then the foreigner meets Africans
who point out that white people don't talk about 'tribalism' when

they analyse their own conflicts; that the European colonists have exploited tribal distinctions to retain power; and that 'tribalism' obscures the complexities of African politics and history. And so the well-meaning foreigner stops using the word: we are embarrassed by it, become frightened to ask about ethnicity in Africa in case it causes offence. Afraid of the words, we gloss over what the words are trying to describe.

In Rwanda, the idea of tribalism is particularly inappropriate. Most of the distinctions – language, customs, territory – that mark one tribe from another elsewhere in Africa do not apply. The people who live in Rwanda speak the same language, Kinyarwanda; share the same culture; and farm together on the same hills. And yet there is a division. There are the Hutus, who form the great majority (perhaps as much as 90 per cent of the population, though the census is unreliable). There are the Tutsis. And there are the Twa. A child's guide to Rwanda would say that Tutsis are tall compared with Hutus, generally speaking, and then be stuck to find other obvious signs of difference.

Rwandans know better. They can tell each other's *ethnie* through conversations about family and lineage. Foreigners are not so artful, so don't know how to ask. Yet *ethnie* – a complex sense of self shaped by history and ideology – is the defining point of identity for Rwandans. It is something at once more subtle and more consuming than tribalism. Foreigners might believe that ignoring the politics of ethnic division is the safest course of action, but we didn't understand it, and if we had understood it, we wouldn't have believed its consequences. For *ethnie* was to determine who was to live and who to die.

2

I suppose I'd known for some years what this business of *ethnie* could do because I'd met Rwandan refugees in Uganda. They were the evidence that Rwanda, where the sole and ruling party described itself as a movement for development, had known violence and political strife. The refugees were Tutsis, the minority that had ruled Rwanda in the pre-colonial age and continued to dominate it during its time as a colony. They had been driven out after the Hutus, the majority, seized power when the Belgians left in 1962. The Tutsis lived in camps close to Uganda's border with Rwanda, but they were a successful community; some sent their children to universities in Europe and North America. Then, in 1990, an army of these Tutsi exiles, calling themselves the Rwandan Patriotic Front (RPF), invaded Rwanda. They were almost immediately beaten back, but they regrouped, and war began. By 1994, the RPF had become a sophisticated guerrilla army that had advanced and retreated and advanced again.

War had forced up to a million Hutu peasants to leave their homes. Several hundred thousand were camped uncomfortably on hillsides outside Kigali, but the plan was that soon they – and the Tutsi refugees from previous decades – would be able to return to their homes. A peace treaty had been signed at Arusha, in northern Tanzania, in August 1993 – a power-sharing arrangement between government and rebels and United Nations troops brought in to oversee it. Rebel leaders would become ministers in a transition government. Diplomats began to talk of the Arusha Accords as a model for the resolution of conflict in Africa. (And there was certainly a lot to resolve. Rwanda had another displaced population of about 400,000 people who had crossed its southern border from Burundi after an attempted military coup in that country in October, in which Burundi's Hutu president had been killed. The Burundi army was dominated by Tutsis; the refugees in Rwanda were Hutus. They lived in miserable camps, which were marked on the map on our office wall. The international community had failed to provide enough food; many of their children were dying.)

In March, I went to an RPF rally on the Ugandan border. Busloads of RPF supporters, all Tutsi, drove up from Kigali, talking of the good times to come. Thérèse, a secretary with the UN, was excited at the prospect of finding a husband among the RPF. 'These boys are handsome – when the RPF comes to town, we'll even find one for you, if you want.'

She had spent four months in prison in 1990 on suspicion of supporting the RPF. She was in her mid-thirties and had never married. Her explanation was *ethnie*. 'Hutu men who have good jobs like civil servants aren't allowed to marry Tutsis,' she said. That wasn't strictly true. Only soldiers were banned from marrying Tutsi women – among powerful men, Tutsi wives were a status symbol. The real issue, I thought, is that well-educated, middle-class Tutsi women like Thérèse don't want to marry Hutus.

I tried to settle into my rented house. With the foreigner's tact, I had never asked Evariste his *ethnie*, but he was quite tall and slim, with a narrow nose, a typical Tutsi physique, and the owner of the house told me that she believed he was a Tutsi.

Anyway, I scarcely knew him, and his *ethnie* was none of my business. He was simply the nightwatchman. Expatriates and the native rich in Kigali employ watchmen, known as *zammu*, for their houses, as they do all over urban Africa. The wealthy live besieged and guarded by the poor. In Kigali, as crime and shooting increased, the *zammu* learned to open the gate only to whites or to black people who came in cars marked with the symbols of aid agencies.

Our exchanges were the routine greetings of employer and employed: '*Bonjour, madame.*' '*Bonjour, Evariste, ça va?*' His French was hesitant, and he didn't invite conversation. He helped us install the generator. In the tense weeks before the president was killed, electricity in our part of town was restricted to two evenings a week. The growl of the generator masked occasional grenade explosions and gunshots; the light it powered enabled us to work or read. I didn't go out much at night.

During my first weeks in Kigali, I had stayed at a hotel. I would sit at one of the rough wooden tables under the thatched roof of the bar and watch people. One evening, a young man in a leather jacket came over and started talking. He told me that he had a university place in Belgium but had been refused a visa.

I wanted to find out about *ethnie* – it was easier to talk to a stranger – so I asked to see his identity card. He pulled it out of his wallet.

Name, father's name, place of birth, place of residence, *ethnie*. The choices were Hutu, Tutsi, Twa, *naturalisé*. The last category was for foreigners who had taken Rwandan citizenship.

'It's the fault of the Belgians,' he said. 'The Belgians made us carry this card.'

'But the Belgians left thirty years ago! Why didn't you ditch the cards then? That's what the Kenyans did,' I said.

'You don't understand what the Belgians were like,' he said. 'They colonised us and gave us these identity cards. Now they won't even let me have a visa. It's racism.'

One Saturday night, a group of men threw grenades into the hotel bar. Eight people were killed and thirty injured. The hotel was owned by the only prominent Tutsi politician in the country. A few days later, fragmentation grenades were thrown into some Tutsi homes. The hospitals were filled with people slashed with machetes and injured by shrapnel. Soon after, I moved from the hotel to the house. I stayed at home in the evenings and read *Middlemarch*. And then, the president's plane was shot down.

3

Evariste and I developed a routine in those few days after the president was killed. I would sleep a few hours at night, after the shooting died down; at dawn, as the gunfire started up again, I would start work by the telephone. Foreigners were scrambling to leave the country, but I reverted to my role as reporter and stayed.

The killers were murdering people at roadblocks and in their homes. Once a day, Evariste would call a neighbour to try and find out if his wife and two children were still alive.

I thought: their targets are Tutsis. At any moment, they could come for Evariste.

I tried to persuade him to sleep in my absent landlady's bedroom, where I believed he would be safe from the mob, but he refused, saying first that it was not his place to sleep in the bed of *la patronne*;

and then that the patrolling soldiers had told all the *zammu* in the neighbourhood to stay outside and keep to their duties, protecting the rich people's houses. The soldiers' authority was greater than mine.

Fragments of news came in by phone for me to piece together and relay to London. A group of men had been to one aid worker's house and demanded that he hand over his Tutsi cook. He refused, but they found the cook and killed him anyway. The prime minister, Agathe Uwilingiyimana, a Hutu, and the Tutsi hotel owner were dead. Ten Belgian UN soldiers had been killlled, because Belgium was regarded as pro-RPF; the killers were saying that Belgium was behind the shooting down of the president's plane. The RPF had left their bases in the north and were heading for Kigali.

The Rwandans I knew from Unicef called me from the suburbs. They had abandoned their reserve, the opacity that I'd found so impenetrable in the office, and were desperate for help. One Rwandan colleague, François, was a Hutu, but his son, who was tall like a Tutsi, had lost his ID. 'They said they would kill him, so I gave them the radio, and they spared him. What shall I do when they come again?'

'Give them money bit by bit, don't give them everything at once,' I suggested.

'But there's another problem. They killed my next-door neighbour, Monsieur Albert. They say I was his friend, but it's not true. I don't really know him. He was Belgian, but I've called the Embassy, and they won't come and get the body. Now the body is beginning to smell.'

'Bury it,' I said. 'It's a health risk.'

'But he's a white man; he should have a proper burial.'

'It doesn't matter what colour he is; he's dead. Just bury him and say a prayer.'

'But what if the soldiers say I buried him because he was my friend?'

'Tell them you didn't know him, but you had to bury him because of the smell.'

François rang back the next day. 'Thank you,' he said. 'I did what you said. You were right. We dug a grave at the front and buried him. Maybe the Belgians will come for him after the war.'

'Maybe they will,' I said, thinking: is this it, is this all I can do? Tell someone to bury a body?

The phone kept ringing. Another colleague, Françoise, rang. She was a classic Tutsi – tall, light-skinned and lithe – one of the women I'd travelled with on the bus to the RPF rally the previous month. Now, she was sobbing hysterically and hiding in a cupboard. Her cousin had been killed on the road outside her house, she knew that her family was next on the list. 'They don't kill you if you give them money and jewellery, but we have given them everything.' She wanted the UN to receive her, but the UN was evacuating only foreigners.

An RPF contingent had broken out of the old parliament building and taken on the Presidential Guard; fighting blocked the road to the airport. All the politicians who supported the Arusha Accords were dead or in hiding. A new government had appointed itself.

I tried to plan how to rescue the people I knew. I was fooling myself – I couldn't do it. Tutsis trying to escape were being pulled from vehicles and slaughtered on the road. I had scarcely any petrol in my car. I didn't know the suburbs where the people lived.

One afternoon, a delegate from the International Red Cross rang. He had seen hundreds, maybe thousands of bodies, evidence of a slaughter far worse than we had imagined. I knew that I had to see for myself if I was to report first-hand. The next morning, I drove through the streets, past soldiers swigging beer, and abandoned bodies, to the Red Cross headquarters, and from there, with a medical team, to a Red Cross depot in the suburbs. Two women lay inside, moaning from the pain of bullet wounds. Five bodies lay round the back. Up a hill, two soldiers shifted uneasily outside a house and watched us go in. The bodies of five women lay piled in the flower bed. Their faces were fixed in terror; flies crawled over the blood of their machete wounds. A woman who had watched from the other side of the valley said that some Tutsis had gathered at the Red Cross depot for safety. In the morning, twenty soldiers had come. Those they did not slaughter on the spot, they marched to the house up the hill and murdered there.

In the house, we walked through shards of glass, torn paper, wrecked furniture and broken crockery. The mess spoke of a frenzy of killing, of anger and madness.

We took the wounded to the central hospital. The dying lay two or three to a bed and on the floor, blocking the entrance to the ward. Nurses stepped over them. Blood ran down the steps and along the gutters. Trucks kept arriving, loaded high with more bodies. A woman came into the ward carrying a baby whose leg was partially severed, the tendons and muscles exposed. Relatives patiently told their stories, always the same – Hutu neighbours and soldiers had thrown grenades in their house because they were Tutsis.

That night, after we left, the soldiers went into the wards and finished off most of the patients.

I went back to the house. Evariste was still there. The next morning, after a sleepless night, I went into the living room, sat down and started to cry.

Evariste sat silently opposite me. Eventually, he said, in French, 'Why are you crying, madame?'

'Because I'm scared,' I replied. He waited.

'Don't be scared,' he said, at last.

I told him I would have to leave; I couldn't stay much longer in the house because the telephone would soon be cut off and, without the telephone, I couldn't work. I needed to go to the hotel where other journalists were. But I didn't want to abandon him. To Evariste, the answer was simple.

'You are a European; you should be with other Europeans,' he said.

The UN security officer, a flamboyant French former policeman known by his radio call-sign, 'Moustache', was driving around town with a single armed guard rescuing foreigners. When he asked his headquarters in New York if he could help Rwandan UN staff, he was told no. He had no support from the UN troops because they had retreated to barracks. Two months earlier, when all UN staff had been asked to mark their house on a map in case of emergency, I had decided not to bother. In case of emergency, I might want to stay. Now I rang Moustache.

'At last you ring me!' he said. 'Tell me where you are and I am coming for you.'

He took me to a house where, as Evariste had predicted, I found other Europeans. Other journalists began to arrive, and I moved into a hotel. After a few more days, I left Kigali for Nairobi, and then Nairobi for Burundi, where I would go to the border to meet the first refugees heading south, away from the charnel house Rwanda had become.

4

The Rwandan president, Juvénal Habyarimana, who died in the plane crash on 6 April, had been hated by the RPF Tutsis, but extremists close to his own Hutu family and political party had come to hate him even more.

Habyarimana had done everything he could to avoid implementing the Arusha Accords. Under the agreement, the presidency would have lost most of its power, and his party, the National Republican Movement for Development and Democracy (MRNDD), would have had to govern not only with opposition Hutu parties, but with the Tutsi-dominated RPF. His negotiators had let him down, and the rebels had struck a hard bargain. After twenty-one years of unfettered rule, he was committed to a policy which would destabilise his power. His wife was not pleased.

In Rwandan politics, every institution had its unofficial counterpart. The president ruled, but then there was the *akazu* – the 'little house', a clique named after the court that surrounded the Tutsi kings during the nineteenth century. The president's wife, Agnès, and her brothers controlled the *akazu*, and with it access to wealth and power. And while the president's party supported the Arusha Accords, the Committee for the Defence of Democracy (CDR), secretly funded by Habyarimana, propounded a Hutu extremist ideology, against all compromise with the rebels.

The parties had militias masquerading as youth wings: the MRNDD militia was the *inherahamwe* – 'those who attack together';

LINDSEY HILSUM

while the CDR militia was called the *impuzamugambi* – 'those with the same goal'. The militias carried out politicians' orders by bombing, shooting and stabbing, while the party leaders talked peace. Even the army and the government radio station had their shadows. A ceasefire in 1993 had, in theory, confined the army to barracks, but members of it, the death squads known as the Zero Network, went on operating under the command of an army colonel. And while the state-owned Radio Rwanda supported the official line – brotherhood and amity – the commercial station, Radio Mille Collines, broadcast Hutu extremist propaganda, folk songs and chants – '*I hate the Hutus who eat with the Tutsis*' – as well as lists of Tutsis who were to be killed.

Habyarimana manipulated and schemed and split the opposition parties with a mixture of bribery and threats. The Arusha Accords had specified which portfolios would go to which parties. By March, the parties were in disarray. Twice, the diplomats and dignitaries were in their seats waiting for the president to swear in the new assembly. Twice, he failed to turn up. He consulted his friends, Presidents Mobutu of Zaire and Eyadéma of Togo, past masters at staying in power without popular support. The UN peacekeeping force, there to oversee the transition, began to mutter about withdrawal.

In the end, at a summit in Tanzania, Habyarimana bowed to pressure from other regional leaders and agreed to stop prevaricating and to implement the Accords. It was on his way back to Rwanda that his plane was shot down. It is not known who was responsible, but the evidence points to Hutu extremists who had once been close to Habyarimana.

5

G enocide in a small country with little access to sophisticated technology relies on bombs, guns, sticks and knives; people to wield them; and a plan – whom to kill and when. Then there is the question of motive. Ideology supplies that. Thus, you could argue, genocide requires three kinds of people: killers, strategists and ideologues. Rwanda's shadow armies and political parties and radio broadcasts provided all three: the CDR, the *inherahamwe* and Radio Mille Collines. But they were all recent institutions; none could have existed without history and myth.

All societies are sustained by myth, and in Rwanda the myths are especially potent. Stories of the past blend history with legend, and are reworked and retold to justify the power of rulers or the protest of the ruled. The past – who are we? where did we come from? – resonates in the present: who has the right to land or a country, who is condemned to exile? One well-known Rwandan myth is this:

> At the beginning of time, Kigwa, the first king of Rwanda, descended from heaven and sired three sons: Ga-twa, Ga-hutu and Ga-tutsi. He asked each of them to take care of a gourd of milk overnight. Ga-twa became thirsty and drank the milk.Ga-hutu fell asleep and knocked the gourd over. Ga-tutsi guarded the milk carefully and was guarding it still when Kigwa returned in the morning. Kigwa decreed everyone's social status – Ga-tutsi would be his successor, own cattle and be excused manual labour. Ga-hutu and his people would only be allowed cattle if they worked for Ga-tutsi. Ga-twa would have no cattle and would be an outcast.

The idea of Tutsi superiority is in the subconscious of all Rwandans; denying the attitudes it engenders requires conscious self-defiance. Ideology rather than knowledge is the tool; you choose your interpretation of history to back up political propaganda, or to justify murder.

European explorers searching for the source of the Nile first came across Rwanda in the second half of the nineteenth century. They found three groups of people in this part of Africa, each playing a distinct social role. The state was embodied by the king – the *mwami* – who had a sacred drum or *kalinga*. The Tutsis gave the Hutus the right to rear and tend cattle and to cultivate land in exchange for labour. Social divisions were permeable – a Hutu could become a Tutsi by acquiring cattle, and then marrying a Tutsi woman – though they were becoming more rigid under the last of the precolonial kings. Many questions could have been asked of this society: were the Hutus merely serfs who were repressed by the Tutsi aristocracy, or was the relationship of benefit to both? But the question that obsessed the Europeans was much simpler: why were the Tutsis so tall? In a Darwinian age which was beginning to develop racial theory and was equipped with a set of sub- or pseudo-sciences – anthropometry, craniology, phrenology – there was no shortage of answers. The Tutsis had captured the European imagination. John Hanning Speke, the British explorer who discovered the source of the Nile in 1862, decided that they had descended from the Oromos of southern Ethiopia – that they were a superior race which had conquered the inferior Bantu people, the Hutus. Colonial rule, first by Germany from 1890 to 1916 and thereafter by Belgium, brought further theories: the Tutsis were the lost tribe of Christendom, they were survivors of Atlantis, they were descended from ancient Egyptians, they were refugees from Asia Minor. Eventually, a consensus emerged that was close to Speke's original idea: the Tutsis were 'Nilo-Hamites' – Nilo from the River Nile, Hamites because they had descended from Noah's son Ham – who had migrated south from Ethiopia in the sixteenth century.

The Duke of Mecklenburg, an early German explorer, wrote lyrically: 'Unmistakable evidence of a foreign strain is betrayed in their high foreheads, the curve of their nostrils and the fine oval shape of their faces.' The Hutu, by contrast, 'are medium-sized people whose ungainly figures betoken hard toil, and who patiently bow themselves in abject bondage to the later-arrived yet ruling race, the Tutsi'.

Belgian anthropologists instituted a programme of measurement. The average Tutsi nose, one study noted, was 55.8mm long and 38.7mm wide; an average Hutu nose was 52.4mm long and 43.6mm wide. Stature, weight, 'nasal index', face height and 'facial index' were also measured, the results tabulated and sent back to Brussels. From the perspective of the late twentieth century, this obsession with the human physique may sound risible, but in Rwanda, a month after the president's plane was shot down, I watched doctors bandaging the hands of children whose fingers had been sliced off by Hutus because long fingers were thought to be a Tutsi characteristic. Hutus also cut off Tutsis' legs at the knee, to make them 'as short as us'.

Size was too crude a mark of identity for the Belgian administration, and in the 1930s, such categorisation was refined with the introduction of identity cards. Anyone with more than ten cattle was defined as Tutsi, those with fewer were Hutu. By the 1950s, the few Hutus who had been educated in mission schools were agitating for change, for government jobs, for access to power. Elsewhere in Africa, anti-colonial movements were encouraging Africans to burn identity cards that specified 'tribe'. In Rwanda, however, Hutu political leaders wanted to keep the cards so that the Tutsis could be identified, and their social, economic and political dominance ended.

The Tutsis were, in any case, becoming unfashionable. Social democracy was gaining currency in post-war Europe, and many of the missionary priests who came to Rwanda found the Tutsi monarchy, with its assumption of superiority and its monopoly on power, distasteful. Moreover, as independence approached, the Tutsis adopted the rhetoric of pan-Africanism and anti-colonialism; the Belgians began to worry that they would take Rwanda into the Chinese or Soviet camp. The Belgians decided to save Rwanda from feudalism and communism in one smart move. After forty years of shoring up Tutsi power, they changed sides and backed the Hutus. The violence began in 1959, two years before independence, and Belgium did little to stop it. Tutsi political activists assassinated Hutu leaders, and in retaliation Hutu peasants swept through the countryside in bands of ten, each led by a 'president' with a whistle, burning Tutsi homes. The peasants called it the *muyaga*, the wind that blows itself into a hurricane. By 1963, it had forced 135,000 Tutsis to flee Rwanda, and the fact that many children of these refugees later formed the core of the RPF was never forgotten by Hutu leaders. Léon Mugesera, a Hutu extremist ideologue, told a gathering of Hutu peasants in 1992: 'Our fatal error back in 1959 was to let them flee.' By 1994, Hutu leaders were advocating mass slaughter: 'This time, we will kill them all.' Those who murdered children used a Rwandan proverb: 'If you want to exterminate rats, you mustn't spare the little ones.'

And so, after independence, a new Rwanda was established which turned the old hierarchy on its head. Quotas were introduced; as always, *ethnie* determined whether you got a job or went to school or could hold political office, only now the powerful *ethnie* was Hutu. The *kalinga* or drum that had been the symbol of Rwanda at the time of the *mwami* was rejected as an emblem of Tutsi domination. Instead of a symbol, post-independence Rwanda had an ideology: Hutu power, rooted in a culture of obedience and control. From birth all Rwandans were members of President Habyarimana's Republican Movement for National Development, the only political organisation. A group of households comprised a *cellule*; every *cellule* had a spokesman who reported to the *conseiller* who was in charge of the next administrative unit up the ladder, the *secteur*. He, in turn, reported to the *bourgmestre*, who was in charge of the *commune*. And the *bourgmestre* reported to the *préfet* in charge of the *préfecture* ... and so on, to the highest reaches of the government. If a Rwandan wanted to leave his hill, he first asked the authorities for permission. Unlike most African capitals, Kigali remained small and largely immune to urban drift; Rwanda had pass laws stricter than those of South Africa.

What outsiders saw, or chose to see, was an ideology of discipline, development and conservative Christianity which made a pleasant contrast to countries such as Zaire or Sudan, where political breakdown and apparent chaos rendered Western ideas of development meaningless. What outsiders did not hear, or chose not to hear, was the idea of *ethnie* that fuelled the ideology; the fear that history in the shape of the old Tutsi hierarchy would return. After all, to the south, in Burundi, where the Tutsi army continued to slaughter Hutu peasants, it had never gone away.

Hutus, therefore, were taught the lessons of history as it was interpreted by the new Hutu elite. Ferdinand Nahimana, professor of history at Rwanda's National University and the founder of Radio Mille Collines, tried to demystify the Tutsis by explaining that while European scholars studied subjugated Hutus in Tutsi kingdoms, few had examined the Hutu principalities that had resisted Tutsi expansion until the 1920s. This demonstrated that Tutsi rule was not inevitable, so long as the Tutsis were kept in check. Tutsis were to be denied not only citizenship, but life itself, because they were *inyangarwanda* – 'haters of Rwanda'.

Léon Mugesera, who was vice president of Habyarimana's party in the president's home *préfecture*, adapted history in a different way. He subscribed to the European belief that the Tutsis were relative newcomers who had arrived in Rwanda from Ethiopia four centuries before. In a speech in 1992 – by which time Hutu ideology was well-developed – Mugesera said the Tutsis should be returned to their original home via the expedient route of the River Nyawarungu. Two years later, the bodies of murdered Tutsis were floating down the Nyawarungu and into the Kagera River, in which they could be seen passing under a road bridge on the Tanzanian border at the rate of one per minute. Ethiopia, given the river-flows of Africa, was an unreachable destination. The bodies came to rest on the shores of Lake Victoria, where they rotted in the sun.

6

Two months after I left Kigali, I returned to Rwanda, to Butare, a city in the south of the country that had once been well known for its tolerance and spirit of liberalism. The Hutu *inherahamwe* were now in charge of the roadblocks (though they would not be for long: the RPF, having dislodged the 'interim government' that had appointed itself in Kigali after Habyarimana's death, was now advancing south), and thousands of Tutsis had been slaughtered there, as well as Hutu students and lecturers at the university, who were seen as the RPF's fellow travellers.

I went to Gikongoro, a town in the hills a few miles to the west of Butare. French troops on a 'humanitarian mission' had occupied the area, which was filling up with Hutu refugees. Two young men, a teacher and a Red Cross volunteer, were among them. They tried to explain to me what had happened in Butare during the previous ten weeks of murder.

'The Tutsis formed an association,' the teacher said. 'They were planning to kill all the Hutus, and there were documents to prove it in their houses. When the people found these papers, they grew angry, and that's why they killed the Tutsis.'

I asked about the Hutus at the university who had been killed by other Hutus.

'They were plotting, too.'

'So who was responsible?'

'The victims were responsible.'

I persisted with my questions. 'The children who were killed, were they responsible for their own deaths?'

'That was a question of hatred between families,' the Red Cross worker said. 'Many Tutsis sent their children to join the RPF, so people said: "I don't want the child of a person who does such bad things."'

These were educated men, fluent in French. They spoke without irony; I believe they were convinced of their own story. They faltered just a little when I asked if they had taken part in killings themselves.

'No, I didn't personally take part,' the teacher said, and the other concurred. 'But we understand why people did it. This is war. It's sad that people die.'

'Are you sad the Tutsis died?' I asked.

The teacher quoted a proverb: 'If there's a trap ahead of you, and someone removes that trap before you fall in, then you're happy. So we're happy.'

7

B y the time I reached Kibuye, in the west of the country, in August, the bodies of the four thousand Tutsis who had been killed in a church there were long buried. The church stands among trees on a promontory above the calm blue of Lake Kivu. The Tutsis had been sheltering inside when a mob, drunk on banana beer, had thrown grenades through the doors and windows and then run in to club and stab to death the people who remained alive. It had taken about three hours. A few days later, another organised mob did much the same at the local sports stadium where the *préfet*, Clément Kayishema, had told Tutsis to assemble. Eleven thousand people were gathered there. They couldn't kill them all on the first day, so they came back the following morning. Once, there had been 60,000 Tutsis in Kibuye *préfecture*, about 20 per cent of the population – an unusually high proportion. French troops now estimated that about nine in every ten Tutsis had been killed, and that half the male Hutu population, and a smaller proportion of the female, had taken part in the killings.

A Lutheran pastor, Bernard Ndutiye, was – as he put it – a 'passive participant' in the slaughter. When I met him in Kibuye, he had turned a local primary school into a home for orphaned and abandoned children. He was thin and anxious; he said he couldn't find enough food for his charges. There was also the matter of his conscience. During the months of killing, he said, the *inherahamwe*, their faces and genitals covered with banana fronds, had moved through Kibuye at dawn every day, blowing whistles and beating drums. 'They went from house to house, saying: "Come on, attack. The RPF are killing people. We must kill all accomplices of the RPF."' At Ndutiye's house, they found three Tutsi children, school friends of his own children, whom he was hiding. They took the two girls away; the seven-year-old boy they clubbed to death then and there. 'They said I had hidden the children of the RPF, so I was an RPF supporter. Afterwards, they forced me to follow them. They wanted everyone to participate,' he said. 'The people who put up resistance were forced.

To prove you weren't RPF, you had to walk around with a club or stick. We followed behind and buried the bodies.'

'Did you try to resist?' I asked.

'I bandaged my leg as an excuse. Being a priest was no answer because they told me there are priests who are RPF. They said: "You can have religion afterwards." '

I asked how it was possible that so many had taken part in the slaughter, and that men like him hadn't refused.

Ndutiye searched his vocabulary for words a foreigner might understand.

'There are times when you lose faith, when a man loses control and is under the influence of the devil.'

Some people did resist. When I went back to Kigali later that year, I met an elderly Hutu who risked his life to hide seventeen Tutsis. He was a hero in his neighbourhood. He wasn't the only one, but he was unusual. People struck bargains – their own Tutsi relatives would be spared if they took up a machete to kill Tutsis on another hill. Some Hutu women married to Tutsis were forced to kill their own children, while others saved their own children by agreeing to kill those of their neighbours.

During the genocide, one academic handed me a sheaf of papers marked 'Ministry of Defence' and ostentatiously stamped SECRET. It was entitled 'Definition and Identification of the Enemy', and I was told that it had been widely circulated in Rwanda from late 1992 onwards. The primary enemy was defined as 'Tutsis inside and outside the country, extremists nostalgic for power'. Other enemies included Tutsi refugees, Hutus discontented with the current regime, Nilo-Hamitic people of the region, criminals on the run and foreigners married to Tutsi women.

Despite what the Tutsi women had told me on the bus to the RPF rally, intermarriage between Hutus and Tutsis had increased during Habyarimana's regime in the 1970s, especially between Hutu men and Tutsi women. Foreign men preferred Tutsis too, especially the archetypal long-legged, light-skinned young women. Foreign-aid agencies tended to employ Tutsis because many came from successful families and had studied abroad. The Hutu magazine *Kangura* published the 'Hutu Ten Commandments', which began:

> 1. Every Hutu should know that a Tutsi woman, wherever she is, works for the interest of her Tutsi ethnic group. As a result, we shall consider a traitor any Hutu who marries a Tutsi woman, befriends a Tutsi woman or employs a Tutsi woman as a secretary or concubine.
>
> 2. Every Hutu should know that our Hutu daughters are more suitable and conscientious in their role as woman, wife and mother of the family. Are they not beautiful, good secretaries and more honest?'

The fourth commandment condemned as a traitor any Hutu who did business with a Tutsi. The tenth stated that:

> The Hutu ideology must be taught to every Hutu at every level. Every Hutu must spread this ideology widely. Any Hutu who persecutes his brother Hutu for having read, spread and taught this ideology is a traitor.

The efficiency of the Rwandan state made sure that this message was spread to every corner of the country. The same efficiency – the discipline and order so admired by foreign-aid workers – meant that when the orders came on 7 April for the killing to begin, they were usually obeyed. Numerous witnesses have told how the *bourgmestres* in conjunction with local military or police instructed people to kill. Fear drove the killers on – fear of the invading enemy, fear of their neighbours, fear of execution if they refused to obey orders. If everyone breaks the rules which govern society, the rules no longer apply; group solidarity is strengthened, guilt becomes collective.

8

From April into June, the rest of the world did nothing. The UN peacekeepers withdrew. Diplomacy was at best misguided and at worst damaging – the UN kept calling for a ceasefire, when an RPF victory was the only hope of ending the genocide. Eventually, late in June, the West sent its envoys: aid workers, representing individual altruism, a belief in the power of good; and soldiers.

By the time the French troops arrived, the genocide had continued unchecked for ten weeks. A few thousand gaunt and terrified Tutsis emerged from their hiding places in roofs and banana plantations and gathered in camps to be guarded by French legionnaires. The *inherahamwe* still controlled the surrounding hills.

The motives for French intervention were complex. The French were playing on a larger stage, pointing up the incompetence of the UN and the autonomy of France as a world power. But France did have an attachment to Rwanda. For many years, the head of President Mitterrand's Africa Unit at the Elysée Palace was his son, Jean-Christophe, who formed a friendship with President Habyarimana. When his plane – a gift from the French – was shot down, his widow and her family were flown straight to Paris. The French regarded the Rwandan government as a protector of *francophonie* in Africa, a bulwark against encroaching Anglo-Saxon influence. Here was Europe's ancient tribal rivalry played out in the heart of Africa in a clash of culture and language: the RPF, schooled in Uganda, spoke English, while the Hutu government spoke French. France empathised with the Hutus: the French too had overthrown a monarchy and staged a revolution.

The French troops on the ground, however, were none too sure which side they were on. President Mitterrand had sent them on a 'humanitarian mission', and they were saving the Tutsis, who had been attacked by murderous bands of Hutus. But the Hutus thought the French were there to save them from the advance of the RPF. Roadblocks where Tutsis had been killed were decorated with

Tricouleur flags and signs saying VIVE LA FRANCE; the Hutu militia drove around in pickups brandishing machetes and singing songs of welcome. The French army knew about Africa and its wars; they had played an important part in French colonial history, and French troops still did regular tours of duty in the Central African Republic and Djibouti. But nothing had prepared them for Rwanda. One day, I was talking to the commander of a marine unit, Lieutenant Colonel Erik de Stabenrath, about his experience. He was a career soldier, from an old-established army family, and he had served in Bosnia and Beirut, but the intensity of the killing in Rwanda had shocked him. 'It was the most terrible massacre in world history,' he said, 'not in terms of numbers, but in the manner in which it was carried out.'

He had come upon thousands of bodies buried in shallow graves, churches where hasty scrubbing had failed to remove the blood from the walls. The stories told by survivors were often worse than the evidence: Tutsis hunted down and slashed with machetes, beaten with nail-studded clubs, shot with small arms, gang-raped and blown up by fragmentation grenades. His own estimate was that half a million had been killed, a rate of 7,000 deaths a day.

Another French officer, Colonel Patrice Sartre, the commander in Kibuye, was more cynical: 'Elsewhere in Africa people don't like to work. They beg,' he said. 'People here are more educated and hard-working. They don't beg, but they kill.'

I asked if, given the atrocities perpetrated by the Hutu government, France would now support the RPF. 'No,' he said. 'France will always be on the side of the slaves.'

9

The RPF never forgave the French for their support of Habyarimana's government, nor for occupying part of Rwanda and preventing a complete RPF victory, nor for allowing the key leaders of the genocide to escape across Rwanda's borders. Nonetheless, the government army, the Forces Armées Rwandaises, knew by June that it had lost the war. In mid-July, its commander-in-chief, General Augustin Bizimungu, fled with his army to Goma, just inside Zaire. They had been defeated, but their forces had survived largely intact.

Much of the civilian population went with them. This was the awful, spectacular exodus, witnessed by hundreds of reporters and dozens of television crews, who never tired of repeating that it was the largest recorded exodus in history, meaning that a million people had come through one point in an international boundary within the space of three days.

It is difficult to forget: dust, children lost and weeping, the weak trampled underfoot in the crush. Fear drove them on – the terror that, if they stayed in Rwanda, the RPF would exact revenge from the Hutu population for what they had done to the Tutsis (and their fear, as I and others discovered later, was not misplaced).

The flight to Goma was chaotic, but it was also stage-managed. Entire communities moved together. They were still following the same leaders and obeying their instructions: Radio Mille Collines and the *bourgmestres* told them to flee to Zaire, just as some weeks earlier they had told them to kill their Tutsi neighbours. Many of them, however, did not escape death by fleeing Rwanda, because Goma became for them an act of collective suicide. Human excrement piled up in the gutters, while the bodies of those who collapsed of exhaustion lay unburied along the road. Cholera set in. Thousands died on a great black plain of volcanic rock, where graves could not be dug. Instead, bodies wrapped in rush matting lay two and three deep along the road to the airport, some with children whimpering beside them. Eventually, French soldiers in masks used a mechanical digger to carve out a large trench, into which they bulldozed the dead.

Goma was a trap for the refugees, but also an escape route for the guilty among them. International agencies talked about separating the *inherahamwe* from the innocent, but the threads of guilt and responsibility were too deeply woven into Hutu society for outsiders to tease them out. The Hutu leaders, meanwhile, rented large houses in Goma and Bukavu, another town in Zaire, at the other end of Lake Kivu, and set about recreating their structures of control. The aid agencies needed these structures as the only efficient way to distribute their aid. Compassion worked against justice: if the aid workers wanted to save lives, including those of the thousands of dying children, they would have to shore up the system which had produced the *inherahamwe* and turned peasants into murderers.

Here, in the middle of this pitiful chaos, while I waited to interview an aid worker in his office in a Goma backstreet, I heard a familiar voice: '*Bonjour, madame.*' It was Evariste, the nightwatchman. Three months had passed since I had last seen him. We had spoken once by phone at the end of April, but then the line had been cut. I couldn't believe he was still alive. He had stayed in the house, he said, until the RPF entered Kigali. No one had touched it, or him. His wife and children were safe.

What was he doing here, among the Hutus and their leaders? At last, I asked, 'What *ethnie* does it give on your identity card?'

'Hutu,' he replied.

I had been stupid. Why had I assumed he was a Tutsi and a potential victim? Perhaps because he was employed by an aid agency, or because I had needed to trust him when I was afraid. Perhaps because even when the killing was at its height, one of my main emotions was embarrassment – I assumed he was Tutsi so I could avoid talking about *ethnie*.

Evariste handed me the keys to the house which he had carried with him after he had locked up. I gave him money. He disappeared into the crowd, one refugee among a million, facing the possibility of death more acutely now than ever before.

10

In December, I visited the Oxfam office in Kigali to see one of its staff, Esther Mujawayo. During the first week of killing, she had hidden, together with her husband and their three children, in the school where her husband taught French; in April, I had tried and failed to get messages to her from friends in England. In early May, soldiers took away her husband and shot him. Esther and the children spent another two months in hiding.

Esther has an intense, energetic way of talking, leaning forward in an effort to make her listener understand. If you ask her, she will show you photographs of her wedding. She will point to her father, mother and aunt – all of whom were killed in the village where she was born. Then she will point to the people who killed them – neighbours, people she grew up with.

Thirty-one members of Esther's family were killed. Her seventy-eight-year-old invalid mother and an eighty-year-old aunt were dragged from their bed and thrown live onto a pile of corpses. It took nearly a week for them to die as they lay exposed to the sun and rain while village boys threw stones at them. Her cousin died in a pit latrine; when she reached up to struggle out, a Hutu cut off her hands.

'What is very sad is that I don't think my family tried to hide,' Esther said. 'I can understand that people have been manipulated – politicians and the radio can change people – but how could they use such horrible ways of killing?'

Esther told me that she had forced herself to return to the village to try to discover what had happened.

'I thought it would be safe to go to my parents' place to be clear with myself that it's finished, and to see the hole where they are. It's very impressive. They wanted to erase everything. They killed people, they completely destroyed the house, they cut down all the trees and they started to cultivate everywhere. They even ploughed up the road leading to our home to show us that we were finished.

'I have no roots in Rwanda now. I can go anywhere as long as I am with my three children.'

The survivors of genocide, unable to bear the prospect of remaining where their families were slaughtered, have drifted to Kigali. Many of them feel guilty because they are still alive. They feel as though they are ghosts – strangers without a home. Monica Uwimana, one of those who had called me for help during the first week of killing, survived, though her five children were killed. When I met her again, she had no sense of future. She said, 'There's a saying these days, when you meet somebody: you say, Oh! you're still alive! As if it's a miracle. As if you were supposed to die.'

But Kigali, in December, was flourishing. Tutsi refugees who fled the violence in 1959 – 'Fifty-niners' – had returned from Belgium, Canada, Burundi and Uganda to reclaim the homeland. The disco had reopened; my old hotel had been repaired. There was a wave of weddings among former guerrilla fighters celebrating their new life. In the countryside, the newcomers had begun to cultivate their fields left by the dead or by those who fled to Zaire or Tanzania. The Arusha Accords stated that those who left in 1959 had no right to reclaim their lands, but who was to stop them?

11

And now, in the summer of 1995, Rwanda has become the new draw for the emergency aid industry. One hundred and fifty non-governmental organisations are there, along with myriad branches of the UN. Eager young Europeans and North Americans drive white Toyotas with logos on the doors and radio aerials thick as whips waving on the bonnet. They talk in acronyms, walkie-talkies strapped to the belts on their jeans.

Each new foreigner is issued with a white laminated card produced by the UN peacekeeping force, which failed to stop the genocide and now fails to prevent continued killing. The card shows a map of Rwanda and an explanation of the UN Security system – Green Alert, Yellow Alert, Red Alert. There is a list of useful phrases, the words in Kinyarwanda for: 'Yes', 'No', 'Stop', 'Hello', 'My name is Bob', 'Where is Kigali?' and 'Do not shoot'.

Until the end of May 1995, aid was concentrated in the former French zone in the south-west of the country, where a quarter of a million Hutus were still living in camps. It was easier to feed refugees than to start rebuilding the country, and it felt more urgent.

But the new RPF government saw the camps as cover for the *inherahamwe* and weapons that had been smuggled from Zaire. In May, it ordered troops to break them up. According to government figures, 338 people died, mostly trampled in a stampede. Foreign doctors said that they saw 4,000 dead and thousands more injured, mainly shot in the back by RPF soldiers. The government's message to the foreigners was clear: national security is more important than humanitarianism. Its message to the Hutus was unequivocal: we are in charge.

Foreigners, struggling to think of a solution, often come up with the word 'reconciliation'. Esther Mujawayo told me that was a concept she found difficult. 'It's a word I hate because I don't know what it means,' she said. 'Even if I were ready to reconcile – with whom? I've never met anybody who felt guilty, who said sorry. Who is asking me for pardon?'

No one is likely to ask Esther or any other survivor for pardon as long as the authors of the genocide – the old members of the *akazu*, the organisers of the Zero Network, the ministers of the government that appointed itself in April – remain at liberty. They fly between Zaire, Kenya, Tanzania, West Africa and Europe drumming up support, doing arms deals, planning their comeback and promulgating their own version of what happened in Rwanda. They include General Augustin Bizimungu and Jean Kambanda, the prime minister of the April government. Kambanda now calls himself 'prime minister of the government in exile' and lives in a lakeside house at Bukavu in Zaire, from where, across Lake Kivu, he can see Rwanda.

The Hutus in exile like to present the killings in the context of an ethnic war between the Hutus and the Tutsis, the result of an uncontrollable hatred between two peoples. The RPF, on the other hand, says that the killings were prompted by a government that tried to wipe out the Tutsis and all opposing Hutus in a brutal attempt to ensure that they would hold power forever. The RPF, which likes to see itself as a non-sectarian force, says that its quarrel is not with Hutus, but with the former regime (to the RPF, the history of injustice in Rwanda begins and ends with the past thirty years of Hutu power; the centuries of Tutsi dominance – and the repression of the Hutus – are seen as a benign old order). The RPF has filled Rwanda's jails with people 'arrested on suspicion of participating in genocide', but locking up or even executing hundreds or thousands of peasants will not exorcise the collective crime.

The organisers of the genocide are well known, and the evidence against them is well documented. But only a handful have been arrested. A faltering and poorly funded International Tribunal is gathering more evidence. If arrest warrants are ever issued, the accused will no doubt get adequate warning and retreat into the more chaotic reaches of Africa to evade capture.

Those who led the genocide still have authority over the mass of Hutu peasants in Zaire and Tanzania. There is no pressure on them to acknowledge what they did, let alone atone for it.

The wealthy world's fault in all this is not that it does not care – many millions of dollars have been spent to keep the refugees alive – but that it does not understand. Rwanda lurched into view only when Habyarimana's plane exploded, and because we denied its history, the genocide had no meaning. We knew nothing, so we could do nothing. We could not comprehend that ideology and culture can subsume individuals into the mass, that collective identity can come to matter more than personal feeling and character.

Foreign governments say the RPF must share power with 'moderate Hutus', but the 'moderate Hutus' were the first to be killed; certainly, the RPF government contains Hutus, but its centre of power is the top rank of the Tutsi army which won the war.

Across Lake Kivu, just inside Zaire, the *inherahamwe* and Hutu soldiers look east to their homeland. They dream of return and train with new weapons, even as the sons and daughters of Tutsi exiles from thirty years ago stream in from Uganda with great herds of long-horned cattle, their dream of returning fulfilled.

12

The last time I went to Kigali, I looked for people who had known Evariste. By the time Esther Mujawayo took me to meet a driver who had news of him, I had guessed what the news would be. The driver told me he had crossed a roadblock near the house where I had stayed about a week after the killing started and had seen Evariste on one of the barricades.

'What was he doing?' I asked.

'He was carrying a gun.'

'Could he have been forced to do it?'

'They only gave guns to certain people, those they trusted. He was with them – he was one of them. We know that.'

The driver, who was a Tutsi, faced death as he approached the roadblock. He pretended that he was employed by the Belgian Red Cross. 'Evariste didn't look at me, and I didn't look at him. I pretended not to know him, but I saw him.'

I wondered whether Evariste had waited until I left before beginning his work, or whether he had already started, those nights when he refused to sleep inside the house. I wondered what deals he had done with the soldiers outside. What had he been thinking, why did he do it, what did it mean to him? Had he been a member of the *inherahamwe* before, or did it start then? Was he forced or did he believe in what he was doing? I wondered at how I could not have known, at my foolishness, at my painful ignorance, at my inability to understand or just to see. The days we had spent together in the house in Kigali had been the most terrifying of my life. I had been through all that with Evariste, yet I had known nothing of him, nor his people, nor where he came from, nor how he felt and thought. ∎

Big Timber, Montana, November 8, 2014
Courtesy of 303 Gallery, New York

AGNES OF IOWA

Lorrie Moore

GRANTA 54: SUMMER 1996

Her mother had given her the name Agnes, believing that a good-looking woman was even more striking when her name was a homely one. Her mother was named Cyrena and was beautiful to match but had always imagined her life would have been more interesting, that she herself would have had a more dramatic, arresting effect on the world and not ended up in Cassell, Iowa, if she had been named Enid or Hagar or Maude. And so she named her first daughter Agnes, and when Agnes turned out not to be attractive at all but puffy and prone to a rash between her eyebrows, her hair a flat and bilious hue, her mother backpedaled and named her second daughter Linnea Elise (who turned out to be a lovely, sleepy child with excellent bones, a sweet, full mouth and a rubbery mole above her lip which later in life could be removed without difficulty, everyone was sure).

Agnes herself had always been a bit at odds with her name. There was a brief period in her life, in her mid-twenties, when she had tried to pass it off as French – she had put in the *accent grave* and encouraged people to call her 'On-yez'. This was when she was living in New York City and often getting together with her cousin, a painter who took her to parties in TriBeCa lofts or at beach houses or at mansions on lakes upstate. She would meet a lot of not very bright rich people who found the pronunciation of her name intriguing.

It was the rest of her they were unclear on. 'On-yez, where are you from, dear?' asked a black-slacked, frosted-haired woman whose skin was papery and melanomic with suntan. 'Originally.' She eyed Agnes's outfit as if it might be what in fact it was: a couple of blue things purchased in a department store in Cedar Rapids.

'Where am I from?' Agnes said it softly. 'Iowa.' She had a tendency not to speak up.

'Where?' the woman scowled, bewildered.

'Iowa,' Agnes repeated loudly.

The woman in black touched Agnes's wrist and leaned in confidentially. She moved her mouth in a concerned and exaggerated way, like an exercise. 'No, dear,' she said. '*Here* we say *O-hi-o.*'

That had been in Agnes's mishmash decade, after college. She had lived improvisationally then, getting this job or that, in restaurants or offices, taking a class or two, not thinking too far ahead, negotiating the precariousness and subway flus and scrimping for an occasional facial or a play. Such a life required much expendable self-esteem. It engaged gross quantities of hope and despair and set them wildly side by side, like a Third World country of the heart. Her days grew messy with contradictions. When she went for walks, for her health, cinders would spot her cheeks, and soot would settle in the furled leaf of each ear. Her shoes became unspeakable. Her blouses darkened in a breeze, and a blast of bus exhaust might linger in her hair for hours. Finally her old asthma returned and, with a hacking, incessant cough, she gave up. 'I feel like I've got five years to live,' she told people, 'so I'm moving back to Iowa so that it'll feel like fifty.'

When she packed up to leave she knew she was saying goodbye to something important, which was not that bad in a way because it meant that at least you had said hello to it to begin with, which most people in Cassell, Iowa, could not claim to have done.

A year later she married a boyish man twelve years her senior, a Cassell realtor named Joe, and together they bought a house on a little street called Birch Court. She taught a night class at the Arts

Hall and did volunteer work on the Transportation Commission in town. It was life like a glass of water: half-full, half-empty, half-full; oops, half-empty. Over the next six years she and Joe tried to have a baby, but one night at dinner, looking at each other in a lonely way over the meatloaf, they realized with a shock that they probably never would. Nonetheless they still tried, vandalizing what romance was left in their marriage.

'Honey,' she would whisper at night when he was reading under the reading lamp, and she had already put her book away and curled toward him, wanting to place the red scarf over the lampshade but knowing it would annoy him and so not doing it. 'Do you want to make love? It would be a good time of month.'

And Joe would groan. Or he would yawn. Or he would already be asleep. Once, after a long hard day, he said, 'I'm sorry, Agnes. I'm just not in the mood.'

She grew exasperated. 'You think *I'm* in the mood?' she said. 'I don't want to do this any more than you do.' He looked at her in a disgusted way, and it was two weeks after that they had the identical sad dawning over the meat loaf.

At the Arts Hall, formerly the Grange Hall, Agnes taught the Great Books class but taught it loosely, with cookies. She let her students turn in poems and plays and stories that they themselves had written; she let them use the class as their own little time to be creative. Someone once even brought in a sculpture: an electric one with blinking lights.

After class she sometimes met with students individually. She recommended things for them to write about or read or consider in their next project. She smiled and asked if things were going well in their lives. She took an interest.

'You should be stricter,' said Willard Stauffbacher, the head of the Instruction Department. He was a short, balding musician who taped to his door pictures of famous people he thought he looked like. Every third Monday he conducted the monthly departmental meeting – aptly named, Agnes liked to joke, since she did indeed depart mental. 'Just because it's a night course doesn't mean you shouldn't impart standards,' Stauffbacher said in a scolding way. 'If it's piffle, use the word *piffle*. It's meaningless? Write *meaningless* at the top of every page.' He had once taught at an elementary school and once at a prison. 'I feel like I do all the real work around here,' he added. He had posted near his office a sign that read:

RULES FOR THE MUSIC ROOM
I WILL STAY IN MY SEAT UNLESS (SIC) PERMISSION TO MOVE
I WILL SIT UP STRAIGHT
I WILL LISTEN TO DIRECTIONS
I WILL NOT BOTHER MY NEIGHBOR
I WILL NOT TALK WHEN MR STAUFFBACHER IS TALKING
I WILL BE POLITE TO OTHERS
I WILL SING AS WELL AS I CAN

Agnes stayed after one night with Christa, the only black student in her class. She liked Christa a lot – Christa was smart and funny, and Agnes would sometimes stay late with her to chat. Tonight Agnes had decided to talk Christa out of writing about vampires all the time.

'Why don't you write about that thing you told me about that time?' Agnes suggested.

Christa looked at her skeptically. 'What thing?'

'The time in your childhood, during the Chicago riots, walking with your mother through the police barricades.'

'Man, I lived that. Why should I want to write about it?'

Agnes sighed. Maybe Christa had a point. 'It's just I'm no help to you with this vampire stuff,' Agnes said. 'It's formulaic genre fiction.'

'You would be of more help to me with my *childhood*?'

'Well, with more serious stories, yes.'

Christa stood up, perturbed. She grabbed her paperback. 'You with all your Alice Walker and Zora Hurston. I'm not interested in that anymore. I've done that already. I read those books years ago.'

'Christa, please don't be annoyed.' *Please do not talk when Mr Stauffbacher is talking.*

'You've got this agenda for me.'

'Really, I don't at all,' said Agnes. 'It's just that – you know what it is? It's that I'm sick of these vampires. They're so roaming and repeating.'

'If you were black, what you're saying might have a different spin. But the fact is you're not,' Christa said, and picked up her coat and strode out – though ten seconds later she gamely stuck her head back in and said, 'See you next week.'

'We need a visiting writer who's black,' Agnes said in the next depart mental meeting. 'We've never had one.'

They were looking at their budget, and the readings this year were pitted against Dance Instruction, a program headed up by a redhead named Evergreen.

'The Joffrey is just so much central casting,' said Evergreen, apropos of nothing. As a vacuum cleaner can start to pull up the actual thread of a carpet, her brains had been sucked dry by too much yoga. No one paid much attention to her.

'Perhaps we can get Harold Raferson in Chicago,' Agnes suggested.

'We've already got somebody for the visiting writer slot,' said Stauffbacher coyly. 'An Afrikaner from Johannesburg.'

'What?' said Agnes. Was he serious? Even Evergreen barked out a laugh.

'W.S. Beyerbach. The university's bringing him in. We pay our four hundred dollars and we get him out here for a day and a half.'

'Who?' asked Evergreen.

'This has already been decided?' asked Agnes.

'Yup.' Stauffbacher looked accusingly at Agnes. 'I've done a lot of work to arrange for this. *I've* done all the work!'

'Do less,' said Evergreen.

W hen Agnes had first met Joe, they'd fallen madly upon each other. They'd kissed in restaurants; they'd groped under coats at the movies. At his little house they'd made love on the porch, or the landing of the staircase, against the wall in the hall, by the door to the attic, filled with too much desire to make their way to a real room.

Now they struggled self-consciously for atmosphere, something they'd never needed before. She prepared the bedroom carefully. She played quiet music and concentrated. She lit candles – as if she were in church praying for the deceased. She donned a filmy gown. She took hot baths and entered the bedroom in nothing but a towel, a wild fish-like creature of moist, perfumed heat. In the nightstand drawer she still kept the charts a doctor once told her to keep, still placed an X on any date she and Joe actually had sex. But she could never show these to her doctor, not now. It pained Agnes to see them. She and Joe looked like worse than bad shots. She and Joe looked like idiots. She and Joe looked dead.

Frantic candlelight flickered on the ceiling like a puppet show. While she waited for Joe to come out of the bathroom, Agnes lay back on the bed and thought about her week, the stupid politics of it – the Arts Hall, the Transportation Commission, all those loud, smacking collisions of public good and private power. She was not very good at politics. Once, before he was elected, she had gone to a rally for Bill Clinton, but when he was late and had kept the crowd waiting for over an hour, and when the sun got hot and bees began landing on people's heads, when everyone's feet hurt, and tiny children began to cry, and a state assemblyman stepped forward to announce that Clinton had stopped at a Dairy Queen in Des Moines and that was why he was late – Dairy Queen! – she had grown angry and resentful and apolitical in her own sweet-starved thirst and she'd joined in with some other people who had started to chant, 'Do us a favor, tell us the flavor.'

Through college she had been a feminist – more or less. She shaved her legs, *but just not often enough,* she liked to say. She signed day-care petitions and petitions for Planned Parenthood. And although she had never been very socially aggressive with men, she felt strongly that she knew the difference between feminism and Sadie Hawkins Day – which some people, she believed, did not.

'Agnes, are we out of toothpaste or is this it? – Oh, OK, I see.'

And once, in New York, she had quixotically organized the ladies'-room line at the Brooks Atkinson Theater. Because the play was going to start any minute, and the line was still twenty women long, she had got six women to walk across the lobby with her to the men's room. 'Everybody out of there?' she'd called in timidly, allowing the men to finish up first, which took a while, especially with other men coming up impatiently and cutting ahead in line. Later at intermission, she saw how it should have been done. Two elderly black women, with greater expertise in civil rights, stepped very confidently into the men's room and called out, 'Don't mind us, boys. We're coming on in. Don't mind us.'

'Are you OK?' asked Joe, smiling. He was already beside her. He smelled sweet, of soap and minty teeth, like a child.

'I think so,' she said and turned toward him in the bordello light of their room. He had never acquired the look of maturity-anchored-in-sorrow that burnished so many men's faces. His own sadnesses in life – a childhood of beatings, a dying mother – were like quicksand, and he had to stay away from them entirely. He permitted no unhappy memories spoken aloud. He stuck with the same mild cheerfulness he'd honed successfully as a boy, and it made him seem fatuous – even, she knew, to himself. Probably it hurt his business a little.

'Your mind's wandering,' he said, letting his own eyes close.

'I know.' She yawned, moved her legs onto his for warmth, and in this way, with the candles burning into their tins, she and Joe fell asleep.

Spring arrived, cool and humid. Bulbs cracked and sprouted, shot up their green periscopes, and on April 1 the Arts Hall offered a joke lecture by T.S. Eliot, visiting scholar. 'The Crudest Month', it was called. 'You don't find it funny?' asked Stauffbacher.

April 4 was the reception for W.S. Beyerbach. There was to be a dinner afterward, and then Beyerbach was to visit Agnes's Great Books class. She had assigned his second collection of sonnets, which were spare and elegant, with sighing and diaphanous politics. The next afternoon there was to be a reading.

Agnes had not been invited to the dinner, and when she asked about this, in a mildly forlorn way, Stauffbacher shrugged as if it were totally out of his hands. 'I'm a *published poet*,' Agnes wanted to say. She had had a poem published once – in the *Gizzard Review*, but still!

'It was Edie Canterton's list,' Stauffbacher said. 'I had nothing to do with it.'

She went to the reception anyway, annoyed, and when she planted herself like a splayed and storm-torn tree near the cheese, she could feel the crackers she was eating forming a bad paste in her mouth and she became afraid to smile. When she finally introduced herself to W.S. Beyerbach, she stumbled on her own name and actually pronounced it 'On-yez'.

'On-yez,' repeated Beyerbach in a quiet Englishy voice. Condescending, she thought. His hair was blond and white, like a palomino, and his eyes were blue and scornful as mints. She could see he was a withheld man; although some might say *shy*, she decided it was *withheld*: a lack of generosity. Passive-aggressive. It was causing the people around him to squirm and nervously improvise remarks. He would simply nod, the smile on his face faint and vaguely pharmaceutical. Everything about him was tight and coiled as a doorspring. From living in *that country*, thought Agnes. How could he live in that country?

Stauffbacher was trying to talk heartily about the mayor. Something about his old progressive ideas and the forthcoming convention center. Agnes thought of her own meetings on the Transportation Commission, of the mayor's leash law for cats, of his new squadron of meter maids and bicycle police, of a councilman the mayor once slugged in a bar. 'Now, of course, the mayor's become a fascist,' said Agnes in a voice that sounded strangely loud, bright with anger.

Silence fell in the room. Edie Canterton stopped stirring the punch. Agnes looked around. 'Oh,' she said. 'Are we not supposed to used *that word* in this room?' Beyerbach's expression went blank. Agnes's face burned in confusion.

Stauffbacher looked pained, then stricken. 'More cheese, anyone?' he asked, holding up the silver tray.

After everyone left for dinner, she went by herself to the Dunk 'N Dine across the street. She ordered a California BLT and a cup of coffee, and looked over Beyerbach's work again: dozens of images of broken, rotten bodies, of the body's mutinies and betrayals, of the body's strange housekeeping and illicit pets. At the front of the book was a dedication – *To D.F.B. (1970–1989).* Who could that be? A political activist maybe, 'a woman who had thrown aside the unseasonal dress of hope' only to look for it again 'in the blood-blooming shrubs'. Perhaps if Agnes got a chance, she would ask him. Why not? A book was a public thing, and its dedication was part of it. If it was too personal a question for him, tough. She would find the right time, she decided, paying the check and putting on her jacket, crossing the street to the Hall. She would wait for the moment, then seize it.

He was already at the front door when she arrived. He greeted her with a stiff smile and a soft 'Hello, On-yez'. His accent made her own voice ring coarse and country-western.

She smiled and then blurted, 'I have a question to ask you.' Her voice sounded like Johnny Cash's.

Beyerbach said nothing, only held the door open for her and then followed her into the building.

She continued as they stepped slowly up the stairs. 'May I ask you who your book is dedicated to?'

At the top of the stairs they turned left down the long corridor. She could feel his steely reserve, his lip biting, his shyness no doubt garbed and rationalized with snobbery, but so much snobbery to handle all that shyness that he could not possibly be a meaningful critic of his country. She was angry with him. *How can you live in that country?* she wanted again to say, although she remembered when someone once said that to her – a Danish man, on Agnes's senior trip abroad to Copenhagen. It was during the Vietnam War, and the man had stared meanly, righteously. 'The United States: how can you live in that country?' the man had asked. Agnes had shrugged. 'A lot of my stuff is there,' she said, and it was only then that she first felt all the dark love and shame that came from the pure accident of home, the deep and arbitrary place that happened to be yours.

'It's dedicated to my son,' Beyerbach said finally.

He would not look at her, but stared straight ahead along the corridor floor. Now Agnes's shoes sounded very loud.

'You lost a son,' she said.

'Yes,' he said. He looked away, at the passing wall, past Stauffbacher's bulletin board, past the men's room, the women's room, some sternness in him broken, and when he turned back she could see his eyes filling with water, his face reddened with unbearable pressure.

'I'm so sorry,' Agnes said.

They walked side by side, their footsteps echoing down the corridor toward her classroom. All the anxieties she felt with this mournfully quiet man now mimicked the anxieties of love. What should she say? It must be the most unendurable thing to lose a child. Shouldn't he say something of this? It was his turn to say something.

But he would not. And when they finally reached the classroom, she turned to him in the doorway and, taking a package from her purse, said simply, in a reassuring way, 'We always have cookies in class.'

Now he beamed at her with such relief that she knew she had for once said the right thing. It filled her with affection for him – perhaps, she thought, that's where affection begins: in an unlikely phrase, in a moment of someone's having unexpectedly but at last said the right thing. *We always have cookies in class.*

She introduced him with a bit of flourish and biography. Positions held, universities attended. The students raised their hands and asked him about apartheid, about shanty towns and homelands, and he answered succinctly, after long sniffs and pauses, only once referring to a question as 'unanswerably fey', causing the student to squirm and fish around in her purse for something, nothing, Kleenex perhaps. Beyerbach did not seem to notice. He went on, speaking of censorship: how a person must work hard not to internalize a government's program of censorship, since what a government would like best is for you to do it yourself; how he himself was not sure he had not succumbed. Afterward, a few students stayed and shook his hand, formally, awkwardly, then left. Christa was the last. She too shook his hand and then started chatting amiably. They knew someone in common – Harold Raferson in Chicago! – and as Agnes quickly wiped the seminar table to clear it of cookie crumbs, she tried to listen but couldn't really hear. She made a small pile of crumbs and swept them into one hand.

'Goodnight,' sang out Christa when she left.

'Goodnight, Christa,' said Agnes, brushing the crumbs off her hand and into the wastebasket.

She straightened and stood with Beyerbach in the empty classroom. 'Thank you so much,' she said, finally, in a hushed way. 'I'm sure they all got quite a lot out of that. I'm very sure they did.'

He said nothing but smiled at her gently.

She shifted her weight from one leg to the other. 'Would you like to go somewhere and get a drink?' she asked. She was standing close to him, looking up into his face. He was tall, she saw now. His shoulders weren't broad, but he had a youthful straightness to his carriage. She briefly touched his sleeve. His suit coat was corduroy and bore a faint odor of clove. This was the first time in her life that she had ever asked a man out for a drink.

He made no move to step away from her; he actually seemed to lean toward her a bit. She could feel his dry breath, see up close the variously hued spokes of his irises, the grays and yellows in the blue. There was a sprinkling of small freckles near his hairline. He smiled, then looked at the clock on the wall. 'I would love to, really, but I have to get back to the hotel to make a phone call at ten-fifteen.' He looked a little disappointed – not a lot, thought Agnes, but certainly a *little*. She would have bet money on it.

'Oh, well,' she said. She flicked off the lights, and in the dark he carefully helped her on with her jacket. They stepped out of the room and walked together in silence, back down the corridor to the front entrance of the Hall. Outside on the steps the night was balmy and scented with rain. 'Will you be all right walking back to your hotel?' she asked. 'Or –'

'Oh, yes, thank you. It's just around the corner.'

'Right. That's right. Well, my car's parked way over there. So, I guess I'll see you tomorrow afternoon at your reading.'

'Yes,' he said. 'I shall look forward to that.'

'Yes,' she said. 'So shall I.'

The reading was in the large meeting room at the Arts Hall and was from the sonnet book she had already read, but it was nice to hear the poems again in his hushed, pained tenor. She sat in the back row, her green raincoat sprawled beneath her on the seat like a large leaf. She leaned forward on to the seat ahead of her, her back an angled stem, her chin on double fists, and she listened like that for some time. At one point she closed her eyes, but the image of him before her, standing straight as a compass needle, remained caught there beneath her lids, like a burn or a speck or a message from the mind.

Afterward, moving away from the lectern, Beyerbach spotted her and waved, but Stauffbacher, like a tugboat with a task, took his arm and steered him elsewhere, over toward the side table with the little plastic cups and warm Pepsi. *We are both men*, the gesture seemed to say. *We both have* bach *in our names*. Agnes put on her green coat. She went over toward the Pepsi table and stood. She drank a warm Pepsi, then placed the empty cup back on the table. Beyerbach finally turned toward her and smiled familiarly. She thrust out her hand. 'It was a wonderful reading,' she said. 'I'm very glad I got the chance to meet you.' She gripped his long, slender palm and locked thumbs. She could feel the bones in him.

'Thank you,' he said. He looked at her coat in a worried way. 'You're leaving?'

She looked down at her coat. 'I'm afraid I have to get going home.' She wasn't sure whether she really had to or not. But she'd put on her coat, and it now seemed an awkward thing to take it off.

'Oh,' he murmured, gazing at her intently. 'Well, all best wishes to you, On-yez.'

'Excuse me?' There was some clattering near the lectern.

'All best to you,' he said, something retreating in his expression.

Stauffbacher suddenly appeared at her side, scowling at her green coat, as if it were incomprehensible.

'Yes,' said Agnes, stepping backward, then forward again to shake Beyerbach's hand once more; it was a beautiful hand, like an old and expensive piece of wood. 'Same to you,' she said. Then she turned and fled.

For several nights she did not sleep well. She placed her face directly into her pillow, then turned it for some air, then flipped over to her back and opened her eyes, staring past the stark angle of the door frame at the far end of the room toward the tiny light from the bathroom which illuminated the hallway, faintly, as if someone had just been there.

For several days she thought perhaps he might have left her a note with the secretary, or that he might send her one from an airport somewhere. She thought that the inadequacy of their goodbye would haunt him too, and that he might send her a postcard as elaboration.

But he did not. Briefly she thought about writing him a letter, on Arts Hall stationery, which for money reasons was no longer the stationery but photocopies of the stationery. She knew he had flown to the West Coast, then off to Tokyo, then Sydney, then back to Johannesburg, and if she posted it now, perhaps he would receive it when he arrived. She could tell him once more how interesting it had been to meet him. She could enclose her poem from the *Gizzard*

Review. She had read in the newspaper an article about bereavement – and if she were her own mother she would have sent him that too.

Thank God, thank God, she was not her mother.

M ay settled firmly into Cassell with a spate of thunder showers. The perennials – the myrtle and grape hyacinths – blossomed around the town in a kind of civic blue, and the warming air brought forth an occasional mosquito or fly. The Transportation Commission meetings were dreary and long, too often held during the dinner hour, and when Agnes got home she would replay them for Joe, weeping about the photo radar and the widening interstate.

When her mother called, Agnes got off the phone fast. When her sister, Linnea, now in Minneapolis, called about their mother, Agnes got off the phone even faster. Joe rubbed her shoulders and spoke to her of carports, of curb appeal, of mortgage rates and asbestos-wrapped pipes.

At the Arts Hall she taught and fretted and continued to receive the usual memos from the secretary, written on the usual scrap paper – except that the scrap paper, for a while, consisted of the extra posters for the Beyerbach reading. She would get a long disquisition on policies and procedures concerning summer registration and she would turn it over, and there would be his face – sad and pompous in the photograph. She would get a simple phone message – 'Your husband called. Please call him at the office' – and on the back would be the ripped center of Beyerbach's nose, one minty eye, an elbowish chin. Eventually there were no more, and the scrap paper moved on to old contest announcements, grant deadlines, Easter concert notices.

At night she and Joe did yoga to a yoga show on TV. It was part of their effort not to become their parents, though marriage, they knew, held that hazard. The functional disenchantment, the sweet habit of each other, had begun to put lines around her mouth, lines that looked like quotation marks – as if everything she said had already been said before. Sometimes their old cat, Madeline, a fat and pampered calico reaping the benefits of life with a childless couple

during their childbearing years, came and plopped herself down
with them, between them. She was accustomed to much nestling
and appreciation and drips from the faucet, though sometimes she
would vanish outside, and they would not see her for days, only to spy
her later, in the yard, dirty and matted, chomping a vole or eating
old snow.

For Memorial Day weekend Agnes flew with Joe to New York, to
show him the city for the first time. 'A place,' she said, 'where
if you're not white or not born there, it's no big deal. You're not
automatically a story.' She had grown annoyed with Iowa, the pathetic,
third-hand manner in which the large issues and conversations of the
world were encountered there. The oblique and tired way history
obligingly insinuated itself. If ever. She longed to be a citizen of
the globe!

They roller-skated in Central Park. They looked in the Lord &
Taylor windows. They went to the Joffrey. They went to a hair salon
on Fifty-seventh Street, and there she had her hair dyed a vibrant red.
They sat in the window booth of a coffee shop and got coffee refills
and ate pie.

'So much seems the same,' she said to Joe. 'When I lived here,
everyone was hustling for money. The rich were. The poor were.
But everyone tried hard to be funny. Everywhere you went – a
store, a facial place – someone was telling a joke. A good one.' She
remembered it had made any given day seem bearable, that impulse
toward a joke. It had been a determined sort of humor, an intensity
mirroring the intensity of the city, and it seemed to embrace and
alleviate the hard sadness of people using each other and marring the
earth the way they did. 'It was like brains having sex. It was like every
brain was a sex maniac.' She looked down at her pie. 'People really
worked at it, the laughing,' she said. 'People need to laugh.'

'They do,' said Joe. He took a swig of coffee, his lips out over the
cup in a fleshy flower. He was afraid she might cry – she was getting
that look again – and if she did, he would feel guilty and lost and sorry

for her that her life was not here anymore but in a far and boring place with him. He set the cup down and tried to smile. 'They sure do,' he said. And he looked out the window at the rickety taxis, the oystery garbage and tubercular air, seven pounds of chicken giblets dumped on the curb in front of the coffee shop where they were. He turned back to her and made the face of a clown.

'What are you doing?' she asked.

'It's a clown face.'

'What do you mean, a clown face?' Someone behind her was singing 'I Love New York', and for the first time she noticed the strange irresolution of the tune.

'A regular clown face is what I mean.'

'It didn't look like that.'

'No? What did it look like?'

'You want me to do the face?'

'Yeah, do the face.'

She looked at Joe. Every arrangement in life carried with it the sadness, the sentimental shadow, of its not being something else but only itself. She attempted the face – a look of such monstrous emptiness and stupidity that Joe burst into a howling sort of laughter, like a dog, and then so did she, air exploding through her nose in a snort, her head thrown forward, then back, then forward again, setting loose a fit of coughing.

'Are you OK?' asked Joe, and she nodded. Out of politeness he looked away, outside, where it had suddenly started to rain. Across the street two people had planted themselves under the window ledge of a Gap store, trying to stay dry, waiting out the downpour, their figures dark and scarecrowish against the lit window display. When he turned back to his wife – oh, his sad, young wife – to point this out to her, to show her what was funny to a man firmly in the grip of middle age, she was still bent sideways in her seat so that her face fell below the line of the table, and he could only see the curve of her heaving back, the fuzzy penumbra of her thin spring sweater, and the garish top of her bright, new and terrible hair. ∎

Save up to
37%

Subscribe to the joy of print

Subscribe to The Guardian and The Observer and you'll keep finding more to share with your family and friends. If you're looking to impress the foodie in your life, our brilliant supplements offer recipes, restaurant reviews and more. And you can pass our award-winning sport writing to your favourite football fanatic. Plus our quality, independent coverage of major events is perfect for people who care about the world around them.

When you subscribe, you can save up to 37% on the price of your newspapers - all year round.

Your newsagent won't miss out on a penny, either. With our voucher subscription, they'll receive the same amount as they would if you'd paid for your paper in cash.

Package	Newsstand price	Subscription rate	Saving
Everyday	£17.40	£10.99	37%
Monday to Saturday	£14.20	£9.49	33%
Weekend	£6.40	£4.79	25%

Prices above are weekly. Savings calculation is savings made per week against the retail price.

Become a Guardian and Observer subscriber from just £4.79 a week

Visit gu.com/granta2019
or call 0330 333 6767

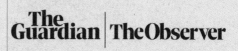

The Guardian | The Observer

NADINE AT FORTY

Hilary Mantel

GRANTA 56: WINTER 1996

Thomas arrived unexpectedly, jolting up the hill in the dust-covered taxi. She paid the fare, and he stayed for the summer. They chose to make love in that hushed grey hour which, in hot climates, can be taken for dawn or dusk. They slept till noon, and then, perfunctorily washed, yawned onto the small side terrace, where they were screened from human eyes. They took their bread and coffee here, overlooking the hillside that tumbled down to the sea. When Dea brought the tray she averted her eyes from the sun-flushed triangle at the neck of his robe, and turned away even more pointedly from the sight of her employer's body, slack and naked under silk.

After the first few days a new routine began. Dea would anticipate them, hurrying the tray to the table the second she heard the click of the latch of their bedroom door. Their breakfast would be waiting for them, as if placed by invisible hands. Sometimes they missed the maid so narrowly that the click of her sandals on the tiles was still fading when he reached out to take an orange from the basket, or her hungry fingers tore into crust and crumb.

The sea moved far below, a purplish blue.

When he left, in the autumn, she discovered that he had tampered with all the clocks. She hurried from room to room, incredulous. Some were running slow. Some had stopped altogether. She had to pack them in straw and take them to the town, where the man in the shop looked at her as if he judged her insane. 'All of these?' he asked in careful English. 'Each one of these requires to be mended?'

'Each one,' she said. 'You can see they all show different times.'

As she left the shop, the man said something to his wife, who was dusting shelves very slowly in the shadows at the back. It was something satirical that she didn't quite catch. His attitude is ridiculous, she thought. Surely he could understand that there must be one consistent time in every room of a house?

Ah, she thought: an Anglo-Saxon attitude.

All the clocks were restored, except her grandmother's tiny drawing-room clock, the clock that had tinkled so gently for tea during years of Kensington twilights, at the hour when the sky had seemed to lower itself and rest tentatively on the treetops of Cornwall Gardens. It was a clock with a china case, roses of china strewn at its base, gilt fingers now indicating seven thirty. She knew, by this, at what hour he had done the deed. But in the morning, or the evening?

Neither seemed possible. At seven in the morning Dea was already in the kitchen, or sweeping the long terrace with a monotonous whisper of brushstrokes that broke into her sleep, transforming itself to the sound of steam trains, of waterfalls. At seven in the evening she herself would be walking from room to room, glass in hand, laughing, her silly skirts flouncing over the polished floors. But perhaps it was at some earlier hour – four o'clock? – that he had picked and probed at the tiny balances and springs . . . so that then the hands would falter, hesitate, move feebly for an hour or two, with less and less conviction, until finally, with a delicate shudder, they came to rest. Pre-dawn, then; he worked while she slept, his rather broad, coarse feet padding the tiles, and the moon a curving hoof, a lively bone, hooking at an open shutter for a chink to gain admission.

She missed the clock's silvery chime, and the loss made her peevish. Anyway it was time to go. The mornings were misty; the fires smoked, and Dea sulked at having to lay them. She packed her bags and closed the house till spring.

In June, unexpectedly, Thomas was back again. You could not say he had changed, except that there was a tension at the outer corner of each eye and the outer corner of each lip. She noticed this tension and saw how, in a year or two, his expression would harden. Age does not creep up, she thought, like a cat burglar – age fells you suddenly. She remembered when she had learned this, the shock it had delivered.

She was seventeen then. On a spree with her schoolgirl's allowance, in the curtained changing room of a London store; out-striding the black-clad women who would have helped her, making clear with a pout and a toss of her head that she would rather be alone with herself, a Narcissa, staring into the triple silver pool of the long mirrors. She recalled the minute click as she dropped onto a gilt hook the hangers of the experimental clothes. A swish of satin; her own frock dropped onto a chair. She saw the turn of her shoulder, ivory polished; her back's long curve.

As she raised her chin to admire herself, an overhead bulb, its rays like a ghost's baton, struck a glancing blow across her face. Gaping, she spun around; her future, in triplicate, bounced at her from the walls. It was a second, a fraction of a second, that Nadine was lost and gone – then her youth slipped back into her, attentive, poised, graceful like a dancer in a line.

But what she had seen, she could not unsee. There was a deep shadow under her chin. There were cavities gouged in the flesh, running from nose to mouth. There were marks under her eyes, as if a fist had made them.

Good morning, the face had said: I am Nadine at forty.

She had left the cubicle in a rush, hastily buttoning her pulled-on frock with one hand, while with the other she thrust into the salesgirl's arms a bundle of gaping bodices and fighting sleeves, of trailing belts and seams indecently turned out. Well, she said, scrutinising herself now, I have passed forty, and it is not so bad; it is not so bad as all that.

There was a house party that year. Thomas sulked, scrambling each morning down to the crescent of shingle to kick at stones. If she had known he was coming, she would not have invited anyone else; both of them knew this.

'Be kind to my friends,' she said. 'You are too old to sulk.'

'You are just too old,' he said.

Etienne was one of her guests. She especially wished she had not asked him; or that he had come alone, for a short visit which would have been in the nature of a rest-cure. In the war, Etienne had been in a camp. He had been at Drancy, and then he was moved east. Sometimes he talked about his arrest and about an unknown person who had betrayed him, but he never talked about what came after that.

Etienne was not a bitter man. But he was aloof and dry. The shadow of what he left unsaid hovered always about his jaw and darkened it, like a nomad bruise, a cloud. His eyes, too, seemed drained of colour, and he kept his hair clipped short, shaved almost, as if in obedience to some harsh regime that might one day march its soldiers south. He ate little, even after dark when it was cool. Something was wrong: he had suffered a digestive disorder, an ulcer of some kind, or perhaps it was typhoid. 'I keep best on bread and milk,' he said, 'the bread not too fresh.' He smiled a little. Dea started to keep rolls for him, yesterday's baking, which once she would have taken home to her children.

Thomas said, turning over in bed, 'That man I hate. He casts a pall of gloom.'

'A long time ago, Etienne's family and my family were friends,' she said.

He said, 'He might at least shave properly.'
She said, 'Why did you stop the clocks?'
He said, 'You know why.'

Her orgasms were regular, each night an efficient fleshly replica of the night before. She wondered about this and decided that, strangely, Thomas was more adept at dealing with the female body than with a clockwork mechanism. There should be more such men, she said, smiling to herself in the glass, pretending to share a crude joke with a female friend.

'One day,' Etienne said, 'sometime in the next century, we will all die, all of us survivors.'

She looked at him for a moment without speaking because she didn't understand what he meant. How can survivors die?

'And there will be no more of our convocations,' he said. 'No more assemblies of the walking dead. No more waking in the night. No more of this weeping and praying. We will be extinguished. We will be forgotten.'

'But you can't be forgotten,' she said. 'They have written books, made films. They have interviewed everyone and recorded what they say. They have opened the camps as museums. You can go to see them. There is a whole room full of shoes. I have seen pictures of it.'

'But I want us to be forgotten,' he said. 'It is a great error to believe the Nazis lost the war. For us, you see, they won it, and they win it each day. Each day we re-enact, on ourselves, what was done to us. They are the masters of our hours, and we are their obedient servants. Our ageing is a war, a long war, and each successive death will be a small victory. Each death will go to the wiping out of their triumph.'

'If you thought that . . .'

'Yes, Nadine?'

'The logical way –'

'Yes, of course. So many do. It is put down as falls on staircases. Sometimes as automobile accidents.'

S tifling August. Thomas said, 'I really want this to last forever.'
Sheets bunched under his body. Her sweat drying. Four in
the afternoon; the garden silent. A tap running somewhere, Dea's
tuneless hum from below, and the scent of falling lilies heavy as spice.

He said, 'You are no company, this summer, Nadine.'

'No.' She frowned. 'Perhaps not.'

'You are absent. Self-absorbed. Gone down the hill to play on the
shingle.'

'Well . . .' She frowned. 'There are things to think about.'

'So suddenly! And so little practice as you've had.'

'You must not –'

Not totally humiliate me, she had been going to say. He cut in on
her. 'You have fallen in love with Etienne.'

'No.' He confused her: was this an accusation or a joke? 'I have
some choices, but that is not one. Etienne has no future.'

'And you have one?' He was laughing. 'Oh, Nadine – and I stopped
your clocks to preserve your past. How ungrateful you are!'

T he days shortened. The guests went away. Birdsong grew
shriller, sharpened, and the air seemed used. This time Thomas
left without touching the clocks. Each hour was in its proper place.
No arrangements had been made for next year. Finding herself alone,
she stared into the mirror, trying to conjure out the woman behind it,
the woman she had seen so briefly in the changing room – trying to
will her into life. Nadine at sixty, she said to herself. ∎

The cortège at Scratchwood services on the M1 motorway

THOSE WHO FELT
DIFFERENTLY

Ian Jack

GRANTA 60: WINTER 1997

The last day of August, a Sunday, eight in the morning. Like many people in Britain, I was asleep. The bedside radio came on. A solemn voice, a plain sentence or two, the tune of 'God Save the Queen' played at its most mournful pitch. (There are two versions of the British national anthem kept at every radio station: solemn and triumphant.)

'Did you hear that?' said my partner, who was waking beside me.

I had. The BBC had done a fine job on our slumbering reflexes. The news was more than merely important or shocking – a plane crash, an IRA bomb. Its delivery evoked feelings more awkward than sadness and surprise. The national memory was being awoken; the story that the nation tells about itself. And because the national memory has become increasingly blurred and contested, it was interesting to discover the old version still alive in oneself, to realise how much of it one knew and felt bound up with. Reflexively, I thought of the pre-war prime minister Neville Chamberlain and his tight little speech on the radio on another Sunday morning – in September 1939 – which disclosed that Britain was at war with Germany: 'I am speaking to you from the Cabinet Room at Number Ten Downing Street.' It was ridiculous to think of this. It happened six years before I was born; and Britain, on 31 August 1997, was not at war with Germany, with anyone (though for a day or two the enemy was identified as freelance photographers, helpfully known by a foreign word, the paparazzi). But the happenings that come into the category of supreme national moments have a grammar of their own, literally so. The BBC announcer usually said, 'You're listening to BBC Radio 4,' but that morning he said, 'This is the BBC,' and with that small reversion from modern, market-minded informality to old-fashioned authority so the death of the Princess of Wales became linked to Mr Chamberlain, air raids on the Ruhr (six of our aircraft are missing), the conquest of Everest, the Falklands War.

Or at least it did in my half-awake mind, not that I noticed the reason at the time. My partner said: 'I feel so sorry for those poor boys.'

We went downstairs and watched television. Eventually the prime minister, Tony Blair, came on and spoke for the first time of 'the People's Princess'. Some journalists later wrote that the phrase had been invented for the occasion by Blair's press secretary (which may well be true, his press secretary having previously worked in tabloid newspapers), but at the time it seemed to fall quite naturally in his statement, in which emotion seemed to battle with articulacy. I write 'seemed' but that does not mean I doubted his sincerity; it was just that, having followed his election campaign, I knew how well he could deploy sincerity in his well-considered outbreaks of spontaneity.

We had lunch. My partner explained to our five-year-old daughter that the princess had died. Our daughter asked: 'Is that the woman you said was awful?' We wondered where we should take the children in the afternoon. The television had pictures of people outside Buckingham Palace, some of them crying. We remembered that the pond in St James's Park had ducks, and that this part of London – central, royal, institutional London – can be enjoyed by the people who live in London as well as by the tourists who have claimed it and made it their own. Also, we were curious – who were these people who had gone to the palace? – but I do not think coldly inquisitive. We were perhaps just a little sad.

We drove. The traffic was thick. The Mall had been closed to all but pedestrians. We parked the car near the monument to the Duke of York and walked down the steps and into the Mall. Whenever I drive down this avenue – always in a car or a taxi; nothing so vulgar as a bus route pollutes it – I am always surprised to see Buckingham Palace, the memorial to Queen Victoria, Horse Guards Parade, the minor palaces and mansions, the statues of explorers, the friezes of army regiments, the sentry boxes, the immobile sentries in scarlet uniforms and black bearskin hats. My surprise is that I live in the same city, so close to this fabled history which in my childhood looked so grand and far away and could only be represented in my home with model soldiers. And yet (another surprise when one investigates it) the setting is not so very historical. There are people still alive who can remember this imperial cityscape under construction. My own father, had he lived in London at that time, could have watched as a boy as masons chiselled the Portland stone of the new facade to Buckingham Palace (finished in 1913), or the bronze statue to Captain Cook (1914) was unveiled, or Admiralty Arch (1910) had its keystones put in place. He could have been there on the day in 1911 when King George V stood beside the new Queen Victoria Memorial and tapped its designer on the shoulder with a sword, transforming him into a knight: Sir Thomas Brock. And then this small boy, my father, could have turned and walked down the new Mall, with its plane trees, flagpoles and galleon-topped lamp posts, which was widened to make a processional route and pushed through to Trafalgar Square in the same year.

This, then, is a twentieth-century stage, post-Victorian, the whole planned as a tribute to the dead queen; as traditional and historic as the machine gun or an early Mercedes.

We did not go to the palace directly. We crossed the Mall and went into the park. How would I describe the situation here? I would say it was normal. The afternoon was fine. Tourists strolled around the lake, young people with backpacks scattered bread for the ducks. For a time, our children stood on the bridge and threw pebbles into the water. A pair of handsome swans and some cygnets slid by. Then, as we lay on the grass, I noticed a little black girl in a bed of roses. She had scissors in her right hand and a small bundle of rose blooms in her left. She was snipping more blooms cleanly and quietly.

I went across to her.

'You know you shouldn't be doing that, don't you?'

'Yes,' she said, 'I know.' Her scissors went on snipping.

A quandary for the civic-minded. She might have a father, or several tough brothers, out of sight behind a tree. I summoned some courage.

'Well, don't do it then.'

She skipped off up the slope to the Mall, where she ran alongside the people who were walking towards the palace and looked up into their faces and offered her flowers. As nobody took them, money may have been involved. She was too far away to hear.

We saw her again among the crowd – then still small – which had gathered in front of the palace railings. She was with a woman, probably her mother, who looked like a Somali. The roses had gone; they must have been on the pile, but the crowd was too thick in front of the flowers to see. The Somali woman stood reverently, I thought, near a mounted policeman who was guiding the flower-bringers to a route which ran along the front of the railings to the place where their flowers could be left. People were arriving with bunches every couple of minutes. The people without flowers looked at these people with flowers. They were the spectacle; there was nothing much else to see. The palace yard was empty apart from the sentries, who occasionally stamped and banged their rifles down and picked them up again, and the palace as usual presented its blank, mysterious face to the world. If the Queen and her family had been at home, it would have looked the same – she does not come to the windows and wave, toodle-oo – but in any case the Queen and her family were on their Scottish holidays in Balmoral.

Further off, behind the Victoria Memorial, hot-dog and ice-cream sellers and television crews had parked their vans. On the memorial itself, men in T-shirts had begun to set up scaffolding for television cameras, their steel tubes rattling on the marble, of which the memorial contains 2,300 tons. We climbed the steps towards Queen Victoria, who is seated, but measures thirteen feet high, and is surrounded by allegorical figures. Above her, winged *Victory* with *Courage* and *Constancy* at *Victory*'s feet. Beside her, *Trust* facing south, *Justice* north and *Charity* west. The queen herself faces east, away from the palace and down the Mall towards her city, her empire, her people.

I had never been here before. It was fascinating; how unlikely it was that one small woman in one small country could represent so much universal principle, at least in the eyes of Sir Thomas Brock. People leaned in the sun on the memorial's balconies and, though I overheard one or two quiet conversations about the dead princess, their behaviour suggested attitudes like our own. They licked ice cream. They were perhaps a little sad, but mainly they seemed curious. Later on television we would all be described as mourners. Meanwhile, pole by pole, the television platforms rose up towards *Charity* and the two marble children she clutched at her knee.

We walked back down the Mall. I noticed that many people going the other way and carrying flowers were black or brown, Africans and African Caribbeans, Asians. I remembered how sixteen years before I had been a reporter at the princess's wedding and how, walking the processional route between the palace and St Paul's, I had seen very few black faces in the crowds. I now remembered writing that, and also a remark about the national anthem being a rotten tune, which had been circled on the galley proofs by the paper's editor with a line drawn to his note in the margin: *No, a jolly good tune in my opinion!*

It seemed long ago; the post-war height of the monarchy's popularity, when newspapers thought royalty could do no wrong and there was a frenzy of good wishes in the streets. We drove home through a city which had changed since then, and (I thought, that day) in some ways for the better.

Later that night the telephone rang. It was a friend who edits a weekly magazine. Could I write 2,500 words on Diana by the next evening?

'But I don't know anything about her,' I said. 'What could I write about?'

'You know – Diana the Icon,' he said.

'The Icon? How do you mean?'

'You know – the clothes, the busted marriage, bulimia, landmines, Aids, all those things. What she meant to us all.'

No, I said, I didn't really think I could.

'Look at it another way,' he said, 'it's worth the price of a new kitchen.'

A new kitchen! Even cheap ones, I thought, came in at about £6,000. And perhaps my friend was thinking bigger than that, somewhere up in the Smallbone range.

A kitchen for 2,500 words. In such small ways does an event become a phenomenon.

September was not a good month for those who imagined that human society is, or might one day be, governed by reason. After the People's Princess came the People's Mall, the People's Funeral, the People's Earl (Spencer), the People's Europe, the People's Television Channel (BBC1), all of them promoted and discussed without irony. In London, a man applied to the International Star Registry to have a star in the Andromeda constellation named 'Diana – the People's Princess' (another application wanted a star in the Lyra constellation named 'Dodi and Diana – Eternally Loved'). The leader of the Conservative Party, William Hague, suggested that Heathrow Airport be renamed Diana Airport. The Chancellor of the Exchequer, Gordon Brown, was said to be seriously considering a proposal that the August Bank Holiday be renamed Diana Day. Letters to newspapers made other suggestions for the renaming of hospitals and coins, for statues, for fountains, for special stamps. Three foreign tourists were sentenced to jail for taking old teddy bears from the tributes to the princess which had been heaped on various pavements (none in fact served their sentences, but one was punched by an onlooker on leaving the court). The wholesale price of flowers rose by 25 per cent in the London markets, despite special shipments from the polythene growing-tunnels of Holland, Israel, Africa and South America. By 9 September, 10,000 tons of them had been piled outside Buckingham Palace and Kensington Palace. Estimates of the number of individual blooms reached 50 million. Estimates of the total weight of tributes reached 15,000 tons, if cards, bottles of champagne, trinkets, teddy bears and items of crockery bearing Diana's picture were included. Public-health officers estimated that the temperature inside these masses of vegetation, cellophane and paper could be 180 degrees Fahrenheit. People waited for up to eight hours to sign the books of condolence and the queue in the Mall sometimes stretched for three-quarters of a mile. As of 15 September, Buckingham Palace had received 500,000 letters and 580,000 email messages of sympathy. By 30 September, 3 million CDs of Elton John singing the song that he had sung at the funeral had been sold in the United Kingdom (21 million copies had been pressed worldwide; the profits went to charity). Ten new or revised books about the princess had been published (two of them headed the lists of hardback and paperback bestsellers). T-shirts, tea towels, videos, 'antique bronzed' busts, commemorative plates and medals were also doing well. The press-clippings agency, Durrants, said that the coverage in the world's magazines and newspapers by far exceeded that generated by any other event, anywhere in the world, at any time in history.

Could grief for one woman have caused all this? We were told so, and it is true that personal grief can have odd, rippling effects: Queen Victoria, mourning her husband, set a fashion for black dress in Britain that was copied throughout Europe. This, on the other hand, was not the replication of clothes but a multiplication of tears. People on television and in the newspapers said that they grieved more for the Princess of Wales than they had for their wives or husbands. It seemed unbelievable, and yet for a time it was difficult in Britain to question it. There was an oppression of grief. People had not only to grieve, they had to be seen to grieve, and in the most pictorial way, by hugging and kissing. The Queen and her family were not seen to grieve enough. They were told to grieve more, and not only by tabloid newspapers (*Show us you care, Ma'am!*). *The Times* told her that she went against the public mood at her peril. The *Independent* said that it would welcome the sight of the royal family in tears and holding on to one another on the steps of Westminster Abbey. The argument became metaphorical, sociological, psychological and political. 'New Labour', a piece of highly successful political rebranding invented by marketeers, spoke for 'New Britain'. New Britain was the princess, the prime minister, flowers, compassion and the therapeutic benefits of touching and crying – *Modernity*, if the princess gets a memorial like Victoria. Old Britain was the Queen, her son and heir, pensioners with 'stiff upper lips', reticence and the neurosis brought about by repression – *History* on the same memorial. As a depiction of 60 million individuals, it was as accurate as Mrs Miniver had been in 1942 or Swinging London in 1966; but it became accepted wisdom that the nation had crossed some kind of emotional fault line.

Two questions arose. Outside the personal sorrow of those who knew the princess, what kind of grief were people feeling? And how many people were feeling it? To judge the quality of other people's grief may be a risky enterprise, but my guess about the first is this: that it was recreational grieving ('look-at-me' grief was how the writer Julian Barnes described it), that it was enjoyable, that it promoted the griever from the audience to an on-stage part in the final act of the opera, which lasted six days. The dead heroine had provided the most marvellous story, and the grief of her spectators may have been genuine in the sense of unfaked. But it was grief with the pain removed, grief-lite. When people telephoned each other that Sunday morning, they spoke eagerly – 'Have you heard that . . . ?' – and not with the dread – 'How can I tell him that . . . ?' – familiar to bearers of seriously wounding news, which the hearer may recover from only in months or years or sometimes never at all. It was possible, after all, for the readers of Dickens to weep at the death of Little Nell, whom they too felt they knew.

In September, in the week that separated her death from her funeral, it was sacrilege to talk openly in this way. I don't think I exaggerate this. The public mood, as relayed and reinforced by the media, became vindictive towards dissension. To be sceptical was to be unfeeling. Organisations which thought that life might go on as normal, as the Scottish football authorities did with an international match that was to be played on the same day (though not at the same time) as the funeral, became enemies of this thing, the public mood. Politicians and newspapers pilloried them and their ways were corrected. And yet privately – or so it seemed to me – it was difficult to meet people who fully shared the emotion that we were meant to feel. Letters began to appear in a few newspapers which suggested another kind of community; the angry, puzzled and beleaguered, the people who were not quite sad enough. How many of them were there – were we? No reliable quantification can exist. In Britain, 31 million people watched the funeral on television, about half the population, but watching (as I did) and feeling tearful (as I did) is no indicator of grief. Still, it was the largest audience that British television has ever had. According to the BBC, the next largest – 30.1 million – was for an episode of the soap, *EastEnders,* in which Angie the barmaid was served divorce papers by Dirty Den. ∎

Edward, aged seven, with his sister Rosy in Gezira Preparatory School uniform, 1943
Courtesy of the author

SELF-CONSCIOUSNESS

Edward W. Said

GRANTA 67: AUTUMN 1999

M y father's strength, moral and physical, dominated the early part of my life. He had a massive back and a barrel chest, and although he was quite short he communicated indomitability and, at least to me, a sense of overpowering confidence. His most striking physical feature was his ramrod-stiff, nearly caricature-like upright carriage. And with that, in contrast to my shrinking, nervous timidity and shyness, went a kind of swagger that furnished another browbeating contrast with me: he never seemed to be afraid to go anywhere or do anything. I was, always. Not only did I not rush forward as I should have done in school games, but I felt seriously unwilling to let myself be looked at, so conscious was I of innumerable physical defects, all of which I was convinced reflected my inner deformations. To be looked at directly, and to return the gaze, was most difficult for me. When I was about ten I mentioned this to my father. 'Don't look at their eyes; look at their nose,' he said, thereby communicating to me a secret technique I have used for decades. When I began to teach as a graduate student in the late fifties I found it imperative to take off my glasses in order to turn the class into a blur that I couldn't see. And to this day I find it unbearably difficult to look at myself on television, or even read about myself.

It was my mother's often melting warmth which offered me a

rare opportunity to be the person I felt I truly was, in contrast to the 'Edward' who failed at school and sports, and could never match the manliness my father represented. And yet my relationship with her grew more ambivalent, and her disapproval of me became far more emotionally devastating than my father's virile bullying and reproaches. One summer afternoon in Lebanon when I was sixteen and in more than usual need of her sympathy, she delivered a judgement on all her children that I have never forgotten. I had just spent the first of two unhappy years at Mount Hermon, a repressive New England boarding school, and this particular summer of 1952 was critically important, mainly because I could spend time with her. We had developed the habit of sitting together in the afternoons, talking quite intimately, exchanging news and opinions. Suddenly she said, 'My children have all been a disappointment to me. All of them.' Somehow I couldn't bring myself to say, 'But surely not me,' even though it had been well established that I was her favourite, so much so (my sisters told me) that during my first year away from home she would lay a place for me at table on important occasions like Christmas Eve, and would not allow Beethoven's Ninth (my preferred piece of music) to be played in the house.

'Why,' I asked, 'why do you feel that way about us?' She pursed her lips and withdrew further into herself, physically and spiritually. 'Please tell me why,' I continued. 'What have I done?'

'Some day perhaps you will know, maybe after I die, but it's very clear to me that you are all a great disappointment.' For some years I would re-ask my questions, to no avail: the reasons for her disappointment in us, and obviously me, remained her best-kept secret, as well as a weapon in her arsenal for manipulating us, keeping us off balance, and me at odds with my sisters and the world. Had it always been like this? What did it mean that I had once believed our intimacy was so secure as to admit few doubts and no undermining at all of my position? Now as I looked back on my frank and, despite the disparity in age, deep liaison with my mother, I realised how her critical ambivalence had always been there.

Hilda, my mother, was born in Nazareth in 1914, the middle child of five, and she was Palestinian, even though her mother was Lebanese. Her father was the Baptist minister in Nazareth. She was sent to boarding school in Beirut, the American School for Girls, a missionary institution that tied her to Beirut first and last, with Cairo a long interlude between. Undoubtedly a star there and at junior college (now the Lebanese American University), she was popular and brilliant – first in her class – in most things. Then, in 1932, she was plucked from what was – or was retrospectively embellished as – a wonderful life and returned from Beirut to dour, old Nazareth, where she was deposited into an arranged marriage with my father, who was at least nineteen years her senior.

My father, Wadie, never told me more than ten or eleven things about his past, all of which never changed and remained hardly more than a series of set phrases. He was born in Jerusalem in 1895 (my mother said it was more likely 1893), which made him at least forty at the time of my birth. He hated Jerusalem, and although I was born and we spent long periods of time there, the only thing he ever said about it was that it reminded him of death. At some point in his life his father was a dragoman who because he knew German had, it was said, shown Palestine to Kaiser Wilhelm. And my grandfather – never referred to by name except when my mother, who never knew him, called him Abu-Asaad – bore the surname Ibrahim. In school, therefore, my father was known as Wadie Ibrahim. I still do not know where 'Said' came from, and no one seems able to explain it. The only relevant detail about his father that my father thought fit to convey to me was that Abu-Asaad's whippings were much severer than his of me. 'How did you endure it?' I asked, to which he replied with a chuckle, 'Most of the time I ran away.' I was never able to do this, and never even considered it.

Today none of us can fully grasp what my parents' marriage was or how it came about, but I was trained by my mother – my father being generally silent on that point – to see it as something difficult at first, to which she gradually adjusted over the course of nearly forty years, and which she transformed into the main event of her life. She never worked or really studied again, and she never spoke about sex without shuddering dislike and discomfort, although my father's frequent remarks about the man being a skilled horseman, the woman a subdued mare, suggested to me a basically reluctant, if also exceptionally fruitful, sexual partnership that produced six children.

But I never doubted that at the time of her marriage to this silent and peculiarly strong middle-aged man she suffered a terrible blow. She was wrenched from a happy life in Beirut. She was given to a much older spouse – perhaps in return for some sort of payment to her mother – who promptly took her off to strange parts and then set her down in Cairo, a gigantic and confusing city in an unfamiliar Arab country. My parents often returned to my father's family home in Jerusalem – once for my birth, in 1935 – but Cairo was where my father had his business (office equipment and stationery), and it was where, mostly, I grew up.

In 1937, when I was two, my parents moved to Zamalek, an island in the Nile between the city of Cairo in the east and Giza in the west, inhabited by foreigners and wealthy locals. Zamalek was not a real community but a sort of colonial outpost whose tone was set by Europeans with whom we had little or no contact: we built our own world within it. Our house was a spacious fifth-floor apartment at 1 Sharia Aziz Osman that overlooked the so-called Fish Garden, a small, fence-encircled park with an artificial rock hill (*gabalaya*), a tiny pond and a grotto; its little green lawns were interspersed with winding paths, great trees and, in the *gabalaya* area, artificially made rock formations and sloping hillsides where you could run up and down without interruption. Except for Sundays and public holidays the Garden, as we called it, was where I spent all of my playtime, always unsupervised and always within range of my mother's voice, which was lyrically audible to me and my sisters.

I played Robinson Crusoe and Tarzan there, and when my mother came with me, I played at eluding and then rejoining her. She went nearly everywhere with us, throughout our little world, one little island enclosed by another one. In the early years we went to school a few blocks away from the house – GPS, Gezira Preparatory School, which I attended from the autumn of 1941 till we left Cairo in May 1942, then again from early 1943 till 1946, with one or two longer Palestinian interruptions in between. For sports there was the Gezira Sporting Club and, on weekends, the Maadi Sporting Club, where I learned to swim. For years, Sundays meant Sunday school; this senseless ordeal occurred between nine and ten in the morning at the GPS, followed by matins at All Saints' Cathedral. Sunday evenings took us to the American Mission Church in Ezbekieh, and two Sundays out of three to evensong at the cathedral. School, church, club, garden, house – a limited, carefully circumscribed segment of the great city – was my world until I was well into my teens.

During the GPS years I began slowly, almost imperceptibly, to develop a contestatory relationship with two of my younger sisters, Rosy and Jean, which played or was made to play into my mother's skills at managing and manipulating us. I had felt protective of Rosy: I helped her along, since she was somewhat younger and less physically adept than I; I cherished her and would frequently embrace her as we played on the balcony; I kept up a constant stream of chatter, to which she responded with smiles and chuckles. We went off to GPS together in the morning, but we separated once we got there since she was in a younger class. She had lots of giggling little girlfriends – Shahira, Nazli, Nadia, Vivette – and I, my 'fighting' classmates such as Dickie Cooper or Guy Mosseri. Quickly she established herself as a 'good' girl, while I lurked about the school with a growing sense of discomfort, rebelliousness, drift and loneliness.

After school the troubles began between us. They were accompanied by our enforced physical separation: no baths together, no wrestling or hugging, separate rooms, separate regimens, mine more physical and disciplined than hers. When Mother came home she would discuss my performance in contrast to my younger sister's. 'Look at Rosy. All the teachers say she's doing very well.' Soon enough, Jean – exceptionally pretty with her thick, auburn pigtails – changed from a tag-along younger version of Rosy into another 'good' girl, with her own circle of apparently like-minded girlfriends. And she also was complimented by the GPS authorities, while I continued to sink into protracted 'disgrace', an English word that hovered around me from the time I was seven. Rosy and Jean occupied the same room; I was down the corridor; my parents in between; Joyce and Grace (eight and eleven years younger than I) had their bedrooms moved from the glassed-in balcony to another room as the apartment was modified to accommodate the growing children.

The closed door of Rosy and Jean's room signified the definitive physical as well as emotional gulf that slowly opened between us. There was once even an absolute commandment against my entering the room, forcefully pronounced and occasionally administered by my father, who now openly sided with them, as their defender and patron; I gradually assumed the part of their dubiously intentioned brother. 'Protect them,' I was always being told, to no effect whatever. For Rosy especially I was a sort of prowling predator-target, to be taunted or cajoled into straying into their room, only to be pelted with erasers, hit over the head with pillows, and shrieked at with terror and dangerous enjoyment. They seemed eager to study and learn at school and home, whereas I kept putting off such activities in order to torment them or otherwise fritter away the time until my mother returned home to a cacophony of charges and countercharges buttressed by real bruises to show and real bites to be cried over.

There was never complete estrangement though, since the three of us did at some level enjoy the interaction of competing, but rarely totally hostile, siblings. My sisters could display their quickness or specialised skill in hopscotch, and I could try to emulate them; in memorable games of blind man's buff, ring-around-the-rosy, or clumsy football in a very confined space, I might exploit my height or relative strength. After we attended the Circo Togni, whose lion tamer especially impressed me with his authoritative presence and braggadocio, I replicated his act in the girls' room, shouting commands like '*A posto, Camelia!*' at them while waving an imaginary whip and grandly thrusting a chair in their direction. They seemed quite pleased at the charade, and even managed a dainty roar as they clambered onto bed or dresser with not quite feline grace.

But we never embraced each other, as brothers and sisters might ordinarily have: for it was exactly at this subliminal level that I felt a withdrawal on all sides, of me from them, and them from me. The physical distance is still there between us, I feel, perhaps deepened over the years by my mother. When she returned from her afternoons at the Cairo Women's Club she invariably interjected herself between us. With greater and greater frequency my delinquency exposed me to her angry reprobation: 'Can't I ever leave you with your sisters without your making trouble?' was the refrain, often succeeded by the dreaded codicil, 'Wait till your father gets home.' Precisely because there was an unstated prohibition on physical contact between us, my infractions took the form of attacks that included punching, hair-pulling, pushing, and the occasional vicious pinch. Invariably I was 'reported' and then 'disgraced' – in English – and some stringent punishment (a further prohibition on going to the movies, being sent to bed without dinner, a steep reduction in my allowance and, at the limit, a beating from my father) was administered.

All this heightened our sense of the body's peculiar, and problematic, status. There was an abyss – never discussed nor examined, nor even mentioned during the crucial period of puberty – separating a boy's body from a girl's. Until I was twelve I had no idea at all what sex between men and women entailed, nor did I know very much about the relevant anatomy. Suddenly, however, words like 'pants' and 'panties' became italicised: 'I can see your pants,' said my sisters tauntingly to me, and I responded, heady with danger, 'I can see *your* panties.' I quite clearly recall that bathroom doors had to be bolted shut against marauders of the opposite sex, although my mother was present for both my dressing and undressing, as well as for theirs. I think she must have understood sibling rivalry very well and the temptations of polymorphous perversity all around us. But I also suspect that she played and worked on these impulses and drives:

she kept us apart by highlighting our differences, she dramatised our shortcomings to each other, she made us feel that she alone was our reference point, our most trusted friend, our most precious love as, paradoxically, I still believe she was. Everything between me and my sisters had to pass through her, and everything I said to them was steeped in her ideas, her feelings, her sense of what was right or wrong.

None of us of course ever knew what she really thought of us, except fleetingly, enigmatically, alienatingly (as when she told me that we had all been a disappointment to her). It was only much later in my life that I understood how unfulfilled and angry she must have felt about our life in Cairo; its busy conventionality, forced rigours and the peculiar lack of authenticity. She had a fabulous capacity for letting you trust and believe in her, even though you knew that a moment later she could either turn on you with incomparable anger and scorn or draw you in with her radiant charm. 'Come and sit next to me, Edward,' she would say, inviting you into her confidence, and allowing you an amazing sense of assurance; of course, you also felt that by doing this she was keeping out Rosy and Jean, even my father then, as well.

But who was she really? Unlike my father, whose general solidity and lapidary pronouncements were a known and stable quantity, my mother was energy itself, all over the house and our lives, ceaselessly probing, judging, sweeping all of us, plus our clothes, rooms, hidden vices, achievements and problems into her always expanding orbit. But there was no common emotional space. Instead there were bilateral relationships with my mother, as colony to metropole, a constellation only she could see as a whole. What she said to me about herself, for instance, she also said to my sisters, and this characterisation formed the basis of her operating persona: she was simple, she was a good person who always did the right things, she loved us all unconditionally, she wanted us to tell her everything. I believed this unquestioningly. There was nothing so satisfying in the outside world, a merry-go-round of changing schools (and hence friends and acquaintances), in which, as a non-Egyptian of uncertain, not to say suspicious, composite identity, I felt habitually out of place. My mother seemed to take in and sympathise with my general predicament. And that was enough for me. It worked as a provisional support, which I cherished tremendously.

It was through my mother that I grew more aware of my body as incredibly fraught and problematic, first because in her intimate knowledge of it she seemed better able to understand its capacity for wrongdoing, and second because she would never speak openly about it, but approached the subject either with indirect hints or, more troublingly, by means of my father and maternal uncles, through whom she spoke like a ventriloquist. When I was about fourteen I said something she thought was tremendously funny; I did not realise at the time how astute I was. I had left the bathroom door unlocked (a telling inadvertence, since I had gained some privacy as an adolescent, but for some reason wanted it occasionally infringed upon), and she suddenly entered. For a second she didn't close the door, but stood there surveying her naked son as he hastily dried himself with a small towel. 'Please leave,' I said testily, 'and stop trying to catch up where you left off.' She burst out laughing, quickly closed the door, and walked briskly away. Had she ever really left off?

I knew much earlier that my body and my sisters' were inexplicably taboo. My mother's ambivalence expressed itself in her extraordinary physical embrace of her children – covering us with kisses, caresses and hugs, cooing, making expostulations of delight about our beauty and physical endowments – and at the same time offering a great deal of devastating negative commentary on our appearance. Fatness was a dangerous and constant subject when I was nine and Rosy was seven. As my sister gained weight it became a point of discussion for us throughout childhood, adolescence and early adulthood. Along with that went an amazingly detailed consciousness of 'fattening' foods, plus endless prohibitions. I was quite skinny, tall, coordinated; Rosy didn't seem to be, and this contrast between us, to which was added the contrast between her cleverness at school and my shabby performance there, my father's special regard for her versus my mother's for me (they always denied any favouritism), her greater *savoir faire* when it came to organising her time, and her capacity for pacing herself, talents I did not at all possess – all this deepened the estrangement between us, and intensified my discomfort with our bodies.

It was my father who gradually took the lead in trying to reform, perhaps even to remake, my body, but my mother rarely demurred, and regularly brought my body to a doctor's attention. As I look back on my sense of my body from age eight on, I can see it locked in a demanding set of repeated corrections, all of them ordered by my parents, most of them having the effect of turning me against myself. 'Edward' was enclosed in an ugly, recalcitrant shape with nearly everything wrong with it. Until the end of 1947, when we left Palestine for the last time, our paediatrician was a Dr Grünfelder, a German Jew, and known to be the finest child-doctor in Palestine. His office was in a quiet and leafy area of the parched city that seemed distinctly foreign to me then. He spoke to us in English, although there was a good deal of confidential whispering between him and my mother that I was rarely able to overhear. Three persistent problems were referred to him, for which he provided his own idiosyncratic solutions; the problems themselves indicate the extent to which certain parts of my body came in for an almost microscopic, and needlessly intense, supervision.

One concerned my feet, which were pronounced flat early in my life. Grünfelder prescribed the metal arches that I wore with my first pair of shoes; they were finally discarded in 1948, when an aggressive clerk in a Dr Scholl's store in Manhattan dissuaded my mother from their use. A second was my odd habit of shuddering convulsively for a brief moment every time I urinated. My mother observed me for a couple of weeks, then brought the case to the world-renowned 'child specialist'. Grünfelder shrugged his shoulders. 'It is nothing,' he pronounced, 'probably psychological' – a phrase I didn't understand but could see worried Mother just a little more, or was at least to worry *me* until I was well into my teens, after which the issue was dropped.

The third problem was my stomach, the source of numerous ills and pains all my life. It began with Grünfelder's scepticism about my mother's habit of wrapping and tightly pinning a small blanket around my midsection in both summer and winter. She thought this protected me against illness, the night air, perhaps even the evil eye; later, hearing about it from different friends, I realised it was common practice in Palestine and Syria. She once told Grünfelder about this strange prophylactic in my presence, his response to which I distinctly remember was a knitted brow. 'I don't see the need,' he said, whereupon she pressed on with a rehearsal of all sorts of advantages (most of them preventive) that accrued to me. I was nine or ten at the time. The issue was also debated with Wadie Baz Haddad, our family GP in Cairo, and he too tried to dissuade her. It took another year for the silly thing to be removed once and for all; my mother later told me that still another doctor had warned her against sensitising my midsection so much, since it then became vulnerable to all sorts of other problems.

My eyes had grown weaker because I had spring catarrh and a bout of trachoma; for two years I wore dark glasses at a time when no one else did. At age six or seven, I had to lie in a darkened room every day with compresses on my eyes for an hour. As my short-sightedness developed I saw less and less well, but my parents took the position that glasses were not 'good' for you, and were positively bad if you 'got used' to them. In December of 1949 at the age of fourteen, I went to see *Arms and the Man* at the American University of Cairo's Ewart Hall, and was unable to follow the action on stage, until a friend loaned me his glasses. Six months later, after a teacher's complaint, I did get glasses with express parental instructions not to wear them all the time: my eyes were already bad enough, I was told, and would get worse.

At the age of twelve I was informed that the pubic hair sprouting between my legs was not 'normal', increasing my already overdeveloped embarrassment about myself. The greatest critique, however, was reserved for my face and tongue, back, chest, hands and abdomen. I did not know I was being attacked, nor did I experience the reforms and strictures as the campaigns they were. I assumed they were all elements of the discipline that one went through as part of growing up. The net effect of these reforms, however, was to make me deeply self-conscious and ashamed.

The longest-running and most unsuccessful reform – my father's near obsession – concerned my posture, which became a major issue for him just as I reached puberty. In June 1957, when I graduated from Princeton, it culminated in my father's insisting on taking me to a brace and corset maker in New York in order to buy me a harness to wear underneath my shirt. What still distresses me about the experience is that at the age of twenty-one I uncomplainingly let my father feel he was entitled to truss me up like a naughty child whose bad posture symbolised some objectionable character trait that required scientific punishment. The clerk who sold us the truss remained expressionless as my father amiably declared, 'See, it works perfectly. You'll have no problems.'

The white cotton and latex truss with straps across my chest and over the shoulders was the consequence of years of my father trying to get me to 'stand up straight'. 'Shoulders back,' he would say, 'shoulders back,' and my mother – whose own posture, like her mother's, was poor – would add in Arabic, 'Don't slump.' As the offence persisted she resigned herself to the notion that my posture came from the Badrs, her mother's family, and would routinely emit a desultory sigh, fatalistic and disapproving at the same time, followed by the phrase '*Herdabit beit Badr*', or 'the Badr family humpback', addressed to no one in particular, but clearly intended to fix the blame on my ancestry, if not also on her.

The Badrs' or not, my father persisted in his efforts. These later included 'exercises', one of which was to slip one of his canes through both my armpits and make me keep it there for two hours at a stretch.

Another was to make me stand in front of him and for half an hour respond to the order 'One' by thrusting my elbows back as hard and as quickly as possible, supposedly straightening my back in the process. Whenever I wandered across his line of vision he would call out, 'Shoulders back.' This of course embarrassed me when others were around, but it took me weeks to ask him to please not call out to me so loudly on the street, in the club, or even walking into church. He was reasonable about my objection. 'Here's what I'll do,' he said reassuringly. 'I'll just say "Back", and only you and I will know what it means.' And so 'Back' I endured for years and years – until the truss.

A corollary to the struggle over my posture was how it affected my chest, whose disproportionately large size and prominence I inherited from my father. Very early in my teens I was given a metal chest expander with instructions to use it to develop the size and disposition of the front of my body. I was never able to master the gadget's crazy springs, which leapt out at you threateningly if you did not have the strength to keep them taut. The real trouble, as I once explained to my mother who listened sympathetically, was that my chest was already too large; thrusting it forward aggressively, making it even bigger, turned me into a grotesque, barrel-chested caricature of a well-developed man. I seemed to be caught between the hump and the barrel. My mother understood and tried to persuade my father of this, without any observable result. When he was in America before the First World War my father had been influenced by Eugen Sandow, the legendary strongman who even turns up in *Ulysses*, and Sandow featured an overdeveloped chest and erect back. What was good for Sandow, my father once told me, ought to do 'for you too'.

Yet on several occasions my resistance exasperated my father enough for him to pummel me painfully around my shoulders, and once even to deliver a solid fist to my back. He could be physically violent, throwing heavy slaps across my face and neck, while I cringed and dodged in what I felt was a most shameful way. I regretted his strength and my weakness beyond words, but I never responded or called out in protest, not even when, as a Harvard graduate student in my early twenties, I was bashed by him humiliatingly for being rude, he said, to my mother. I learned how to sense that a cuff was on its way by the odd fashion in which he drew his top lip into his mouth and the heavy breath he suddenly took in. I much preferred the studied care he took with my canings – using a riding crop – to the frightening, angry and impulsive violence of his slaps and swinging blows to my face. When she suddenly lost her temper, my mother also flailed at my face and head, but less frequently and with considerably less force.

As I write this now it gives me a chance, very late in life, to record the experiences as a coherent whole that very strangely have left no anger, some sorrow, and a surprisingly strong residual love for my parents. All the reforming things my father did to me coexisted with an amazing willingness to let me go my own way later on; he was strikingly generous to me at Princeton and Harvard, always encouraging me to travel, to continue piano studies, to live well, always willing to foot the bill, even though my journey took me further from him as an only son and the only likely successor in the family business. What I cannot completely forgive, though, is that the contest over my body, and my father's reforms and physical punishment, instilled a deep sense of generalised fear in me, which I have spent most of my life trying to overcome. I still sometimes think of myself as a coward, with some gigantic lurking disaster waiting to overtake me for sins I have committed and will soon be punished for. ∎

reply 17/2

La Résidence des Fleurs,

Avenue Pasteur,

06600 Antibes

27 January 1986

Dear Buford,

I think this monstrous error is explicable if not
excusable. The whole passage from September 14 on page
25 to the end should have been inserted on page 21 after
September 12. I cant check now with the manuscript book
as it is in Georgetown. I think what probably happened
was this: I dictated the parts I wanted used onto a
dictabel& and I was in a very tired condition. My hand
may well have slipped and what is imexcusable I didn't
note this when the typescript was returned Brom the
typist. I was in a hurry as well as tired and if I
remember rightly you too were in a hurry and I didn't
have proofs. Oh well, such things happen.

I am glad that your circulation is doing so well,
but you must forgive me if I dont join you at the
Pompidou Centre. I hate public appearances, even though
sometimes I have to give way. I dont want to give way
on this occasion. I have a mass of correspondence and I
am struggling with a book and want to give all my energies
to that.

Yours sincerely

Graham Greene

Diana Athill with André Deutsch (centre) and Nicholas Bentley, outside their office in Bloomsbury, London, early 1960s
Courtesy of the author

EDITING VIDIA

Diana Athill

GRANTA 69: SPRING 2000

G ood publishers are supposed to 'discover' writers, and perhaps
they do. To me, however, they just happened to come. In 1956,
four years after the launch of André Deutsch Limited, of which
I was a director, Mordecai Richler (whose first novel we had just
published) introduced me to Andrew Salkey. Andrew was a writer
from Jamaica who was then keeping a roof over his head by working
for the BBC's Caribbean Service and who was always generous
towards other writers. When he heard that I was Mordecai's editor
he immediately asked if he could send me a young friend of his
who regularly freelanced for the same service and had just written
something very good. A few days later V. S. Naipaul came to a coffee
bar near our office and handed over *Miguel Street*.

He was in his very early twenties and looked even younger, but his
manner was grave – even severe – and unsmiling. This I attributed
to nervousness – but I felt that it was the nervousness of someone
essentially serious and composed, and that it would be impertinent
to think in terms of 'putting him at his ease'. It was a surprise to
discover that *Miguel Street* was funny: delicately funny, with nothing
overdone. It was a portrait of a street in Trinidad's Port of Spain,
in the form of stories which each centred on a street character; its
language that of the street, and its balance between amusement and

sympathy perfectly judged. I was delighted by it, but worried: it was a publishing dogma to which André Deutsch strongly adhered that stories didn't sell unless they were by Names. So before talking to him about it I gave it to Francis Wyndham who was with us as part-time 'Literary Adviser', and Francis loved it at once and warmly. This probably tipped the balance with André, whose instinct was to distrust as 'do-gooding' my enthusiasm for a little book by a West Indian about a place which interested no one and where the people spoke an unfamiliar dialect. I think he welcomed its being stories because it gave him a reason for saying 'no': but Francis's opinion joined to mine made him bid me find out if the author had a novel on the stocks and tell him that if he had, then that should come first and the stories could follow all in good time. Luckily Vidia was in the process of writing *The Mystic Masseur.*

In fact we could well have launched him with *Miguel Street,* which has outlasted his first two novels in critical esteem, because in the fifties it was easier to get reviews for a writer seen by the British as black than it was for a young English writer, and reviews influenced readers a good deal more then than they do now. Publishers and reviewers were aware that new voices were speaking up in the newly independent colonies, and partly out of genuine interest, partly out of an optimistic if ill-advised sense that a vast market for books lay out there, ripe for development, they felt it to be the thing to encourage those voices. This trend did not last long, but it served to establish a number of good writers.

Vidia did not yet have the confidence to walk away from our shilly-shallying, and fortunately it did him no real harm. Neither he nor we made any money to speak of from his first three books, *The Mystic Masseur, The Suffrage of Elvira* and *Miguel Street,* but there was never any doubt about the making of his name, which began at once with the reviews and was given substance by his own work as a reviewer, of which he got plenty as soon as he became known as a novelist. He was a very good reviewer, clearly as widely read as any literary critic of the day, and it was this rather than his first books which revealed that here was a writer who was going to reject the adjective 'regional', and with good reason.

We began to meet fairly often, and I enjoyed his company because he talked well about writing and people, and was often funny. At quite an early meeting he said gravely that when he was up at Oxford – which he had not liked – he once did a thing so terrible that he would never be able to tell anyone what it was. I said it was unforgivable to reveal that much without revealing more, especially to someone like me who didn't consider even murder literally unspeakable, but I couldn't shift him and never learned what the horror was – though someone told me later that when he was at Oxford Vidia did have some kind of nervous breakdown. It distressed me that he had been unhappy at a place which I loved. Having such a feeling for scholarship, high standards and tradition he ought to have liked it . . . but no, he would not budge. Never for a minute did it occur to me that he might have felt at a loss when he got to Oxford because of how different it was from his background, still less because of any form of racial insult: he appeared to me far too impressive a person to be subject to such discomforts.

The image Vidia was projecting at that time, in his need to protect his pride, was so convincing that even when I read *A House for Mr Biswas* four years later, and was struck by the authority of his account of Mr Biswas's nervous collapse, I failed to connect its painful vividness with his own reported 'nervous breakdown'. Between me and the truth of his Oxford experience stood the man he wanted people to see.

At that stage I did not know how or why he had rejected Trinidad, and if I had known it, still wouldn't have understood what it is like to be unable to accept the country in which you were born. Vidia's books (not least *A Way in the World,* not written until thirty-seven years later) were to do much to educate me; but then I had no conception of how someone who feels he doesn't belong to his 'home' and cannot belong anywhere else is forced to exist only in himself; nor of how exhausting and precarious such a condition (blithely seen by the young and ignorant as desirable) can be. Vidia's self – his very being – was his writing: a great gift, but all he had. He was to report that ten years later in his career, when he had earned what seemed to others an obvious security, he was still tormented by anxiety about finding the matter for his next book, and for the one after that . . . an anxiety not merely about earning his living, but about existing as the person he wanted to be. No wonder that while he was still finding his way into his writing he was in danger; and how extraordinary that he could nevertheless strike an outsider as a solidly impressive man.

This does not mean that I failed to see the obvious delicacy of his nervous system. Because of it I was often worried by his lack of money, and was appalled on his behalf when I once saw him risk losing a commission by defying the *Times Literary Supplement*. They had offered their usual fee of twenty-five pounds (or was it guineas?) for a review, and he had replied haughtily that he wrote nothing for less than fifty. 'Oh silly Vidia,' I thought. 'Now they'll never offer him anything again.' But lo! they paid him his fifty and I was filled with admiration. Of course he was right: authors ought to know their own value and refuse the insult of derisory fees.

I was right to admire that self-respect, at that time, but it was going to develop into a quality difficult to like. In all moral qualities the line between the desirable and the deplorable is imprecise – between tolerance and lack of discrimination, prudence and cowardice, generosity and extravagance – so it is not easy to see where a man's proper sense of his own worth turns into a more or less pompous self-importance. In retrospect it seems to me that it took eight or nine years for this process to begin to show itself in Vidia, and I think it possible that his audience was at least partly to blame for it.

For example, after a year or so of meetings in the pubs or restaurants where I usually lunched, I began to notice that Vidia was sometimes miffed at being taken to a cheap restaurant or being offered a cheap bottle of wine – and the only consequence of my seeing this (apart from my secretly finding it funny) was that I became careful to let him choose both restaurant and wine. And this carefulness not to offend him, which was, I think, shared by all, or almost all, his English friends, came from an assumption that the reason why he was so anxious to command respect was fear that it was, or might be, denied him because of his race; which led to a squeamish dismay in oneself at the idea of being seen as racist. The shape of an attitude which someone detests in themselves, and has worked at extirpating, can often be discerned from its absence, and during the first years of Vidia's career in England he was often coddled for precisely the reason the coddler was determined to disregard.

Later, of course, the situation changed. His friends became too used to him to see him as anything but himself, and those who didn't know him saw him simply as a famous writer – on top of which he could frighten people. Then it was the weight and edge of his personality which made people defer to him, rather than consideration for his sensitivity, and it was easy to underestimate the pain and strain endured by that sensitivity when he had first pulled himself up out of the thin, sour soil in which he was reared and was striving to find a purchase in England where, however warmly he was welcomed, he could never feel that he wholly belonged.

W hat began to wear me down in my dealings with Vidia (it was a long time before I allowed myself to acknowledge it) was his depression.

With every one of his books – and we published eighteen of them – there was a three-part pattern. First came a long period of peace while he was writing, during which we saw little of him and I would often have liked to see more, because I would be full of curiosity about the new book. Then, when it was delivered, there would be a short burst of euphoria during which we would have enjoyable meetings and my role would be to appreciate the work, to write the blurb, to hit on a jacket that pleased both him and us, and to see that the script was free of typist's errors (he was such a perfectionist that no editing, properly speaking, was necessary). Then came part three: post-publication gloom, during which his voice on the telephone would make my heart sink – just a little during the first few years, deeper and deeper with the passing of time. His voice became charged with tragedy, his face became haggard, his theme became the atrocious exhaustion and damage (the word damage always occurred) this book had inflicted on him, and all to what end? Reviewers were ignorant monkeys, publishers (this would be implied in a sinister fashion rather than said) were lazy and useless: what was the point of it all? Why did he go on?

It is natural that a writer who knows himself to be good and who is regularly confirmed in that opinion by critical comment should expect to become a bestseller, but every publisher knows that you don't necessarily become a bestseller by writing well. Of course you don't necessarily have to write badly to do it: it is true that some bestselling books are written astonishingly badly, and equally true that some are written very well. The quality of the writing – even the quality of the thinking – is irrelevant. It is a matter of whether or not a nerve is hit in the wider reading public as opposed to the serious one which is composed of people who are interested in writing as an art. Vidia has sold well in the latter, and has pushed a good way beyond its fringes by becoming famous – at a certain point many people in the wider reading public start to feel that they *ought* to read a writer – but it was always obvious that he was not going to make *big* money. An old friend of mine who reads a great deal once said to me apologetically, 'I'm sure he's very good, but I don't feel he's for me' – and she spoke for a large number of reading people.

Partly this is because of his subject matter, which is broadly speaking the consequences of imperialism: people whose countries once ruled empires relish that subject only if it is flavoured, however subtly, with nostalgia. Partly it is because he is not interested in writing about women, and when he does so usually does it with dislike: more women than men read novels. And partly it is because of his temperament. Once, when he was particularly low, we talked about surviving the horribleness of life and I said that I did it by relying on simple pleasures such as the taste of fruit, the delicious sensations of a hot bath or clean sheets, the way flowers tremble very slightly with life, the lilt of a bird's flight: if I were stripped of those pleasures . . . better not to imagine it! He asked if I could really depend on them and I said yes. I have a clear memory of the sad, puzzled voice in which he replied: 'You're very lucky. I can't.' And his books, especially his novels (after the humour which filled the first three drained away), are coloured – or perhaps I should say 'discoloured' – by this lack of what used to be called animal spirits. They impress, but they do not charm.

He was, therefore, displeased with the results of publication, which filled him always with despair, sometimes with anger as well. Once he descended on me like a thunderbolt to announce that he had just been into Foyle's of Charing Cross Road and they didn't have a single copy of his latest book, published only two weeks earlier, in stock: not one! Reason told me this was impossible, but I have a lurking tendency to accept guilt if faced with accusation, and this tendency went into spasm: suppose the sales department really had made some unthinkable blunder? Well, if they had I was not going to face the ensuing mayhem single-handed, so I said: 'We must go and tell André at once.' Which we did; and André Deutsch said calmly: 'What nonsense, Vidia – come on, we'll go to Foyle's straight away and I'll show you.' So all three of us stumped down the street to Foyle's, only two minutes away, Vidia still thunderous, I twittering with nerves, André serene. Once we were in the shop he cornered the manager and explained: 'Mr Naipaul couldn't find his book: will you please show him where it is displayed.' – 'Certainly, Mr Deutsch,' and there it was, two piles of six copies each, on the table for 'Recent Publications'. André said afterwards that Vidia looked even more thunderous at being done out of his grievance, but if he did I was too dizzy with relief to notice.

Vidia's anxiety and despair were real: you need only compare a photograph of his face in his twenties with one taken in his forties to see how it had been shaped by pain. It was my job to listen to his unhappiness and do what I could to ease it – which would not have been too bad if there had been anything I *could* do. But there was not: and exposure to someone else's depression is draining, even if only for an hour or so at a time and not very often. I felt genuinely sorry for him, but the routine was repeated so often . . . The truth is that as the years went by, during these post-publication glooms I had increasingly to force myself into feeling genuinely sorry for him, in order to endure him.

S elf-brainwashing sometimes has to be a part of an editor's job. You are no use to the writers on your list if you cannot bring imaginative sympathy to working with them, and if you cease to be of use to them you cease to be of use to your firm. Imaginative sympathy cannot issue from a cold heart so you have to like your writers. Usually this is easy; but occasionally it happens that in spite of admiring someone's work you are – or gradually become – unable to like the person.

I thought so highly of Vidia's writing and felt his presence on our list to be so important that I simply could not allow myself not to like him. I was helped by a foundation of affection laid down during the early days of knowing him, and I was able to believe that his depressions hurt him far more than they hurt me – that he could not prevent them – that I ought to be better at bearing them than I was. And as I became more aware of other things that grated – his attitude to his wife Pat and to his brother Shiva (whom he bullied like an enraged mother hen in charge of a particularly feckless chick) – I called upon a tactic often employed in families: Aunt Emily may have infuriating mannerisms or disconcerting habits, but they are forgiven, even enjoyed, because they are *so typically her.* The offending person is put into the position of a fictional, almost a cartoon, character, whose quirks can be laughed or marvelled at as though they existed only on a page. For quite a long time seeing him as a perpetrator of 'Vidia-isms' worked rather well.

I n 1975 we received the thirteenth of his books – his eighth work of fiction – *Guerrillas.* For the first time I was slightly apprehensive because he had spoken to me about the experience of writing it in an unprecedented way: usually he kept the process private, but this time he said that it was extraordinary, something that had never happened before: it was as though the book had been given to him. Such a feeling about writing does not necessarily bode well. And as it turned out, I could not like the book.

It was about a Trinidad-like island sliding into a state of decadence, and there was a tinge of hysteria in the picture's dreadfulness, powerfully imagined though it was. A central part of the story came from something that had recently happened in Trinidad: the murder of an Englishwoman called Gail Benson who had changed her name to Halé Kimga, by a Trinidadian who called himself Michael X and who had set up a so-called 'commune'. Gail had been brought to Trinidad by her lover, a black American known as Hakim Jamal (she had changed her name at his bidding). Both of the men hovered between being mad and being con men, and their linking-up had been Gail's undoing. I knew all three, Gail and Hakim well, Michael very slightly: indeed, I had written a book about them (which I had put away – it would be published sixteen years later) called *Make Believe*. This disturbed my focus on large parts of *Guerrillas*. The people in the book were not meant to be portraits of those I had known (Vidia had met none of them). They were characters created by Vidia to express his view of post-colonial history in places like Trinidad. But the situation in the novel was so close to the situation in life that I often found it hard to repress the reaction: 'But that's not true!' This did not apply to the novel's Michael X character who was called Jimmy Ahmed: Jimmy, and the half-squalid half-pathetic ruins of his 'commune', is a brilliant and wholly convincing creation. Nor did it apply to Roche, Vidia's substitute for Hakim Jamal. Roche is a liberal white South African refugee working for a big commercial firm, whose job has involved giving cynical support to Jimmy. Roche was so evidently not Hakim that the question did not arise. But it certainly did apply to Jane, who stood in for Gail in being the murdered woman.

The novel's Jane, who comes to the island as Roche's mistress, is supposed to be an idle, arid creature who tries to find the vitality she lacks by having affairs with men. Obtuse in her innate sense of her superiority as a white woman, she drifts into such an attempt with Jimmy: an irresponsible fool playing a dangerous game for kicks with a ruined black man. Earlier, Vidia had written an account for a newspaper of Gail's murder which made it clear that he saw Gail as that kind of woman.

She was not. She was idle and empty, but she had no sense of her own superiority as a white woman or as anything else. Far from playing dangerous games for kicks, she was clinging on to illusions for dear life. The people she had most in common with were not the kind of secure Englishwomen who had it off with black men to demonstrate their own liberal attitudes, but those poor wretches who followed the American 'guru' Jones to Guyana in 1977, and ended by committing mass suicide at his bidding. She was so lacking in a sense of her own worth that it bordered on insanity.

It was therefore about Jane that I kept saying to myself, 'But that's not true!' Then I pulled myself together and saw that there was no reason why Jane should be like Gail: an Englishwoman going into such an affair for kicks was far from impossible and would be a perfectly fair example of fraudulence of motive in white liberals, which was what Vidia was bent on showing.

So I read the book again – and this time Jane simply fell to pieces. Roche came out of it badly, too: a dim character, hard to envisage, in spite of revealing wide-apart molars with black roots whenever he smiled (a touch of 'clever characterisation' which should have been beneath Vidia). But although he doesn't quite convince, he almost does; you keep expecting him to emerge from the mist, while Jane becomes more and more like a series of bits and pieces that don't add up, so that finally her murder is without significance. I came to the conclusion that the trouble must lie with Vidia's having cut his cloth to fit a pattern he had laid down in advance: these characters existed in order to exemplify his argument, he had not been *discovering* them.

So they did not live; and the woman lived less than the man because that is true of all Vidia's women.

From the professional point of view there was no question as to what I ought to do: this was one of our most valuable authors; even if his book had been really bad rather than just flawed we would certainly have published it in the expectation that he would soon be back on form; so what I must say was 'wonderful' and damn well sound as though I meant it.

Instead I sat there muttering, 'Oh my God, what am I going to say to him?' I had never lied to him – I kept reminding myself of that, disregarding the fact that I had never before needed to lie. 'If I lie now, how will he be able to trust me in the future when I praise something?' The obvious answer to that was that if I lied convincingly he would never know that I had done it, but this did not occur to me. After what seemed to me like hours of sincere angst I ended by persuading myself that I 'owed it to our friendship' to tell him what I truly thought.

Nothing practical would be gained. A beginner writer sometimes makes mistakes which he can remedy if they are pointed out, but a novelist of Vidia's quality and experience who produces an unconvincing character has suffered a lapse of imagination about which nothing can be done. It happened to Dickens whenever he attempted a good woman; it happened to George Eliot with Daniel Deronda. And as for my own attitude – I had often seen through other people who insisted on telling the truth about a friend's shortcomings: I knew that *their* motives were usually suspect. But my own were as invisible to me as a cuttlefish becomes when it saturates the surrounding water with ink.

So I told him. I began by saying how much I admired the many things in the book which I did admire, and then I said that I had to tell him (*had* to tell him!) that two of his three central characters had failed to convince me. It was like saying to Conrad, '*Lord Jim* is a very fine novel except that Jim doesn't quite come off.'

Vidia looked disconcerted, then stood up and said quietly that he was sorry they didn't work for me, because he had done the best he could with them, there was nothing more he could do, so there was no point in discussing it. As he left the room I think I muttered something about its being a splendid book all the same, after which I felt a mixture of relief at his appearing to be sorry rather than angry, and a slight (only slight!) sense of let-down and silliness. And I supposed that was that.

The next day Vidia's agent called André to say that he had been instructed to retrieve *Guerrillas* because we had lost confidence in Vidia's writing and therefore he was leaving us.

André must have fought back because there was nothing he hated more than losing an author, but the battle didn't last long. Although I believe I was named, André was kind enough not to blame me. Nor did I blame myself. I went into a rage. I fulminated to myself, my colleagues, my friends: 'All those years of friendship, and a mere dozen words of criticism – *a mere dozen words!* – send him flouncing out in a tantrum like some hysterical prima donna!' I had long and scathing conversations with him in my head; but more satisfying was a daydream of being at a huge and important party, seeing him enter the room, turning on my heel and walking out.

For at least two weeks I seethed . . . and then, in the third week, it suddenly occurred to me that never again would I have to listen to Vidia telling me how damaged he was, and it was as though the sun came out. *I didn't have to like Vidia any more!* I could still like his work, I could still be sorry for his pain; but I no longer faced the task of fashioning affection out of these elements in order to deal as a good editor should with the exhausting, and finally tedious, task of listening to his woe. 'Do you know what,' I said to André, 'I've begun to see that it's a release.' (Rather to my surprise, he laughed.) I still, however, failed to see that my editorial 'mistake' had been an act of aggression. In fact I went on failing to see that for years.

Guerrillas was sold to Secker & Warburg the day after it left us.

A month or so after this I went into André's office to discuss something and his phone rang before I had opened my mouth. This always happened. Usually I threw myself back in my chair with a groan, then reached for something to read, but this time I jumped up and grabbed the extension. 'Why – Vidia!' he had said. 'What can I do for you?'

Vidia was speaking from Trinidad, his voice tense: André must call his agent *at once* and tell him to recover the manuscript of *Guerrillas* from Secker & Warburg and deliver it to us.

André, who was uncommonly good at rising to unexpected occasions, became instantly fatherly. Naturally, he said, he would be delighted to get the book back, but Vidia must not act too impetuously: whatever had gone wrong might well turn out to be less serious than he now felt. This was Thursday. What Vidia must do was think it over very carefully without taking action until Monday. Then, if he still wanted to come back to us, he must call his agent, not André, listen to his advice, and if that failed to change his mind, instruct him to act. André would be waiting for the agent's call on Monday afternoon or Tuesday morning, hoping – of course – that it would be good news for us.

Which – of course – it was. My private sun did go back behind a film of cloud, but in spite of that there was satisfaction in knowing that he thought himself better off with us than with them, and I had no doubt of the value of whatever books were still to come.

Vidia never said why he bolted from Seckers, but his agent told André that it was because when they announced *Guerrillas* in their catalogue they described him as 'the West Indian novelist'.

The books still to come were, indeed, worth having (though the last of them was his least important): *India: A Wounded Civilization, The Return of Eva Perón, Among the Believers, A Bend in the River* and *Finding the Centre*. I had decided that the only thing to do was to behave exactly as I had always done in our pre-*Guerrillas* working relationship, while quietly cutting down our extracurricular friendship, and he apparently felt the same. The result was a smooth passage, less involving but less testing than it used to be. Nobody else knew – and I myself was unaware of it until I came to look back – that having resolved never again to utter a word of criticism to Vidia, I was guilty of an absurd pettiness. In *Among the Believers*, a book which I admired very much, there were two minor points to which in the past I would have drawn his attention, and I refrained from doing so: thus betraying, though luckily only to my retrospecting self, that I was still hanging on to my self-righteous interpretation of the *Guerrillas* incident. Vidia would certainly not have 'flounced out like some hysterical prima donna' over matters so trivial. One was a place where he seemed to draw too sweeping a conclusion from too slight an event and could probably have avoided giving that impression by some quite small adjustment; and the other was that when an Iranian speaking English said 'Sheep' Vidia, misled by his accent, thought he said 'ship', which made some dialogue as he reported it sound puzzling. To keep mum about that! There is nothing like self-deception for making one ridiculous.

When Vidia really did leave us in 1984 I could see why – and even why he did so in a way which seemed unkind, without a word of warning or explanation. He had come to the conclusion that André Deutsch Limited was going downhill. It was true. The recession, combined with a gradual but relentless shrinkage in the readership of books such as those we published, was well on the way to making firms of our size and kind unviable; and André had lost his vigour and flair. His decision to sell the firm, which more or less coincided with Vidia's departure, was made (so he felt and told me) because publishing was 'no fun any more', but it was equally a matter of his own slowly failing health. The firm continued for ten years or so under Tom Rosenthal, chuntering not-so-slowly downwards all the time (Tom had been running Seckers when they called Vidia a West Indian, so his appearance on the scene did nothing to change Vidia's mind).

A writer of reputation can always win an even bigger advance than he is worth by allowing himself to be tempted away from publisher A by publisher B, and publisher B will then have to try extra hard on his behalf to justify the advance: it makes sense to move on if you time it right. And if you perceive that there is something going seriously wrong with publisher A you would be foolish not to do so. And having decided to go, how could you look in the eye someone you have known for over twenty years, of whom you have been really quite fond, and tell him, 'I'm leaving because you are getting past it'? Of course you could not. Vidia's agent managed to conceal from André what Vidia felt, but André suspected something: he told me that he thought it was something to do with himself and that he couldn't get it out of the agent, but perhaps I might have better luck. I called the agent and asked him if there was any point in my getting in touch with Vidia, and he – in considerable embarrassment – told me the truth; whereupon I could only silently agree with Vidia's silence, and tell poor André that I'd been so convincingly assured of the uselessness of any further attempt to change Vidia's mind, that we had better give up.

So this leaving did not make me angry, or surprised, or even sad, except for André's sake. Vidia was doing what he had to do, and it seemed reasonable to suppose that we had enjoyed the best of him, anyway. Many years later Mordecai Richler, in at the story's end, oddly enough, as well as its beginning, told me that he had recently seen Vidia with his new and much younger wife, Nadira (they met in Pakistan in 1995 and married the next year, soon after Pat's death). He was, said Mordecai, 'amazingly jolly'; and I was pleased to find that this news made me very glad indeed. ■

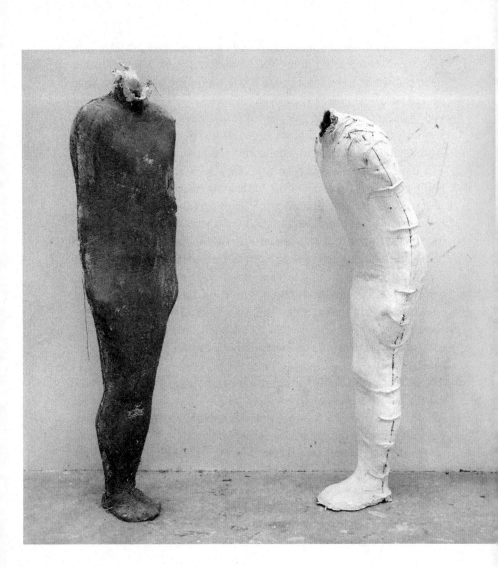

Sculptures by Antony Gormley, at his studio.
London, *c*.1997

SHRINKS

Edmund White

GRANTA 71: AUTUMN 2000

In the mid-1950s, when I was fourteen or fifteen, I told my mother I was homosexual: that was the word, back then, homosexual, in its full satanic majesty, cloaked in ether fumes, a combination of evil and sickness.

Of course I'd learned the word from her. She was a psychologist. Throughout my early childhood, she'd been studying part-time for a master's degree in child psychology. Since I was not only her son but also her best friend, she confided everything she was learning about me – her live-in guinea pig – to me. For instance, I was enrolled in an 'experimental' kindergarten run by Dr Arlett, my mother's mentor in the department of child psychology at the University of Cincinnati. Dr Arlett, however, decided after just one semester that I was 'too altruistic' to continue in the school. I was dismissed. I suspect that she meant I was weirdly responsive to the moods of the female teachers-in-training, for whom I manifested a sugary, fake concern, just as I'd learned to do with my mother. No doubt I was judged to be an unhealthy influence on the other kids. But my mother, who chose against all evidence to interpret my vices as virtues, my defeats as victories, decided that what Dr Arlett really meant was that I was too advanced spiritually, too mature, to hang back in the shallows with my coevals.

My reward was a return to loneliness. We lived at the end of a lane in a small, rented mock-Tudor house. My older sister, who disliked me, was attending Miss Daugherty's School for Girls; she sometimes brought friends home, but she didn't let them play with me. I played alone – or talked to my mother when she wasn't at school or studying.

My mother wrote her master's thesis on the religious experiences of children. She herself was intensely spiritual; at least she spoke often of her inner life and said she prayed, though I never saw her pray. She'd been brought up a Baptist in Texas, but she'd converted to Christian Science, initially to please my father but later out of a genuine affinity with the thinking of Mary Baker Eddy. Like Mrs Eddy, my mother denied the existence of evil (except as it was embodied by my father's mistress). Like Mrs Eddy, my mother believed in thinking mightily positive thoughts. She had a pantheistic, nearly Hindu conviction that every living creature was sacred and formed a wave cresting out of, then dissolving back into, Universal Mind. When my mother was distraught, which occurred on a daily basis, she found consolation in bourbon and Eddy's *Science and Health with Key to the Scriptures*. Eddy's hostility to medicine my mother dismissed as an ideal beyond our grasp given our current state of imperfect evolution.

My mother detected signs in me of a great soul and highly advanced spirituality.

When I was seven my parents divorced. My mother had ordered my father to choose between her and his mistress (who doubled as his secretary); he chose the mistress. My mother was devastated. Although she had a giant capacity for reinterpreting every loss as a gain, even she couldn't find something positive in divorce.

It was a good thing she'd taken that degree in psychology because now, at age forty-five, she had to go to work to supplement her meagre alimony. She labored long hours for low pay as a state psychologist in Illinois and Texas, and later in Illinois again, administering IQ tests to hundreds of grade-school students and even 'projective' tests (the

Rorschach, the House-Tree-Person) to children suspected of being 'disturbed'.

True to my status as guinea pig, I was tested frequently. She who was so often overwrought at home, given to rages or fits of weeping, would become strangely calm and professional when administering a test. Her hands would make smoothing gestures, as though the lamp-lit table between us were that very sea of mind that needed to be stilled back into universality. Her voice was lowered and given a storytelling sweetness ('Now, Eddie, could you tell me everything you see in this ink blot?'). I, too, was transformed when tested, but toward anxiety, since a psychological test was like an X-ray or a blood test, likely to reveal a lurking disease: hostility, perversion or craziness or, even worse, a low intelligence.

She wrote down everything I saw in each plate and exactly where in each ink blot I detected a tomb or a diamond. She then went off for a few hours and consulted her thick dark-blue-bound manual of interpretation with its burgundy label. I was afraid of the results, as absolute and inarguable in their objectivity as they were mysterious in their encoding and decoding.

My mother was nearly gleeful when she told me I was a 'borderline psychotic' with 'strong schizophrenic tendencies'. Apparently the most telling sign of my insanity was my failure to see anything human in the ink blots. All I saw were jewels and headstones.

What remained unclear was whether I was inevitably sliding over the frontier toward full-blown psychosis or whether the process was reversible. Did the Rorschach lay bare my essence or my becoming? Was I becoming better or worse?

There was nothing consistent or logical about my mother's thinking. She found me wise to the point of genius and often said she wanted to write a book about raising the Exceptional Child ('Let him take the lead – he will teach you what he wants to learn'). I was, she suggested, possessed of almost divine understanding and profundity. But then (and here, on alternating days, she could get on a similar roll) I was also half-crazy, dangerously unbalanced, suspiciously apt at imitating wisdom and understanding, a flatterer, a robot programmed to resemble a thinking, feeling human being.

I'd read in one of my mother's psychological manuals a long entry on homosexuality that I could scarcely understand. But I did take in that whereas adult homosexuality was an entrenched ego disorder caused by an unresolved Oedipus complex and resulting in secondary narcissistic gains that were especially hard to uproot, in every early adolescence the individual, the *boy*, passes through a homosexual *stage* that is perfectly normal, a brief swirl around the Scylla of orality and the Charybdis of anality before surging to the sunny open seas of mature genitality. I could only hope that I was just passing through a phase.

I was afire with sexual longing and looked for partners everywhere. The same maniacal energy I'd devoted to playing a succession of dying kings right out of *The Golden Bough* I now consecrated to scoring. I haunted the toilets at the Howard Street elevated station, the one that marked the frontier between Chicago and Evanston. A few men let me touch them and twice a man drove me in a car full of children's toys down to the beach. I wasn't ugly but I *was* jailbait and life even for a part-time homosexual was hard enough during the Eisenhower years.

When I was fourteen my mother announced that she was thinking of marrying Mr Hamilton, a Chicago newspaperman. I had had sex with Mr Hamilton's twenty-year-old son Bob who had pretended he drank too much one night and was forced to stay over – in my room. Now with Wilde-like fatality I said, 'Then it will have to be a double wedding.'

Because of this quip my mother called up Bob Hamilton in a cold fury and denounced him – and the marriage to Mr Hamilton never came to anything.

Betraying my partners was something I felt drawn to. At Camp Towering Pines I'd let an older boy 'hypnotize' me and press my willing mouth down on his penis, but I couldn't resist informing my mother, nominally the camp psychologist, of what he'd 'attempted'.

Did I hope to shift the blame for unhealthy desires and practices on to someone else? Or did I merely hope to stir up trouble, create a drama? Or was I trying to draw my mother's attention to behavior I was horrified by the moment I'd ejaculated? Or was I angry with these young men for not loving me as much as they desired me? If they had loved me they would have attempted to run away with me, wouldn't they? Love was what I wanted, though I don't think I could have been loved any more than a porcupine can be embraced.

My mother sent me to a Freudian psychiatrist in Evanston for an evaluation. I had just read Oscar Wilde and was determined to be as brittle and brilliant as his characters. I sat on the edge of my chair, hectic red flowers blowing in my cheeks, and rattled on and on about my condition, my illness, which I was no more able to defend than Wilde could. All he or I had to offer was defiance and a dandified insolence. If we were pinned down, by a prosecutor or an examining psychiatrist, what could we say – that homosexuality was defensible? Neither of us was that clever; no one could escape his particular moment in history, especially since I, as an American living during the tranquilized 1950s, scarcely believed in history at all. For us nature had replaced history. What I was doing was against nature, anti-physical.

The psychiatrist told my mother that I was 'unsalvageable'. That I should be locked up and the key thrown away. My mother promptly reported this harsh, scary judgment to me, and to my father, though I begged her not to. Of course neither she nor I was capable of dismissing this diagnosis as a dangerously narrow-minded prejudice held by a banal little suburbanite in a brown suit. No, it came from a doctor and was as unquestionable as a diagnosis of diabetes or cancer. The doctor's level of sophistication or humanity was irrelevant.

M y mother had a younger friend named Johanna Tabin who had studied with Anna Freud in London and was now practising as a psychoanalyst in Glencoe. We occasionally spent social evenings with her and her husband and two sons in their big suburban house or at our much smaller apartment beside the lake. They represented everything we aspired to – wealth and calm intelligence and respectability, social and professional importance and family love. Johanna's husband, Julius, had been a nuclear physicist and had become a patent lawyer for nuclear inventions.

Johanna's sons, a few years younger than my sister and I, were treated with elaborate respect by their mother. Whenever they would ask her a question or say something to her, she would immediately turn her attention to them, even if she was on the phone listening to my mother. This indulgence was very unhealthy, my mother decided, and she resented it as much as she disapproved of it. But Johanna was intractable. The second there was a treble squeak in the background, she'd put the receiver aside and say, 'Yes, darling, I'm listening. What is it, darling?' She analysed their dreams and games with an equal attentiveness. I remember when Geoffrey, the younger son, kept singing a song he'd made up about a tumbleweed, she'd decided that he was the little tumbleweed who makes the big horse, his father, rear back in fright – a perfectly normal desire to intimidate the patriarch, she said with a happy smile.

Rather mournfully I thought my mother was too self-absorbed ever to have interpreted my behavior so ingeniously, and if she'd managed to detect a sign of defiance in me she would have squelched it rather than nourished it. Now I can see that she was all alone in the world, poor and overworked and profoundly wounded by my father's rejection after their divorce. Even though she called us the Three Musketeers, we were in fact painfully divided each from the other. My sister was convinced that our mother and I were shamefully bizarre. She herself was unpopular and withdrawn. I was obviously a freak. Only when my mother was administering a test or diagnosing a child did she feel calm and whole and professional.

She must have been jealous of Johanna's happy marriage, because she was always picking up hints of its imminent collapse. 'Poor Johanna,' she'd say. 'The poor little thing is terribly neglected by Julius. It's only a matter of days before he abandons her.'

Despite these dire predictions, Johanna's marriage continued to flourish stubbornly, her career to become more and more distinguished, her husband more and more successful, her sons increasingly brilliant. 'Poor Johanna,' Mother would croon. 'She buries herself in her work because she's so unhappy in her marriage.'

The only thing that amazed me was that Johanna remained so attached to my mother. Did my mother possess undetectable attractions? In a similar way I'd been disconcerted when I'd read my mother's thesis on the religious career of children and discovered in it so many big words I didn't know and had never heard my mother pronounce.

One evening at Johanna's, I talked to her about my homosexuality. I don't remember how the subject came up. Had my mother already set it up? All I remember was that we were seated briefly on the glassed-in sun porch just two steps down from the more brightly lit living room. Dinner was over. Johanna kept casting sunny smiles back at her boys, who were out of earshot and racing around the couch, but when she returned her attention to me she lowered her big sad eyes behind the pale, blue-rimmed glasses and a delicate frown-line was traced across her pure brow. She wore no makeup beyond a faintly pink lipstick. She didn't really follow fashion; she was content to appear neat, of which my mother, who got herself up as elaborately as an *onnagata* in the kabuki, thoroughly disapproved. Johanna scrunched forward and rested her chin on her palm. She was as lithe as a girl. She had beautiful teeth (her mother was a dentist).

'I'm very worried,' I said. 'I don't seem to be moving out of the normal homosexual stage of development.' I was fifteen.

'Yes, dear,' she said, 'I can feel you're very concerned.' She had a way of reflecting through re-statement what her interlocutor had just said, a technique ascribed to Carl Rogers that my mother found insulting and maddeningly condescending but that I liked because it seemed so focused and nonjudgmental. Johanna's life was so manifestly a success that I was happy to bask for an instant in her attention.

'Do you think I should see a therapist?'

She studied my face with her huge, sympathetic eyes and said nothing.

'Could I see you?' I asked. I knew that she received many patients a day in the soundproof office in the basement. My mother had also told me that Johanna had cured a lesbian who was now happily married to a New York writer.

'Have you,' she asked with a tentativeness that suggested a sensitivity in me I was far from enjoying, 'Have you, dear, ever actually . . .'

'Had sex?' I asked brightly. 'Oh, yes, many times.' For an instant I was proud of my experience until I saw my admission shocked and saddened her.

'I had no idea,' she said, shaking her head as if it suddenly weighed much much more, 'that you'd actually gone on to act out, to act on your impulses.' She looked mournful. Whereas Christianity had taught me that the thought was as bad as the deed, Johanna seemed to think acting out was much worse than merely desiring. By realizing my fantasies I'd – what? Made them harder to root out? Coarsened myself?

'You thought I just had a few fantasies?' I was almost insulted, certainly amused, although I could also see I should downplay the extent of my debauchery if I didn't want to break her heart.

She peered deeply into my eyes, perhaps searching for some reassuring signs of remorse or the pain I must undoubtedly be feeling. She shook herself free of her thoughts and said, 'I'm afraid I can't see you as a patient, dear, since we're all such friends. But I can recommend someone who . . .' here she put her words together carefully, '. . . who might help you find your way toward a life that would fully express you, who you really are.'

With a brilliant flash of lightning over the dark landscape of my personality, I suddenly saw that homosexuality, far from being saturnine or interestingly artistic, was in fact a lack, an emptiness, a deformity preventing a full and happy development.

Already I hoped to be a writer but, as I was beginning to realize, successful writing entailed a grasp of universal values and eternal truths, which were necessarily heterosexual. Foolishly I had imagined I could transform the dross of homosexuality into the gold of art, but now I saw I could never be a great artist if I remained ignorant of the classical verities of marriage and child-rearing, adultery and divorce. But if psychoanalysis could convert me into a heterosexual, might it not at the same time ablate the very neurosis that made me want to write? Should I tamper with my neurosis?

I began to read books about psychoanalysis – Freud himself, especially the *Introduction to Psychoanalysis* and *The Interpretation of Dreams*, but also the softer, less pessimistic American adaptations of his thought by Erich Fromm. I learned that making art was an act of neurotic compensation and sublimation – although Theodor Reik made his unorthodox mark by arguing that art was the highest form of mental health. I couldn't find much about homosexuality in any book, but enough to know it was sterile, inauthentic, endlessly repetitious and infantile.

Somewhere I came across the theory that homosexuality was caused by an absent father and a suffocating mother. Perhaps my mother herself had been the one to suggest that my father's absence had queered me, for she was always eager to work out the multiple ways in which his desertion had harmed us all. To bring me the benefits of a suitable father figure she was eager to remarry – but no man was willing to take on the burden. I was sent to live with my father for one year back in Cincinnati, but he ignored me – and I had sex on a regular basis with the neighbor boy.

When I realized that I wasn't getting any better, that I was just as obsessed with men as ever, I begged my parents to enrol me in a boys' boarding school. My reasoning was that if I was homosexual because I was suffocated by my mother and deprived of male models, then a tough, almost military school would be sure to shape me up. Reluctantly they complied, but after a year away from home, when I realized I was more besotted with boys than previously, I asked my father to send me to a shrink.

I had one all picked out. Half the students at my school, Cranbrook, outside Detroit, Michigan, were day boys and half were boarders. We boarding students were occasionally allowed to spend a weekend with a day boy's family if we got written permission from our parents. I was invited home by Stephen Schwartz. His family played classical music (the Mozart Clarinet Concerto, Bach's cantatas) on a stereo that was piped into every room of the compact wood house which, to my eyes, looked half-Hopi, half-Japanese. He was a shaggy-haired mouth-breather, arty and intelligent, who was neither scandalized by nor interested in my perversion. He liked to write and knew a lot about jazz; he was neither a grade-grubber nor an athlete, the only two admissible types at Cranbrook. He had a crazy sense of humor. All the grim striving of his fellow students and the severity of our anti-intellectual, martinet masters only made him laugh. We worked together on the student literary magazine, to which he contributed satires.

His father was a psychiatrist who recommended me to James Clark Moloney. I made an appointment with Moloney and my mother wrote a note granting me permission to take a taxi to his office in a Detroit suburb. I wrote about Moloney in *A Boy's Own Story*, published in 1982, more than two decades after the event, though I was still angry with him.

My father was reluctant to take on the expense of regular psychiatric fees, which amounted to fifty dollars an hour at a time when a good dinner at a restaurant cost five dollars, for instance, and a general practitioner charged only ten dollars a visit. Someone wealthy at that time earned seventy or eighty thousand dollars a year. Dr Moloney wanted to see me three times a week, which came to six hundred dollars a month, a sum that exceeded my mother's alimony by a hundred dollars.

My father also objected just as strenuously to the whole notion of psychoanalysis, which he saw as a form of soak-the-rich charlatanism, an ineffectual and dangerously self-indulgent stewing over problems engendered by idleness and entrenched through the principle of the more you scratch the more it itches. As a good businessman he made me put all my arguments for psychoanalysis in clear, terse letters, which he countered in short missives printed in his neat hand on stationery that read 'From the desk of E. V. White'. He addressed me as 'Dear Ed V.,' (I was Edmund Valentine White III, a dynastic custom typical of even quite ordinary families in the South). I wrote to him explicitly about my unsuccessful struggle against homosexuality and about the smothering-mother, absent-father aetiology, intended as an indirect reproach against him. I knew the divorce was a sore spot, since he considered it a blot on his rectitude, not because he loved my mother (he didn't) but because he believed divorce under any circumstances was morally reprehensible. He was privately an eccentric, even violent man, but he could tolerate no demerit on his public record. He wanted to appear, if not actually be, irreproachable.

I had no idea what to expect at Dr Moloney's, but I certainly thought he'd be a small man with a varnished pate and an inky comb-over, many books (some in German) and in his waiting room the sorry smell of old tobacco. I was in no way prepared for the cages of shrieking birds, the Papuan deities and, in the garden as seen through a plate-glass window, a gilt statue of a meditating *bodhisattva*. I fancied myself a Buddhist but of the austere Theravada sort, and I sniffed at Dr Moloney's idolatry, even though I'd come here precisely because I sought a compassionate intercessor, a *bodhisattva* of my own.

He didn't have a secretary. Another patient let me in and we sat uncomfortably staring at each other, rigid with sibling rivalry. At last Moloney stumbled out, escorting a sniffing little woman. He appeared surprised that he'd double-booked his next hour.

'Don't worry,' he said to me. 'There are enough teats to suckle the whole litter.' He chuckled, revealing neatly spaced teeth in a handsome red face. He cocked an eye at me.

He had a leonine mane of white hair, a bulbous nose with a sore on one side, close to the tip, which he kept vaguely clawing at, as an old dog will half-heartedly try to free itself of its collar. He wore sandals on big, yellow-nailed feet, shapeless trousers held up with a rope, a short-sleeved Hawaiian shirt. He licked his lips constantly.

He made me feel very prim, especially since I'd put on my favorite Brooks Brothers sack suit with the brown-and-black twill. I didn't like the idea that he'd already decided I was a famished pup before I'd said even a word.

He chose to see the other patient first, though not for a full hour, he explained, but more for a patch-up. If I sat in the inner waiting room I could hear the drone of the patient's voice and the grunt of the doctor's. Not their words, just the rhythm and intonation of their voices, but the mere possibility of eavesdropping frightened and attracted me.

Moloney had but one master theory and he proposed it to everyone as an answer to every ill. He believed in the introjected mother. Every infant has the right to expect and enjoy unconditional love from his mother, at full throttle and all the time. Modern American women, however, are deformed by societal inhibitions and their own deprivations as children. They are incapable of giving complete, nourishing love; when I told Dr Moloney that my mother hadn't breastfed me because she had inverted nipples, he slapped his knees, let out a great cry and leaped to his feet. 'You see!'

The emotionally starved, alienated child decides to mother himself. The faint, elusive image of his mother's face and warmth he incorporates into his inner pantheon. Now he is no longer dependent on her vagaries, caprices and eclipses. Now he can beam her up whenever he needs her. If he sucks his thumb he is nursing himself. He has become a closed circuit – with only one crucial disadvantage: such total independence is virtually synonymous with madness. He has lost all vital connection to the outside world. He's self-sufficient, but at a terrible price. When he thinks he has fallen in love with a real woman, in point of fact all he's done is to project his mother's *imago* onto a neutral screen. He is enamored of half of his inner cast of characters. Since he's not relating to a real person in all her shifting specificity but instead to the crude, fixed outlines of the introjected mother, he cannot interact with the flesh-and-blood woman. If she should break through his defences by smiling her real smile, breathing her real breath on his cheek, he will panic and break it off. As an infant he learned how dangerous it was to open up to an actual, autonomous Other.

I was taught all this during my very first hour with Dr Moloney – or rather my first ninety minutes, since he was eager to prove to me he was not like one of those goddamn tightass Freudians with their finicky, fucking fifty-minute hours. He also needed to lay out his entire theory during our first encounter so that it could begin to sink in.

As I learned in session after session, Dr Moloney had served in the Pacific as an army doctor. There, in Okinawa, he had observed that infants were fearless and happy because they never left their mother's side; they were carried everywhere, papoose-style, bound to their mother's back, their heads looking out *above* hers – 'That way they feel united to her but in charge.' Once I saw an elegant young father on the streets of Birmingham, a baby peering out at the world from his back, and I recognized one of Dr Moloney's Michigan Okinawans.

Moloney gave me his books to read and even one of his manuscripts to improve. 'Don't think I'm a castrating asshole like your father, an anal perfectionist who can't admit that another man can help him. I need all the help I can get.' He loved to insult my parents, whom he'd never met and who were not at all the straw men he'd set up. They were as eccentric as he – impoverished rural Texans unprepared for the world they'd created for themselves by earning money and moving North. Moloney cursed them for being uptight patricians, unfeeling aristocrats, but in fact they were self-made crazy people, all too full of dangerous feelings. I would never sink to the indignity of going into Moloney's backyard and hacking away at the logs he painted with the words 'Mom' and 'Dad'.

Moloney was a warm man, an easy-going bohemian with ethnographic interests who believed he could give me the unconditional love that he thought I craved and that his version of my mother had denied me. He would often interrupt me to say, 'I love you, goddamn it.' His eyes would fill with tears and he'd idly pick at his infected nose, or come at the sore on his forehead from above, fat fingers stretching down, his elbow cocked to the ceiling. But on some days he had to search for my name.

As best I could figure out he'd had a more conventional past, reflected in his first, unimpeachably Freudian book, but now he'd become cracked over the introjected mother and the Okinawan papoose cure. He wore heavy turquoise and silver bracelets, black amulets on his hairy chest, and lived surrounded by bobbing, chiming deities from the Pacific, Asia and Africa (Freud had inaugurated this taste for carved African statues, as photos of his Vienna cabinet revealed).

The other Freudian remnant was the couch. After a few intimidating sessions in a chair I was graduated to the couch, while out of sight behind me, at a desk, Moloney took notes (or wrote something, perhaps one of his pamphlets). I could hear him back there coughing or rummaging around for something or scratching with his pen. More than once I caught him dozing. That he was asleep changed his preceding silence in my eyes from a sharp, therapeutic instrument into an obtuse abnegation. I bored him. This man who claimed to love me was zoning out on me. 'I know what you're thinking!' he shouted. 'You're probably mad as hell. And you have a right to be. You have a right to unqualified love. No time limits, no lapses, eternal, unqualified love. But even Homer nods. The baby squalls, and he's completely in his rights. If I were perfect – and you deserve perfection, it's your birthright –' Here he got confused and ended up scratching his nose.

When Johanna asked me during Christmas vacation how things were going, I said, 'I'm very disappointed. He's a nice man. But he doesn't remember anything about me and each time I mention a friend I have to situate that person all over again.'

'Surely you're exaggerating –'

'Not at all. He's not really interested in the details of my life. Or my life. I don't think he likes men. Or they don't catch his interest. He constantly accuses me of over-intellectualizing, although he's happy enough to exploit my proofreading skills.'

Over-intellectualizing was considered one of my most serious defenses. If I disagreed with one of Moloney's interpretations he'd laugh, show his small white teeth and say, 'If you go on winning every argument this way you'll soon enough lose every chance at happiness. No one around here doubts your intelligence. It's just that I want you to break out of your closed circuit and touch another living human being, goddamn it. Come on, take a chance on life –' And here he groped for my name before sketching in a feeble gesture that ended in a shrug. I learned to question all my impulses, to second-guess my motives, to ascribe a devious unconscious purpose to my most unobjectionable actions. If I had a dream about making love to Marilyn Monroe, Moloney would interpret it as a 'flight into health', a ruse I'd invented to throw him off my track by appearing normal, cured. 'In this dream I'm Marilyn Monroe,' he'd say, perfectly seriously. 'Like her I have long hair, a wide mouth, I'm voluptuously put together.'

Now I'd say the worst consequence of my years in psychoanalysis was the way it undermined my instincts. Self-doubt, which is a cousin to self-hatred, became my constant companion. If today I have so few convictions and conceive of myself as merely an anthology of opinions, interchangeable and equally valid, I owe this uncertainty to psychoanalysis. Fiction is my ideal form because a character, even a stand-in for me, occupies a dramatic moment, wants one thing rather than another, serves the master narration. The novel is a contrived simplification of the essay I actually inhabit; it is a story rather than an assertion, a development in time rather than a statement in the eternal present of truth. Fiction suggests that no one is ever disinterested. It does not ask the author to adjudicate among his characters. It is the ultimate arena of situationist ethics. ■

Freud's desk chair, made of crimson-brown leather, designed by Felix Augenfeld, *c.*1930

KILTYKINS

Ved Mehta

GRANTA 72: WINTER 2000

When I was seeing Kilty (how, even today, the word 'seeing' mesmerizes me), the fact of my blindness was never mentioned, referred to, or alluded to. My recent friends cannot believe that could have been the case – indeed, from my present vantage point, I myself can scarcely believe it, especially since Kilty and I were so intimate in everything else. But in this respect my relationship with Kilty was not unusual; I was equally reticent about the subject with practically everyone else. The silence must have been a testament to the force of my will.

I now understand that, at the time, I was in the grip of the fantasy that I could see. The fantasy was unconscious and had such a hold on me, was so intense and had so many ramifications, that my girlfriend's indulgence in it was the necessary condition of my loving her. Indeed, if I got interested in a woman and she interfered by hint or gesture with it, I would avoid her, feeling sad and frustrated. Yet there was hardly a day that I did not feel defeated, patronized and humiliated – when I did not wish to be spared the incessant indignities that assaulted me. To give a fairly innocuous example, I still come across a man I have known since my university days, several days a week, in a club to which we both belong, and every time I see him he tells me his name. I have gently told him many times that I recognize him by his voice, but to no effect. Although this man is a historian of international stature, he seems to lack the sensitivity to realize that a voice, in its way, is as distinctive as a face. Could it be that the fantasies that sighted people have about the blind are based less on reality than those that blind people have about the sighted?

I needed to be accepted on my own terms by Kilty and anyone else I was close to – it was easier for me to conduct myself as if I could see. So the fantasy was not wholly irrational. In order for me to live as if I could see, it had to remain largely unconscious. I had to function as if I were on automatic pilot. Talking about the fantasy, analyzing it, bringing it out into the open would have impeded my functioning. Or, at least, that was my unconscious fear. I went overboard. I allowed the fantasy to pervade every part of my life: the way I dressed myself, wrote books and articles, collected furniture and paintings. But even when I was most under the influence of my fantasy, I maintained the habit of checking external reality. I never walked off a cliff, for instance. Without such continual verification, I could not have survived in the sighted world.

Over the years, I have often asked myself, How was it that my girlfriends all played along without once slipping up? Was my fantasy contagious? Did I seek these women out because they were susceptible to my reality and, in their own way, could take leave of that reality and mold themselves to mine? Anyway, isn't that the sort of thing that all people do when they are in love – uniting, as it were, to become, as Genesis has it, 'one flesh'? Yet I wonder if, in my case, their accommodation prevented them from really getting to know me and me from really getting to know them, thereby condemning me to devastating isolation. But then, the fault was mine. I no doubt impressed them with my mastery of my surroundings. I did not feel limited in any way, and I think I must have felt that from the moment I became blind, two months short of my fourth birthday, as a result of an attack of cerebrospinal meningitis. When I was twenty-three, I published a youthful autobiography, which dealt with my illness and my blindness, but by the time I met Kilty eleven years later I had all but disowned the book as juvenilia, so I never mentioned it to her.

When I bounced back from my bout of meningitis, which lasted some two months, I probably forgot in my conscious mind what it had been like to see. Unconsciously, I assumed that I could do everything that anyone else could do – indeed, I was scarcely aware of any change, for I was incapable of distinguishing between sight and the absence of sight. Keats says that in 'darkness there is light', but the entire experience of darkness and light became, in a sense, meaningless to me. As a four-year-old child, I imagined that my world was everybody's world. If I had been older, I might have experienced my blindness differently – hesitating, perhaps, to put one foot in front of the other, moving about with outstretched hands, or clinging to the end of my mother's sari. Had that been the case, I would have experienced blindness as frightening, tragic, debilitating. As it was, I laughed and played, jumped around, ran about, hopped and skipped, climbed up and fell down – much as I had done when I could see.

This happened in Lahore, in then undivided India. At the time, my four sisters and one brother were all younger than twelve, and, like children anywhere, they made no concessions for me. My Westernized father, a born optimist, did not curtail his aspirations for me. Instead of equating me with the blind beggars outside the gate, he took inspiration from what Milton had attained and wished the best for me. Only my mother, a religious woman with very little schooling, was unable to extend herself to my new condition. Believing that blindness, like poverty, was a curse for misdeeds done in a previous incarnation, she would search my face for some sign of my bad deed and, finding it innocent, was sure that my blindness was merely a passing curse of the evil eye. No matter how much or how often my father, a medical doctor, explained to her that the long, raging fever had damaged my optic nerves and that I would be permanently blind, she insisted that my condition was temporary. She carted me around to healers and astrologers who prescribed Ayurvedic or Unani treatments, along with a variety of penances. She tried all of them. That was her form of denial, and it must have reinforced my own denial – my habit of living as if I could see. Within seconds of meeting a woman, I was able to surmise what they looked like – even the shade of their lipstick. But what they were not to know was that I had reached that level of mastery only after years upon years of using alchemy to transform my ears into my eyes – of developing, in Keats's words, 'blindness keen'.

At that time, in India, the blind were considered uneducable, and there were years at a time when I was not sent to school. Eventually I went to a school for the blind in Arkansas and then to college in southern California and then to Oxford and Harvard. I became a writer. Paradoxically, in order to live in the world, I had to live as if I could see, and yet that very way of living was a hurdle to acceptance by others, especially by any woman I loved, for, as long as I continued to hide from myself, how could I expect her to truly know and love me? Still, I met women and fell in love with them. One such case was Kilty.

It was November 1968 when, as if to soften the edge of a miserable wintry day, a shy young woman whom I had encountered at parties around town walked into my office at the *New Yorker* magazine. When I was first introduced to her I'd remarked on her unusual first name and she had told me that actually it was Katherine, but then when she was being brought home from the hospital her mother had proposed several nicknames, including Kathy, Katrina and Kat, but her father had said that the baby looked too uncommon for any of them, and had come up on the spot with 'Kilty'. It had stuck.

'I see you're busy,' she now said, backing out of my office and starting quickly down the hall.

I dashed after her and caught up with her near the elevator.

'Don't go away, Kilty.'

'I don't want to disturb you,' she said.

'You are not disturbing me – you're brightening my day.' I was surprised at my words, but her shyness encouraged me.

Kilty laughed in a girlish, high-pitched way, and her laughter rippled along the corridors. As we walked back to my office she would, now and again, fall behind or step ahead, to make way for curious colleagues, who had come out of their offices to look at the source of the laughter.

Sitting down and facing me across my desk, she said, 'I think you know my father from the Century.'

Every now and then, I had indeed encountered her father, Timothy Chaste, at the Century, a men's club for writers, artists and amateurs of the arts, situated on West 43rd Street.

'I am a fan of yours, and I wonder if I could trouble you to read my poems,' Kilty said, and pushed a folder across the desk. She had a little girl's voice.

'I'd love to read your poems,' I said, and asked where I should return them to her. I seemed to remember she lived somewhere outside the city. She said she used to live in Pleasantville, but her parents had recently bought a co-op apartment, with a big mortgage, on Fifth Avenue. Last spring, when she graduated from college, she had moved in with them. She added quickly, 'Maybe instead of your just sending your comments by mail we could have coffee somewhere near here and talk about my poems.'

We agreed to meet at Schrafft's the next day, and I walked with her to the elevator.

Kilty's poems turned out to be all about love and were rather elegiac. The voice was that of a confused college girl. The verses seemed formless and incomplete. Still, when we met for coffee, I had no trouble saying encouraging things about them.

'Thank you – you can't imagine how much your opinion means to me,' she said. Her little girl's voice, though shy, sounded to me like the jingling of bangles on a beckoning hand.

'Gosh, I wouldn't have thought my opinion would be so important to you,' I said, and then, realizing that I seemed to be inviting compliments, I looked away.

'I think of you more than you know,' she replied.

*

Christmas was approaching. Kilty persuaded me to install a Christmas tree in my apartment – I had never had one before – and came round one evening to decorate it. She arrived with a sewing basket containing, among other things, pipe cleaners and colorful scraps of fabric and pieces of felt. While we sat and talked, she started stitching together some birds. Her sitting on my Italian-silk sofa and bending over the sewing in her lap – even as my mother, my sisters and my aunts had done, knitting, stitching and embroidering at home – gave the room a family touch.

When she had an assemblage of colorful birds, she showed me how to bend their little pipe-cleaner legs around the branches of the tree and we worked rapidly until much of the front of the tree was alive with the small, auspicious things. Now and again, by design as much as by accident, I touched Kilty's hand: it was long, shapely and competent.

On Christmas Eve she invited me to dinner with her parents and her younger sister, Bronwyn, at their apartment. Mr Chaste seated me between Kilty and himself and talked to me as a friend, while his wife went through all the correct motions of a cordial hostess and treated me as one of the family. Nevertheless, the evening seemed a little stiff and forced, especially because Kilty acted as if I were her parents' guest, conspicuously avoiding speaking to me. Yet the more she ignored me the more I felt drawn to her.

Early in the new year we had dinner with two friends at a German restaurant. When I walked her home, she seemed excited, almost hyper.

As we approached her building, I cautiously put my arm around her, and fully expected her to disengage herself gently. Instead, she turned her face toward me and rested her head on my shoulder.

I found myself kissing her. We circled the block, kissed again, crossed over to the park side of Fifth Avenue, kissed again and yet again.

*

In the morning, just as I walked into my office and was wondering about the appropriate time to call Kilty, the telephone rang.

'It's me,' Kilty said. Perhaps because of her little girl's voice, the greeting sounded very intimate. 'Beware,' I told myself. 'Go slow. It takes you forever to recover from a love affair.'

'Last night was wonderful,' I said, not quite certain whether I was saying the right thing.

'What are you doing tonight?' she asked.

That's a question that I should have asked, I thought.

'I'm taking you out to dinner,' I said quickly.

In speaking to her, I seemed to veer from caution to boldness, from one extreme to the other.

'Same German restaurant?' she asked.

'I thought you might like a change.'

'This little mouse is a homebody. She likes the same nibbles again and again.'

I found the way she talked in her little girl's voice about nibbles both exciting and threatening. I was reminded of my mother, who had a girlish side, and who, like a child, was by turns sweet and arbitrary. I recalled how the atmosphere of the household would change from rational discourse to arbitrary fiat whenever my father went away and we were left under my mother's thumb. One moment she'd be very cuddly when all I wanted to do was go outside and play, and the next moment she would start shouting at me for no reason I could imagine.

When Kilty and I went out to dinner that night, we happened to get the same table and the same waiter that we'd had the night before.

'The same as before,' she said. 'This little mouse –'

'I know. The mouse doesn't like change.'

'Yes!'

We both laughed.

Over dinner, Kilty told me that at boarding school and at college in Toronto she had painted posters and watercolors and sold them to fellow students in order to help pay for her education. When she came to New York, she felt that she had no practical skills for getting an ordinary job, so for the first month or two after graduation she had tried out painting as a career, and had made the rounds of galleries in SoHo and Greenwich Village. Although the gallery owners were very taken with her paintings, she didn't sell any. Her father then suggested that she try modeling – she was stunning, with a delicate face and deep blue eyes set off by long jet-black hair – and that was what she was doing now.

Modeling: what an odd suggestion for a father to make, I thought, and I asked her if she liked being a model.

'No, I don't – it's horrible. Many of the models I have to hang around with at the agencies have never set foot in a college, and they shamelessly offer themselves to slimy hustlers just to get one measly little job. Outright prostitution would be more honest than modeling.'

'Doesn't your mother object to your modeling?' I asked.

'What's wrong with people admiring a beautiful body? It makes me happy that God has given me good looks to share.'

I was taken aback by her abrupt change of stance. I quickly turned to another subject, and asked her whether she had ever thought of going to graduate school.

'After you've lived and worked in New York City as an adult, it's hard to go back to campus living,' she said.

'I suppose anything would be better than the dreary life of a graduate student,' I said, trying to be agreeable.

'How can you say that?' she asked sharply. 'I thought that, as an Oxford man, you had the highest regard for academic life. As it happens, I've been seriously considering going on to Yale for a PhD. I love studying. I could even become fond of New Haven.'

Glossing over her contradictions, I told her about my experience as a graduate student – how I had loved Oxford but found Harvard cold and uncaring.

'What was Oxford like?' Kilty asked eagerly. 'Bronwyn talks about going there when she finishes college.'

There was so much to say about Oxford that I could think of no one concrete thing. I finally said, 'I had my happiest years there.'

'What were your friends there like?'

I told her about Dom Moraes, a vivid poet friend of mine, and, on an impulse, described the funny way we'd sometimes talked, inserting 'tiny' before certain words and attaching 'kins' to others.

She suddenly became excited. 'You mean I might say to Dom, "I'm having a tiny dinner with Vedkins"?'

'That's about right. And sometimes, if we were especially silly, we would call each other "ducks". I think that was a take-off on "duckie", which is what English shop assistants used to call us.'

'How wonderful! Can we talk like that to each other?'

'You don't scorn such talk as precious and adolescent?'

'I'd love calling my tiny boyfriend Vedkins.'

Gosh, what have I let myself in for? I thought. That stuff had sounded pretty silly even at Oxford when we were undergraduates.

'I don't think that kind of fatuous Oxford talk would go over in America,' I said.

'Why do you always think in big categories, like women and America? The "tiny" stuff will be our private talk, just between you and me. You know, I still call Bronwyn "Roo", and she calls me "Piggy-winks". And sometimes when we really don't want anyone to know what we're saying, we talk pig Latin, lickety-split. So you see that we Americans have silly talk, too.'

'What are you thinking?' Kilty said a moment later.

'I was just wondering if you minded that I wasn't an American.'

'You are such a wondrous bird. Don't you know that we Americans are all originally immigrants?'

'So you don't mind?'

'I find you very exotic – like baklava!'

On the street corner, I hesitated between turning south and taking her to her parents' apartment and turning north and inviting her to my apartment. Kilty instinctively turned north, and I fell in step.

Once we were inside my apartment, she sat down on the sofa. I sat down next to her, and we embraced.

Later, as I switched off the lamp on the bedside table, I remembered an episode with Gigi, my first serious girlfriend, when I had suddenly become impotent. I started shivering.

'Why are you shivering so?'

'It's no good!' I cried, pulling away from her. 'I'm good for nothing.'

'Shhh.'

'You should have nothing to do with me,' I cried into the pillow.

'Shhh.'

'I can't stop shivering. It's all over.' I was getting maudlin. 'You don't know awful things about me,' I said. 'I'm not a man.'

I expected Kilty to say, as Gigi had done, that I shouldn't worry, that it didn't matter – I wanted her to console me – but she did nothing of the kind. Instead, she said, 'First-time jitters.' She threw herself on me and wrapped herself around me, biting and licking me. I remember thinking that she was as voluptuous as a Zola heroine.

I revived in a rush. She was initiating me into making love with my whole body. My relief, however, was momentary. Her wild passion stirred a new fear in me, different from the earlier, paralyzing one but equally intense – that she would be demanding and uncontrollable. I never stopped to think whether she was actually wild or I simply perceived her that way, because I was still ignorant of the true scope of a woman's passion and needs. Even as I was delighting in her unrestrained lovemaking, I worried that I might not measure up to her expectations, and so a more desirable man would materialize and tear her away from me.

'You're scowling. What's the matter?' she asked.

'Nothing. Just for a moment, I had a bad thought.'

'What was it?'

'I was remembering some losses.'

'You are my strange, tiny Vedkins. My very own tiny Vedkins.'

I take things too seriously, I thought. I must learn to enjoy things. She's being playful. That's part of lovemaking.

I fell asleep with my cheek resting on her shoulder.

W here shall I put the question? I asked myself. The apartment? There's no romance in that. In a restaurant? That's a public place. On the Top of the Sixes, with a stunning view of the city I love? That's touristy. On a boat on the Circle Line? That's certainly romantic, but also public and a bit tacky. Take her away to an inn somewhere in the Catskills? That's sort of middle-aged – OK for divorcées and widowers but not right for young love. Walking along the Brooklyn Bridge? That's all right for spring, but not for the winter. Still, I didn't want to let another day go by. We'd been together now for only a few weeks, but I was deeply and irrevocably in love. Trying to learn from what I thought of as mistakes with other women, I was determined not to be tardy and casual. I felt that I had to take control and act quickly.

When I was in high school, I had fallen under the spell of J.D. Salinger and his toy epic, *The Catcher in the Rye*, and had been mesmerized by Holden Caulfield's ingenuous question to a New York taxi driver: 'You know those ducks in that lagoon right near Central Park South? That little lake? By any chance, do you happen to know where they go, the ducks, when it gets all frozen over?' In my adolescence, I had identified with those migrating ducks.

I decided that as soon as Kilty and I got together that evening, I would coax her to take a walk with me in Central Park and steer her to the duck pond. We had generally been meeting for dinner at my apartment after she finished her day of modeling – or, what was more likely, looking for modeling jobs. But that day she was held up during some modeling session and didn't get to my apartment until about nine-thirty, by which time it was dark and not safe to be out in the Park. It was also fiercely cold. I had to put off my proposal until the next day, and I thought that that was just as well, because it happened to be Saturday and I could take her to the Park in the afternoon, when the sun might be out.

After we'd had a potluck – since I was incompetent in the kitchen, she always did the preparing – she slumped down on the bed, uncharacteristically neglecting to wash the dishes, and said, 'I hate my body. I hate men gawking at me. It makes me shy all over. When I'm posing for the camera, I always squirm and fidget, and then they have me start all over again. That just makes the sessions longer and more agonizing.'

'You are tired, sweet – just close your eyes and rest,' I said, lying down next to her and reaching for her.

'Leave me alone,' she said, and she turned to the wall and began crying into the pillow. 'I hate you,' she sobbed.

'You can't mean that,' I said, trying to get close to her.

She edged away from me, toward the wall.

'Has something happened?' I asked weakly.

'You should know.'

'Kiltykins,' I said, 'what has happened to my tiny girlfriend?'

'Don't you dare call me that.'

She had never spoken to me that way before, and she seemed so remote that I myself started crying.

'Please turn to me, please look at me,' I pleaded, but she kept her face averted and pressed into the pillow. I ventured to stroke her back, but she didn't respond.

'I hate being a kept woman. Why haven't you asked me to marry you?' she demanded, her voice muffled by the pillow.

'Oh, no! Is that what's rankling you? This very evening, I was going to ask you to ma-ma-marry.' I still couldn't say the word without stammering, so the sentence remained unfinished. I was now almost thirty-five. The long years of wanting to be married hadn't helped me overcome the feeling that I could never be married.

'You were really going to ask me?' Suddenly warm and tender, she wiped my tears away with the end of the bed sheet and snuggled up next to me, as abruptly as she had earlier turned her back on me. 'I feel like a bad girl. Will you forgive your tiny Kiltykins? Sometimes demons take hold of me. I don't know where they come from, but they come and go like dog days.'

'I was going to propose to you this very night, and then we could have tied the knot whenever you wanted.'

'What were you going to say?'

'Some sweet things,' I said, and I told her of my plans.

'Well, let's go there tomorrow, just as you planned – by the duck pond,' she said.

'You don't think I've ruined the surprise?'

'But I haven't given my answer. A lady needs to be properly wooed and given time to think.'

She then threw herself on me passionately.

The next day I took Kilty for lunch at a little Italian restaurant on Madison Avenue, and afterward we walked over, through a cold, sunless afternoon, to the pond. It was windswept and bleak, and there was not a single duck or child in sight.

'Well?' she prompted.

I was flustered. 'Will you marry me?' My words came out in a single breath. I wondered whether I had surrendered to her what should have been entirely my initiative.

'In books, men kneel on one knee.'

I knelt down, and she seemed happy.

'But I'm waiting for your answer,' I said.

'You know so little about me. I gave you my answer when I slept with you.'

'I was hoping for a definitive response, sweet.'

She flung her arms around me and kissed me powerfully, murmuring, 'Yes . . . yes . . . yes . . . yes.'

As Kilty and I were walking back to my apartment, after the formalities at the duck pond, I said to her giddily, 'The moment we get home, I'm going to telephone my parents in New Delhi, and Jasper and Miriam, my friends in Oxford . . .'

Her hand in mine went rigid.

'Are you all right?'

'Yes,' she said, in a distant voice. Then she said, 'You aren't to breathe a word about marriage to a soul.'

'I won't if you don't want me to – but why not?'

'Don't ask me any questions unless you want me to flip.'

'I won't,' I said accommodatingly.

H er spell – or whatever it was – passed, but the rest of the way home I stepped along in a gingerly fashion, as if my very balance had been shaken. Finally, in the evening, when she was her relaxed, flirtatious self again, I asked her the reason for the secrecy.

'I must speak to Pappy and Mother before anyone else hears about our marriage. You can't have any idea how much persuading it will take to get them to agree. I'll have to find just the right moment, or everything may go kaput.'

'I don't understand,' I said. 'You talk as if your parents regarded me as a pariah.'

'The problem is not with you, sweet. It's with them. You don't know my parents. Mother is so moral, with such strict principles, that she would never give her consent – never accept you into the family if she knew that you'd already slept with me.'

'Why does your mother have to know anything about that?'

'She has her ways of finding out. Ever since I was small, she has been able to look right through me and know whether I'm lying.'

I tried another approach. 'Maybe I could have a word with your father in the club.'

'You don't know Pappy. He's very possessive of me. Only Mother can bring him around.'

'I know he's eccentric,' I said, 'but he has always been friendly to me at the club. I think I can talk to him man-to-man.' I realized as I spoke that I owed such self-confidence to Kilty.

'Please don't even think of talking to Pappy,' she protested. 'If you love me, you will let me handle my parents in my own way.'

'I will, but I need to understand what I'm up against.'

'If you must know, Pappy and Mother want for their daughters blond, blue-eyed, tall, all-American boys, who are good Protestants like themselves. And you are dark, and unconventional in looks and on top of it, an Indian and a Hindu. Another thing against you is that you are a writer. Pappy has had so little success with his drawings that he never wanted us girls to go near anyone who was in the arts. He wants us to marry doctors or lawyers.'

I said to Kilty, 'You've got to lead your own life. It may take your parents some time but they are good people and they will accept anyone you love.'

'I know that. And time is the very thing I want to give them. All I ask of you is patience.'

Patience, I thought. How can I forget how patient she was on our first night together?

So it was that what should have been our joyous news became our miserable secret. When we were together near my apartment, we'd skulk around in case her parents might catch sight of us and she even stopped meeting me anywhere in the vicinity of the club, in case we should run into her father.

At the time Muriel Spark had an office across the corridor from mine at the *New Yorker*, and we became fast friends. Hardly anyone was more fun to be with than Muriel. She dressed like a schoolgirl but had a muscular intelligence, and was full of tart observations and laughter. I was so taken with her and her books that within a few weeks of meeting her I'd read nearly all her novels.

I told Muriel about Kilty, and after that Muriel would always ask me, 'How are you and Kilty getting along, Veders? When am I going to hear some wedding bells?' Not knowing that all the resistance came from Kilty, she used to badger me for holding back.

One evening, she had dinner with Kilty and me in the apartment, and after she had gone Kilty said, 'I found your friend Muriel cold and frightening. I couldn't wait for her to leave. I'm sure she has X-ray eyes and she could see right through me.'

'I don't think she has X-ray eyes at all,' I said. 'Nor is she particularly cold.'

'If you say so,' Kilty said in a resigned tone. Then she picked up and opened Muriel's novel *The Bachelors*, which Muriel had brought as a present. 'Look, she has inscribed it to you: "To my favourite bachelor." What a wonderful inscription.'

'Actually, it's a bloody insult, à la Muriel,' I said. 'She's comparing me to the criminal-protagonist of the novel. As she sees it, I am leading a barren life. She's as acerbic with her pen as she's sweet with her tongue. On second thought, maybe she just wishes me well and is trying to hasten me on toward marriage.'

'So she guessed our secret?'

'It's no secret that we are seeing each other,' I said.

'I'm sure she thinks I'm a witch.' Kilty's voice quavered so eerily that I almost had the illusion that it belonged to someone else.

'I'm sure she thinks no such thing,' I said.

One evening, soon after Muriel Spark's visit, both Kilty and I got off work a little early, and we walked over to a market and bought shrimp, rice, asparagus, onions, thyme and bay leaf. When we got home, laden with our purchases, I put *Don Giovanni*, a favorite opera of ours, on the gramophone while Kilty prepared an East-West combination of shrimp curry and wild rice. As always, it was exciting to have Kilty puttering about in my kitchen and filling the apartment with homey aromas. She deftly cut, mixed and ground – at every stage cleaning up after herself, so that the kitchen was almost as neat as when she started. Perhaps because for most of my life I had been living in a solitary environment, I was disturbed by disorder and so was especially taken with her standards of neatness.

When Kilty finished in the kitchen, we went into the living room, turned the opera down and ate at the dining table. After dinner I poured a little brandy into a couple of crystal snifters and we settled down together on the sofa.

'Coby called today, and I'm going to Philadelphia to see him tomorrow,' she said without any preliminaries. 'I broke up with him last October, just before I went to Paris with Michael.'

I knew about Michael – he was a good friend of mine – but Coby was news. I was stunned.

'You've never mentioned Coby before,' I said.

'You've never mentioned any of your ex-girlfriends to me, either.' Her tone was defiant – one of tit for tat.

Why had I never stopped to think about her earlier involvements, I wondered. Why hadn't I learned something from my experience with Gigi? Why had I simply assumed that I was Kilty's first love, even though every woman I had previously been involved with seemed to bring with her the memory of another lover?

'But there hasn't been a woman in my life for a long time,' I protested.

'I know,' she said, putting her head affectionately on my shoulder. 'Don't be alarmed.'

'But I am, very alarmed. How many beaux have you had?'

'You know about my liaison with Michael, and I had a beau when I was at boarding school, but Coby, whom I started dating in college, was the only serious one.'

'How long were you together?'

'Two, three years, but why is that important?'

'Do you still think about him?'

'I still sometimes wake up from dreaming about him.'

'Do you dream much about me?'

'Do you feel competitive with him?'

'Yes, and desperately jealous.'

'I can't swear that you have no reason not to be.' She cuddled up to me. 'Sweet, don't put me through an inquisition.'

'I must know, Kilty. I can't –' I broke off.

'Before I can be really all yours I must take leave of Coby properly. I will have no peace unless I do.'

'Kilty, I've gone through this business of waiting for a girlfriend to say goodbye to an old boyfriend before,' I said. 'I'm not going through it again.'

She pulled away and half stood up. 'You want me to walk out the door and never come back?' Her voice quavered, as it had after she met Muriel.

Her threat was so unexpected and so at variance with my perception of her character that I wondered in passing whether I knew the woman I had so recently proposed to at all.

'Please don't talk like that,' I said. 'I'll do anything you want. Sit back down. Relax.'

On the gramophone, Leporello was singing '*Madamina, il catalogo è questo*'.

'There is no way I could ever be happy with you – or with anyone else – unless I squared things up with Coby,' she said, sitting down and sounding like a little girl again.

I didn't want to hear anything more about Coby. Images of her kissing him were already disturbing me. I felt as though I needed a Wailing Wall. I told myself that instead of sweeping away thoughts about Coby I should try to learn every last thing about him.

Inwardly, I was crying, but I said, in my most encouraging voice (the one I used for interviewing reluctant subjects), 'Tell me more about Coby. He sounds fascinating.'

'You know the way people refer to Frank Sinatra as "Old Blue Eyes"? Well, everyone at Toronto used to refer to Coby as "Bedroom Eyes".'

The nickname was so unexpected that I flinched.

'What does "Bedroom Eyes" mean?' I demanded. 'It tells me nothing about his eyes. Are they restless, or deep, or penetrating, or seductive? Is his gaze so intense that you feel you are in his power? Are they those X-ray eyes that can see through you, unclothe you?'

'Don't overdo it,' she said. 'I know how you feel.'

'I'd really like to know who my competition is,' I said.

'To begin with, he's not your competition. Besides, you must control your jealous impulses.'

'It's only fair that I should know something about him,' I said. 'What did he major in? What is he doing in Philadelphia?'

'Please, don't. Not so fast.'

'Who is he? How long have you known him?' I knew I was beginning to sound prosecutorial, but I couldn't seem to check myself.

'If you must know, we met at Toronto. We were taking the same class and he started passing notes to me.'

Exchanging billets-doux right under the nose of the unsuspecting professor – how sly and intimate.

'Now Coby's at the University of Pennsylvania Law School,' she said. 'He's the top student there.'

Oh, God! Unlike me, he will have a real profession, I thought. He can give her financial security, while I can only struggle to make ends meet.

'Why do you look so sad?' she asked.

'Is Coby very handsome?' I asked.

'When I first saw him, I ran in the other direction, because he looks like a movie star. But, sweet, don't torture yourself. I've broken up with him, and that's the end of it.'

'But it's not the end of it if you want to go and see him.'

'I want to go and be with him, not for my sake but for his. He can be really violent, and I want to make sure he doesn't do harm to himself.'

'Why couldn't you just talk to him on the telephone?'

'As I told you, I am finished with him, but he's not finished with me. I have to help him get over me.'

'If I were you, I'd make myself scarce – cut off all communication,' I said. 'Otherwise, you'll simply be reminding him of what he's lost, and prolonging his misery.'

'How little you understand about women.'

Understand women! Was I as ignorant about them as she seemed to think I was? And how different from men were they, really?

'It's true. I don't have much knowledge of women,' I said.

'But at college you must have gone on a lot of dates.'

'I didn't,' I said. 'I must know where you will be staying if you go to Philadelphia.'

'In Coby's apartment.'

'Why do you have to stay with him?'

'Why not? I've always stayed with him. If you think Coby would let me stay anywhere else, you're crazy.'

I could contain myself no longer. 'Kilty, I'll go mad if you stay with Coby. It's cruel. It's unbearable.'

I half expected her to get up and head for the door, but she didn't make a move. Instead, she said, in a bantering tone, 'I thought that as a writer you would have a greater range of sympathies – that you'd be tolerant of people who are quirky and do unconventional things.'

'I might like to write about someone who's quirky and does unconventional things, and I might even be drawn to such a person, but it doesn't follow that I would want to live with her.'

'So my Vedkins doesn't want to live with me.'

'Kilty, be serious. You know that's not what I was saying. I just find the idea of your staying with Coby insane.'

'I am disappointed in you.'

'*I* am disappointed in *you.*'

'I'm going.'

Kilty went to Philadelphia on Friday without giving me Coby's number. She asked me merely to wait for her calls, and then she didn't telephone until Saturday afternoon. She explained that she hadn't been able to call earlier, because she couldn't talk privately to me from Coby's apartment.

'Where are you calling from, then?' I asked.

'From a telephone booth.'

I knew that I was being blunt, but I asked her, 'You aren't sleeping with him, are you?'

'What do you think?'

'Of course not.'

'Then why do you ask?'

'Look, Kilty, I'm going crazy. Just swear to me that you're not.'

'I swear.'

'Do you cuddle?'

'What kind of question is that?'

'Kilty, I have to know.'

'He tries, but I tell him I'm spoken for. Don't you trust your Kiltykins?'

'I do, but I grew up hearing my father say, "All men are wolves." '

'Then your father has Coby's number.' She laughed.

'Don't you see why I have these head-splitting images? Can't you just say goodbye to Coby and get on the next train and come back?'

'I gave Coby my word that I would stay with him for three days.'

'Tell him that your fiancé is about to check into the mental hospital – that he needs you.'

'Shhh. I told you that has to be a secret.'

'What? My going into the loony bin?'

'No, silly, the duck pond.'

'Why can't you say "our engagement"? Coby isn't there, is he?'

'I think of it as "duck pond". Do you mind?'

'But why does that have to be a secret from him?'

'Because he's my mother's pet. He still talks to her. Or when he's feeling lonely he calls Bronwyn. They call each other Buddy, and they're very close.'

'I myself need some comforting.'

'Why don't you take Bronwyn out to lunch?'

My anger was mounting.

'I'm sorry I'm putting you through all this, but it's necessary,' she said. 'Do you know why I love you so much? Because you're the strongest man I've ever known. Stronger than Coby, stronger than Pappy. Just let me get through this in my own way.'

'But I don't feel strong. I have these nightmares. I seem to be always shivering.'

'In a little more than two days, I'll be back, dear heart.'

'Where do you sleep?'

'You know that law students are very poor. He just has a studio apartment.'

'How many beds does he have?'

'One.'

'One? So where do you camp out?'

'He has a sofa.'

'Where do you get dressed?'

'In the bathroom.'

'What do you wear when you sleep?'

'A nightie.'

'Does he turn off the lights, or does he see you in your nightie?'

'Of course, he sees me in my nightie. I told you, he lives in a one-room apartment.'

'Is there a lock on the bathroom door?'

'What questions you ask! I don't know. Vedkins, I trust him. He would never do anything stupid. If he did, that would be the end of everything.'

'But I thought everything had already ended.'

'I mean, after something like that we couldn't even be friends.'

'I don't think you can be friends with someone with whom you had a deep involvement. There is too much history.'

'Most of the time, I forget you're not an American, but sometimes you really talk like an Indian.'

'I am an Indian.'

'But you're living in America.'

'Your toilet things.'

'What about them?'

'Do you keep them in a toilet bag or are they spread around the bathroom?'

'I don't have a toilet bag. When have you ever seen me with a toilet bag?'

'I don't want your toothbrush to be touching his toothbrush.'

'What did you say?'

'Dammit, I don't want him to be mucking around with your toilet things.'

'He would never do that. I must go. Coby is calling me.'

'I thought you were telephoning from someplace other than his apartment.'

'I'm calling from a bank, but he's waiting outside the booth.'

When she finally came back from Philadelphia, I asked her, 'Are you over and done with Coby?'

'You talk as if I'd gone to bury him.'

'Kilty, you know what I mean.'

'I don't.' There was a sharpness in her voice that made me wince. 'Do you think you can finish a relationship over a weekend? Is that how you finish your relationships? You should have warned me if that's the kind of person you are.'

'But, Kilty, you told me –'

'I told you that I will be all yours, but only after I have nursed Coby through this terrible black period.'

'You don't mean to say you'll have to go back to Philadelphia?'

'I think I can handle it over the telephone, and take care of things when he comes to New York – or, at least, that's what I think now. But I must be free to do whatever I think is right.'

'Why in hell would he be coming to New York?'

'To see me, Bronwyn and Mother. Besides, he has some family here.'

'Did your mother find him suitable for you?'

'Of course. He is so handsome and presentable.'

'In other words, I'm not.'

'What do you expect? He looks like a movie idol.'

'Then your mother is dumb to prefer him to me. I mean "would be" when she gets to know about us.'

'Now you're getting personal. In America, we are not rude about people's mothers.'

Listening to her, I sometimes felt that she was the reasonable one and I was the unreasonable one. How could I expect Coby to stop loving Kilty, just like that? Would I have Kilty treat Coby with any less kindness than my last girlfriend had treated me? The truth was that I was beginning to discover in myself sympathy for Coby. I told myself, 'You've been behaving like an ogre. Stop persecuting Kilty. Show some understanding for Coby.'

'You must help him to get over you,' I said. 'In his place, I would expect nothing less from my Kilty.'

Summer came and went. Every two or three weeks either Kilty would go to Philadelphia or Coby would turn up unexpectedly in New York. And she so arranged matters – unconsciously, I presumed – that I was never able to meet Coby and judge for myself how much of a threat he really was. On top of all that, she would frequently swear that she was going to talk to her parents about our engagement and would later come up with an excuse for not doing so. Whenever I pushed her on the subject, her voice would harden and her hands would tense up. At first, I didn't know what to do, but eventually I caught on that if I hugged her she would immediately relax, almost as if she had been playing a little game.

One Saturday evening, when I was walking Kilty home after dinner, she was especially warm and forthcoming and I seized the opportunity to bring up something that had been puzzling me about her.

'I sometimes feel that I know two Kiltys. I mean, there is this Kilty I am walking with. But there is also the other Kilty, who, without any warning, can become as stiff as a poker.'

'You're talking about the demon Kilty. I'd like to be free of her, too, but I have no control over her.' There was an undertone of deep distress in her little girl's voice.

'Why don't you have control over those demons?' I asked, gently.

'Because Libbie takes me over.'

'Who is Libbie?' I pressed.

'Libbie was our little sister.'

'I've never heard you mention her before.'

'We never talk about her, because Pappy was watching her on the beach. She was just a little girl when she drowned. Maybe Pappy's attention wandered, or maybe Bronwyn and I distracted him. Please don't ask me for any more details.' She seemed on the verge of tears.

As I was kissing Kilty goodbye just outside her building, she said, 'I'll be leaving for New Haven tomorrow. I've been accepted at Yale.' She was going to study for a PhD in English literature.

I berated her for never telling me about her plans.

'I applied just as a lark. I was sure I wouldn't get in.'

'I can't bear the thought that you'll be in New Haven while I'm in New York. If you want to go to graduate school, why don't you go to Columbia?'

'It's too late to apply anywhere else now, and Yale is giving me money.'

The next day, I took Kilty to Grand Central Station, and hauled her suitcase full of clothes and books from the taxi to the platform.

'It won't be too bad for you, sweet, will it?' she asked.

I felt like yelling, 'What do you think? Why are you doing this to us?' But instead I said, 'No, it won't be too bad. I'll try to come up on weekends.'

'Wouldn't that be very disruptive to your work?'

'It will be OK.'

'It will be expensive – what with taxis, trains, hotels and restaurants.'

'I'll manage,' I said.

'So you'll come up next Friday?'

I hadn't planned on it, but I said yes.

'So we'll be separated for only five days – right?'

'Right.'

'And every night I'll call you and wish you goodnight.'

'Yes, of course.'

'Once I get used to graduate school, maybe I'll be able to come down for weekends and spare you the trouble. And, you know, I don't have to stay at Yale the whole year. Your Kiltykins might be fed up to her gills by December.'

'Since you're going, you should make the best of it,' I told her. Why am I saying things that I don't mean, I wondered. By not being honest about my feelings, I'm playing games with her. But what choice do I have?

'Dealing with my parents will be so much easier once I'm not living under their roof. I could announce our wedding to Mother and Pappy over the phone, and if they didn't agree we could just go down to City Hall in December and get married.'

'Yes, of course.' I felt old and tired.

Within hours of her departure, Kilty sent me a telegram saying
that unless I objected she would arrive in New York City the following
Friday evening. That made me wonder why she hadn't waited until
the end of the day, when we would be talking on the telephone.

Kilty arrived in the city late that Friday. I suggested that the next day
we go to Cartier so that I could get her an engagement ring. 'Even if
you shouldn't wear the ring, it would be a testament of our promise
at the duck pond,' I said.

Kilty agreed with such alacrity that I reproached myself for not
having suggested the expedition earlier.

At the jeweler's, the salesman, a vice president of the company,
announced in a manner both deferential and unctuous, 'I have never
failed to satisfy a bride with just the right ring.' As he brought out
a tray of rings with ornate settings of single diamonds flanked by
smaller diamond baguettes, he added, 'Diamonds are forever.'

Kilty shyly slipped one or two of the rings on to her finger but
then said firmly, 'I don't like diamonds.'

The salesman was clearly surprised but, turning to me, he said,
'Madam is right. Diamonds are not for everybody.' He turned to
Kilty and asked her if she had a favorite stone.

'Gravestone,' she said to me, under her breath in pig Latin, but
brightly asked the salesman if he could show her some rubies, and he
brought out another tray of rings. Kilty chose a modest platinum ring
discreetly set with a blood-red stone, and, putting it on her finger,
examined it, back and front.

'I love it,' she said. 'I think I read somewhere that this is a stone of
passion.' Taking it off and playing with it, she asked the salesman if there
was any danger of the stone's falling off while she was washing the dishes.

Another educated girl might look down on domesticity, but my
Kilty thrives on it – goes public with it, I thought. Maybe we really are
on our way to being married.

'I can guarantee, madam, that the ruby is well set and that the ring
can undergo a lot of punishment,' the salesman said.

'We'll take it,' I said, without asking the price.

'Spoken like a bridegroom,' the salesman remarked.

I started. The word 'groom' made me think of someone taking care of a horse, rather than a woman, and, in any case, it did not quite fit me.

I made out a cheque for $1,102.40. While the salesman was writing the receipt, with his back to us, Kilty put the engagement ring back on her finger and said, in a whisper, 'This tiny duckie now has a duck-pond souvenir.'

She might go about things in a lighthearted way, but she fully savors them, I thought. Her way is much better than my serious approach.

One day in early October, Kilty announced on the telephone, without any preliminary, 'I may never be able to do it.'

'Do what, sweet?'

'Marry you.'

For a moment, I imagined that she was in the middle of one of her demon fits.

'You're not being serious,' I said soothingly.

'I am too,' she said petulantly.

As we talked on, it appeared that she had made up her mind to call the whole thing off.

'Is there another man in the picture?'

'Boys are constantly ogling me in the classroom and on the streets. It's very flattering. But you know your Kilty isn't fickle.'

Your Kilty – the words confused me.

'You don't know what you are saying,' I said.

'I need time, lots of time.'

'If you are so unsure, maybe we should stop seeing each other,' I responded, but as soon as my words were out I regretted them.

The last thing that I imagined was that she'd take me up on it, but she said, 'If that's the way you feel, I think we should stop seeing each other, but remember the onus is on you.' She hung up.

I was too proud to call her back, and she didn't call me. A few days
went by. All that time, I kept thinking that this was merely a lovers'
quarrel – a temporary impasse, which we would somehow soon get
over. Then I received a letter from her with a protruding object, which
turned out to be a pink seashell. Its outside was so crinkly and knotty
that it could have been a piece of bark, while the inside was so smooth
and fine that it could have been a piece of glass. She might have had
any number of reasons for choosing that particular seashell – she
liked it, she'd just been to a beach, and so on – but I imagined that she
was telling me to take the rough with the smooth. Her letter, however,
said that she loved me.

I felt I could now initiate a call to her without injury to my pride.

'Are you very sad?' These were the first words from her on the
telephone.

'Overwhelmingly so,' I said.

'I know,' she said. 'I can't help it. I'm very sorry. I'll be a good girl
from now on, I promise. But I warn you, sometimes those roaming
demons take over your Kilty, and it's as if I had no control over what
I say and do.'

One weekend I took a train to New Haven and there, on a glorious day
in late fall, we sat under a tree on the campus with students sprawled
all around us – eating, talking, or simply basking in the warmth of a
brief Indian summer.

'Being in these surroundings reminds me of my failures at
Harvard,' I said, and then, thinking that I was being too gloomy, I
added, 'I'm told that in Japan people glorify failure, as if success were
ignoble.'

'Maybe, after we get married, we should go and live in Japan. I'm
ready for something different.'

Her mention of marriage, unprompted, lifted my spirits, and set
the tone for the rest of the weekend.

A day or two later, in New York, I received a letter from Kilty. It
was written on a sheet torn from a Latin notebook with declensions

of the three pronouns ego, nos and vos on one side and on the other this message:

> Darling, I love you. I miss you. I could only be writing this to you. Do you believe me? The radiator bings. Also a cold draft hits our legs. Our heads are hot. For the class, he has put aside his pipe. The dullest are in the class. He wears a college blazer, consumes our time with impossibly dull genius. Because of him, us are uniformly restless. How can we let him know that he is bound by the social contract to be quiet.

The letter, if a little incoherent, was so evocative of damp New Haven and self-absorbed Yale, that it seemed sheer poetry to me. Another delightful and loving letter followed. I wrote and told her that I could no longer go on living without her, that she had to take her parents into her confidence and stop wavering. She immediately responded with two telegrams, dispatched within a half an hour of each other. Because they were sent to the office over the weekend, I didn't get them until the following Monday. The first telegram read:

> SATURDAY NOVEMBER 22 SORRY TO SEND THIS TO THE OFFICE CANT REACH YOU BY PHONE I LOVE YOU AND WANT TO MARRY YOU NOW OR WHEN EVER YOU CHOOSE IF YOU DONT CALL BY MONDAY NIGHT I WILL KNOW THAT YOU HAVE DECIDED NO LOVE KILTY

And the second telegram went,

> DARLING PLEASE TELEPHONE I LOVE YOU AND WANT TO BE WITH YOU FOR ALWAYS KILTY

On the one hand, her telegrams filled me with hope and excitement, but, on the other, they made me weary. Could she really think that my failure to call her within forty-eight hours would indicate that I didn't want to marry her? And why send the telegrams on a weekend to my office rather than to my apartment? Was she just being absent-minded or did she consciously want me to miss her deadline? I should have noticed a kind of danger signal in these telegrams, but as soon as I read them I got her on the telephone. She said that she was determined to get married before Christmas and would be coming down to New York on Friday to make all the necessary arrangements.

Kilty had vacillated so much that I didn't allow myself to take her coming for granted until she actually arrived on Friday November 28. This was such a heady period that for years afterward I remembered each date as if I were marking off days in an Advent calendar. That weekend, she talked about quitting Yale, arranging the wedding, and going on a honeymoon to Merano, in northern Italy; her friend Sophie had been there, and reported that it was an incomparable place. For myself, after all I had lived through, I had trouble thinking beyond the wedding, especially since Kilty had still not broken the news to her parents. I had come to share her dread of approaching her parents, so that I now imagined they had the power to abort our plans.

'You leave Pappy and Mother to me,' she would say stubbornly whenever I brought up the subject. 'They lost Libbie, and they won't want to lose Kilty. But I have to get at them in my own way and in my own time. Actually, I'm sure they have already guessed, and reconciled themselves to everything.'

As luck would have it, I won a free trip to New Delhi in an airline raffle the same Friday that Kilty came down to the city to set our marriage plans in motion. Since coming to the West, I had had such limited funds that I had been able to go home only twice in twenty years. And just then my father, who had heart trouble, was not keeping well. I mentioned the free trip to Kilty and asked her what she thought of it.

Before the words were out of my mouth, I regretted them. Kilty would not hear of my passing up the trip.

'You have to go,' she said. 'It would be easier for me to talk to my parents if my Vedkins wasn't sitting around waiting for an hour-by-hour account.'

Even as Kilty is tackling her parents, I will be giving the good tidings to my family, I thought. For many years, my relatives had been waiting for the news of my marriage. I had now turned thirty-five and, in their eyes, was long past the Hindu stage of a householder – of becoming a family man in my own right. The Hindu life cycle calls for a man to devote his first twenty-five years to learning, his second to raising a family, his third to doing community service, and his fourth to preparing to take leave of worldly cares.

'I'll just go for a week,' I said. 'Two days and two nights will be taken up by flying there and back, but I will have five days at home. That will be plenty.' I remember noticing that she seemed to be relieved that I was going, but I told myself that that was natural, given the pressure of making wedding plans in such a short time.

On Monday December 1, in order to fulfill a requirement for the marriage license, Kilty and I got our blood drawn by my doctor. The next morning, furnished with the blood-test reports, we rode down in the subway to City Hall and obtained a marriage license, stamped DECEMBER 2, 1969, 11:53 A.M. It admonished us: THE MARRIAGE SOLEMNIZATION MAY NOT BE PERFORMED WITHIN 24 HOURS AFTER THIS DATE. If the date had been left up to me, we would have returned to City Hall on December 3 and got married. But Kilty wanted a proper wedding, so we settled on December 20 – the Saturday before Christmas and almost a year to the day since she had trimmed the Christmas tree in my apartment. She thought that would give her enough time to find a wedding dress and to invite the few guests we wanted. We got in touch with Judge J. Howard Rossbach in Riverdale, a friend of mine, and he agreed to save the date and perform the ceremony.

'The marriage plans are going lickety-split,' Kilty said. 'Now I feel we are going to be married, for real.'

'I feel that, too,' I said.

Postscript: Dr Bak

It was thanks to Kilty – in my despair of her – that I became a patient myself. For two years I went for psychotherapy for two hours a week at forty dollars an hour. For two years after that, I went for deep psychoanalysis for four hours a week at the same hourly rate. For those four years, I saw Dr Bak at his office on the thirteenth floor of a building at the corner of 87th and Park. Bak, a pillar of the New York psychoanalytic establishment, was a large, dark, imposing man; he had the authoritarian air and debonair manner of a European aristocrat. He seemed always to have a Monte Cristo No. 2 in his mouth and the cigar was always lit, which gave me the impression of Dr Bak as a dragon breathing fire. He had a basso voice and an elusive, confusing way of speaking. I fancied that he spoke that way either because English was not his first language (he was a Hungarian Jew who had escaped to the US in 1941) or because, as a psychoanalyst, he thought that he could keep his patients off balance by making them struggle to understand him, and thereby get them to yield more unconscious material. But his English pronunciation was good – with the exception of guttural consonants such as 'k' and 'g' which he often transposed. In sessions with Dr Bak, Kilty became Gilty.

'I feel I'm talked out about Kilty today,' I said at one point in my third session. 'I can't think of anything more to say about her.'

'You have a lot to say about Gilty. That's my impression from the other two times you've come here.'

'It's hard to talk about her to a complete stranger,' I said.

For a couple of minutes he just puffed at his cigar and leaned back in his big chair, waiting for me to go on. 'Maybe all you needed were these three consultations with me.'

For the next three years I talked endlessly about my past loves, among other things. I talked about Kilty and Lola, Vanessa and Gigi, but I

never referred to my blindness, just as the women had never referred
to it. The subject just never came up; even the word itself was never
mentioned. When the dam eventually broke – that's another story – I
flooded Dr Bak with questions. Did I fall for these women because,
like my mother, they denied my blindness? Or did they fall in love
with me because I was blind? By falling in love with me, were they
denying their own beauty? Did they think that in some magical way
I could tell they were beautiful, despite the fact that I couldn't see?
Was it their fantasy that I could actually see, and did their love turn to
ashes when it clashed with reality? Since the fantasy had served me
well in my writing, did I assume that it would serve me well in love?

I asked Dr Bak, 'Why didn't you bring up the subject of my
blindness months or years ago? I wasted all this effort coming here
and paying my hard-earned money by talking about everything else
but the most obvious subject.'

Dr Bak replied, 'But if an insight doesn't come from within you,
it is like reading a book. You feel that it is about someone else – not
you. It doesn't get integrated into your psyche. You continue to resist
the insight.'

'What do you mean?'

'You are forcing me to be very pedantic. Resistance is a psychological
defense mechanism that we all have, but it is also a way of fending off
unpleasant truths.'

'And of course it could be that my blindness played no role in any
of those women falling in love with me or leaving me.'

'Yes, it could be.'

'But then I suppose you would say that if I had been reconciled
to the fact of my blindness I would have fallen for a different kind of
woman. Maybe a woman who wouldn't have ended up hurting me.'

'Yes, it could be.'

One June day, Kilty telephoned and told me that she had gone
into deep psychoanalysis with Dr Aldridge and that he had
reached the conclusion that she was 'unanalyzable'.

'Dr Aldridge says that, though unusual, sometimes that is the case,' she said. 'I feel that a stone has been lifted from my head. Now that I am free of these shrinks once and for all, I can go on, as I always have, like a blunderhead.' She laughed as if she were making a joke, but rather demonically, I thought, as if also to underscore the fact that, in contrast to her freedom, I would be a slave to psychoanalysis for many more years.

I reported Kilty's call to Bak in my penultimate session before the summer break. Like most psychoanalysts, he took a vacation from his patients in July and August.

'Blunderbuss,' he laughed, from his chair at my head. 'Unconsciously, she wants to shoot dead the person who dares to fall in love with her.'

'Utter nonsense.' He didn't rise to the challenge.

'The galling thing is that Kilty is free from psychoanalysis, and I will have to go on with this hateful stuff, until God knows when.'

'How can you justify that, after three years of coming here, you still have intimate conversations with her? Do you see her? Does she write to you?'

'Yes. The other day she sent me a book about Russian literature because she wanted me to have something "valuable" from her. She said she thought of me because she saw me at a party from across the room at a mutual friend's house. She thought I had "the purest, sweetest smile of anyone", that she deeply regretted the "destruction and suffering" that I had gone through out of love for her, and that she wished for the return of my natural strength and energy. But I feel like a heel telling you this, and betraying her trust.'

'As I've often told you, what you think of as betrayal is an inescapable part of therapy and psychoanalysis. Everything you tell me stays with me. You still seem to love her, but maybe she's just a –'

'I didn't catch the word. What did you say?'

'You heard me.'

'I didn't.'

'What do you think I said?'

'It sounded like "itch" or "witch". . .'

'It sounds as if you did hear – your unconscious just doesn't want to acknowledge it.'

Bak stood up – his signal that my hour was up.

I got up from the couch, but instead of walking out of his office as I generally did, I hung back.

The telephone rang. Bak often got calls as I was leaving, as if his friends knew to telephone him during the ten-minute break between patients.

'Go!' Bak said irritably, walking around his desk and picking up the telephone.

'I'm not leaving until you tell me the word,' I said truculently.

He covered the mouthpiece and spat out, 'Bitch.'

Until that moment, I had thought I was over Kilty, but I suddenly had such a surge of anger against Bak that I felt like throttling him. But, being the good patient that I was, I left, quietly closing his office door behind me. ■

THE VIEW FROM THIS END

Alexandra Fuller

GRANTA 88: WINTER 2004

M y first rainy season in Zambia, in 1993, was one of the wettest in decades. By December, the city had flooded and cars drove down Cha Cha Cha Road, right past the government buildings in the centre of Lusaka, up to their hubs and higher in brown sewage-rich water. The privies and drains and the streets and slums, long piled high and overspilling with human waste and refuse, sent their excess belching into the streets. We walked with our skirts held up around our hips, our shoes dangling from the ends of our fingers, and our lips pressed tight against the flies and stench.

The new cholera lorries rocked past us with dangerous urgency, spraying pedestrians and cars with mud and leaving behind them the faint, lingering scent of antiseptic and the nostril-widening scent of ancient disease.

Cholera. Goes with disease words like plague, pox, chigger, delirium.

Those unmistakable white lorries with blue logos painted on their doors and flashing yellow lights on their roofs – there must have been a dozen in the city at that time – had been donated by foreign aid groups. They were shiny under the thin, splattered glaze of mud; polite with a generous aura of Europe. But the bodies in the backs of the lorries were all Zambian. Women and men, crouched over each other, wretched with infection, holding their leaking bodies in check with bright bolts of cloth across their mouths, over their heads. They were people in mourning for themselves.

Every evening the lorries trundled out to Leopard's Hill Road, where the big cemetery lay, bringing with them the dead and the high-wailing relatives of the dead; the ululating women; the sombre men beneath crush-rimmed hats; the wide-eyed children. The cemetery was already spilling beyond capacity with the wasted bodies of Aids victims. Now it was overwhelmed by the carcasses spawned by cholera. In places, big pits had been dug, lime-sprinkled. We were like a people covering up a war crime.

I asked the groom, Day-Freddy, 'Where do they take the sick people?'

He said, 'To the cholera clinics.'

'You mean the hospitals?'

Day-Freddy frowned, 'I don't know.' He shrugged again. 'You should know.'

'Why should I know?'

'You are the one to write for the paper.'

I stared at Day-Freddy. We were sitting outside on the back veranda after our morning ride, drinking tea. 'Well, I do write for the paper.' But not about potentially troublesome issues like cholera. Not since I got into trouble with the article about the Minister of the Environment. I had interviewed him for a new, independent paper. He was famously corrupt, obviously inept and without curiosity or intelligence. The day the article was published, my husband Charlie was pulled into a government official's office and told to keep me under control.

Charlie had shrugged, 'Me keep her under control?'

The official had swung back on his chair and said, casually, 'Your work permit can be revoked at any time, Mr Ross.'

So now I wrote about the great success of Zambia's tobacco crops in the north and the country's potential for tourism in the east and a series of canoe trips I had taken on the middle section of the Zambezi

River. I wrote gently about Zambia's rich wildlife, its heritage of forests.

'Anyway, we Zambians die like chickens,' said Day-Freddy, soaking a thick doorstop of bread in his sweet, milky tea. 'Maybe it's not news for the paper.' He took a mouthful of soggy bread and told me, 'More people die of cholera. So? What's the news in that?' He swallowed and added, 'And you can't write this story.'

'Why not?'

Day-Freddy drained his tea and turned his cup over, flicking tea leaves and drops on the ground. 'Because you have fear,' he said.

The next morning Day-Freddy and I drove into the second-class district to buy maize bran for the horses. We were on our way home when a cholera lorry, swaying dangerously as it avoided potholes, tore past us. On impulse, I turned across the road and banked off the steep edge where tarmac had receded to expose red gums of eroded soil.

'What are you doing, madam?' asked Day-Freddy, clutching the edge of the seat.

'We're going to follow the cholera lorry,' I told him. 'We're going to find a cholera clinic.'

The lorry led us out of Lusaka, past Soweto market with its stalls of stolen car parts and second-hand clothes, and deep into the centre of George Compound. Day-Freddy kept shaking his head, 'Very dangerous,' he told me. 'This is not a good plan, madam.'

'Why not?'

'You are white, you are a woman. They will attack you. They will steal this pickup,' his eyes rolled wildly, 'they will beat me.'

'Don't be silly.'

'Look around here. They are poor, you are rich. You are crazy.'

'You're afraid,' I told him.

Day-Freddy nodded.

We were spinning through thick mud. House spilled upon house, each one made of more imaginative and desperate material than the last; houses of cloth sacks, plastic bags, road signs, cardboard and unravelled tyres. Tin roofs, or roofs made up of patched-together stop signs were held down with rocks. Great piles of refuse as high as the car towered next to each house on either side of the road. At times the water was so deep it threatened to seep under the doors and onto our feet. Day-Freddy pressed his shoes firmly against the dashboard and wrinkled his nose. 'How can people live like dogs?'

'It's not their fault.'

'I didn't say it was a fault, madam. I was simply asking this: How can people live like this?'

'I don't know.'

'I'm not getting out to push,' Day-Freddy informed me, 'if you get stuck.'

I kept the revs high, clutched the steering wheel tightly and followed closely in the wake left by the cholera lorry, hoping I would not accidentally slide off the road altogether. Children balanced high and victorious on top of the piles of refuse called after me, '*Mzungu! Mzungu!*' and waggled their hips at me.

We stopped, finally, at a school that had undergone a hasty conversion into a cholera clinic. Day-Freddy wouldn't leave the car. 'I've read the posters,' he told me. 'You will catch cholera and die if you step in there.' He covered his nose and mouth with his hands and made a face. 'I think you can catch it through breathing.' His voice was muffled and anxious.

'No you won't,' I scolded him. 'Only if you don't wash your hands.' But the smell was overpowering when I opened the car door and for a moment I hesitated. Then I saw Day-Freddy's expression and I stepped gingerly out of the car.

'Can I help you?' asked a man who was stirring a huge drum of yellow liquid at the foot of the steps.

'I was just . . .' I cleared my throat, 'I was wondering if you'd let me look around?'

'Around?'

'Yes. I've seen the cholera lorries, I was just –'

'Who are you?'

'No one.'

The man frowned at me suspiciously.

'I was just curious, that's all.'

Behind me, still in the pickup, I heard Day-Freddy snort with derision. I turned around to glare at him. He quickly covered his face again.

'I was thinking . . . I write for the paper.'

The man stopped stirring the liquid in the drum and frowned at me again, fiercely this time. 'Which paper? No journalists allowed,' he said. He put down the broom handle with which he was stirring the liquid in the drum and made shooing motions at me. 'You must go.'

'But don't you think people should know what is happening here?'

'What people?'

'I mean people who read the papers.'

'The people who read the papers already know what is going on,' the man said, returning to his drum.

I squinted back against the sun at Day-Freddy who was flapping frantically at the air, trying to get flies out of the cab.

'What's in the drum?' I asked the man.

'Clothes,' the man replied, 'contaminated clothes. We are supposed to burn them, but how can you burn clothes if they are all somebody has to wear?'

There were over a hundred people in that school turned cholera clinic, most of them naked but for a single covering of cloth. There were not enough cholera beds (stretchers with holes cut into them, with buckets under the holes), or beds of any description, so patients shared stretchers. Their bottoms could not fit over the holes, with two of them like that, and they were shitting on one another. Other patients had been lined up on soggy cardboard on the veranda where intravenous drips hanging from washing lines fed into upturned arms. Babies slept in the nook of their sick mothers' arms. Vomit and shit, like watery rice, were mopped up from the floor, scraped off the beds, sloshed off the cardboard sheets, by a nurse wearing a plastic apron and gumboots.

There was a single flush toilet which had long since ceased to flush – its contents slopped out onto the veranda. The two long-drops in the yard wafted disease and exhaustion, flooded and sagging precariously. The morgue was a black tent, steaming in the afternoon sun, next to the long-drops. It was from the morgue that the pervasive, sweet-rotten smell was coming.

This was not a humanitarian disaster on the vast scale Africa is so capable of producing, just a heartless indignity imposed upon a few thousand unlucky Zambians, one hundred of whom happened to be dribbling slowly to death right here.

While I was there, the cholera lorry left with bodies from the morgue and another appeared with freshly ill victims.

While I was there, a patient was brought from a distant village in a wheelbarrow by his relatives and had to be helped onto a corner of cardboard, where he died before the orderly could put the needle of the intravenous drip into his arm.

A baby, kept with its sick mother on a cholera bed in one of the old classrooms, died of pneumonia. It lay like a sodden comma, curled up against its mother, and no one realised it was dead until she began to bleat, her trilling thin with dehydration and despair. A pretty young nurse, in a white uniform with black gumboots and a white plastic apron, held the tiny body away from her as she hurried to the morgue.

I was only there an hour.

I drove home too fast, grim and guilty with what I had seen. Day-Freddy occupied himself trying to hunt down and kill flies.

'They'll bring the illness back to us,' he said, his voice squeaky with hysteria.

'Oh, don't be silly.'

'If a fly lands on you, you'll be sick. Sure, sure.'

When we got back to Lilayi Road, I left the pickup running and ran inside to collect blankets, clothes, towels, soap, aspirin, tins of food and shoes. I put them into cardboard boxes which I carried out to the vehicle.

'What are you doing?' asked Day-Freddy.

'You saw those people.' I could still smell the clinic in my hair, on my skin. I had been made to wash my hands and feet in a drum of caustic antiseptic before I could leave the clinic. The tyres of my car had been doused with the same yellow fluid.

'But I need these things,' Day-Freddy said plaintively, fingering a pile of towels.

'No you don't.'

'All of this?' he asked, holding up some tennis shoes.

'Yes,' I said firmly. 'You've had enough from me, wouldn't you say.'

Day-Freddy returned my accusing look steadily. 'You're too soft-soft,' he told me.

'That may be. Or maybe I'm not soft-soft enough.'

'They'll just sell everything,' he said, sulkily.

'So? Don't you?'

Day-Freddy sulked.

Two weeks later I could still smell the clinic when the wind lifted my hair. And my cholera article was rejected by the independent newspaper whose editor had recently been arrested and accused of slander towards a government minister.

Day-Freddy and I rode the horses up to the game farm at the top of the road and turned east into the rising sun. We were smiling into the cool breeze picked up off the previous night's rain.

'Race you,' I told him, which was no competition. He was on the faster mare, and he was a gutsier rider. 'Give me a head start and watch for antbear holes.' I trotted ahead. Gozzy tossed his head and flecked my leg with saliva. I could hear Day-Freddy muttering softly, reassuring Kalamo. 'On your marks,' I shouted over my shoulder, gathering up the reins and crouching forward. 'Get set,' I let Gozzy's rear end bunch up under the saddle. 'Go!'

Kalamo streaked past us before we had reached the first gate; by then I had lost all but the most rudimentary control of Gozzy. I was holding on hard, muscles tight with crouching, my breathing loud and rasping in my ears. I pulled up next to Day-Freddy, who was grinning like a fool, panting, his face shining with sweat even in the cool morning. 'I won, madam.'

'You won.' I leaned forward on my saddle and looked up at him, panting. I was wondering if I'd eaten something a bit off the night before. Suddenly I didn't feel very well. Day-Freddy swam in front of me. His smile melting into his face – dripping red, black, white like smudging paint.

'Jesus, Freddy.' I was still breathing hard. 'I think I'm . . . I think I need to . . .' I slid off Gozzy and my legs buckled.

'Madam?'

Day-Freddy jumped off the mare and the two horses sauntered off to graze. Day-Freddy crouched next to me, tried to hold me up. I retched and yellow vomit splattered out onto the green Rhodes grass and dribbled down my chin.

'Oh,' cried Day-Freddy, dropping my shoulders and letting me fall over, 'you have the cholera, madam! You have for sure the cholera.' He held his hands up in the air in horror and stepped back from me.

I shook my head, but could not speak. My body was racked with another bout of retching. When I could catch my breath I said, 'Fetch the horses now, let's ride home.'

'But you are sick, madam.'

'It's okay, Freddy, don't call the cholera lorry yet.' But I was only half joking.

The rainy season leaked on through March, by which time I had forgotten what it felt like to live without nausea and exhaustion. For hours at a time, I watched rain cry down the windows in the bedroom. Heat and humidity settled like breath somewhere north of my stomach. I began to have fantasies about strawberries and snow and chocolate breakfast cereal, none of which were available but which all seemed to promise a reprieve from my condition.

At weekday lunchtimes, the *mzungu* doctor in Lusaka was usually to be found drinking deeply of South African wine at the Marco

Polo restaurant, indifferent to the constraints of the conventional lunch hour. He didn't bother to remove his white clinical coat or his stethoscope when leaving his offices at noon. This being Zambia, a medical emergency could arise at any moment. Surgery using knife and fork and red wine.

He was the acknowledged authority on malaria, bilharzia and rabies, and though he couldn't treat you, he would tell you – without frills – if you were among the one-in-three Zambians to have acquired HIV.

He carelessly dispensed the few medications available to him for the treatment of dysentery, tuberculosis, ringworm, giardia, syphilis, witchcraft and tick fever. But he did not consider the possibility of pregnancy a medical condition.

For the third time in three months, the pregnancy test administered by the doctor's nurse had come back without a red stripe in the right-hand window. 'Are you sure the tests aren't out of date? Perhaps they've expired.' I cleared my throat and the doctor looked at his watch again. I was making him late for his customary bottle of South African wine. I thought about how else I might phrase this and at last I said, 'You may want to just have a quick peek up there. Just to make sure.'

'A peek?' said the doctor with distaste.

'A little peek,' I tried.

Which he wouldn't do. Especially before lunch.

'You have an IUD installed, no?'

'Well, yes.'

'So?'

So, for the third time in as many months he declared my pregnancy hysterical and for the third time in as many months I waved my gratitude and farewell at him, mouth covered, and hurried off to the clinic loos where I vomited noisily and prolifically, to the distress of the patients waiting for their prescriptions at the pharmacy.

*

'I must have a tummy bug after all,' I told Charlie.

But then the hard lump of baby in my belly became impossible to deny. And I must have been throwing up for a reason.

If it wasn't cholera. Which it wasn't. And if I hadn't had my period for three months, which I hadn't.

Dad, up from the farm, said, 'Well of course, you're in calf.'

'But the pregnancy tests came back negative.'

'Tests? Pah.'

'Damn.'

Dad lit a cigarette. 'Don't worry. Half of all heifers lose their first take.'

'No, it's not that,' I said. 'No, Dad. I want the baby.'

'Oh.' He was embarrassed and didn't know what to say. He stirred more sugar into his tea. 'Well, then . . .' Dad was trying, in his rough way, to protect me from what he thought I didn't know. 'Ja, well don't be disappointed, that's all. You know, if . . . It's common to have a practice run.'

I didn't have the heart to tell him that I had already had a practice run.

Years ago I took care of that. On an anonymous, thin, plastic-sheeted bed, a stranger's white-gloved hands in a Canadian hospital took care of that. I didn't tell Dad that I cried for days into a friend's pillow and smoked all my friend's cigarettes and bled into his toilet until he came and carried me, inexpertly, to bed, and let me bleed on to his sheets. He was not the father of the child I had chosen to lose, just an old friend with a car and a basement apartment near campus and a big heart.

The old friend, holding me, had said, 'I had a hamster I really loved when I was a kid. And one day I hugged the little fucker to death, by mistake.' He stroked my head. 'So I know how you feel.' Then we put a towel under me and he said, 'Shit, how much blood is there to lose? You need fluids,' and fetched me a cold beer.

I told Dad that there were worse things than finding out you're pregnant.

We decided I should drive through the border at Chirundu and up to Harare, Zimbabwe, for the advice of a medical expert. We had to stop periodically so I could throw up: after the winding Zambezi escarpment and at the urine-smelling border post and behind the diesel-belching buses at Cloud's End.

The Zimbabwean gynaecologist confirmed via ultrasound that I was pregnant. He showed me where the baby lay, a little pulse in my womb. I looked up at the pictures on the doctor's wall describing foetal development and I imagined my baby, her tiny fists curled in a Black Power salute ('Free Nelson Mandela! Send him home to So-wet-oh!') and then the doctor showed me where the intrauterine device might hinder her growth.

'If you leave the IUD in situ, you risk losing the baby. Or worse.'

'What can be worse?'

The doctor shrugged, an African educated in London, with the schooling of the West, but his own people's matter-of-factness about life, death, loss. 'It's for you to decide. Perhaps some . . . impediment to growth.'

'And if I have IUD removed?'

'You still risk losing the baby.'

I stared up at the wall, at the little defiant fist on the smudgy black-and-white photograph of someone else's baby. I said, 'I don't think I'll lose this one.'

Then I offered my arm to the clinic's nurse and blood was siphoned off to test for HIV, syphilis, gonorrhoea.

Charlie had gone outside to the car and I went out to look for him. There were other potential fathers kicking their heels in the dust and smoking cigarettes, leaned up against farm pickups while their pregnant wives were inside the whitewashed walls of the clinic.

'Well, I'm definitely pregnant.' I crossed my arms and looked away so Charlie couldn't see my tears and I said, 'Bugger, bugger, bugger. He says I might lose it.'

Charlie reached out for me again and this time I let him rock me against his shoulder. And then morning sickness took over and I fought my way out of his embrace to throw up in the gynaecologist's beautiful orange cannas.

We chose a small clinic in a village east of Harare to have the IUD removed. I didn't want to lose the baby, but if I did, I wanted to bury her somewhere I would find her again. Somewhere small and quiet and where I could come back and find the flowers I'd planted for her.

I was bedded next to an old-timer in a tiny ward for two that overlooked a pine forest and a comforting, bright new garden of English country flowers: nasturtiums, rhododendrons, lavender and roses.

'What you here for?' asked my neighbour, patting her covers happily and eyeing me over the top of her glasses.

'I'm pregnant,' I said.

'Well, you don't look it,' she said suspiciously.

'That's because I'm not very far along.'

'Good, then we won't have any squawking kids in here any time soon.'

'No.'

The old lady had been prescribed sherry before lunch, 'To stimulate my appetite,' she explained. 'I can tell you something else, I haven't had so much fun . . .' She sipped her sherry appreciatively. 'Underestimated for the digestion,' she confided. Then added, 'I can't stand babies.' She offered me a sip from her glass which I declined weakly, nauseated. 'They won't let me smoke though.'

'Oh.'

'Call me old-fashioned, but I don't have a problem with smoking. Do you? You wouldn't mind if I smoked, would you?'

I grunted.

The pre-op drugs were starting to take effect. My mouth was dry and my legs felt as if they were floating.

'I hate visiting day,' said my neighbour with sudden vehemence. 'They all come to see me and sit on my bed and I can't read. I can't knit. And they're so boring.'

'Who?' I asked feebly.

'My children. Their children. The whole bloody lot of them. They whinge.'

The last thing I heard and saw before they wheeled me into the operating room was the old lady, raising her sherry glass in salute and asking loudly, urgently, 'From what? You didn't say from what? What are you pregnant from?' and looking around the place as if expecting an attack from an unknown quarter.

Charlie was there when I woke up. For a man not given to emotion, he looked close to tears as he said, 'It's going to be okay.'

'I'm still pregnant?'

'So far. They're going to give you something to help you sleep. I'll come get you tomorrow.'

I drifted in and out for the next twelve hours, unable to struggle out of the deep, drugged sleep completely, even as I fought it. During the night, a long green snake found its way into our ward. My old neighbour, assisted by a man whom I vaguely remember as being attached by a pole to an intravenous drip, killed it with a walking stick and draped it on the end of a broom handle.

It had only been a poor, fat house snake.

The doctor told me to take it easy for the next few days.

'Any idea when she's due?' I asked.

'How do you know it's a she?'

I shrugged. 'Just do,' I replied.

The doctor sighed and pressed her hands to my belly. 'You're three months along, I'd say.' She shut her eyes and felt along the ridges of my ribs. 'The end of August,' she announced, 'maybe early September.'

We came back in late August to wait for the baby. We stayed in the highlands for a fortnight, hiking in the relief of cool, pine-scented air and then the doctor decided that there was no more room for the baby to be in my great swinging belly, it was time for us to persuade her to come out.

The local vicar's wife was found to have the same blood group as mine and was told to stand by for a couple of days, veins at the ready, in case I should need her blood. A seventy-year-old, tennis-playing farmer's wife who had, forty years earlier, delivered twins (vaginally and without medical intervention or pain relief) was summoned to give me a few pointers on the birthing process. She kept her lesson brief, swinging her tennis racquet around experimentally all the time. 'Piece of old tackie, really,' she said, sending an imaginary lob over my shoulder. 'Women have been doing this since Adam and Eve, so just remember – you're not doing anything special.' *Slam!* 'Just keep breathing, don't bother with the hollering, and you'll be fine.'

'Thank you.'

She turned to Charlie, 'I've rafted the Zambezi,' she announced, twisting to execute an air-backhand. 'That's what childbirth is like,' she informed me unhelpfully, 'wave after wave.' *Wa-boom!* 'And then you hit an eddy.'

'I see.'

'An enema will really help get this labour going,' the Shona midwife told me. I was already pinned to the bed with pain and, as far as I had been told, we were not even close to a cigar. The midwife loomed in and out of my range of vision, which was mostly the pale blue tent made by the blanket hung between my knees and a high barred window that leaked in a pale, spring light.

'A what?'

'Come on,' she said, producing a length of thin red hosepipe, 'roll over on your side.'

'Oh my God, no, you're not going to . . .'

Mum, who had driven down with us from Zambia to help me deliver the baby, grinned unhelpfully.

'Mu-um!'

She said, 'I heard of a movie star that got a gerbil stuck in his bottom once. Just think about that. That's got to be worse than an enema.'

'Out,' I said, glaring at Mum and Charlie, 'both of you out!' I groaned through a contraction.

'Keep an eye out for gerbils, ha, ha.'

'Not funny, Mum.'

The door slammed behind my mother and husband.

'And stay there,' I shouted, 'till I tell you.'

The midwife said, 'This is a good remedy for a slow labour.'

'It's humiliating is what it is.' I had imagined a placid labour, set to gentle music while I smiled bravely through the pain and effortlessly produced a perfect baby.

She laughed, 'Humiliating? My dear, a day from now you will know what true humiliation is.'

'Oh God.' I held on to the edge of the bed and gritted my teeth.

By four o'clock in the afternoon the baby had been stuck for hours. The doctor put the kettle on. 'Keep pushing,' she told me, 'and you'll get this baby out in time for tea.' Now that anything I had to say had been reduced to words of one syllable, Mum and Charlie had been called back into the room. I grabbed Mum's arm on one side and the midwife's arm on the other, dug my chin into my chest and pushed. Charlie peered hopefully at my bottom.

'Nope,' he announced.

I came up for air. 'Fuck off. Please.'

Charlie got out of range.

Now the kettle was boiling. The doctor scooped tea leaves into a pot and poured hot water over them, the steamy, sweet smell of brewing tea adding to the close, sweaty atmosphere in the room.

I dug my nails into Mum's hand. 'I don't think I can do this,' but then another contraction came and I pushed into the endless, deep pain of it.

The doctor glanced at the teapot ruefully. 'Time to get this baby out,' she told me, rolling up her sleeves. She brought out a knife and something that looked like a toilet plunger. I shut my eyes.

'Just keep breathing,' said Charlie, re-emerging from his corner.

'Fuck off.'

Mum held on to my shoulders and the midwife held on to my legs (like a cow, I thought), and the doctor pulled. If she'd brought out a rope and chain and pulled the child out with the help of a tractor, I would not have been surprised.

I thought of the men at the dip pulling a difficult calf from a cow, singing as they heaved, '*Potsi, piri, tatu, ini.*'

Somewhere far away, somewhere else in the hospital, I heard a woman scream.

Mum said, 'Shhhhh.' And I realised the scream had come from me.

'Push,' said the Shona midwife.

I pushed, the doctor pulled and Mum held on.

Then the baby was on my stomach and I was crying. She was long-limbed, dark-haired, blood-smeared and perfect. She had lips like rosebuds. I put my arms over her and I knew, suddenly and unexpectedly, that I had been put on this earth for one reason only: to give life to this child.

'Cup of tea?' asked the midwife, propping a cup next to me on the bed.

'That'll do you good,' said Mum, 'put a bit of sugar in it.'

'I hate sugar in my tea.'

At a basin in the corner of the ward, a fourteen-year-old girl who had come into the clinic hours after me was preparing to leave. She was up, fully dressed, and was bathing and dressing her new baby. If she can do it, I can do it, I thought. I felt for the edge of my bed and swung my feet on to the floor. Supporting myself against the bed frame, I had a brief vision of the young girl's face and her pink-clothed baby. Then a swimming and indistinct sense that the floor was slipping away from me and rolling up to become the ceiling. Blackness rushed into my head and I was on the floor.

Mum fetched a basin of water and a bar of soap. 'I'll give you a bed bath,' she said, 'you can try getting up tomorrow.' The nurse came through to see how I was getting on and gave me a little white pill to help with the pain. As I drifted out of my mind in a comfortably drugged state I asked, slurring a little, 'What's the pill?'

'Valium,' said the nurse, drawing the curtains, 'we find most . . . ladies need a little something to calm them after birth.'

I sighed and sank back against the pillows. 'The baby?' I asked, indistinctly.

'She's fine,' someone murmured.

I heard Mum say to Charlie, 'Ready for something a bit stiffer than tea?'

Charlie leaned over me and planted a kiss on my forehead. A cigar leered out of his top pocket. 'Well done, babe.'

It wasn't until much later, in the middle of the night, that I struggled out of my fog and lay breathing into the darkness trying to remember where I was. Why did I feel as if I'd been torn in half. Jesus Christ! The baby! Where did I put the baby! I patted the bed next to me and groped wildly around the bedclothes. 'Nurse!' No one came. I swung out of bed and hurried (clutching my bottom which felt as if it might slip out onto the floor) towards a mild light at the end of a dark passage.

'Is the baby here?'

The nurse on duty smelled of cigarettes and coffee. She was knitting, her feet comfortably propped up on the desk in front of her. 'What are you doing out of bed, sweetie?'

'I'm looking for my baby.'

'You can't have her until morning.'

'It is morning,' I said, letting myself behind the desk and looking around, fighting the panic that had swelled in my chest. 'Where did you put her?'

'It's okay, darling. You go back and sleep. It's the last bit of shut-eye you'll be getting for a while.'

'Where is she?' I insisted, planting myself firmly in front of the nurse and holding myself together. I'd seen a cow with a prolapsed uterus on the farm once.

The nurse counted her stitches and put her knitting down reluctantly. 'Come.'

The baby was alone in a plastic box, with a bright light bulb hanging over her. 'The light keeps her warm,' said the nurse. Like baby chickens.

I scooped up the swaddled infant from the plastic box.

'I promise we can keep her here for you. I've been feeding her sugared water.' The nurse sounded defensive, a little offended.

'It's all right,' I said. 'I'll take her now.'

I held the soft sleeping thing up to my face and inhaled the fresh breath of her new lungs, the soft-kitten-blood smell of her recent birth.

I went back to bed, undressed myself and unrolled the baby, holding her next to my skin. She nestled into my breast, her rosebud mouth opened and closed over my nipple. I shut my eyes and closed my arms around her. 'I promise I won't let you go,' I told the baby. We fell asleep like that, both of us naked, with her mouth soft and wet over my nipple and her breathing warm and steady against my neck. ■

Shift, 2019

HOW TO WRITE ABOUT AFRICA

Binyavanga Wainaina

GRANTA 92: WINTER 2005

Always use the word 'Africa' or 'Darkness' or 'Safari' in your title. Subtitles may include the words 'Zanzibar', 'Masai', 'Zulu', 'Zambezi', 'Congo', 'Nile', 'Big', 'Sky', 'Shadow', 'Drum', 'Sun' or 'Bygone'. Also useful are words such as 'Guerrillas', 'Timeless', 'Primordial' and 'Tribal'. Note that 'People' means Africans who are not black, while 'The People' means black Africans.

Never have a picture of a well-adjusted African on the cover of your book, or in it, unless that African has won the Nobel Prize. An AK-47, prominent ribs, naked breasts: use these. If you must include an African, make sure you get one in Masai or Zulu or Dogon dress.

In your text, treat Africa as if it were one country. It is hot and dusty with rolling grasslands and huge herds of animals and tall, thin people who are starving. Or it is hot and steamy with very short people who eat primates. Don't get bogged down with precise descriptions. Africa is big: fifty-four countries, 900 million people who are too busy starving and dying and warring and emigrating to read your book. The continent is full of deserts, jungles, highlands, savannahs and many other things, but your reader doesn't care about all that, so keep your descriptions romantic and evocative and unparticular.

Make sure you show how Africans have music and rhythm deep in their souls, and eat things no other humans eat. Do not mention rice and beef and wheat; monkey-brain is an African's cuisine of choice, along with goat, snake, worms and grubs and all manner of game meat. Make sure you show that you are able to eat such food without flinching, and describe how you learn to enjoy it – because you care.

Taboo subjects: ordinary domestic scenes, love between Africans (unless a death is involved), references to African writers or intellectuals, mention of school-going children who are not suffering from yaws or Ebola fever or female genital mutilation.

Throughout the book, adopt a *sotto* voice, in conspiracy with the reader, and a sad *I-expected-so-much* tone. Establish early on that your liberalism is impeccable, and mention near the beginning how much you love Africa, how you fell in love with the place and can't live without her. Africa is the only continent you can love – take advantage of this. If you are a man, thrust yourself into her warm virgin forests. If you are a woman, treat Africa as a man who wears a bush jacket and disappears off into the sunset. Africa is to be pitied, worshipped or dominated. Whichever angle you take, be sure to leave the strong impression that without your intervention and your important book, Africa is doomed.

Your African characters may include naked warriors, loyal servants, diviners and seers, ancient wise men living in hermitic splendour. Or corrupt politicians, inept polygamous travel-guides, and prostitutes you have slept with. The Loyal Servant always behaves like a seven-year-old and needs a firm hand; he is scared of snakes, good with children, and always involving you in his complex domestic dramas. The Ancient Wise Man always comes from a noble tribe (not the money-grubbing tribes like the Gikuyu, the Igbo or the Shona). He has rheumy eyes and is close to the Earth. The Modern African is a fat man who steals and works in the visa office, refusing to give work permits to qualified Westerners who really care about Africa. He is an enemy of development, always using his government job to make it difficult for pragmatic and good-hearted expats to set up NGOs or Legal Conservation Areas. Or he is an Oxford-educated intellectual turned serial-killing politician in a Savile Row suit. He is a cannibal who likes Cristal champagne, and his mother is a rich witch doctor who really runs the country.

Among your characters you must always include The Starving African, who wanders the refugee camp nearly naked, and waits for the benevolence of the West. Her children have flies on their eyelids and pot bellies, and her breasts are flat and empty. She must look utterly helpless. She can have no past, no history; such diversions ruin the dramatic moment. Moans are good. She must never say anything about herself in the dialogue except to speak of her (unspeakable) suffering. Also be sure to include a warm and motherly woman who has a rolling laugh and who is concerned for your well-being. Just call her Mama. Her children are all delinquent. These characters should buzz around your main hero, making him look good. Your hero can teach them, bathe them, feed them; he carries lots of babies and has seen Death. Your hero is you (if reportage), or a beautiful, tragic international celebrity/aristocrat who now cares for animals (if fiction).

Bad Western characters may include children of Tory Cabinet ministers, Afrikaners, employees of the World Bank. When talking about exploitation by foreigners mention the Chinese and Indian traders. Blame the West for Africa's situation. But do not be too specific.

Broad brushstrokes throughout are good. Avoid having the African characters laugh, or struggle to educate their kids, or just make do in mundane circumstances. Have them illuminate something about Europe or America in Africa. African characters should be colourful, exotic, larger than life – but empty inside, with no dialogue, no conflicts or resolutions in their stories, no depth or quirks to confuse the cause.

Describe, in detail, naked breasts (young, old, conservative, recently raped, big, small) or mutilated genitals, or enhanced genitals. Or any kind of genitals. And dead bodies. Or, better, naked dead bodies. And especially rotting naked dead bodies. Remember, any work you submit in which people look filthy and miserable will be referred to as the 'real Africa', and you want that on your dust jacket. Do not feel queasy about this: you are trying to help them to get aid from the West. The biggest taboo in writing about Africa is to describe or show dead or suffering white people.

Animals, on the other hand, must be treated as well-rounded, complex characters. They speak (or grunt while tossing their manes proudly) and have names, ambitions and desires. They also have family values: *see how lions teach their children?* Elephants are caring, and are good feminists or dignified patriarchs. So are gorillas. Never, ever say anything negative about an elephant or a gorilla. Elephants may attack people's property, destroy their crops, and even kill them. Always take the side of the elephant. Big cats have public-school accents. Hyenas are fair game and have vaguely Middle Eastern accents. Any short Africans who live in the jungle or desert may be portrayed with good humour (unless they are in conflict with an elephant or chimpanzee or gorilla, in which case they are pure evil).

After celebrity activists and aid workers, conservationists are Africa's most important people. Do not offend them. You need them to invite you to their 30,000-acre game ranch or 'conservation area', and this is the only way you will get to interview the celebrity activist. Often a book cover with a heroic-looking conservationist on it works magic for sales. Anybody white, tanned and wearing khaki who once had a pet antelope or a farm is a conservationist, one who is preserving Africa's rich heritage. When interviewing him or her, do not ask how much funding they have; do not ask how much money they make off their game. Never ask how much they pay their employees.

Readers will be put off if you don't mention the light in Africa. And sunsets, the African sunset is a must. It is always big and red. There is always a big sky. Wide empty spaces and game are critical – Africa is the Land of Wide Empty Spaces. When writing about the plight of flora and fauna, make sure you mention that Africa is overpopulated. When your main character is in a desert or jungle living with indigenous peoples (anybody short) it is okay to mention that Africa has been severely depopulated by Aids and War (use caps).

You'll also need a nightclub called Tropicana, where mercenaries, evil nouveau riche Africans and prostitutes and guerrillas and expats hang out.

Always end your book with Nelson Mandela saying something about rainbows or renaissances. Because you care. ■

LOST CAT

Mary Gaitskill

GRANTA 107: SUMMER 2009

Last year I lost my cat Gattino. He was very young, at seven months barely an adolescent. He is probably dead but I don't know for certain. For two weeks after he disappeared people claimed to have seen him; I trusted two of the claims because Gattino was blind in one eye, and both people told me that when they'd caught him in their headlights, only one eye shone back. One guy, who said he saw my cat trying to scavenge from a garbage can, said that he'd 'looked really thin, like the runt of the litter'. The pathetic words struck my heart. But I heard something besides the words, something in the coarse, vibrant tone of the man's voice that immediately made another emotional picture of the cat: back arched, face afraid but excited, brimming and ready before he jumped and ran, tail defiant, tensile and crooked. Afraid but ready; startled by a large male, that's how he would've been. Even if he was weak with hunger. He had guts, this cat.

Gattino disappeared two and a half months after we moved. Our new house is on the outskirts of a college campus near a wildlife preserve. There are wooded areas in all directions, and many homes with decrepit outbuildings sit heavily, darkly low behind trees, in thick foliage. I spent hours at a time wandering around calling Gattino. I put food out. I put a trap out. I put hundreds of flyers up, I walked around knocking on doors, asking people if I could look in their shed or under their porch. I contacted all the vets in the area. Every few days, someone would call and say they had seen a cat in a parking lot or behind their dorm. I would go and sometimes glimpse a grizzled adult melting away into the woods, or behind a building or under a parked car.

After two weeks there were no more sightings. I caught three feral cats in my trap and let them go. It began to snow. Still searching, I would sometimes see little cat tracks in the snow; near dumpsters full of garbage, I also saw prints made by bobcats or coyotes. When the temperature went below freezing, there was icy rain. I kept looking. A year later I still had not stopped.

Six months after Gattino disappeared my husband and I were sitting in a restaurant having dinner with some people he had recently met, including an intellectual writer we both admired. The writer had considered buying the house we were living in and he wanted to know how we liked it. I said it was nice but it had been partly spoiled for me by the loss of our cat. I told him the story and he said, 'Oh, that was your trauma, was it?'

I said yes. Yes, it was a trauma.

You could say he was unkind. You could say I was silly. You could say he was priggish. You could say I was weak.

A few weeks earlier, I had an email exchange with my sister Martha on the subject of trauma, or rather tragedy. Our other sister, Jane, had just decided not to euthanize her dying cat because she thought her little girls could not bear it; she didn't think she could bear it. Jane lives in chronic pain so great that sometimes she cannot move normally. She is under great financial stress and is often responsible for the care of her mother-in-law as well as the orphaned children of her sister-in-law who died of cancer. But it was her cat's approaching death that made her cry so that her children were frightened. 'This is awful,' said Martha. 'It is not helping that cat to keep him alive, it's just prolonging his suffering. It's selfish.'

Martha is in a lot of pain too, most of it related to diabetes and fibromyalgia. Her feet hurt so badly she can't walk longer than five minutes. She just lost her job and is applying for disability which, because it's become almost impossible to get, she may not get, and which, if she does get, will not be enough to live on, and we will have to help her. We already have to help her because her COBRA payments are so high that her unemployment isn't enough to cover them. This is painful for her too; she doesn't want to be the one everybody has to help. And so she tries to help us. She has had cats for years, and so knows a lot about them; she wanted to help Jane by giving her advice, and she sent me several emails wondering about the best way to do it. Finally she forwarded me the message she had sent to Jane, in which she urged her to put the cat down. When she didn't hear from Jane, she emailed me some more, agonizing over whether or not Jane was angry at her, and wondering what decision Jane would make regarding the cat. She said, 'I'm afraid this is going to turn into an avoidable tragedy.'

Impatient by then, I told her that she should trust Jane to make the right decision. I said, this is sad, not tragic. Tragedy is thousands of people dying slowly of war and disease, injury and malnutrition. It's Hurricane Katrina, it's the war in Iraq, it's the earthquake in China. It's not one creature dying of old age.

After I sent the email, I looked up the word 'tragic'. According to *Webster's College Dictionary*, I was wrong; their second definition of the word is 'extremely mournful, melancholy or pathetic'. I emailed Martha and admitted I'd been wrong, at least technically. I added that I still thought she was being hysterical. She didn't answer me. Maybe she was right not to.

I found Gattino in Italy. I was in Tuscany at a place called Santa Maddalena run by a woman named Beatrice von Rezzori who, in honor of her deceased husband, a writer, has made her estate into a small retreat for writers. When Beatrice learned that I love cats, she told me that down the road from her two old women were feeding a yard full of semi-wild cats, including a litter of kittens who were very sick and going blind. Maybe, she said, I could help them out. No, I said, I wasn't in Italy to do that, and anyway, having done it before, I know it isn't an easy thing to trap and tame a feral kitten.

The next week one of her assistants, who was driving me into the village, asked if I wanted to see some kittens. Sure, I said, not making the connection. We stopped by an old farmhouse. A gnarled woman sitting in a wheelchair covered with towels and a thin blanket greeted the assistant without looking at me. Scrawny cats with long legs and narrow ferret hips stalked or lay about in the buggy, overgrown yard. Two kittens, their eyes gummed up with yellow fluid and flies swarming around their asses, were obviously sick but still lively – when I bent to touch them, they ran away. But a third kitten, smaller and bonier than the other two, tottered up to me mewing weakly, his eyes almost glued shut. He was a tabby, soft gray with strong black stripes. He had a long jaw and a big nose shaped like an eraser you'd stick on the end of a pencil. His big-nosed head was goblin-ish on his emaciated pot-bellied body, his long legs almost grotesque. His asshole seemed disproportionately big on his starved rear. Dazedly, he let me stroke his bony back – tentatively, he lifted his pitiful tail. I asked the assistant if she would help me take the kittens to a veterinarian and she agreed; this had no doubt been the idea all along.

The healthier kittens scampered away as we approached and hid in a collapsing barn; we were only able to collect the tabby. When we put him in the carrier, he forced open his eyes with a mighty effort, took a good look at us, hissed, tried to arch his back and fell over. But he let the vets handle him. When they tipped him forward and lifted his tail to check his sex, he had a delicate, nearly human look of puzzled dignity in his one half-good eye, while his blunt muzzle expressed stoic animality. It was a comical and touching face.

They kept him for three days. When I came to pick him up, they told me he would need weeks of care, involving eye ointment, ear drops and nose drops. Beatrice suggested I bring him home to America. No, I said, not possible. My husband was coming to meet me in a month and we were going to travel for two weeks; we couldn't take him with us. I would care for him and by the time I left, he should be well enough to go back to the yard with a fighting chance.

So I called him 'Chance'. I liked Chance as I like all kittens; he liked me as a food dispenser. He looked at me neutrally, as if I were one more creature in the world, albeit a useful one. I had to worm him, de-flea him and wash encrusted shit off his tail. He squirmed when I put the medicine in his eyes and ears, but he never tried to scratch me – I think because he wasn't absolutely certain of how I might react if he did. He tolerated my petting him, but seemed to find it a novel sensation rather than a pleasure.

Then one day he looked at me differently. I don't know exactly when it happened – I may not have noticed the first time. But he began to raise his head when I came into the room, to look at me intently. I can't say for certain what the look meant; I don't know how animals think or feel. But it seemed that he was looking at me with love. He followed me around my apartment. He sat in my lap when I worked at my desk. He came into my bed and slept with me; he lulled himself to sleep by gnawing softly on my fingers. When I petted him, his body would rise into my hand. If my face were close to him, he would reach out with his paw and stroke my cheek.

Sometimes, I would walk on the dusty roads surrounding Santa Maddalena and think about my father, talking to him in my mind. My father had landed in Italy during the Second World War; he was part of the Anzio invasion. After the war he returned as a visitor with my mother, to Naples and to Rome. There is a picture of him standing against an ancient wall wearing a suit and a beret; he looks elegant, formidable and at the same time tentative, nearly shy. On my walks I carried a large, beautiful marble that had belonged to my father; sometimes I took it out of my pocket and held it up in the sun as if it might function as a conduit for his soul. My father died a slow painful death of cancer, refusing treatment of any kind for as long as he was able to make himself understood, gasping, 'No doctors, no doctors.' My mother had left him years before; my sisters and I tended to him, but inadequately, and too late – he had been sick for months, unable to eat for at least weeks before we became aware of his condition. During those weeks I thought of calling him; if I had I would've known immediately that he was dying. But I didn't call. He was difficult, and none of us called him often.

My husband did not like the name Chance and I wasn't sure I did either; he suggested McFate, and so I tried it out. McFate grew stronger, grew a certain one-eyed rakishness, an engaged forward quality to his ears and the attitude of his neck that was gallant in his fragile body. He put on weight, and his long legs and tail became *soigné*, not grotesque. He had strong necklace markings on his throat; when he rolled on his back for me to pet him, his belly was beige and spotted like an ocelot. In a confident mood, he was like a little gangster in a zoot suit. Pensive, he was still delicate; his heart seemed closer to the surface than normal, and when I held him against me, it beat very fast and light. McFate was too big and heartless a name for such a small fleet-hearted creature. '*Mio Gattino*,' I whispered, in a language I don't speak to a creature who didn't understand words. '*Mio dolce piccolo gatto.*'
    One night when he was lying on his back in my lap, purring, I saw something flash across the floor; it was a small, sky-blue marble rolling out from under the dresser and across the floor. It stopped in the middle of the floor. It was beautiful, bright, and something not visible to me had set it in motion. It seemed a magical and forgiving omen, like the presence of this loving little cat. I put it on the windowsill next to my father's marble.

I spoke to my husband about taking Gattino home with us. I said I had fallen in love with the cat, and that I was afraid that by exposing him to human love I had awakened in him a need that was unnatural, that if I left him he would suffer from the lack of human attention that he never would have known had I not appeared in his yard. My husband said, 'Oh no, Mary . . .' but in a bemused tone.

I would understand if he'd said it in a harsher tone. Many people would consider my feelings neurotic, a projection onto an animal of my own need. Many people would consider it almost offensive for me to lavish such love on an animal when I have by some standards failed to love my fellow beings: for example, orphaned children who suffer every day, not one of whom I have adopted. But I have loved people; I have loved children. And it seems that what happened between me and the children I chose to love was a version of what I was afraid would happen to the kitten. Human love is grossly flawed, and even when it isn't, people routinely misunderstand it, reject it, use it or manipulate it. It is hard to protect a person you love from pain because people often choose pain; *I* am a person who often chooses pain. An animal will never choose pain; an animal can receive love far more easily than even a very young human. And so I thought it should be possible to shelter a kitten with love.

I made arrangements with the vet to get me a cat passport; Gattino endured the injection of an identifying microchip into his slim shoulder. Beatrice said she could not keep him in her house, and so I made arrangements for the vet to board him for the two weeks Peter and I traveled.

Peter arrived; Gattino looked at him and hid under the dresser. Peter crouched down and talked to him softly. Then he and I lay on the bed and held each other. In a flash, Gattino grasped the situation: the male had come. He was friendly. We could all be together now. He came onto the bed, sat on Peter's chest and purred thunderously. He stayed on Peter's chest all night.

We took him to the veterinarian the next day. Their kennel was not the quiet, cat-only quarters one finds at upscale American animal hospitals. It was a common area that smelled of disinfectant and fear. The vet put Gattino in a cage near that of a huge enraged dog that barked and growled, lunging against the door of its kennel. Gattino looked at me and began to cry. I cried too. The dog raged. There was a little bed in Gattino's cage and he hid behind it, then defiantly lifted his head to face the gigantic growling; that is when I first saw that terrified but ready expression, that willingness to meet whatever was coming, regardless of its size or its ferocity.

When we left the vet I was crying absurdly hard. But I was not crying exclusively about the kitten, any more than my sister Jane was crying exclusively about euthanizing her old cat. At the time I didn't realize it, but I was, among other things, crying about the children I once thought of as mine.

Caesar and his sister Natalia are now twelve and sixteen respectively. When we met them they were six and ten. We met him first. We met him through the Fresh Air Fund, an organization that brings poor urban children (nearly all of whom are black or Hispanic) up by bus to stay with country families (nearly all of whom are white). The Fresh Air Fund is an organization with an aura of uplift and hope about it, but its project is a difficult one that frankly reeks of pain. In addition to Caesar, we also hosted another little boy, a seven-year-old named Ezekial. Imagine that you are six or seven years old and that you are taken to a huge city bus terminal, herded onto buses with dozens of other kids, all of you with big name tags hung around your neck, driven for three hours to a completely foreign place, and presented to total strangers with whom you are going to live for two weeks. Add that these total strangers, even if they are not rich, have materially more than you could ever dream of, that they are much bigger than you and, since you are staying in their house, you are supposed to obey them. Add that they are white as sheets. Realize that even very young children 'of color' have often learned that white people are essentially the enemy. Wonder: who in God's name thought this was a good idea?

We were aware of the race–class thing. But we thought we could override it. Because we wanted to love these children. I fantasized about serving them meals, reading to them at night, tucking them in. Peter fantasized about sports on the lawn, riding bikes together. You could say we were idealistic. You could say we were stupid. I don't know what we were.

We were actually only supposed to have one, and that one was Ezekial. We got Caesar because the FAF called from the bus as it was on its way up, full of kids, and told us that his host family had pulled out at the last minute due to a death in the family, so could we take him? We said yes because we were worried about how we were going to entertain a single child with no available playmates; I made the FAF representative promise that if it didn't work out, she would find a backup plan. Of course it didn't work out. Of course there was no backup plan. The kids hated each other, or, more precisely, Ezekial hated Caesar. Caesar was younger and more vulnerable in every way; less confident, less verbal, possessed of no athletic skills. Ezekial was lithe, with muscular limbs and an ungiving facial symmetry that sometimes made his naturally expressive face cold and mask-like. Caesar was big and plump, with deep eyes and soft features that were so generous they seemed nearly smudged at the edges. Ezekial was a clever bully, merciless in his teasing, and Caesar could only respond by ineptly blustering, 'Ima fuck you up!'

'Look,' I said, 'you guys don't have to like each other, but you have to get along. Deep down, don't you want to get along?'

'No!' they screamed.

'He's ugly!' added Ezekial.

'Oh dry up Ezekial,' I said, 'we're all ugly, okay?'

'Yeah,' said Caesar, liking this idea very much. 'We're all ugly!'

'No,' said Ezekial, his voice dripping with malice, 'you're ugly.'

'Try again,' I said. 'Can you get along?'

'Okay,' said Caesar. 'I'll get along with you Ezekial.' And you could hear his gentle, generous nature in his voice. You could hear it, actually, even when he said, 'Ima fuck you up!' Gentleness sometimes expresses itself with the violence of pain or fear and so looks like aggression. Sometimes cruelty has a very charming smile.

'No,' said Ezekial, smiling. 'I hate you.'

Caesar dropped his eyes.

*

We were in Florence for a week. It was beautiful, but crowded and hot, and I was too full of sadness and confusion to enjoy myself. Nearly every day I pestered the vet, calling to see how Gattino was. 'He's fine,' they said. 'The dog isn't there anymore. Your cat is playing.' I wasn't assuaged. I had nightmares; I had a nightmare that I had put my kitten into a burning oven, and then watched him hopelessly try to protect himself by curling into a ball; I cried to see it, but could not undo my action.

Peter preferred the clever, athletic Ezekial and Caesar knew it. I much preferred Caesar, but we had made our original commitment to Ezckial and to his mother, whom we had spoken with on the phone. So I called the FAF representative and asked her if she could find another host family for Caesar. 'Oh great,' she snapped. But she did come up with a place. It sounded good: a single woman, a former schoolteacher, experienced host of a boy she described as responsible and kind, not a bully. 'But don't tell him he's going anywhere else,' she said. 'I'll just pick him up and tell him he's going to a pizza party. You can bring his stuff over later.'

I said, 'Okay,' but the idea didn't sit right with me. So I took Caesar out to a park to tell him. Or rather I tried. I said, 'You don't like Ezekial do you?' and he said, 'No, I hate him.' I asked if he would like to go stay at a house with another boy who would be nice to him, where they would have a pool and – 'No,' he said. 'I want to stay with you and Peter.' I couldn't believe it – I did not realize how attached he had become. But he was adamant. We had the conversation three times, and none of those times did I have the courage to tell him he had no choice. I pushed him on the swing set and he cried, 'Mary! Mary! Mary!' And then I took him home and told Peter I had not been able to do it.

Peter told Ezekial to go into the other room and we sat Caesar down and told him he was leaving. 'No,' he said. 'Send the other boy away.'

Ezekial came into the room.

'Send him away!' cried Caesar.

'Ha ha,' said Ezekial, 'you go away!'

The FAF woman arrived. I told her what was happening. She said, 'Why don't you just let me handle this.' And she did. She said, 'Okay Caesar, it's like this. You were supposed to go stay with another family but then somebody in that family *died* and you couldn't go there.'

'Somebody *died*?' asked Caesar.

'Yes, and Peter and Mary were *kind* enough to let you come stay with them for a little while and now it's time to –'

'I want to stay here!' Caesar screamed and clung to the mattress.

'Caesar,' said the FAF woman, 'I talked to your mother. *She* wants you to go.'

Caesar lifted his face and looked at her for a searching moment. 'Lady,' he said calmly, 'you a liar.' And she was. I'm sure of it. Caesar's mother was almost impossible to get on the phone and she spoke no English.

This is probably why the FAF woman screamed, actually screamed, 'How dare you call me a liar! Don't you ever call an adult a liar!'

Caesar sobbed and crawled across the bed and clutched at the corner of the mattress; I crawled after him and tried to hold him. He cried, 'You a liar too, Mary!' and I fell back in shame.

The FAF lady then made a noble and transparently insincere offer: 'Caesar,' she said, 'if you want, you can come stay with me and my family. We have a big farm and dogs and –'

He screamed, 'I would never stay with you, lady! You're gross! Your whole family is gross!'

I smiled with pure admiration for the child.

The woman cried, 'Oh, I'm gross, am I!' And he was taken down the stairs screaming, 'They always send me away!'

Then Ezekial did something extraordinary. He threw his body across the stairs, grabbing the banister with both hands to block the exit. He began to whisper at Caesar, and I leaned in close, thinking, if he is saying something to comfort, I am going to stop this thing cold. But even as his body plainly said please don't do this, his mouth spitefully whispered, 'Ha ha! You go away! Ha ha!'

I stepped back and said to Caesar, 'This is not your fault!' He cried, 'Then send the other boy away!' Peter pried Ezekial off the banister and Caesar was carried out. I walked outside and watched as Peter put the sobbing little boy into the woman's giant SUV. Behind the screen door, Ezekial was dancing, incoherently taunting me as he sobbed too, breathless with rage and remorse.

If gentleness can be brutish, cruelty can sometimes be so closely wound in with sensitivity and gentleness that it is hard to know which is what. Animals are not capable of this. That is why it is so much easier to love an animal. Ezekial loved animals; he was never cruel with them. Every time he entered the house, he greeted each of our cats with a special touch. Even the shy one, Tina, liked him and let him touch her. Caesar, on the other hand, was rough and disrespectful – and yet he wanted the cats to like him. One of the things he and Ezekial fought about was which of them Peter's cat Bitey liked more.

On the third day in Florence I called Martha – the sister I later scolded for being hysterical about a cat – and asked for help. She said she would communicate psychically with Gattino. She said I needed to do it too. 'He needs reassurance,' she said. 'You need to tell him every day that you're coming back.'

I know how foolish this sounds. I know how foolish it is. But I needed to reach for something with a loving touch. I needed to reach even if nothing was physically there within my grasp. I needed to reach even if I touched darkness and sorrow. And so I did it. I asked Peter to do it too. We would go to churches and kneel on pews and pray for Gattino. We were not alone; the pews were always full of people, old, young, rich and poor, of every nationality, all of them reaching, even if nothing was physically there. 'Please comfort him, please help him,' I asked. 'He's just a little thing.' Because that was what touched me: not the big idea of tragedy, but the smallness and tenderness of this bright, lively creature. From Santa Annunziata, Santa Croce and Santa Maria Novella, we sent messages to and for our cat.

I went into the house to try and comfort Ezekial, who was sobbing that his mother didn't love him. I said that wasn't true, that she did love him, that I could hear it in her voice – and I meant it, I *had* heard it. But he said, 'No, no, she hates me. That's why she sent me here.' I told him he was lovable and in a helpless way I meant that too. Ezekial was a little boy in an impossible situation he had no desire to be in, and who could only make it bearable by manipulating and trying to hurt anyone around him. He was also a little boy used to rough treatment, and my attempts at caring only made me a sucker in his eyes. As soon as I said 'lovable' he stopped crying on a dime and starting trying to get things out of me, most of which I mistakenly gave him.

Caesar was used to rough treatment too – but he was still looking for good treatment. When I went to visit him at his new host house, I expected him to be angry at me. He was in the pool when I came and as soon as he saw me, he began splashing toward me, shouting my name. I had bought him a life jacket so he would be more safe in the pool and he was thrilled by it; kind treatment did not make me a sucker in his eyes. He had too strong a heart for that.

But he got kicked out of the new host's home anyway. Apparently he called her a bitch and threatened to cut her. I could see why she wouldn't like that. I could also see why Caesar would have to let his anger out on somebody if he didn't let it out on me.

Ezekial was with me when I got the call about Caesar's being sent home. The FAF woman who told me said that Caesar had asked her if he was going back to his 'real home, with Peter and Mary'. I must've looked pretty sick when I hung the phone up because Ezekial asked, 'What's wrong?' I told him, 'Caesar got sent home and I feel really sad.' He said, 'Oh.' There was a moment of feeling between us – which meant that he had to throw a violent tantrum an hour later, in order to destroy that moment – a moment which could scarcely have felt good to him.

After Ezekial left I wrote a letter to Caesar's mother. I told her that her son was a good boy, that it wasn't his fault that he'd gotten sent home. I had someone translate it into Spanish for me, and then I copied it onto a card and sent it with some pictures I had taken of Caesar swimming. It came back: MOVED, ADDRESS UNKNOWN. Peter told me that I should take the hint and stop trying to have any further contact. Other people thought so too. They thought I was acting out of guilt and I was. But I was acting out of something else too. I missed the little boy. I missed his deep eyes, his clumsiness, his generosity, his sweetness. I called the Fresh Air Fund. The first person I talked to wouldn't give me any information. The next person gave me an address in East New York; she gave me a phone number too. I sent the letter again. I prayed the same way I did later for Gattino: 'Spare him. Comfort him. Have mercy on this little person.' And Caesar heard me – he did. When I called his house nearly two months after he'd been sent back home, he didn't seem surprised at all.

When Peter and I returned to the veterinary hospital to claim Gattino, he purred at the sight of us. When we went back to Santa Maddalena, his little body tensed with recognition when he saw the room we had lived in together; then he relaxed and walked through it as if returning to a lost kingdom. My body relaxed too; I felt safe. I felt as if I had come through a kind of danger, or at least a kind of complex maze, and that I had discovered how to make sense of it.

The next day we went home. The trip was a two-hour ride to Florence, a flight to Milan, a layover, an eight-hour Atlantic flight, then another two-hour drive. At Florence Peter was told that because of an impossible bureaucratic problem with his ticket, he had to leave the terminal in Florence, get his bag and recheck it for the flight to Milan. The layover wasn't long enough for him to recheck the bags and make it onto the flight with me, and the airline (Alitalia) haughtily informed him that there was no room on the next flight. I boarded the plane alone; Peter had to spent the night in Milan and buy a ticket on another airline; I didn't find this out until I landed in New York with Gattino peering intrepidly from his carrier.

And Gattino *was* intrepid. He didn't cry in the car, or on the plane, even though he'd had nearly nothing to eat since the night before. He settled in patiently, his slender forepaws stretched out regally before him, watching me with a calm, confidently up-raised head. He either napped in his carrier or sat in my lap, playing with me, with the person sitting next to me, with the little girl sitting across from me. If I'd let him, he would've wandered up and down the aisles with his tail up.

The first time I called Caesar, he asked about Bitey; he asked about his life jacket. We talked about those things for a while. Then I told him that I was sad when he left. He said, 'Did you cry?' And I said, 'Yes. I cried.' He was silent; I could feel his presence so intensely, like you feel a person next to you in the dark. I asked to talk to his mother; I had someone with me who could speak to her in Spanish, to ask her for permission to have contact with her son. I also spoke to his sister Natalia. Even before I met her, I could hear her beauty in her voice – curious, vibrant, expansive in its warmth and longing.

I sent them presents – books mostly, and toys when Caesar's birthday came. I talked more to Natalia than to her brother; he was too young to talk for long on the phone. She reached out to me with her voice as if with her hand, and I held it. We talked about her trouble at school, her fears of the new neighborhood and movies she liked, which were mostly about girls becoming princesses. When Caesar talked to me, it was half-coherent stuff about cartoons and fantasies. But he could be suddenly very mature. 'I want to tell you something,' he said once. 'I feel something but I don't know what it is.'

I wanted to meet their mother; I very much wanted to see Caesar and meet his sister. Peter was reluctant because he considered the relationship inappropriate – but he was willing to do it for me. We went to East New York with a Spanish-speaking friend. We brought board games and cookies. Their mother kissed us on both cheeks and gave us candles. She said they could come to visit for Holy Week – Easter. Natalia said, 'I'm so excited'; I said, 'I am too.'

And I was. I was so excited I was nearly afraid. When Peter and I went into Manhattan to meet them at Penn Station, it seemed a miracle to see them there. As soon as we got to our house Caesar threw a tantrum on the stairs – the scene of his humiliation. But this time I could keep him, calm him and comfort him. I could make it okay, better than okay. Most of the visit was lovely. We have pictures in our photo album of the kids riding their bikes down the street on a beautiful spring day and painting Easter eggs; we have a picture of Natalia getting ready to mount a horse with an expression of mortal challenge on her face; we have another picture of her sitting atop the horse in a posture of utter triumph.

On the way back to New York on the train, Caesar asked, 'Do you like me?' I said, 'Caesar, I not only like you, I love you.' He looked at me levelly, and said, 'Why?' I thought a long moment. 'I don't know why yet,' I said. 'Sometimes you don't know why you love people, you just do. One day I'll know why and then I'll tell you.'

When we introduced Gattino to the other cats we expected drama and hissing. There wasn't much. He was tactful. He was gentle with the timid cats, Zuni and Tina, slowly approaching to touch noses, or following at a respectful distance, sometimes sitting near Tina and gazing at her calmly. He only teased and bedeviled the tough young one, Biscuit – and it's true that she didn't love him. But she accepted him.

Then things began to go wrong – little things at first. I discovered I'd lost my passport; Peter lost a necklace I'd given him; I lost the blue marble from Santa Maddalena. For the sixth summer in a row, Caesar came to visit us and it went badly. My sister Martha was told she was going to be laid off. We moved to a new house and discovered that the landlord had left old junk all over the house; the stove was broken and filled with nests of mice; one of the toilets was falling through the floor; windowpanes were broken.

But the cats loved it. Especially Gattino. The yard was spectacularly beautiful and wild, and when he turned six months old, we began letting him out for twenty minutes at a time, always with one of us in the yard with him. We wanted to make sure he was cautious and he was: he was afraid of cars, he showed no desire to go into the street, or really even out of the yard, which was large. We let him go out longer. Everything was fine. The house got cleaned up; we got a new stove. Somebody found Peter's necklace and gave it back. Then late one afternoon I had to go out for a couple of hours. Peter wasn't home. Gattino was in the yard with the other cats; I thought, 'He'll be okay.' When I came back he was gone.

Because he had never gone near the road I didn't think he would cross the street – and I thought if he had, he would be able to see his way back, since across the street was a level, low-cut field. So I looked behind our house, where there was a dorm in a wooded area, and to both sides of us. Because we had just moved in, I didn't know the terrain and so it was hard to look in the dark – I could only see a jumble of foliage and buildings, houses, a nursery school and what I later realized was a deserted barn. I started to be afraid. Maybe that is why I thought I heard him speak to me, in the form of a very simple thought that entered my head, plaintively, as if from outside. It said, 'I'm scared.'

I wish I had thought back: 'Don't worry. Stay where you are. I will find you.' Instead I thought, 'I'm scared too. I don't know where you are.' It is crazy to think that the course of events might've been changed if different sentences had appeared in my mind. But I think it anyway.

The next day I had to go into Manhattan because a friend was doing a public reading from her first new book in years. Peter looked for Gattino. Like me he did not look across the street; he simply didn't think he would've gone there.

The second day we made posters and began putting them up in all the dorms, houses and campus buildings. We alerted campus security, who put out a mass email to everyone who had anything to do with the college.

The third night, just before I went to sleep, I thought I heard him again. 'I'm lonely,' he said.

The fifth night we got the call from a security guard saying that he saw a small, thin, one-eyed cat trying to forage in a garbage can outside a dorm. The call came at two in the morning and we didn't hear it because the phone was turned down. The dorm was very close by; it was located across the street from us, on the other side of the field.

I walked across the field next day and realized something about it that I had not noticed before: from a human perspective it was flat enough to easily look across; from the perspective of a creature much lower to the ground, it was made of valleys and hills too big to see over.

Something I didn't say correctly: I did not lose the blue marble from Santa Maddalena. I threw it away. When Peter lost his necklace I decided that the marble was actually bad luck. I took it out into a field and threw it away.

A friend offered to pay for me to see a psychic. He hadn't seen her, he doesn't see psychics. But a pretty girl he was flirting with had seen this psychic, and been very impressed by her; my friend wanted me to tell him what the psychic was like, I guess in order to get some sideways knowledge of the girl. So I made the appointment. She told me that Gattino was 'in trouble'. She told me he was dying. She couldn't tell me where he was, except that it was down in a gulley or ditch, someplace where the ground dropped down suddenly; water was nearby and there was something on the ground that crunched underfoot. Maybe I could find him. But maybe I wasn't meant to. She thought maybe it was his 'karmic path' to 'walk into the woods and close his eyes', and, if that was so, that I shouldn't interfere. On the other hand, she said, I might still find him if I looked in the places she described.

I told my friend that I was not impressed with the pretty girl's choice of psychics. And then I went to the places she described and looked for Gattino. I went every day and every night. At the end of one of those nights, when I was about to go to sleep, words appeared in my head again. They were 'I'm dying' and then 'Goodbye'. I got up and took a sleeping pill. Two hours later I woke with tears running down my face.

Who decides which relationships are appropriate and which are not? Which deaths are tragic and which are not? Who decides what is big and what is little? Is it a matter of numbers or physical mass or intelligence? If you are a little creature or a little person dying alone and in pain, you may not remember or know that you are little. If you are in enough pain you may not remember who or what you are; you may know only your suffering, which is immense. Who decides? What decides – common sense? Can common sense dictate such things? Common sense is an excellent guide to social structures – but does it ever have anything to do with who or what moves you? ∎

THE DREADFUL MUCAMAS

Lydia Davis

GRANTA 115: SPRING 2011

They are very rigid, stubborn women from Bolivia. They resist and sabotage whenever possible.

They came with the apartment. They were bargains because of Adela's low IQ. She is a scatterbrain.

In the beginning, I said to them: *I'm very happy that you can stay, and I am sure that we will get along very well.*

This is an example of the problems we are having. It is a typical incident that has just taken place. I needed to cut a piece of thread and could not find my six-inch scissors. I accosted Adela and told her I could not find my scissors. She protested that she had not seen them. I went with her to the kitchen and asked Luisa if she would cut my thread. She asked me why I did not simply bite it off. I said I could not thread my needle if I bit it off. I asked her please to get some scissors and cut it off – now. She told Adela to look for the scissors of *la Señora Brodie,* and I followed her to the study to see where they were kept. She removed them from a box. At the same time I saw a long, untidy piece of twine attached to the box and asked her why she did not trim off the frayed end while she had the scissors. She shouted that it was impossible. The twine might be needed to tie up the box sometime. I admit that I laughed. Then I took the scissors from her and cut it off myself. Adela shrieked. Her mother appeared behind her. I laughed again and now they both shrieked. Then they were quiet.

I have told them: *Please, do not make the toast until we ask for breakfast. We do not like very crisp toast the way the English do.*

I have told them: *Every morning, when I ring the bell, please bring us our mineral water immediately. Afterwards, make the toast and at the same time prepare fresh coffee with milk. We prefer 'Franja Blanca' or 'Cinta Azul' coffee from Bonafide.*

I spoke pleasantly to Luisa when she came with the mineral water before breakfast. But when I reminded her about the toast, she broke into a tirade – how could I think she would ever let the toast get cold or hard? But it is almost always cold and hard.

We have told them: *We prefer that you always buy 'Las Tres Niñas' or 'Germa' milk from Kasdorf.*

Adela cannot speak without yelling. I have asked her to speak gently, and to say *señora*, but she never does. They also speak very loudly to each other in the kitchen.

Often, before I have said three words to her, she yells at me: *Sí . . . sí, sí, sí . . . !* and leaves the room. I honestly don't think I can stand it.

I say to her: *Don't interrupt me!* I say: *No me interrumpe!*
    I have asked them: *First listen to what I have to say!*

The problem is not that Adela does not work hard enough. But she comes to my room with a message from her mother: she tells me the meal I have asked for is impossible, and she shakes her finger back and forth, screaming at the top of her voice.

They are both, mother and daughter, such willful, brutal women. At times I think they are complete barbarians.

I have told her: *If necessary, clean the hall, but do not use the vacuum cleaner more than twice a week.*
    Last week she refused point-blank to take the vacuum cleaner out of the front hall by the entrance. Just when we were expecting a visit from the Rector of Patagonia!

I have asked her: *Please, do not leave the dirt and the cleaning things in the hall.*
    I have asked her: *Please, collect the trash and take it to the incinerator immediately.*

They have such a sense of privilege and ownership.

I took my underthings out to them to be washed. Luisa immediately said that it was too hard to wash a girdle by hand. I disagreed, but I did not argue.
    When I go to them to inquire about the tasks I have given them, I find they are usually engaged on their own occupations – washing their sweaters or telephoning.
    The ironing is never done on time.

Adela refuses to do any work in the mornings but house-cleaning.

I say to them: *We are a small family. We do not have any children.*

Today I reminded them both that my underthings needed to be washed. They did not respond. Finally I had to wash my slip myself.

I say to them: *We have noticed that you have tried to improve, and in particular that you are doing our washing more quickly now.*

Today I said I needed her there in the kitchen, but she went to her mother's room, and came back with her sweater on, and went out anyway. She was buying some lettuce – for them, it turned out, not for us.

At each meal, she makes an effort to escape.

As I was passing through the dining room this morning I tried, as usual, to chat pleasantly with Adela. Before I could say two words, however, she retorted sharply that she could not talk while she was setting the table.

Adela rushes out of the kitchen even when guests are present and shouts: *Telephone for you in your room!*

Although I have asked her to speak gently, she never does. Today she came rushing in again saying: *Telephone, for you!* and pointed at me. Later she did the same with our luncheon guest, a professor.

I say to Luisa: *I would like to discuss the program for the days to come. Today I do not need more than a sandwich at noon, and fruit. But* el señor *would like a nutritious tea.*

Tomorrow we would like a rather nourishing tea with hard-boiled eggs and sardines at six, and we will not want any other meal at home.

At least once a day, we want to eat cooked vegetables. We like salads, but we also like cooked vegetables. Sometimes we could eat both salad and cooked vegetables at the same meal.

We do not have to eat meat at lunchtime, except on special occasions. We are very fond of omelettes, perhaps with cheese or tomato.

Please serve our baked potatoes immediately after taking them from the oven.

We had had nothing but fruit at the end of the meal for two weeks.

I asked Luisa for a dessert. She brought me some little crêpes filled with apple sauce. They were nice, though quite cold. Today she gave us fruit again.

I said to her: *Luisa, you cannot refer to my instructions as 'illogical'.*

Luisa is emotional and primitive. Her moods change rapidly. She readily feels insulted and can be violent. She has such pride.

Adela is simply wild and rough, a hare-brained savage.

I say to Luisa: *Our guest, Señor Flanders, has never visited the park. He would like to spend several hours there. Can you make sandwiches of cold meat for him to take with him? It is his last Sunday here.*

For once, she does not protest.

I say: *Please, I would like Adela to polish the candlesticks. We are going to have them on the table at night.*

When setting the dining table, Adela puts each thing down with a bang.

I ring the bell at the dining table, and a loud crash follows instantly in the kitchen.

I have told them: *There should not be these kitchen noises during our cocktail and dinner hour.*

Luisa, I say, *I want to make sure we understand each other. You cannot play the radio in the kitchen during our dinner time. There is also a lot of shouting in the kitchen. We are asking for some peace in the house.*

But they are hitting each other again and yelling.

If we ask for something during a meal, she comes out of the kitchen and says: *There isn't any.*

It is all so very nerve-racking. I often feel worn out after just one attempt to speak to her.

We do not believe they are sincerely trying to please us.

Adela sometimes takes the bell off the dining table and does not put it back. Then, I cannot ring for her during the meal, but have to call loudly from the dining room to the kitchen, or go without what I need, or get the bell myself so that I can ring it. My question is: does she leave the bell off the table on purpose?

I instruct them ahead of time: *For the party we will need tomato juice, orange juice and Coca-Cola.*

I tell her: *Adela, you will be the one in charge of answering the door and taking the coats. You will show the ladies where the toilet is, if they ask you.*

I ask Luisa: *Do you know how to prepare* empañadas *in the Bolivian style?*

We would like them both to wear uniforms all the time.

I say to Adela: *Please, I would like you to pass among the guests frequently with plates of hors d'oeuvres that have been recently prepared.*
    When the plates no longer look attractive, please take them back out to the kitchen and prepare fresh ones.

I say to her: *Please, Adela, I would like there always to be clean glasses on the table, and also ice and soda.*

I have told her: *Always leave a towel on the rack above the bidet.*

I say to her: *Are there enough vases? Can you show them to me? I would like to buy some flowers.*

I see that Adela has left a long string lying on the floor next to the bed.

She has gone away with the wastebasket. I don't know if she is testing me. Does she think I am too meek or ignorant to require her to pick it up? But she has a cold, and she isn't very bright, and if she really did not notice the string, I don't want to make too much of it. I finally decide to pick up the string myself.

We suffer from their rude and ruthless vengeance.

A button was missing from my husband's shirt collar. I took the shirt to Adela. She shook her finger and said no. She said that *la Señora Brodie* always took everything to the dressmaker to be mended.

Even a button? I asked. Were there no buttons in the house?

She said there were no buttons in the house.

I told Luisa they could go out on Sundays, even before breakfast. She yelled at me that they did not want to go out, and asked me, where would they go?

I said that they were welcome to go out, but that if they did not go out, we would expect them to serve us something, even if it was something simple. She said she would, in the morning, but not in the afternoon. She said that her two older daughters always came to see her on Sundays.

I spent the morning writing Luisa a long letter, but I decided not to give it to her.

In the letter I told Luisa: *I have employed many maids in my life.*

I told her that I believe I am a considerate, generous and fair employer.

I told her that when she accepts the realities of the situation, I'm sure everything will go well.

If only they would make a real change in their attitude, we would like to help them. We would pay to have Adela's teeth repaired, for instance. She is so ashamed of her teeth.

But up to now there has been no real change in their attitude.

We also think they may have relatives living secretly with them behind the kitchen.

I am learning and practising a sentence that I will try on Luisa, though it may sound more hopeful than I feel: *Con el correr del tiempo, todo se solucionará.*

But they give us such dark, Indian looks! ∎

Gertrude Stein with Alice B. Toklas, and her dog, Basket, in front of her home, France, 1944

ALL I KNOW ABOUT GERTRUDE STEIN

Jeanette Winterson

GRANTA 115: SPRING 2011

In 1907 a woman from San Francisco named Alice B. Toklas arrived in Paris. She was going to meet a fellow American living there already. She was excited because she'd heard a lot about Gertrude Stein.

In 2011 a woman from London named Louise was travelling by Eurostar to Paris. Louise was troubled. Louise was travelling alone because she was trying to understand something about love.

Louise was in a relationship; it felt like a ship, though her vessel was a small boat rowed by herself with a cabin for her lover. Her lover's ship was much bigger and carried crew and passengers. There was always a party going on. Her lover was at the centre of a busy world. Louise was her own world; self-contained, solitary, intense. She did not know how to reconcile these opposites – if opposites they were – and to make things more complicated, it was Louise who wanted the two of them to live together. Her lover said no – they were good as they were – and the solitary Louise and the sociable lover could not be in the same boat.

And so Louise was travelling alone to Paris.

I am Louise.

*

I took the Metro to Cité. I walked past Notre-Dame and thought of the hunchback Quasimodo swinging his misshapen body across the bell-ropes of love for Esmeralda. Quasimodo was a deaf mute. Cupid is blind. Freud called love an 'overestimation of the object'. But I would swing through the ringing world for you.

Alice Toklas had no previous experience of love.

Her mother died young – young for the mother and young for Alice – and Alice played the piano and kept house for her father and brothers. She ordered the meat, managed the budget, supervised the kitchen. And then she came to Paris and met Gertrude Stein.

Gertrude Stein's mother died young too – and you never fully recover from that – actually you never recover at all; you take it with you as an open wound – but with luck that is not the end of the story.

Gertrude had a modest but sufficient private income. She and her brother Leo had long since left the USA to set up house in Paris in the rue de Fleurus. Gertrude wrote. Leo painted. They bought modern art. They bought Matisse when no one did and they bought Picasso when no one did. Pablo and Gertrude became great friends.

But Gertrude was lonely. Gertrude was a writer. Gertrude was lonely.

I find myself returning again and again to the same familiar condition of solitariness. Is it sex that makes this happen? If it were not for sex, wouldn't we each be content with our friends, their companionship and confidences? I love my friends. I am a good friend. But with my lover I begin to feel alone.

A friend of mine can be happy without a lover; she will have an affair if she wants one, but she doesn't take the trouble to love.

I do very badly without a lover. I pine, I sigh, I sleep, I dream, I set the table for two and stare into the empty chair. I could invite a friend – sometimes I do – but that is not the point; the point is that I am always wondering where you are even when you don't exist.

Sometimes I have affairs. But though I enjoy the bed, I feel angry at the fraud; the closeness without the cost.

I know what the cost is: the more I love you, the more I feel alone.

On 23 May 1907 Gertrude Stein met Alice B. Toklas.
Gertrude: Fat, sexy, genial, powerful.
Alice: A tiny unicorn, nervous, clever, watchful, determined.
When Gertrude opened the door to the atelier of 27 rue de Fleurus, Alice tried to sit down but couldn't, because the chairs were Stein-size and Alice was Toklas-size and her feet did not reach the floor.
'The world keeps turning round and round,' said Gertrude, 'but you have to sit somewhere.'

I sat opposite you and I liked your dishevelled look; hair in your eyes and your clothes a strategic mess. We were both survivors of other shipwrecks. You looked sad. I wanted to see you again.
For a while we corresponded by email, charming each other in fonts and pixels. Did you . . . do you . . . would you like to . . . I wonder if . . .

Every day Miss Toklas sent a petit bleu *to Miss Stein to arrange a walk in the Luxembourg Gardens or a visit to a bookshop or to look at pictures.*
One day Alice was late. Gertrude was so angry. Alice picked up her gloves to leave but as she was walking across the courtyard Gertrude called out, 'It is not too late to go for a walk.'

We went walking on Hampstead Heath. We walked for two hours straight ahead going round in circles. The circles were the two compass-turns of your desire and mine. The overlap is where we kissed.
The Stein and Toklas love affair was about sex.
They went on holiday together – the dripping heat of Italy and Gertrude liking to walk in the noonday sun.
They talked about *The Taming of the Shrew* – that play by Shakespeare – the one where Petruchio breaks Kate into loving him – a strange play. Not a poster-play for feminism.
GERTRUDE: A wife hangs upon her husband – that is what Shakespeare says.

ALICE: But you have never married.

GERTRUDE: I would like a wife.

ALICE: What kind of a wife would she be?

GERTRUDE: Ardent, able, clever, present. Yes, very present.

ALICE: I am going back to San Francisco in ten days.

GERTRUDE: I have enjoyed your visits every day to the rue de Fleurus . . .

And they walked in silence up the hill into the crest of the sun and Alice began to shed her clothes – her stockings, her cherry-red corset. Alice began to undress the past. At the top of the hill they sat down and Gertrude did not look at her.

GERTRUDE: When all is said one is wedded to bed.

It was the beginning of their love affair.

I met my lover two years ago and I fell in love. I fell like a stray star caught in the orbit of Venus. Love had me. Love held me. Love like wrist-cords. Love like a voice from a long way off. I love your voice on the phone.

Below me on the *quai* there's a skinny boy singing to his guitar: All You Need is Love. Couples holding hands throw him coins because they want to believe that it is true. They want to believe that they are true.

But the love question is harder to solve than the Grand Unified Theory of Everything.

If you were Dante you'd say they were the same thing – 'the love that moves the sun and the other stars'.

But love is in trouble.

Women used to be in charge of love – it was our whole domain, the business of our lives, to give love to make love to mend love to tend love.

Men needed women to be love so that men could do all the things you can't do without love – but no one acknowledged the secret necessity of love. Except in those dedications: To My Wife.

Now we have our own money and we can vote. We are career-women. (No such word as career-man.) We are more than the love interest. More than love. We are independent. Equal.

But . . . What happened to love?

We were confident that love would always be there, like air, like water, like summer, like sun. Love could take care of itself. We didn't notice the quiet tending of love, the small daily repairs to the fabric of love. The faithful gigantic work that kept love as regular as light.

Love is an ecosystem like any other. You can't drain it and strip-mine it, drill it and build over it and wonder where the birds and the bees have gone.

Love is where we want to live. Planet Love.

When we met, the most surprising and touching thing to me was that you always answered your phone when I called. You were not too important to be available. You are important but you recognised love as more important.

I started to believe you. I started to believe in you. Love has a religious quality to it – it depends on the unseen and it makes miracles out of itself. And there is always a sacrifice. I don't think we talk about love in real terms any more. We talk about partnership. We talk about romance. We talk about sex. We talk about divorce. I don't think we talk about love at all.

Alice Toklas never went back to San Francisco. She never saw her family again. Gertrude's brother Leo soon moved out of the rue de Fleurus and Alice moved in. They were together every day for the next forty years. Shall I write that again? *They were together every day for the next forty years* . . . And they never stopped having sex.

Gertrude Stein liked giving Alice an orgasm – she called it 'making a cow come out'. Nobody knows why – unless Alice made *moo* noises when she hit it. Gertrude said, 'I am the best cow-giver in the world.' Gertrude Stein liked repetition too – of verbs and words and orgasms.

We love the habits of love. The way you wear your hair. The way you drink your coffee. The way you turn your back on me in the mornings so that I will shift to fit myself round you. The way you open the door when you see me coming home. When I leave I look up at the window and I know you will be watching me, watching over me go.

And at the same time love needs to be new every day. The fresh damp risen-up feel of love.

Gertrude Stein said – *There is no there there* – at once refusing materiality and consolation.

I am lonely when I love because I feel the immensity of the task – the stoking and tending of love. I feel unable, overwhelmed. I feel I can only fail. So I hide and I cling all at once. I need you near me, in my house, but I don't want you to find my hiding place. Hold me. Don't come too close.

I decided to walk to the Musée Picasso because the Picasso portrait of Gertrude Stein was on loan there from the Metropolitan Museum of Art, New York. It is a famous picture. Gertrude is massy in the frame, her head almost a kabuki mask. It doesn't look like her but it couldn't be anyone else. Picasso took ninety sittings to paint it and couldn't get the head right. Gertrude said, '*Paint it out and paint it in when I am not there.*'

Picasso did that and Gertrude was very pleased. She hung the picture over her fireplace, and during the Second World War she and Alice took it to the countryside for five years, wrapped in a sheet, in their old open-topped Ford.

Gertrude said to Picasso, '*Paint what is really there. Not what you can see, but what is really there.*'

How can I trust myself like that? To see through the screens that shield me from love and not be so afraid of what I see that I break up, break off, or settle for the diluted version?

I have done all those things before.

And when I am not doing those things I am telling myself that I am an independent woman who should not be limited by/to love.

But love has no limits. Love seems to be a continuous condition like the universe. But the universe is remote except for this planet we call home, and love means nothing unless it is real and in our hands.

Give me your hand.

There's a school party at the museum. They are not looking at Picasso; they are giggling over an iPhone. Poor kids, they're all on Facebook posting themselves at a party. They are all having sex all the time because fucking is the new frigid. Look at their Facebook faces, defiant, unhappy. The F-words. Facebook, fucking, frigid, faking it.

Gertrude Stein called the generation between the wars 'the lost generation'. We are the upgrade generation. Get a new model; phone girlfriend car. Gertrude Stein hated commas. You can see why when car phone girlfriend are the same and interchangeable. Why would I work with love when I can replace the object of love?

Men still trade in their women – nothing feminism can do about that. Now women trade in themselves – new breasts, new face, new body. What will happen to these girls giggling over their iPhones?

They are the upload generation. Neophytes in the service of the savage god of the social network.

Fear. F is for fear.

In this bleak and broken world, what chance is there for love? Love is dating sites and bytes of love. Love is a stream of body parts. But if we part, I want to know that love had time enough. It takes a long time to be close to you.

Gertrude Stein could not be rushed, although she did not like to be kept waiting. Her time was her own. She had a big white poodle called Basket and she walked herself and her poodle round Paris.

Sometimes Basket went in the car with Gertrude and Alice and Alice went into the shops – and she liked that – and Gertrude stayed in the car – and she liked that. She wrote things in her notebook. She wrote every day but only for half an hour.

'*It takes a lot of time to write for half an hour,*' said Gertrude.

She wrote unpublished for thirty years. And then, in 1934, written in six weeks, *The Autobiography of Alice B. Toklas* by Gertrude Stein became a huge bestseller. Gertrude and Alice boarded the SS *Champion* and sailed for New York. Alice got a fur coat. Gertrude got a leopard-skin cap. Their travelling suits were made by Pierre Balmain. He was just a boy in those days.

When they and their outfits arrived in New York City, the ticker tape in Times Square tweeted:

GERTRUDE STEIN HAS LANDED IN NEW YORK.

'*As if we did not know it . . .*' said Alice.

The pressmen surrounded the Algonquin Hotel. The vendors selling frankfurters and pretzels watched from across the street.

VENDOR 1: The fat one built like a boulder, that's Gertrude Stein.

VENDOR 2: The thin one cut like a chisel . . .

VENDOR 1: That's Alice B. Toklas.

The press bulbs flashed like they were movie stars.

PRESSMAN: Hey, Miss Stein, why don't you write the way you talk? (Laughter.)

GERTRUDE: Why don't you read the way I write?

Everyone is laughing. Gertrude loves fame. Fame loves Gertrude.

VENDOR 2: Where's the husbands?

VENDOR 1: They got no husbands. (He passes a frankfurter through a pretzel and nods significantly.)

VENDOR 2: (low whistle) No kidding? But ain't they American gals?

VENDOR 1: Sure, but they been living in Paris.

Living with you would be the ultimate romance. I am a romantic and that is my defence against the love-commodity. I can't buy love but I don't want to rent it either. I would like to find a way to make the days with you be ours. I would like to bring my bag and unpack it.

You say we will fail, get frustrated, fall out, fight. All the F-words.

But there is another one: forgive.

In 1946 Gertrude Stein was suddenly admitted to the American Hospital at Neuilly. She had stomach cancer.

Only a few months earlier they had come back to Paris, in 1945 – the war over at last – to find the seal of the Gestapo on their apartment. Their silver and linen had been taken and the pictures were packed up ready to be removed to German art collections – that's what happened if you were a Jew.

Alice had been so upset, but Gertrude wanted to get her portrait by Picasso hung over the fireplace again, sit down in their two armchairs either side of the fire, and have some tea.

'*The apartment is here. You are here. I am here,*' she said.

At the hospital the doctor came into the room. They administered the anaesthetic. Gertrude had been advised against an operation but she did not believe in death – at least not for her. She did not believe in the afterlife either. There was no *there there*. Everything was *here*. Gertrude Stein was present tense.

She held Alice's hand. She said to Alice, *What is the answer?* But Alice was crying and only shook her head. Gertrude laughed her big rich laugh. 'Then what is the question?'

The trolley bearing Gertrude was wheeled away. Alice walked beside her lover as though she were walking beside her whole life. Gertrude never came back.

The question is: How do we love?

It is a personal question each to each, intense, private, frightening, necessary. It is a world question too, angry, refusing, demanding, difficult.

Love is not sentimental. Love is not second best.

Women will have to take up arms for love.

Take me in your arms. This is the Here that we have. ■

ALWAYS THE SAME
SNOW AND ALWAYS
THE SAME UNCLE

Herta Müller

TRANSLATED FROM THE GERMAN BY GEOFFREY MULLIGAN

GRANTA 125: AUTUMN 2013

S een from behind, the women's hairdos were sitting cats. Why do I have to say sitting cats to describe hair?

Everything always became something else. At first unobtrusively something else, if you just happened to look at it. But then demonstrably something else when you had to find the right words to describe it. If you want to be precise in your description, you have to find something completely different within the sentence to allow you to be precise.

Every woman in the village had a long, thick plait. The plait was folded back on itself and directed vertically upwards, and a rounded horn comb kept it standing proud above the middle of the head. The teeth of the horn comb vanished into the hair, and only the corners of its curved edge peeked out like small, pointed ears. With those ears and the thick plait, the back of the women's heads looked like a cat sitting bolt upright.

These vagabond qualities that turned one object into another were unpredictable. They distorted one's perception in the blink of an eye, made of it what they wished. Every thin branch swimming in the water resembled a water snake. Because of my constant fear of snakes I have been afraid of water. Not out of fear of drowning, but out of fear of snake wood, I never learned to swim for fear of scrawny, swimming branches. The imagined snakes had a more powerful effect than real ones could have, they were in my thoughts whenever I saw the river.

And whenever funerals approached the cemetery the bell was sounded. One long tug on the rope followed by the small bell with its rapid, urgent ringing – for me that was the cemetery snake that lured people towards death with its saccharine tongue, and the dead towards the caress of the grave. And those caresses soothed the dead, you could sense it from the breath of wind in the cemetery. What soothed the dead revolted me. The more it revolted me, the more I had to think about it. For there was always a breeze, always some cool or warm and dry wind. I was distressed by it. But instead of hurrying, only my breath came in a rush, and I carried the water slowly, watered the flowers slowly, lingered. Those imagined objects in my head with their vagabond qualities may have been an addiction. I was constantly looking for them, so they came looking for me. They ran after me like a mob, as if my fear could feed them. But they probably fed me, gave an image to my fear. And images, above all threatening ones, don't have to console, and therefore they don't have to disappoint, and therefore they never shatter. You can conjure up the same image again and again in your head. Thoroughly familiar, it becomes a support. The repetition made it new every time, and took care of me.

When my best friend came to say goodbye the day before I emigrated, as we embraced thinking we would never see each other again, because I would not be allowed back into the country and she would never be allowed out – as my friend was saying goodbye, we couldn't tear ourselves apart. She went to the door three times and each time she came back. Only after the third time did she leave, walking in a steady rhythm the length of the road. It was a straight road, so I could see her bright jacket getting smaller and smaller, and strangely enough becoming more garish as she went into the distance. I don't know, did the winter sun shine, it was February, did my eyes shine with tears, or did the material of her jacket gleam – one thing I do know: my eyes followed my friend and, as she walked away, her back shimmered like a silver spoon. So I was able to sum up our separation intuitively in two words. I called it silver spoon. And that was the simplest, most precise way to describe the whole event.

I don't trust language. At best I know from my own experience that, to be precise, it must always take something that doesn't belong to it. I have no idea why verbal images are so light-fingered, why the most valid comparison steals qualities it's not entitled to. The surprise comes about only through invention, and time and again it proves true that one gets close to the truth only with the invented surprise in the sentence. Only when one perception steals from another, one object seizes and uses the substance of another – only when that which is impossible in real life has become plausible in the sentence can the sentence hold its own before reality.

My mother believed that in our family fate always intervened during winter. When she emigrated with me from Romania it was winter, February. Twenty years ago.

A couple of days before departure, one was allowed to send seventy kilos of luggage per person in advance from the customs post near the border. The luggage had to be packed in a large wooden crate with prescribed measurements. The village carpenter built it out of pale acacia wood.

I had completely forgotten this emigration crate. I hadn't given it a thought since 1987, since I got to Berlin. But then there came a time when I had to think about it for days on end, for it played an important role in world events. Our emigration crate made history, it was at the centre of world events, it had become a celebrity, was on television for days on end. What with one thing and another, when objects become independent, when in your head they slide for no reason whatsoever into other things, ever more into other things, the better your head knows that they have absolutely nothing to do with these other things: so I kept seeing our emigration crate on television because the Pope had died. His coffin looked just like the emigration crate. Then the whole emigration resurfaced.

At four in the morning my mother and I left on a lorry with the emigration crate. The journey to the customs post was five or six hours. We sat on the floor of the trailer and sheltered behind the crate. The night was ice cold, the moon was rocking up and down, your eyeballs felt too bulky, like frozen fruit in your forehead. Blinking was painful, as if a dusting of frost were in your eyes. At first the rocking of the moon was mild and gently curved, then it got colder, it began to sting, had been sharpened to a point. The night was not dark, but transparent, the snow seemed like a reflection of daylight. It was too cold to talk on this journey. You don't want to keep opening your mouth if your gums are freezing. I wasn't about to breathe a word. And then I had to speak, because my mother, perhaps intending only to mutter to herself, said out loud:

'It's always the same snow.'

She was referring to January 1945 and her deportation to the Soviet Union for forced labour. There were sixteen-year-olds on the Russians' lists. Many people hid. My mother spent four days in a hole in the ground in the neighbour's garden, behind the barn. Then the snow came. They couldn't bring her food in secret any more, every step between house, barn and hole in the ground became visible. Throughout the village, the way to every hiding place could be seen in all that snow. Footsteps could be read in the garden. People were denounced by the snow. Not just my mother, many people had to abandon their hiding places voluntarily, forced out voluntarily by the snow. And that meant five years in the work camp. My mother never forgave the snow.

Later, my grandmother said to me, 'You can't imitate freshly fallen snow, you can't rearrange snow so it looks undisturbed. You can rearrange earth,' she said, 'sand, even grass, if you take the trouble, water rearranges itself because it swallows everything including itself and closes over once it has swallowed. And air,' she said, 'is always arranged, because you can't even see it.'

Hence every substance other than snow would have remained silent. And to this day my mother believes the thick snow was mainly responsible for her being carted off. She felt that the snow fell on the village as if it knew where it was, as if it were at home here. But then it behaved like a stranger, straight away at the service of the Russians. Snow is a white betrayal. That is exactly what my mother meant by her sentence: It's always the same snow.

My mother never said the word BETRAYAL, she didn't need to. The word BETRAYAL was there because she didn't say it. And the word BETRAYAL even grew over the years the more she told her story without using the word BETRAYAL, in repeated sentences always with the same formulations that had no need of the word BETRAYAL. Much later, when I had long known the stories of being carted off, it occurred to me that by dint of systematic avoidance the word BETRAYAL had become monstrous in the telling, in fact so fundamental that, had you wished, you could have summed up the entire story with the words SNOW BETRAYAL. The experience was so powerful that in the years to come perfectly common words were sufficient to tell the story, no abstractions, no exaggerations.

SNOW BETRAYAL is my phrase, and it's like SILVER SPOON. For long, complicated stories, a simple word contains so much that's unspoken because it avoids all details. Countless possibilities stretch out in the listener's imagination, because such words curtail the course of the action to a single point. A phrase such as SNOW BETRAYAL allows many comparisons, because none has been made. A phrase like that leaps out of the sentence, as if made of a different material. I call this material: the trick with language. I am always afraid of this trick with language, and yet it's addictive. Afraid because, as I am engaged in the sleight of hand, I feel that if the trick succeeds, something beyond the words will become true. Because I am taken up for so long with succeeding, it is as if I wanted to prevent it. And because I know the gap between success and failure swings like a jump rope, I know that in this instance it is the temples and not the feet that are jumping. Invented by means of the trick, and therefore entirely artificially, a phrase like SNOW BETRAYAL resonates. The material it is made of changes and becomes no different from a natural physical sensation.

I was responsible for the first betrayal I can remember: the betrayal with the calf. I had two calves in my head, and I measured one calf against the other, if not there would have been no betrayal. One calf was carried into the room, the other calf's foot was broken. One calf was carried into the room shortly after it was born and placed on the sofa in front of my grandfather's bed. My grandfather had lain paralysed in this bed for years. And for fully half an hour he looked at the newborn calf in total silence with piercing, greedy eyes. I sat on the sofa at the foot of the bed and at the foot of the calf. And I watched my grandfather. Sympathy for him almost broke my heart, just as I was repulsed by his gaze. It was a thieving gaze, aimed directly at the calf, it stretched tight like a glass string in the air between bed and calf. It was a look in which the pupils shone like freshly soldered metal droplets. An obscene, despairing admiration that consumed the calf with the eyes. My grandfather could only see the new calf, he couldn't see me – thank God. For I could feel how all-consuming that gaze was, how shameless. What hunger in the eyes, I thought. Then HUNGER IN THE EYES was another phrase that kept coming into my head.

That was one calf. The other calf had its foot broken with an axe just after it was born, so that we could slaughter it. Killing calves was forbidden. They had to be handed over to the state after a couple of weeks, once they had reached the right weight. Only in the case of an accident did the vet allow enforced slaughter, and then one was allowed to keep and eat the meat. When my father explained the accident with the calf to the vet, how the cow had placed its heavy foot on the calf, I shouted, 'You're lying, you did it yourself with the axe!'

I was seven years old, I knew from my parents that one should never lie. But I also knew that the state was bad, and that it locked people up in prison because they told the truth. I knew too that the vet was a stranger in the village, against us and for the state. I almost caused my father to go to prison because he instinctively trusted me to distinguish between the lies that were not allowed at home and the white lies that were permitted because so much was forbidden. Once the vet had gone, after a hefty bribe, I understood, without knowing the word, what I had done, what betrayal is. I felt scorched. I felt sick from head to toe.

For years we had faithfully handed over every calf to the state. Now we wanted to eat veal. That's what it was about. But it was also about several principles, which got confused. Lies, truth and dignity. It was permissible to lie to the state whenever possible, because it was the only way to get your due, this I knew. My father's lie was effective, it was flexible, and necessary too. So what was it that caused me to betray my father in front of this vet? I was thinking of the other calf in my paternal grandparents' house, the one the selfsame father carried from the stall into the room in his arms and placed on the velvet sofa. The calf on the sofa was not beautiful, because a calf has no place on a sofa. It was ugly, the way it just lay there, even if it could do nothing about the fact that it was a calf on a velvet sofa, that it was being so spoiled. But the calf whose foot had been broken with the axe was beautiful. Not out of pity, because we wanted to slaughter it. If you want to eat meat, you have to slaughter – no, the calf was beautiful precisely because we couldn't slaughter it but were obliged to put it on show and torment it. To my peasant eyes, that turned it into an impressive creature. Countless times every day I watched without the slightest problem as chickens, hares or goats were slaughtered. I knew how young cats were drowned, dogs slain, rats poisoned. But an unfamiliar feeling came over me because of the broken foot, I was taken by the natural beauty of the calf, its almost notoriously mawkish innocence, a kind of pain on witnessing the abuse. My father could have ended up in prison. Prison – the word struck me like a knife, in the emptiness of my betrayal my heart pounded up to my brow.

That was a different betrayal to SNOW BETRAYAL.

Perhaps I was reminded of the betrayal with the calf, with the two calves, because this night journey by lorry across the plain and the empty fields was as translucent as thin milk. Sitting in the slipstream of the emigration crate my mother had spoken only of SNOW BETRAYAL.

Then she was travelling to the camp in a sealed cattle wagon, and now she was travelling with me in a lorry to the customs point. Then she was guarded by soldiers with guns, now only the moon was watching. Then she was locked in, now she was emigrating. Then she was seventeen, now she was over sixty.

It was tough travelling on a lorry by moonlight through the February snow with sixty years and seventy kilos and an emigration crate, but it was nothing compared to 1945. After many years of harassment I wanted out of this country. Even if my nerves were shot, even if I had to do it to escape the Ceauşescu regime and its secret service, and so as not to lose my mind, STILL it was something I wanted to do, not had to do. I wanted to get out, and she wanted to because I wanted to. I had to say that to her on the lorry, even if my gums froze as I was talking. 'Stop comparing, it's not the snow's fault,' I had to say to my mother, 'the snow didn't force us out of our hiding place.'

At that time I was not far from losing my mind. I was so exhausted my nerves were playing tricks on me, the fear I felt came through every pore and onto every object I tinkered with. They then tinkered with me. If you look just a little over the edge, manoeuvre just a little in that tiny space in your head between the abstruse and the normal, and if you watch yourself doing it, you have reached the farthest point of normality. Not much more can be added. One must keep an eye on oneself, try to separate thinking and feeling. One wants to absorb everything into the head as usual, but not into the heart. Inside yourself two versions stalk: one enlarged but totally strange, the other familiar but unrecognisably tiny and blurred. You feel yourself becoming increasingly unrecognisable, indistinct. This is a dangerous state to be in, however closely you pay attention you don't know when it will topple over. Only that it will topple over if this shitty life doesn't change.

It wasn't just that there was no hiding place in the snow, as I said to my mother, there was none in my head: it was clear to me I had to get away. I was at the end of my tether, for several months I had confused laughing and crying. I knew when not to cry, when not

to laugh, but it was of no use. I knew what was right, and I did it all
wrong. I was no longer able to keep to what I already knew. I laughed
and I cried.

It was in this state that I arrived at the Langwasser transit hostel
in Nuremberg. It was a tall tower block opposite the site of Hitler's
rallies. The block contained little boxes for sleeping in, corridors with
no windows, neon light only, countless offices. On day one there was
an interrogation by the German Counter-Intelligence Service. Then
again on the second day, repeatedly, with breaks, and on the third,
and on the fourth. I understood: the Securitate weren't here with me
in Nuremberg, only the German Counter-Intelligence Service. I was
now where he was, but where was I, how the hell did I get here. Their
interrogators were known as inspectors. The signs on the doors read
Inspection Office A and Inspection Office B. Inspector A wanted to
know if in fact I had 'an assignment'. The word 'spy' didn't come up,
but they asked, 'Did you have anything to do with the secret service
there?' 'It did with me, there is a difference,' I said. 'I'll be the judge
of that, it's what I'm paid for,' he said. It was disgraceful. Inspector B
then asked, 'Did you want to overthrow the regime? You can admit it
now. It's yesterday's snow.'

Then it happened. I couldn't stand it that some inspector was
dismissing my life with a saying. I leapt up from the chair and said,
far too loud, 'It's always the same snow.'

I have never liked the saying 'yesterday's snow', because it has
no curiosity about what happened in the past. Now I knew clearly
what it was I couldn't abide about the saying, the snows of yesteryear.
I couldn't stand the meanness of it, the contempt. This expression
must be very insecure to puff itself up like that, to appear so arrogant.
We can gather from the expression that this snow was presumably
important in the past, otherwise we wouldn't be talking about it,
wouldn't be trying to rid ourselves of it today. What went through my
head next I didn't say to the inspector.

In Romanian there are two words for snow. One is the poetic
word, *nea*. In Romanian *nea* also means a man whom we know too

well to address formally but not well enough to address familiarly. One might use the word UNCLE. Sometimes words determine their own uses. I had to defend myself against the inspector and against the suggestion in Romanian that said to me, it's always the same snow and always the same uncle.

And something else happened when, newly arrived from the dictatorship to a Nuremberg transit hostel, I was being interrogated by a German Secret Service man. I've just been rescued, I thought, and I'm sitting here in the West like the calf on the sofa. Only when I saw the HUNGER IN THE EYES of the official did I understand that it was not only the tormented calf with the broken foot that had been abused, but also, every bit as much – only more insidiously – the spoiled calf on the sofa.

Every winter the white seamstress came to our house. She stayed for two weeks, ate and slept with us. We called her white because she only sewed white things: shirts and undershirts and nightshirts and brassieres and suspenders and bedclothes. I spent a lot of time near the sewing machine and watched the flow of the stitches, how they formed a seam. On her last evening in our house I said to her at dinner, 'Sew something for me to play with.'

She said, 'What should I sew for you?'

I said, 'Sew a piece of bread for me.'

She said, 'Then you'll have to eat everything you've played with.'

Eat everything you've played with. You could also describe writing that way. Who knows: what I write I must eat, what I don't write – eats me. The fact that I eat it doesn't make it disappear. And the fact that it eats me doesn't make me disappear. The same thing happens when words turn into something else as you write, to be precise, when objects proclaim their independence and verbal images steal what is not theirs. Especially when writing, when words become something different, to be precise, what is taking place is perhaps always the same snow and always the same uncle. ■

CONTRIBUTORS

Diana Athill (1917–2019) was a British writer and editor. For forty years she was the editorial director of André Deutsch, where she worked with authors such as Jean Rhys, Margaret Atwood and V.S. Naipaul. Her memoir, *Somewhere Towards the End*, was published by Granta Books in 2008 and won the Costa Biography Award. The following year, four volumes of her memoirs, including *Stet: An Editor's Life*, were reissued as *Life Class*. The full version of 'Editing Vidia' was published in *Granta* 69: The Assassin (Spring 2000).

John Berger (1926–2017) was a novelist, essayist, screenwriter and critic. His extensive bibliography includes the book-length essay on art criticism *Ways of Seeing*, the *Into their Labours* fiction trilogy and the study of migrant workers *A Seventh Man*. His novel *G.* was awarded the 1972 Booker Prize, and he was awarded the Golden PEN Award for a Lifetime's Distinguished Service to Literature in 2009. His work has often been featured in *Granta*. 'The Zoo in Basel' was published alongside a photoessay by Jean Mohr in *Granta* 35: The Unbearable Peace (Spring 1991).

William Brand was Ryszard Kapuściński's first literary agent and translated much of his work. He is the author of the documentary films *Jestem polskim Żydem* (*I Am a Polish Jew*) and *The Unexpected Guest*.

Bill Buford launched *Granta* in its current form in 1979 and edited the magazine for sixteen years until its fiftieth issue in 1995; he then resigned with the editorial printed in this issue. He later became the fiction editor of the *New Yorker*. He is the author of two books, *Among the Thugs: The Experience, and the Seduction, of Crowd Violence*, on football hooliganism in the UK, and *Heat*.

Nick Caistor is the editor and translator of *The Faber Book of Contemporary Latin American Short Stories*. He translates regularly for *Granta*, and is a three-time winner of the Valle-Inclán translation prize.

Angela Carter (1940–1992) was a British writer and journalist, best known for her book of stories *The Bloody Chamber*, a collection of her adaptations of fairy tales. Her novels include *The Infernal Desire Machines of Doctor Hoffman*, *Wise Children* and *Nights at the Circus*, which won the 1984 James Tate Black Memorial Prize. 'Cousins' was published in *Granta* 3: The End of the English Novel (Autumn 1980), and was republished in the collection *Black Venus* with the title 'Peter and the Wolf', forming part of her 'wolf quartet'.

Raymond Carver (1938–1988) was an American poet and short-story writer who published seven stories in *Granta* in the 1980s. 'Menudo' was published in *Granta* 21: The Story-Teller (Spring 1987). His works include *Will You Please Be Quiet, Please?*, *What We Talk About When We Talk About Love* and *Cathedral*, which was a finalist for the 1984 Pulitzer Prize for Fiction.

Bruce Chatwin (1940–1989) was a British travel writer and novelist. After working first at Sotheby's, and then for the *Sunday Times*, he made a pilgrimage to Patagonia in 1974, which inspired the book that launched his writing career. *In Patagonia* won the Hawthornden Prize and the E.M. Forster Award. Chatwin went on to write many successful travel memoirs, including *The Songlines*, about Indigenous Australian mythology. 'A Coup' was published in *Granta* 10: Travel Writing (Winter 1983).

Lydia Davis is the author of one novel and seven short-story collections. She is also the translator, from the French, of more than thirty books. Her translation of a selection of Proust's letters appeared in *Granta* 140: State of Mind (Summer 2017). In honour of her literary achievements, she was made Chevalier de l'Ordre des Arts et des Lettres by the French government, and awarded the Man Booker International Prize in 2013. 'The Dreadful Mucamas' was published in *Granta* 115: The F Word (Spring 2011).

Don DeLillo is the author of more than fifteen novels, as well as plays, essays and short fiction. 'At Yankee Stadium' is an excerpt from *Mao II*, which won the 1992 PEN/Faulkner Award, and was published in *Granta* 34: Death of a Harvard Man (Autumn 1990). DeLillo made his first appearance in *Granta* in 1984, and his latest contribution was in *Granta* 117: Horror (Autumn 2011). He was awarded the 2010 PEN/Saul Bellow Award for Achievement in American Fiction and the 2015 Medal for Distinguished Contribution to American Letters.

John Gregory Dunne (1932–2003) was a journalist, novelist, critic and screenwriter. He was married to writer Joan Didion, whose book *The Year of Magical Thinking* describes the aftermath of his death from a heart attack in 2003. He is the author of more than ten books, including *Vegas: A Memoir of a Dark Season*, *True Confessions* and *Playland*. 'Glitches' is an excerpt from his autobiographical novel *Harp*; it was published in *Granta* 27: Death (Summer 1989).

James Fenton has published over twenty books as a poet, journalist and critic. After winning an Eric Gregory Award in 1973 for his poetry collection *Terminal Moraine*, he used his prize money to travel to South East Asia. He has contributed many times to *Granta* and his long-form journalism often formed the centrepiece for an issue, such as the full version of 'The Fall of Saigon', published in *Granta* 15: The Fall of Saigon (Spring 1985). He was Oxford Professor of Poetry from 1994–1999.

Alexandra Fuller is the author of several books, including *Don't Let's Go to the Dogs Tonight*, *Leaving Before the Rains Come* and *Scribbling the Cat*, which won the 2005 Lettre Ulysses Award for the Art of Reportage. She grew up in south-central Africa and now lives in Wyoming. The full version of 'The View from This End' was published in *Granta* 88: Mothers (Winter 2004).

Mary Gaitskill is the author of three novels, three books of short stories, and an essay collection. She was born in Kentucky, sold flowers in San Francisco as a teenage runaway and now lives in Brooklyn. In 2002 she was awarded a Guggenheim Fellowship, and that same year her story 'Secretary', from the collection *Bad Behaviour*, was made into a film. The full version of 'Lost Cat' was published in *Granta* 107 (Summer 2009).

Gabriel García Márquez (1927–2014) was a Colombian writer and the author of over twenty works of fiction and non-fiction, including *One Hundred Years of Solitude*, *Chronicle of a Death Foretold* and *Love in the Time of Cholera*. He was awarded the Nobel Prize in Literature in 1982 and his Nobel Prize lecture, 'The Solitude of Latin America', was featured in *Granta* 9: Boris (Autumn 1983). 'Dreams for Hire' was published in *Granta* 41: Biography (Autumn 1992).

Amitav Ghosh is the author of eight novels and six non-fiction books, including *In an Antique Land*, *The Circle of Reason*, which won the 1990 Prix Médicis étranger, and *Sea of Poppies*, which was shortlisted for the 2008 Man Booker Prize. 'The Imam and the Indian' was published in *Granta* 20: In Trouble Again (Winter 1986) and was later included in a book of the same title in the UK and in *Incendiary Circumstances: A Chronicle of the Turmoil of Our Times* in the US.

Lindsey Hilsum is the International Editor of *Channel 4 News*, and the author of *In Extremis: the Life of War Correspondent Marie Colvin* and *Sandstorm: Libya in the Time of Revolution*. 'Where is Kigali?' was published in *Granta* 51: Big Men (Autumn 1995). Hilsum was the only English-speaking foreign correspondent in Rwanda when the genocide began in 1994. Almost twenty years later, she returned to document the nation's path to recovery in 'The Rainy Season', published in 125: After the War (Autumn 2013).

Kazuo Ishiguro is a novelist and short-story writer whose books include *Never Let Me Go* and *The Remains of the Day*, which won the 1989 Booker Prize. He was born in Nagasaki, Japan, and grew up in Britain. He was twice chosen as one of *Granta*'s Best of Young British Novelists (1983 and 1993), and in 2017 he was awarded the Nobel Prize in Literature. 'The Summer After the War' was published in *Granta* 7: Best of Young British Novelists (Spring 1983).

Ian Jack edited *Granta* for twelve years between 1995 and 2007. 'Those Who Felt Differently' is the editorial from *Granta* 60: Unbelievable (Winter 2008). He is the author of several books, including *The Country Formerly Known as Great Britain* and *Mofussil Junction: Indian Encounters 1977–2011*.

Ryszard Kapuściński (1932–2007) was a Polish journalist, known for his reporting on twenty-seven revolutions and coups around the world over the course of a forty-year career as a foreign correspondent. His work first appeared in *Granta* in 1985, after which he became a regular contributor. 'The Snow in Ghana' was published in *Granta* 28: Birthday Special (Autumn 1989) and was later included in *Nobody Leaves: Impressions of Poland*. An interview between Kapuściński and *Granta*'s then-editor Bill Buford was published alongside the essay 'Outline for a Book' in *Granta* 21: The Story-Teller (Spring 1987). His books *Imperium* and *The Soccer War* are published by Granta Books.

Primo Levi (1919–1987) was an Italian writer and chemist. In 1944 he was deported to Auschwitz, an experience he addressed in the memoir *If This Is a Man* and the essay collection *The Drowned and the Saved*, as well as in other works. 'Tadpoles' was published in *Granta* 18: The Snap Revolution (Spring 1986). His story collection *The Periodic Table* was named by the Royal Institution of Great Britain as the best science book ever. His last contribution to the magazine is 'Weightless', an essay that contemplates being 'freed, even if only for a moment, from the weight' of his body. It was published in *Granta* 21: The Story-Teller (Spring 1987)

Todd McEwen is the author of the essay collection *How Not to be American* and five novels, including *McX*, *The Five Simple Machines* and *Who Sleeps with Katz*, published by Granta Books. 'Evensong' was published in *Granta* 8: Dirty Realism (Autumn 1983).

Hilary Mantel is the author of *Wolf Hall* and *Bring Up the Bodies*, winners of the 2009 and 2012 Man Booker Prize. 'Nadine at Forty' was published in *Granta* 56: What Happened to Us? (Winter 1996). Her most recent work is the story collection *The Assassination of Margaret Thatcher*.

Ved Mehta was a staff writer for the *New Yorker* from 1960 to 1993 and is the author of over twenty books, including the twelve-volume family saga *Continents of Exile*. He has received two Guggenheim Fellowships, the MacArthur Prize Fellowship and was the Rosenkranz Writer-in-Residence at Yale University. He is an Honorary Fellow of Balliol College, Oxford. The full version of 'Kiltykins', an extract from the memoir *All for Love*, was published in *Granta* 72: Overreachers (Winter 2000).

Lorrie Moore is the author of five story collections, three novels and a book for children. 'Agnes of Iowa' was published in *Granta* 54: Best of Young American Novelists (Summer 1996.) Her most recent book is the essay collection *See What Can Be Done*. She teaches at Vanderbilt University.

Herta Müller is the winner of the 2009 Nobel Prize in Literature for her depictions of 'the landscape of the dispossessed'. She was born in Romania in 1953. She worked for a period as a translator, but was fired for her refusal to cooperate with the Securitate secret police. She found work as a teacher and an author, and emigrated to Berlin in 1987. Her books include *The Hunger Angel*, *The Appointment* and *The Land of Green Plums*. 'Always the Same Snow and Always the Same

Uncle' was published in *Granta* 125: After the War (Autumn 2013).

Geoffrey Mulligan is the editor of the Clerkenwell Press and No Exit Press. He is a translator from French, German and Spanish. His translations include *Magic Hoffman* by Jakob Arjouni, which was longlisted for the 2000 International IMPAC Dublin Literary Award, and *Cristina and Her Double: Selected Essays* by Herta Müller.

Simon Rees is a librettist, writer and translator working from Italian, French and German. His novels include *The Devil's Looking-Glass*, *Nathaniel and Mrs Palmer* and *Making a Snowman*. He was dramaturg at the Welsh National Opera from 1989 to 2012, and has also written operas, poetry collections, plays, lyrics and librettos.

Philip Roth (1933–2018) won all three major literary awards in the US numerous times, including the 1960 National Book Award for *Goodbye, Columbus*, the 1998 Pulitzer Prize for *American Pastoral* and the 2001 PEN/Faulkner Award for *The Human Stain*. 'His Roth' was published in *Granta* 24: Inside Intelligence (Summer 1988), and formed the prologue to *The Facts: A Novelist's Autobiography*.

Edward W. Said (1935–2003) was Professor of English and Comparative Literature at Columbia University and is the author of eighteen books, including *Orientalism*, *Culture and Imperialism* and *The Question of Palestine*. The full version of 'Self-Consciousness' was published in *Granta* 67: Women and Children First (Autumn 1999), and is an excerpt from his memoir, *Out of Place*, published by Granta Books.

Binyavanga Wainaina is a Kenyan author and journalist, a Bard Fellow and the director of the Chinua Achebe Center for African Writers and Artists at Bard College. He is a founding editor of the Kenyan literary magazine *Kwani?* Wainaina's first contribution to *Granta*, 'How to Write About Africa', started out as an angry letter to the editor in response to *Granta* 48: Africa, which, Wainaina writes, 'was populated by every literary bogeyman that any African has ever known'. It was then included in *Granta* 92: The View from Africa (Winter 2005).

Edmund White's books include a trio of autobiographical novels, *A Boy's Own Story*, *The Beautiful Room Is Empty* and *The Farewell Symphony*, as well as biographies of Jean Genet, Marcel Proust and Arthur Rimbaud. He first appeared in *Granta* as a translator of Milan Kundera from the French, and is now a contributing editor to the magazine. In 2018, he received the PEN/Saul Bellow Award for Career Achievement in American Fiction. The unabridged version of 'Shrinks' was published in *Granta* 71: Shrinks (Autumn 2000) and later formed part his autobiography *My Lives*.

Joy Williams is the author of eleven books, including the novel *State of Grace*, a finalist for the 1974 National Book Award for Fiction, *The Quick and the Dead*, shortlisted for the 2001 Pulitzer Prize for Fiction, and the book of essays, *Ill Nature: Rants and Reflections on Humanity and Other Animals*, a finalist for the 2001 National Book Critics Circle Award for Criticism. 'The Little Winter' was published in *Granta* 28: Birthday Special! (Autumn 1989). Her most recent book is the story collection *The Visiting Privilege* and her latest contribution to *Granta* is 'Web', in *Granta* 142: Animalia (Winter 2018).

Jeanette Winterson is the author of more than twenty books, which include novels, non-fiction and works for children. Her first book, the autobiographical novel *Oranges are Not the Only Fruit*, won the 1985 Whitbread Award and her adaptation of the novel for television won a BAFTA. Winterson was first published in *Granta* in 1988 and was later chosen as one of the magazine's Best of Young British Novelists in 1993. 'All I Know About Gertrude Stein' was published in *Granta* 115: The F Word (Spring 2011). She teaches creative writing at the University of Manchester, and is currently working on a film about Gertrude Stein and Alice B. Toklas.

COPYRIGHT